The Muvipix.com Guide to
Photoshop Elements &
Premiere Elements 11
Steve Grisetti

The tools in Adobe's amazing suite of programs,
and how to use them together to create
professional-looking movies and great-looking
photos on your personal computer.

Dedications and Thanks

I continually look to my friends and colleagues at Muvipix.com for inspiration, challenge and, more often than not, help. To you, dear friends, I dedicate this book.

Thank you, Jeanne, for once again giving me the time, support and occasional neck massages that enabled me to complete this major project

Thank you, dear daughter Sarah, for blessing my heart by finding the inspiration in my work to take your own video work to the next level.

And thank you, Danielle, for jumping on board and helping me refine my text and chase down those stubborn typos.

And a special thanks to my Muvipix.com co-founders, Ron and Chuck, whose friendship and support for over half a decade have meant more to me than they can know.

About Muvipix.com

Muvipix.com was created to offer support and community to amateur and semi-professional videomakers. Registration is free, and that gets you access to the world's friendliest, most helpful forum and lots of ad-free space for displaying your work. On the products page, you'll find dozens of free tips, tutorials, motion backgrounds, DVD templates, sound effects, royalty-free music and stock video clips. For a small annual subscription fee that we use to keep the site running, you'll have unlimited downloads from the ever-growing library of support materials and media.

We invite you to drop by and visit our thriving community. It costs absolutely nothing – and we'd love to have you join the neighborhood!

http://Muvipix.com

About the author

Steve Grisetti holds a master's degree in Telecommunications from Ohio University and spent several years working in the motion picture and television industry in Los Angeles. A veteran user of several video editing programs and systems, Steve is the co-founder of Muvipix.com, a help and support site for amateur and semi-professional videomakers. A professional graphic designer and video freelancer, he has taught classes in Photoshop, lectured on design and even created classes for Lynda.com. He lives in suburban Milwaukee.

Other books by Steve Grisetti

Adobe Premiere Elements 2.0 In a Snap (with Chuck Engels)
The Muvipix.com Guides to Adobe Premiere Elements 7, 8, 9, 10 and 11
The Muvipix.com Guides to Photoshop Elements & Premiere Elements 7, 8, 9 and 10
Cool Tricks & Hot Tips for Adobe Premiere Elements
The Muvipix.com Guide to DVD Architect Studio 5
The Muvipix.com Guides to Vegas Movie Studio HD 10 and 11

An Introduction

There are lots of reasons to be impressed with the latest versions of Adobe's Premiere Elements and Photoshop Elements, major reworkings of their already-terrific video and photo editing programs – as well as a major overhaul of their companion program, the Elements Organizer.

You should see better performance than ever with all three programs, particularly on higher-end computers – and especially if you're running the 64-bit versions of Windows 7 or 8 or Mac's OSX. You'll also find very welcome improved support in Premiere Elements for non-camcorder video – particularly video from smartphones, iPads, iPods and other portable devices.

But the biggest and most obvious change to the entire bundle of programs is in the interface itself. You'll hardly recognize Premiere Elements, with its tools tucked away until called forth by a click on its Action Bar. And Photoshop Elements and the Organizer have also experienced a major de-cluttering. All three have replaced their murky, dark interfaces with bright, clean backgrounds and black, clear, easy-to-read text.

In addition, Photoshop Elements also now includes:

An Actions panel (just like its big brother, Photoshop CS) that performs complicated actions on your photos with the click of a mouse!

A Tool Options Bin with more and easier ways to customize how its amazing collection of tools work.

Cool new filters and Guided Edits.

Premiere Elements offers even more:

Automatic project set-up, which matches your project specs to whatever video you add to it.

A brand-new Quick Edit timeline for easy assemblage of your quick movie projects.

The amazing Time Remapping effect, which allows you to suddenly shift your video into fast or slow-motion and then back again!

Likewise, the Elements Organizer has added a powerhouse of file management tools:

Categorize and search your photos based on where they were shot, what event they recorded and even who is pictured in them!

A greatly improved Media Analyzer and Smart Tags generator.

Tools for uploading your photos and videos directly to YouTube, Facebook, Vimeo, Flickr, Photoshop Showcase and Adobe Revel.

Adobe has clearly put a lot of thought into creating products that are the best in their class. And, with added improvements in performance and stability, they've largely succeeded.

If you're new to video and photo editing, you should find these programs easier to get to know than ever. And, if you're a veteran or a pro, you'll welcome the improvements in performance – and, once you get used to the new look, you'll likely even embrace the drastically changed interface.

Either way, we hope that our book will help you navigate the surprisingly slight learning curve – and that maybe we'll also show you a few cool tricks along the way.

Muvipix.com was created in 2006 as a community and a learning center for videomakers at a variety of levels. Our community includes everyone from amateurs and hobbyists to semi-pros, professionals and even people with broadcast experience. You won't find more knowledgeable, helpful people anywhere else on the Web. I very much encourage you to drop by our forums and say hello. At the very least, you'll make some new friends. And it's rare that there's a question posted there that isn't quickly, and enthusiastically, answered.

Our learning center consists of video tutorials, tips and, of course, books. But we also offer a wealth of support in the form of custom-created DVD and BluRay disc menus, motion background videos, licensed music and even stock footage. Much of it is absolutely free – and there's even more available for those who purchase one of our affordable site subscriptions.

Our goal has always been to help people get up to speed making great videos and, once they're there, provide them with the inspiration and means to get better and better at doing so.

Why? Because we know making movies and taking great pictures is a heck of a lot of fun – and we want to share that fun with everyone!

Our books, then, are a manifestation of that goal. And my hope for you is that this book helps *you* get up to speed. I think you'll find that, once you learn the basics, making movies on your home computer is a lot more fun than you ever imagined! And you may even amaze yourself with the results in the process.

Thanks for supporting Muvipix.com, and happy moviemaking!

Steve
http://Muvipix.com

Section 1: Adobe Photoshop Elements 11

Table of Contents

Chapter 6

Select and Isolate Areas in Your Photos 71

Working with selections

Table of Contents

Table of Contents

Chapter 19

Explore the Project Assets Panel 247

The parts that will form your movie

Chapter 20

Edit Your Video in Expert View 257

Where your movie comes together

Part VI: The Premiere Elements Action Bar

Chapter 21

Make an InstantMovie Using Movie Themes 273

The easy way to create movies

Chapter 22

Use the Premiere Elements Toolkit............. 277

Powerful tools on the Action Bar

Chapter 23

Make Adjustments to Your Video and Audio 291

Correct and customize your clips' levels

Table of Contents

Chapter 32

A Premiere Elements Appendix.................. 393
More things worth knowing

Section 3: The Elements Organizer

Chapter 33

Manage Your Files with the Organizer.......411
Getting to Know the Media Browser

Table of Contents

Chapter 34
Create Fun Pieces.................................. 427
The Organizer's project templates

Chapter 35
Share Your Photos and Videos 443
The Organizer's output tools

Section 1

Adobe
Photoshop Elements 11

Pixels & Resolution

Raster vs. Vector Graphics

Image Size vs. Canvas Size

Selection

Layers & Alpha

RGB Colors

The Option Bar

Native PSD files

Chapter 1

Things You Need to Know
Principles of photo and graphic editing

Photoshop Elements is a surprisingly powerful photo and graphics editor that borrows a large number of tools from its big brother, Photoshop, the industry standard for photo and graphics work. In fact, both programs can even open and edit the same types of files.

The few limitations Elements does have, in fact, might well be things you'll never even miss (unless you're preparing files that will ultimately go onto a printing press).

But before we go too deeply into the tool set of this fine program, there are a couple of basic principles you'll need to understand.

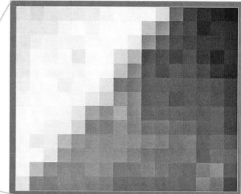

The building blocks of all digital photos are rectangular (usually square) blocks of color known as pixels.

Pixels

Pixels are the building blocks of all digital graphics and photos. Whether you can see them or not, all digital photos as well as photos and graphics created in Photoshop Elements are made up of these little squares of color. Even a tremendously rich, detailed digital photograph, if you blew it up large enough, would reveal itself to be little more than thousands (or millions) of little squares of solid color, each one some mixture of red, green and blue.

This is easier to see on a low resolution image, such as a graphic created for a web site. Zoom in as far as Photoshop Elements will let you go and you'll soon see that even in the apparently smoothest gradation of color there are actually little blocks of solid color.

An understanding of pixels is vital to developing a deeper understanding of how Photoshop Elements works. In order to fully comprehend how virtually any tool does what it does or how any setting affects your image – or how to measure the relative size of your images – you must learn to see your images not merely as pictures of people, animals and places but as compositions of thousands and thousands of little blocks of color.

Non-square pixels – and more than you probably want to know

Like all digital photo devices, video camcorders paint their on-screen images with pixels. But, unlike in a typical photograph, video pixels often aren't square blocks of color – they're rectangular.

Even more confusing, the shapes of these rectangular pixels vary, depending on the nature of the medium.

Standard NTSC, the television and video format used in North America and Japan, uses pixels that are only 90% as wide as they are tall.

Square (photograph) pixels   Narrower NTSC non-square 4:3 pixels   Wider NTSC non-square 16:9 pixels

PAL, the TV format used in most of Europe, uses pixels that are 107% as wide as they are tall. Because of this, a 720x480 pixel NTSC image and a 720x576 pixel PAL image both produce a video frame that is in the same proportion – a 4:3 ratio!

Widescreen standard definition TV uses the same number of pixels to create a video frame as standard TV. The pixels are just proportioned differently. (The pixels are 120% as wide as they are tall in NTSC and 142% as wide as they are tall in PAL.) In other words, there are exactly the same number of pixels in a 4:3 video frame as there are in a 16:9 video image, as illustrated above.

Even many high-definition video camcorders use non-square pixels. In 1440x1080 hi-def TV, the pixels are 133% as wide as they are tall, so that 1440x1080 pixel image produces a 16:9 image. (Though more and more hi-def camcorders are also shooting in 1920x1080, a square pixel format.)

All of this is related to technology dating back to the origins of television. And, unless you're creating graphics for video, it pretty much falls into the "nice to know" rather than "need to know" category. But it *is* nice to know – in case anyone ever asks you why a 720x480 video file becomes a 640x480 web video.

In most cases, as you're designing artwork for your videos, you won't need to concern yourself with whether your pixels are square non-square. This is because Premiere Elements will automatically adapt your square pixel images to the non-square pixel video environment. Just use these **square pixel** equivalents for creating full-screen graphics:

Standard NTSC video	640x480 pixels
Widescreen NTSC video	855x480 pixels
Standard PAL video	768x576 pixels
Widescreen PAL video	1024x576 pixels
High definition video	1920x1080 pixels

Resolution

Resolution means, basically, how many of these pixels are crammed into how much space. Standard definition video, like images created for the Internet, doesn't require a particularly high resolution image. Print, on the other hand, can require a pixel density of two to four times that of an on-screen image.

High resolution photo

Same size photo, at much lower
resolution (fewer pixels per inch)

Just as digital photos are made up of pixels, printed images are made up of little dots of color or ink. A good, press-worthy image may need 300 dots of color per inch (or more) in order to appear to the eye as a smooth color image. Home printed pieces, like the kind you'd print off your desktop printer, can have as few as 150 dots or pixels per inch. Graphics that will be used on-screen (for the Web or in a video) are about 72 pixels per inch. This is why, if you download a graphic from a web site and print it out, you'll often find that the picture prints fuzzy, jagged or "pixelated."

In order to get a good, high-resolution print-out of a 4" x 3" photo, you'd need a photo that measures as much as 1200 pixels wide and 900 pixels tall. That's a lot of pixels when you consider that a standard TV frame measures only 640 x 480 square pixels. In other words, that 1200 x 900 photo you used for your print-out has four times as many pixels as an equivalent full-screen image on a standard definition TV set!

And that's why we say video is a relatively low resolution medium. High-definition video needs a bit more image data – but only a fraction of what print artwork requires (and less than half of the resolution produced by a 5 megapixel digital still camera).

Video images are measured in pixels. In other words, as you're working on images for your videos, their dimensions, in pixels, are the only relevant measurement.

The measurements of any graphics and photos you prepare for video are *never* expressed in inches or centimeters. Even the resolution of your images, in terms of pixels per inch, isn't really relevant.

Why doesn't linear measurement (like inches and centimeters) matter in the world of video graphics? Well, basically, it's because you never know how big the TV is your video is going to be shown on!

TVs and computer monitors come in a variety of sizes and screen settings. A graphic may appear to be 2 inches across on a 17" computer monitor, 4 inches across on a 22" TV set and 30" across on a big screen TV! But the graphic itself is always the same number of *pixels* in size. Those pixels are as large or as small as the screen you're viewing them on.

So, when you're creating your graphics for video (or for the web), always think in terms of measurements in pixels. That's the only constant measurement in on-screen graphics.

Just for convenience sake, most people still do use 72 ppi (pixels per inch) as their resolution setting when creating their on-screen graphics. But ultimately the resolution setting makes no difference in this case. When you create an image for video or for the Web, a 640x480 pixel image is still the same size whether it's 72 ppi or 600 ppi.

Raster vs. vector graphics

All computer-created graphics fit into one of two categories – raster graphics or vector graphics – each behaving in its own unique way.

Raster graphics are graphics or photos that are composed of pixels. Digital photos and videos are both composed of pixels. The graphics files you'll be working with and importing into Premiere Elements will be composed of pixels. And, as we've discussed, all raster art requires a certain density of pixels – or resolution – in order for those pixels to be perceived as a smooth blend of colors. If you stretch or enlarge a photograph so much that its pixels show, it will appear jagged and blurry.

Vector graphics, on the other hand, are defined not by pixels but by shape, outlines and fill colors. Programs like Adobe Illustrator, for instance, create graphics in vector. Vector graphics can be as simple as a square or a circle or nearly as complicated as a photograph.

But vector graphics, because they are defined by *outlines and fill colors rather than pixels*, don't have any resolution. They can be resized indefinitely – even scaled to many times their original size – without breaking up into pixels. They remain simply outlines and fills. If you've used a simple drawing tool, such as the one in Microsoft Word, to draw a circle or square, you've worked with vector art.

Photoshop Elements is predominantly a *raster* art program. It is generally concerned with pixels of color. However, there are a few features in the program that behave as of they were vector art:

Shapes. The **Shape Tools** in Photoshop Elements can draw a variety of useful shapes – from circles and squares to lines and arrows and splashes. The shapes it creates, however, have some unique characteristics, as you'll see once you start using them.

Like vector art, these shapes can be easily resized and stretched without concern for resolution. And, if you'll look at a shape layer in the **Layers** panel (as illustrated to the right), you'll notice that they don't even *look* like most Photoshop art. They also won't share their layer with any other graphics. These shapes are *pseudo vector graphics*. They have all of the editing advantages of vector graphics, and they remain as such until you output your Photoshop Elements file as a graphics file or you select the option to manually render or simplify the shape layer.

Text. We usually don't think of text as vector art, but it essentially behaves the same way. You can stretch or resize text as needed in your Photoshop Elements document without concern for resolution. The text will also remain editable until you output your Photoshop Elements document as a graphics file or you select the option to manually render or simplify the text layer.

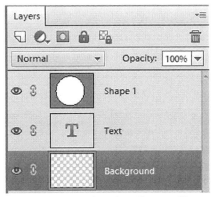

Text and shapes in Photoshop Elements, like vector art, can be resized without regard for the layer's resolution.

Once you output your Photoshop Elements file as a graphics file other than a PSD (a JPEG, TIF or GIF, for instance) or you import the file into Premiere Elements, all of the elements in your graphics file will become raster art. It all becomes pixels. And, because of that, the size (measured in pixels) of your file will determine how large the graphic or photo will be.

Image Size vs. Canvas Size

As you resize your photos or graphics files (under the **Resize** tab, as we'll discuss in **Chapter 7**), it's important to understand the difference between resizing the **Image Size** and the **Canvas Size**.

The distinction is an important one:

If you resize the **Image Size**, the entire image gets bigger or smaller; if you resize the **Canvas Size**, the image remains the same size but you either add more space around it or, if you size your canvas smaller, you trim the sides of the image off, as illustrated below.

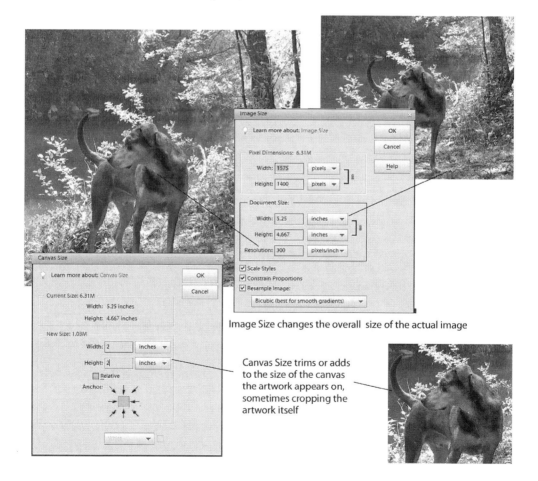

Image Size changes the overall size of the actual image

Canvas Size trims or adds to the size of the canvas the artwork appears on, sometimes cropping the artwork itself

Selections

Selection is a key concept in both Photoshop and Photoshop Elements. A number of the tools in this program are designed to enable you to select – or isolate – areas of your photo or image file and then either remove, add to or add an effect to that area only, without affecting the rest of the image.

Because your photo or graphics work will often involve precise adjustments, understanding how to select areas of your image and then add to, remove from or refine that selection is one of the keys to accessing the program's power.

We'll spend considerable time discussing how to select areas and then use those selections in **Chapter 6, Select and Isolate Areas in Your Photos.**

Many of the tools in Photoshop Elements are designed to allow you to select and isolate areas of your photos so that effects are applied only to your selection.

Layers

The biggest difference between a native Photoshop PSD file and virtually all other photo or raster graphic formats is that PSD files can include layers. These layers can include images, text, shapes or effects – some semi-transparent, some opaque – and it's important to understand how their order affects how they interact with each other.

Think of your layers as a stack of images and other elements. The topmost layers will be entirely seen, while the layers below will be seen "behind" the upper layers or quite possibly obscured completely by them.

Layers can be rearranged. They can also be hidden or made partially transparent or even made to react to certain qualities of the layers below them. And, when the background layer is removed, you can even produce non-rectangular graphics that import into Premiere Elements.

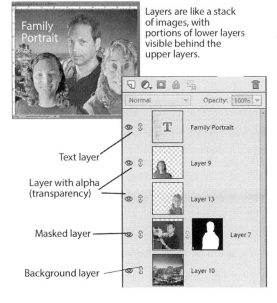

Layers are like a stack of images, with portions of lower layers visible behind the upper layers.

Text layer

Layer with alpha (transparency)

Masked layer

Background layer

Editable text is always on its own layer. Likewise, shapes, until rasterized, are always on their own layers. Layers also give you the advantage of working on your image files in portions, which you can combine, adjust and position in a variety of ways.

In addition, layers and layer groups play a vital role in creating and customizing DVD menu templates for Premiere Elements, as we'll discuss in **Chapter 13, Advanced Photoshop Elements Tools**.

Alpha

Alpha means, essentially, transparency. However, in order for your graphic file to communicate from one program to another that an area of your image file is transparent, it needs to do so using an "alpha channel." An alpha channel is sort of like a color channel except that, in this case, the color is transparent.

Transparent GIFs (see **Chapter 9**) use an alpha channel so that, unlike JPEGs, when used on a web site, GIF graphics can be an other-than-a-square shape, allowing the background of the site to display through them.

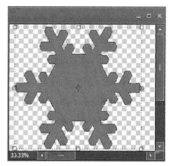

Transparency, represented by default as a checkerboard background in Photoshop Elements, can be carried with the PSD file to Premiere Elements as an "alpha" channel.

Likewise, alpha allows you to create graphics for your videos that have non-rectangular shapes or are text only, with no background.

Some graphics formats can carry alpha channels and some can not. We'll show you how to use alpha channels and which graphics file formats can carry alpha channel information in **Create non-square graphics** in **Chapter 9, Work with Photoshop Elements Layers**.

RGB Color

Virtually every graphic or photo you work with in Photoshop Elements will use either the **Grayscale** (black & white) or **RGB** color mode – meaning that every pixel in that image is a mixture of levels of red, green and blue, the three primary colors in video.

Each red, green and blue in each of those pixels is one of 256 levels of intensity, mixing together to produce a total of 16,777,216 possible color combinations. As we work with colors (**Foreground/Background Colors** in **Chapter 5, The Toolbox**), you'll see the R, the G and the B and those 256 levels of each at work.

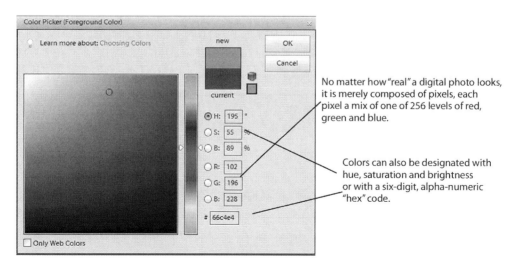

No matter how "real" a digital photo looks, it is merely composed of pixels, each pixel a mix of one of 256 levels of red, green and blue.

Colors can also be designated with hue, saturation and brightness or with a six-digit, alpha-numeric "hex" code.

The **Color Picker** (illustrated on the bottom of the facing page), which launches when you select the option to create a color, builds colors by mixing **red** (R), **green** (G) and **blue** (B) values; or by setting its **hue** (H), **saturation** (S) and **brightness** (B); or by designating the color's six-digit **Hex** value – a color format most often employed when with working with HTML and Web site design.

When the Tool Options Bin is toggled on, the space beneath the Editor will display options for whichever tool you have selected in the Toolbox.

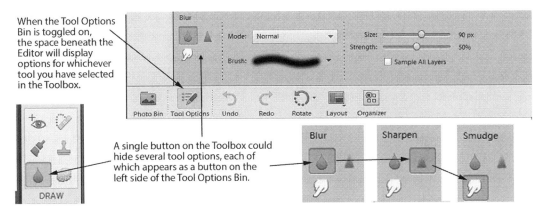

A single button on the Toolbox could hide several tool options, each of which appears as a button on the left side of the Tool Options Bin.

The Tool Options Bin

The **Tool Options Bin** shares the space below the Editor workspace with the **Photo Bin**. To view your **Tool Options** in this area, click on the button in the lower left of the interface, as illustrated above.

Virtually every tool you will use in Photoshop Elements is customizable. Select any tool in the tool panel and its settings and options will appear in the **Tool Options Bin**.

Even something as simple as a line drawing tool can include a myriad of options. The line drawing tool, for instance, includes settings for the width of the line and options for adding arrowheads on either or both ends.

Drop-down menus along this bar allow you to select colors and even unusual textures, like glass, plastic and chrome for your shape.

In addition to settings for each tool, the panel also includes options for switching to other tools, so that more than one tool is available under each button on the **Toolbox** panel.

In other words, as illustrated above, when the **Blur** tool is selected in the **Toolbox** panel, the left side of the **Tool Options Bin** displays not only the **Blur** tool but also the **Sharpen** and **Smudge** tools.

Most buttons on the **Toolbox** access two, three or more tools.

The **Tool Options Bin**, then, greatly extends the function and versatility of every tool. And, in **Chapter 5**, we'll discuss the many options available in this bin for each of the individual tools.

What is a native PSD file?

The basic working file for both Photoshop and Photoshop Elements is the **PSD file** (so named, of course, because that's the suffix the file is assigned on your computer).

There are unique characteristics to PSD files – namely that they can include layers, editable text and pseudo vector shapes. (The word "native" simply means that it's in a native state, the format that all Photoshop files are saved in.)

Photoshop and Photoshop Elements can also export or save your photos and graphics files in a number of other graphics formats, from TIFs to JPEGs to GIFs to PNGs (and a dozen others). These formats, however, don't allow for re-opening layers and text for further editing, as PSDs do.

In the ancient days of technology (like, 15 years ago), Photoshop users had to export their image files to one of these graphics formats in order to import them into another program. But, as Adobe has become the leader in pretty much all facets of print and video production, it's become possible to move graphics files from program to program in their native Photoshop (PSD) state.

In other words, you can import your native PSD files directly from Photoshop Elements into your Premiere Elements project. All of the artwork becomes flattened and the shapes and text become rasterized once the file is added to your video. But any transparent areas in the PSD will remain transparent in your video (which makes them the ideal format for bringing unusually-shaped graphics into Premiere Elements, as we discuss on page 113).

Just as importantly, the original, native PSD file – including the text and layers – remains editable in Photoshop Elements. And , if you are using a PSD file in your Premiere Elements project, whenever you save the file, any updates you've made to the photo or graphic file in Photoshop Elements will automatically be reflected in your graphic in Premiere Elements.

The Welcome Screen

Quick, Guided and Expert Editing

Guides and Rulers

The Photoshop Elements Toolbox

The Panel Bin

The Photo Bin

What's New in Version 11?

Chapter 2

Get to Know Photoshop Elements 11

What's what and what it does

Welcome to Photoshop Elements – a terrific, affordable photo retouching application and graphics editor that just seems to get better and more feature-packed with every generation!

This is a program that seems to offer more wonderful surprises the deeper you dig into it. It provides not only the obvious tools for cleaning, stylizing and creating images, but also lots of not-so-obvious tools for managing your image files, outputting a variety of print projects and even sharing your work online.

In this chapter, we'll look at the various workspaces in Photoshop Elements – and then we'll dig deeper, looking at the dozens of cool tools Adobe has added to make the program even more fun to use.

Launch the Elements Organizer.

Launch the Photoshop Elements Editor.

The Welcome Screen

The **Welcome Screen** is the panel that greets you when you launch the program. (There's a similar **Welcome Screen** for Premiere Elements.)

There are two photo editing workspaces which can be launched from the Photoshop Elements **Welcome Screen**.

- **The Photo Editor button launches the main Editor workspace**, where you'll likely do most of your photo and image file editing.

- **The Organizer button launches the Elements Organizer,** a media file management program that also includes tools for cleaning up photos, creating photo projects and sharing your photo and video projects. We discuss the Elements Organizer and its many powerful tools in **Section 3.**

You can, by the way, re-open this **Welcome Screen** at any time by selecting the option under the Photoshop Elements **Help** menu.

Bypass the Welcome Screen

If you'd prefer not to be greeted by the **Welcome Screen**, you'll find options for launching directly into the Editor workspace by clicking on the gear icon at the top right of the screen.

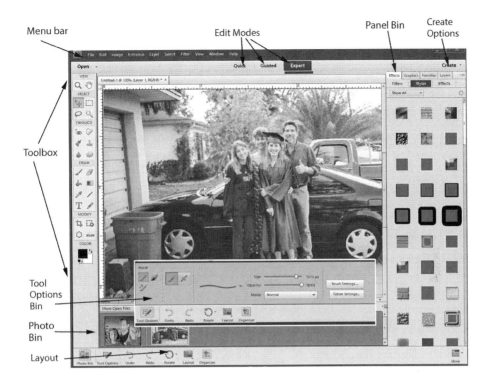

Menu bar · Edit Modes · Panel Bin · Create Options · Toolbox · Tool Options Bin · Photo Bin · Layout

The Editor workspace

The Editor workspace in Photoshop Elements 11 is actually *several* photo editing workspaces, each with its own set of tools and features. It's three main workspaces can be accessed by clicking on the tabs at the top center of the interface.

- In the **Quick Edit** workspace, you'll find a simplified set of tools for cleaning up or enhancing your photos. We'll show you how to use the tools in this workspace in **Chapter 3**.

- In the **Guided Edit** workspace, the programs walks you, step by step, through the editing process. The **Guided Edit** tools can do some pretty advanced things too! Not only will the **Guided Edits** walk you through simple clean-up of your photo, but it will also take you through some pretty high-level photo tricks, like creating a photo that seems to be standing on a reflective surface, an image with a **Tilt-Shift** effect applied and a photo in which someone seems to be popping right out of the frame! We'll show you how these cool edits work in **Chapter 4**.

- The **Full Edit** workspace (illustrated above) includes a comprehensive photo editing and graphics creation **Toolbox**. This is likely where you'll do most of your "serious" editing. It most closely resembles the workspace in the professional version of Photoshop. Needless to say, it's the workspace most of this book is about.

Additionally, the Editor workspace shares a number of tools for creating fun photo pieces with the Elements Organizer under the **Create** tab. We discuss these tools and how to use them in **Chapter 34, Create Fun Pieces**.

By default, all open files are "docked" and appear as tabs along the top of the interface.

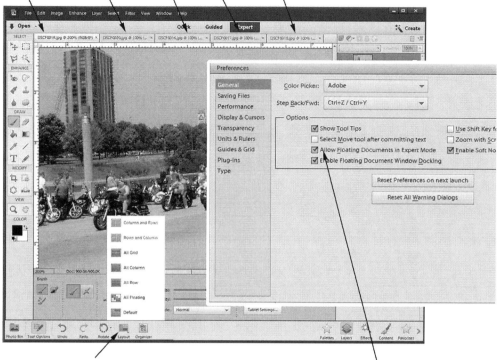

Your docked files can be displayed one at a time or in a variety of arrangements by selecting an option from the Layout menu.

The option to have Floating Windows in your Editor workspace is set in the program's Edit/Preferences.

The Expert Edit Workspace

The **Expert Edit** workspace is modeled after the interface in the professional version of Photoshop.

As illustrated at the top of the facing page, in Photoshop Elements, you can have the option of displaying your open photo and image files as a single tabbed set, each photo filling the Editor workspace panel and each open file represented by a a tab at the top of the workspace – or displaying your open photos as floating windows, a stack of open files that you can drag into any position around your workspace as you edit them.

To float your windows, you must have **Enable Floating Documents** checked on the **General** screen under **Edit/Preferences**, as in the illustration above.

The option to display your files in either mode – as well as a number of optional tabbed arrangements – is found under the **Layout** menu button.

The **Layout** menu button appears along the bottom of the interface, as seen in the illustration.

As many veteran Photoshop users know, there are advantages to displaying your photos as floating windows rather than a tabbed set.

By default, all open photos display maximized in the work panel. You can switch between your photos by clicking on the tabs along the top of the panel.

By dragging on its tab, you can undock a photo from the tabbed set and make it a floating window.

To dock or re-dock a floating window back into a tabbed set, drag it to the top of the tabbed set by its docking header (the top of the frame) until it becomes semi-transparent and a bright blue line displays around the photo. When you release your mouse button, the photo will dock with the rest of the tabbed set.

For instance, when your files are displayed as floating windows, you can copy images, portions of images and even entire layers from one image file to another simply by dragging these elements from one open file to another.

As in the illustration above, there are two ways to switch between displaying your photos as a docked, tabbed set and displaying them as floating windows:

- **Set the Arrange menu to Float All Windows.** When you click on the **Arrange** button and select **Float All Windows**, all of your photo files will display as floating windows.

- **Undock a photo from the tabbed set by dragging on its tab.** When you pull the photo file by its tab from the others in a tabbed set, it becomes a floating window.

Floating windows, by the way, *always float over tabbed photo files*. This means that, in order to get to the photos in your tabbed, docked set, you may have to either minimize any floating windows or drag them out of the way.

To dock or re-dock a photo into a tabbed set, simply drag the floating window by its docking header (the top of the window) to the top of the Editor workspace. When the photo file becomes semi-transparent (as illustrated above) release your mouse button and the photo will dock to the set.

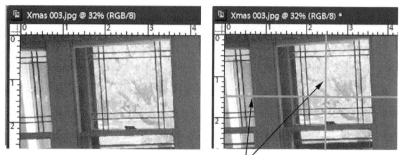

Photoshop Elements can optionally display Rulers and Guides over your image files to help you with placement and measurement of your imagery. To create a guide line, drag onto your photo from one of the rulers.

Guides and Rulers

Optionally, Photoshop Elements will display **Guides** over your image files. These horizontal and vertical lines don't show up on your final piece, of course. But they can be a great help for placing elements and text and ensuring that they are properly lined up.

The program can also display **Rulers** which, like **Guides**, can be very helpful in measuring and placing your imagery.

To display **Rulers**, select the option from the **View** drop-down on the Photoshop Elements Menu Bar.

To create a new **Guide**, click and drag onto your photo from one of the **Rulers** running along the tops and sides of your image files. (Drag from the **Ruler** along the top of your photo to create a horizontal guide or from the **Ruler** along the left of your photo to create a vertical guide.)

To toggle between displaying and hiding the guides on your image files, press **Ctrl+;** on a PC or ⌘**+;** on a Mac or select the option from the **View** menu.

The Toolbox

Along the left side of this workspace is the program's **Toolbox** (as illustrated on the left). The tools in this panel serve a number of functions, from selecting areas in your image file to creating graphics and text to patching and cloning areas of your images. As each tool is selected, that tool's individual settings are displayed in the **Tool Options Bin** that runs along the bottom of the editing workspace.

We'll spend considerable time getting to know the tools in the **Toolbox** and how to use their settings and options in **Chapter 5, Get to Know the Photoshop Elements Toolbox**.

The Panel Bin

To the right of the editing workspace is a column known as the **Panel Bin**, which includes a number of tools and panels that vary, depending on whether you're in **Quick Edit, Guided Edit** or **Expert** mode.

When you first open the program's
Expert edit workspace, this **Panel Bin**
will be in **Basic Workspace** mode.
In **Basic Workspace** mode, you can
view the **Layers, Effects, Graphics** or
Favorites panels in this bin by clicking
on the buttons in the lower right of the
program's interface.

In default Basic Worskpace mode, buttons
along the Action Bar access individual
panels. Clicking the arrow to the right of
the More button allows you to switch to
Custom Workspace mode, in which more
panels are available in a tabbed set.

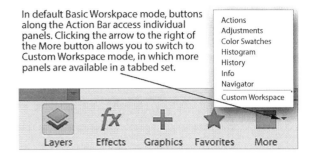

If you click on the arrow to the right
of the **More** button, you will find
the option to set the **Panel Bin** to **Custom Workspace**, which opens the
Layers, Effects and **Graphics** panels (and their respective sub-panels) in
the **Panel Bin** in a tabbed set, as illustrated below

You can click and drag on any tab in the **Panel Bin** to make its panel
a separate, floating panel. (It's common for experienced Photoshop
Elements users to make the **Layers** panel a floating panel so that it is
always available.)

Clicking directly on the **More** button will open an additional bundle of
tabbed panels, including **Info, Navigation, History,** etc. These panels can
likewise be accessed by clicking on the appropriate tab or, by dragging on
the tab, can be made a separate, floating panel.

The panels of the tabbed Panel Bin in Custom Workspace mode.

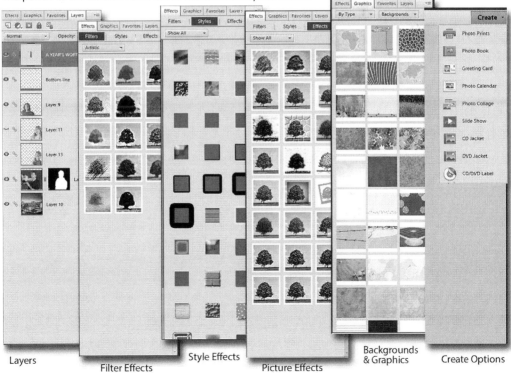

Layers   Filter Effects   Style Effects   Picture Effects   Backgrounds & Graphics   Create Options

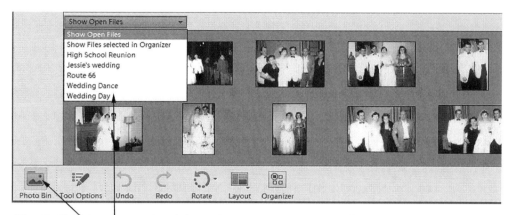

When the Photo Bin option is selected, the area below the Editor worskpace wil display all of the photos you have open in your Photoshop Elements editor, all of the photos you have selected in the Elements Organizer's Media Browser or any photos you've saved to Organizer Album.

The Photo Bin

Running along the bottom of the Editor workspace and sharing space with the **Tool Options Bin** is a small but powerful panel known as the **Photo Bin**.

When the **Photo Bin** button is selected in the lower left of the program's interface, all photos and image files you have open in your Editor workspace will appear as thumbnails in this bin.

To open a file in your **Photo Bin** in the Editor workspace, **double-click** on its thumbnail in the **Photo Bin**.

Although this is the default and most common way to use the **Photo Bin**, it is certainly not its only function. The **Photo Bin** also interfaces with a number of other workspaces.

To access and change the **Photo Bin's** display options, click on the bin's drop-down menu, which reads **Show Open Files** by default, as in the illustration above.

> **Show Open Files.** Displays, as thumbnails, all of the image files you currently have open in your **Editor** workspace.
>
> **Show Files Selected in the Organizer.** If you have both Photoshop Elements and the Elements Organizer open and you have files selected in the Organizer's **Media Browser,** selecting this option displays those files in the **Photo Bin**. These photos or image files can then be launched in the Editor workspace by **double-clicking** on them.
>
> **Albums.** If you have **Albums** created for your image files in the Organizer, these **Albums** will also be listed on this drop-down menu (as in the illustration above), and their images can be accessed as a group simply by clicking on the **Album's** name. To learn more about creating **Albums**, see page 420 of **Chapter 33, Manage Your Files with the Organizer.**

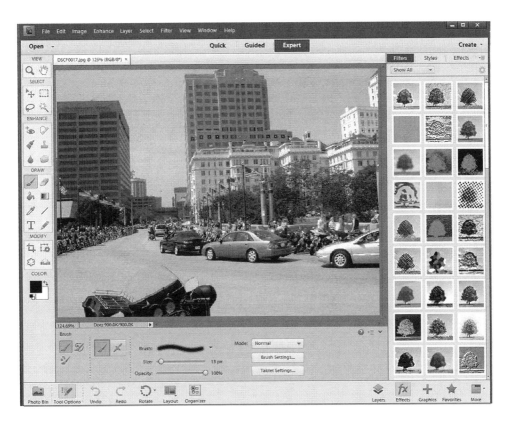

What's new in Photoshop Elements 11?

Adobe has really given Photoshop Elements, as well as Premiere Elements and the Elements Organizer, a major overhaul in version 11.

To improve readability, the program now uses a bigger, brighter interface with its tabs and buttons labeled with big, clean text.

To reduce clutter, more tools are hidden under buttons or stored in tabbed interfaces – easy to access but out of the way.

And the program itself has been tightened up, improving performance and stability, even when working with large photo files.

Additionally, the folks in San Jose have ladled on the new features, particularly in the **Quick** and **Guided Editing** workspaces, where you'll find lots of new tools for cleaning up your pictures and creating photo effects.

Among the highlights are:

An improved Quick Edit workspace

Open your photo in the new **Quick Edit** workspace and you'll find tools for adjusting its exposure levels, correcting its color, shifting its color temperature and sharpening the picture. In addition, this space now includes tools for fixing red eyes, whitening teeth and removing blemishes.

Its lighting and color adjustment tools use an intuitive new **Quick Fix Preview** tool, which allows you to test drive any changes to your photo simply by hovering your mouse over the variations on its tic tac toe-style panel.

We discuss it in depth in **Chapter 3**.

New Guided Edits

There are also many improvements to the **Guided Edits** workspace, with its wizard-like tools that take you step-by-step through the process of correcting or improving your photos or creating special effects.

Nearly every tool in the Photoshop Elements **Toolbox** shows up somewhere in its **Touchup Guided Edits**.

Additionally, Adobe has added some cool, new effects to its **Guided Photos Effects**. Among these are step-by-step wizards for creating a **High Key** and **Low Key** effect, for turning your photo into a **Line Drawing**, for adding a **Vignette Effect** or for creating a **Tilt-Shift** effect that exaggerates depth-of-field so that a scenic photo can appear to be made up of tiny miniatures.

We'll show you some of its highlights in **Chapter 4**.

The Actions Panel

And, as if a larger library of **Guided Edits** weren't enough, Adobe has also included an **Actions** panel, a very cool feature borrowed from the professional version of Photoshop. **Actions** are pre-recorded effects or other tasks that can be applied to your photos simply by "playing" them.

Among the included library are **Actions** that add borders to your photos, resize or crop them, **Actions** that add a faded ink or sepia tone to your image and **Actions** that automatically make your photo look like a Polaroid-style snapshot!

We'll show you how it works in **Chapter 4**.

Quick Fix Preview panels allow you to test drive adjustments by just hovering your mouse over them.

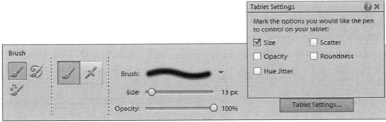

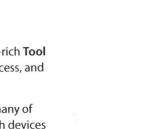

Options for many tools include support to tablets.

The Tool Options Bin

The old **Options Bar** has been replaced by a bigger, more feature-rich **Tool Options Bin**. Customization options for your tools are easier to access, and many include new settings and presets.

This **Tool Options Bin** even includes support for tablets, so that many of your Photoshop Elements tools can more effectively interface with devices like the Wacom Bamboo and other drawing tablets.

New Filters

Some very nice new filters have been added under the **Sketch** category.

> The **Pen & Ink** filter makes your photo look as if it were drawn and painted with ink.

> The **Comic** filter does an amazing job of making your photos look as if they are illustrations in a comic book.

> And the **Graphic Novel** filter gives your photos the look of a highly stylized ink drawing.

We talk more about photo effects and filters in **Chapter 11**.

Improved Camera RAW support

If you're a "serious" photographer, you'll likely also appreciate the improvements to the Camera RAW interface. In fact, it's surprising to see such a powerful Camera RAW interface on a consumer product. But, particularly in the last couple of years, Adobe has put a tremendous amount of effort into making Photoshop Elements more up to the task of working with this advanced digital photo format.

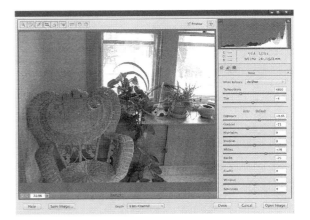

We'll discuss Camera RAW in more detail in **Chapter 13**.

Advanced Refine Edge Options

The **Refine Edge** tool has also been given a major upgrade in version 11. Borrowing some advanced features for refining selections from the professional version of Photoshop, the new **Refine Edge** tool makes selecting around fine details, like fur and hair, not only easier but practically automatic!

We show you how to use this amazing new tool in **Chapter 6**.

Organizer improvements

Adobe has put at least as much time and effort into improving the Elements Organizer as it has Premiere Elements and Photoshop Elements.

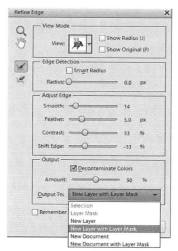

Not only does the program perform more efficiently than ever before, but Adobe has also added or expanded its ability to search and manage your media files by the location the video or photos were shot, the people in the picture, the event they recorded and even by their similarity to other video and photo files.

It's so big we've dedicated the entirety of **Section 3** of the book to it!

Need some Basic Training?

Need more help learning the basics of Photoshop Elements?

Check out my free tutorial series **Basic Training for Photoshop Elements** at Muvipix.com.

This simple, eight-part series will teach you the basics of photo resolution and show you how to adjust lighting and correct color in your photos, work with layers, add effects, scan your pictures and even share your photos and videos online. And, yes, it's absolutely free!

To see the series, just go to http://Muvipix.com and type "Basic Training for Photoshop Elements" in the product search box. (We also offer Basic Training tutorials for other products, include Premiere Elements.)

And while you're there, why not drop by the Community forum and say hi! We'd love to have you become a part of our growing city. Hope to see you there!

Adobe Photoshop Elements

Part I

Quick and Guided Editing

Chapter 3

Quick Fixes
Easy ways to touch up photos

In addition to its more professional photo touch-up and graphic design tools, Photoshop Elements includes a number of simplified and semi-automatic tools for fixing, enhancing and adjusting your image files.

Many of these are Quick Fixes, with simplified controls and automatic functions.

The Quick Fix Work Area

View   Hand Tool   Touch-Up Tools   Set Before & After View

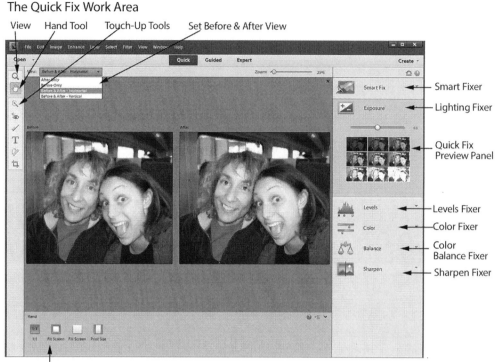

Smart Fixer

Lighting Fixer

Quick Fix
Preview Panel

Levels Fixer
Color Fixer
Color
Balance Fixer
Sharpen Fixer

Tool Options

The Expert Editor workspace is a full-featured toolkit for fixing your photos, correcting color and creating graphic and photographic effects.

However, if you just need a simple fix – or you're intimidated by the multitude of tools and options in the Photoshop Elements Expert workspace, the program also offers simplified **Quick Fix** tools for editing your photos and graphic files.

The **Quick Fix** workspace is launched by clicking the **Quick** tab at the top of the Photoshop Elements interface.

To the left of the workspace is the **Quick Fix Toolbox**, described on the facing page, a simplified version of the **Expert** workspace **Toolbox**.

To the right of workspace are simplified adjustment controls for changing the color, lighting, color temperature and sharpness of your photos. These adjustments can be made using sliders or by using the very intuitive **Quick Fix Preview** panel, as described on page 30.

A drop-down menu in the upper left of the workspace allows you to set your view as **Before Only, After Only** or **Before and After.**

To leave the **Quick Fix** workspace once you have finished applying any fixes to your image file, click the **Expert** button at the top center of the interface.

You may then choose to save the changes you've made to the image file or discard them.

The Quick Fix Toolbox

The **Quick Fix** work area includes a number of tools for viewing and manipulating your image file. The tools on the **Toolbox** to the left of the interface work similarly to their counterparts in the **Expert Editor Toolbox**. (For more information, see **Chapter 5, Get to Know the Photoshop Elements Toolbox**.)

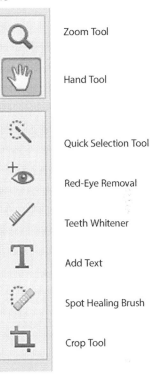

Zoom Tool

Hand Tool

Quick Selection Tool

Red-Eye Removal

Teeth Whitener

Add Text

Spot Healing Brush

Crop Tool

The Zoom Tool (magnifying glass) controls your view.

The Hand Tool allows you to drag your image around in your viewing area.

The Quick Selection Tool selects areas on your image file for manipulation, by "painting" to define the selected area. When an area is selected, any lighting or color adjustments will apply only to that selected area.

Red-Eye Removal removes that annoying red reflection eyes sometimes display when you shoot with a flash in a dimly-lit room. Applying it is as simple as selecting the tool and clicking on the red pupils in your picture, as discussed on page 52.

The Teeth Whitener is a **Smart Brush Tool** (as discussed on page 54 of **Chapter 5, Get to Know the Photoshop Elements Toolbox**). Drag your mouse to **Quick Select** the teeth in your photo and the program will automatically bleach and brighten them.

The Text Tool will add text to your photo. We discuss adding and working with text in your image files in **Chapter 10**.

The Spot Healing Brush automatically removes blemishes and other flaws using a very effective **Content Aware Fill** system. Removing a blemish is as simple as selecting this tool and then dragging over the blemish, as we discuss in more detail on page 53.

The Crop Tool can be used to crop and reshape your image.

The Teeth Whitening Tool will bleach and brighten a selected area of your photo.

Drag the Teeth Whitening Selection Tool to define the whitening area.

Use the Add and Remove options to add to or remove from your selected area.

The Tool Options allow you to set the size, shape and hardness of the edge of your selection.

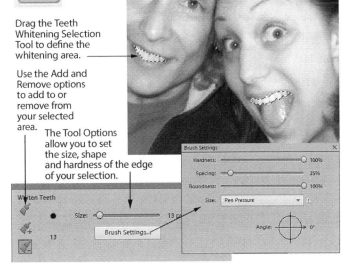

Quick Lighting, Color and Sharpen fixes

The **Quick Fixes** in the panel bin along the right side of the **Quick Edit** interface offer easy, intuitive ways to correct and adjust the color, lighting and sharpness of your photos.

Smart Fix combines adjustments for brightness, contrast and sharpness.

Exposure simulates the adjustments your camera makes, brightening a picture that is too dark or darkening a picture that too light.

Levels adjusts the saturation and contrast of your picture's color for either shadows, midtones or highlights.

Color adjusts saturation (amount of color), hue (tint of color) and vibrance (intensity of color).

Balance adjusts your photo's color temperature (more blue vs. more red) or tint.

Sharpness increases the sharpness of your image.

The tools in this panel include both a slider, for increasing or decreasing intensity of the adjustment, and a **Quick Fix Preview** panel, which allows you to make an adjustment simply by clicking on one of the variations in the tic tac toe-like interface. (You can even preview your change just by hovering your mouse over any of the variations.)

Some adjustments also include an **Auto** button for making automatic color or lighting corrections.

To undo an adjustment, click on the center square in the **Quick Fix Preview** panel or click the ⌕ **Reset** button at the top of the panel.

If you have used the **Quick Selection Tool** described on the previous page to select an area or areas in your photo, your adjustments will be applied only to the selected area.

Organizer Instant Fixes

The Elements Organizer includes a similar set of **Instant Fixes** for doing a quick clean-up of your photos. You can access them by clicking the **Instant Fix** button in the lower right of the Organizer interface.

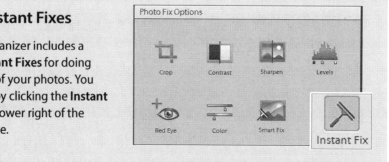

Guided Touchups

Guided Photo Effects

Guided Photo Play Edits

Chapter 4

Guided Edits

Photo adjustments and cool tricks, one step at a time

Guided Edits, as the name implies, are sometimes very high level photo effects made simple through wizards that walk you through each step of the process.

Guided Edits allow you to get professional-looking results with only a basic understanding of the program.

The Guided Edits workspace is opened by clicking the **Guided** tab in the top center of the Photoshop Elements workspace.

A **Guided Edit**, as the name implies, is a simplified and intuitive way of working your image file through a series of adjustments, cleaning up your image or creating special photo effects..

Photoshop Elements walks you through the entire process – explaining how each tool works, offering an automatic fix if available and then giving you the option of either keeping the changes (clicking **Done**) or rejecting the changes and returning to the main menu (**Cancel**).

If you're at all intimidated by the **Expert Edit** workspace, a **Guided Edit** may be the way to go.

The **Guided Edit** panel, which appears down the right side of the **Guided Edit** workspace, offers you three categories of edits:

> **Touchups** clean up your photo's composition or correct its color.
>
> **Photo Effects** apply special effects to your photo, giving it an intriguing or surreal look.
>
> **Photo Play** walks you through some very advanced effects so that people in your pictures seem to pop out of the photo frame or your photo is made to look like a collage of snapshots or your photo seems to be standing on a reflective surface.

Once you've worked through a **Guided Edit**, you'll have the choice of clicking **Done** and **Cancel**.

If you've applied an effect and you'd like to remove it, you can click the **Undo** button in the lower left of the interface or press **Ctrl+z** (⌘+z on a Mac) on your keyboard or by clicking the **Reset** button at the top of the panel.

Touchups

Like the **Quick Fixes** discussed in **Chapter 4**, **Touchups** are designed to offer you a simple workspace for doing color adjustments, cropping and sharpening. In addition, this workspace includes walk-throughs of some advanced photo correction and re-compositing tools, including the **Photomerge Recompose** tool (discussed in detail on page 67).

Brightness and Contrast adjust the blackest and whitest levels of your photo and the contrast between them. This edit includes an **Auto Fix** adjustment button.

Correct Skin Tones is a step-by-step walkthrough of the tool described on page 99.

Crop Photo walks you through the process of trimming down or reshaping your photo.

Enhance Colors opens tools for adjusting your photo's **Hue, Saturation** and **Lightness**. This edit includes an **Auto Fix** adjustment button.

Levels adjusts the black, white and mid-tone levels of your photo (similarly to **Brightness and Contrast**). However, rather than physically change the photo, these adjustments are made to an **Adjustment Layer** (as described on page 100).

Perfect Portrait (the **Guided Edit** panel is illustrated on the right) is a very nice all-purpose edit walkthrough which includes tools for softening or sharpening your photo, adjusting contrast, healing blemishes, removing red-eyes and enhancing eyes and eyebrows.

Recompose is used to move people or elements in a photo closer together without changing their shapes. This tool is discussed in detail on page 67.

Color Cast is a tool that will automatically change the white balance of your photo, based on the area you sample.

Rotate and Straighten guides you through the process of straightening a crooked photo.

Scratches and Blemishes includes tools for softening flaws and erasing blemishes.

Sharpen increases the contrast between pixels, sharpening the look of your photo.

Photo Effects

Photo Effects change the look of your photo in intriguing or surreal ways. As with all **Guided Edits**, the program walks you through the process of creating them, step-by-step:

Depth of Field sharpens the subject in your photo and blurs the background, giving your photo the illusion of being shot with a very short depth of field. We demonstrate this effect on page 34.

High Key washes the color out of your photo and softens its focus to give your picture an ethereal look.

Line Drawing creates the effect that your photo has been hand-drawn in pencil or charcoal.

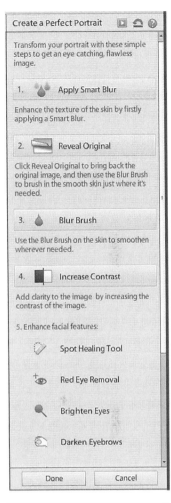

Create a Perfect Portrait

Transform your portrait with these simple steps to get an eye catching, flawless image.

1. Apply Smart Blur

Enhance the texture of the skin by firstly applying a Smart Blur.

2. Reveal Original

Click Reveal Original to bring back the original image, and then use the Blur Brush to brush in the smooth skin just where it's needed.

3. Blur Brush

Use the Blur Brush on the skin to smoothen wherever needed.

4. Increase Contrast

Add clarity to the image by increasing the contrast of the image.

5. Enhance facial features:

Spot Healing Tool

Red Eye Removal

Brighten Eyes

Darken Eyebrows

Done   Cancel

The High Key effect

The Line Drawing effecct

The Tilt-Shift effect gives your scenic photos the exaggerated depth of field of photos of miniatures.

The **Lomo Camera Effect** makes your photos look as if they were shot with a LOMO, a primitive, Soviet-made camera whose weird color and lighting results have given it something of a cult following.

Low Key increases the black levels in your photo, giving it a dark, mysterious look.

Old Fashioned Photo makes your picture look like an old black & white photo.

The Orton Effect softens your photo to give it a gently blurred, dreamy look. You can increase or decrease the effect by custom-adjusting the blur, noise and brightness levels.

Saturated Slide Film Effect imitates the look of photos shot on a film stock that enhances the color saturation.

Tilt-Shift, illustrated above, adds a blur to the top and bottom of a photo shot from an oblique angle, creating the illusion of exaggerated depth of field and making your photo look as if it were composed of miniatures.

The Vignette Effect makes your photo look as if it were shot with a pinhole camera, brighter in the center and darker around the sides.

The Depth of Field Guided Edit

The **Depth of Field Guided Edit** uses a blur and layer mask to create a focused center and blurred background for your photo.

To use the **Depth of Field Guided Edit**:

1   With the photo open in the **Guided Edits** workspace, select **Depth of Field** on the option panel.

2   On the **Depth of Field** panel, select either the **Simple** or **Custom** workspace.

A **Simple Depth of Field** effect will add a blur around the outside of your photo, leaving it unaffected in the center, as in the illustration to the right.

The "Simple" Depth of Field effect

If you select the Simple option.

3 Click the **Add Blur** button, as illustrated on the facing page.

Your entire photo will blur.

4 Click the **Add Focus Area** button.

Click on the focal object in your photo, then drag. The program will mask the effect on your focal object, removing the blur from it – then gradually add blur around the rest of your photo, based on the area defined with your mouse drag.

In a **Custom Depth of Field** effect, you designate the area of your photo that the blur will not apply to, as illustrated below.

If you select the Custom option:

3 Click the **Quick Selection Tool** button.

Drag the tool over the subject of your photo, "painting" to select the area you want to keep in focus.

4 Click the **Add Blur** button.

The area outside of your selection will blur.

If you'd like, you can increase the level of blur around your focal point by dragging the slider at the bottom of the panel.

6 Click **Done** to finish your photo effect.

In Custom Depth of Field mode, use the Quick Selection Tool to draw a selection around your focal object...

...then click Add Blur. The program will automatically add a blur outside of the selection. You can increase or decrease the blur level with the slider.

Photo Play

The **Photo Play** category of **Guided Edits** area includes four fun walkthroughs for creating highly-stylized photographic effects.

The **Out of Bounds Effect** lets you crop your photo, excluding certain elements, so that, say, a person's head, hand or foot extends beyond the borders of the picture. Instructions for using this tool are described below.

Picture Stack breaks your photo into four, eight or twelve photos, making your picture look as if it's been pieced together from several photo segments. For more information on how to use this tool, see page 38.

Pop Art creates a colorful photo series, a la Andy Warhol's famous Marilyn Monroe portrait.

Reflection creates a reflection of your picture, which you can customize so that it appears to be shining off a floor below your photo, a sheet of glass or even rippling water.

An "Out of Bounds" Guided Edit effect

Creating an **Out of Bounds Effect** involves basically two steps. The first is redefining the frame of your photo, which will be cropped down from its current size. The second is designating which elements in the photo will not be affected by this cropping.

For my example I've chosen an action shot of a young girl doing a tae kwon do high kick. To make this shot more interesting, we'll crop the photo's frame around the girl so that her kick seems to be popping right out of the picture.

1   With the photo open in the **Guided Edits** workspace, select **Depth of Field** on the option panel.

The **Panel Bin** will display the **Out of Bounds Effect Guided Edits** options panel.

At the top of this panel is a photo showing an example of the finished effect. If you roll your mouse over it, you'll see the "before" picture that the **Out of Bounds** effect was created from.

Out Of Bounds

2   Click the **Add a Frame** button.

A box will appear over your photo. Drag the corner handles of this box to define what will be your photo's newly cropped frame.

When this cropping box is in your desired position, lock it in place by clicking the green check mark or by pressing the **Enter** key on your keyboard.

The photo will now appear with its new cropping displayed as a semi-opaque overlay, as illustrated on the facing page.

3 Click the **Quick Selection Tool** button on the **Guided Edits** panel. (You may need to scroll down the palette to see this button.)

As we show you in **Chapter 5, Get to Know the Photoshop Elements Toolbox**, the **Quick Selection Tool** works like a paintbrush. Click and drag the tool over the elements in your photo you'd like to extend beyond the photo's newly cropped frame. In my case, this will be the girl and her foot. As you drag the tool over your photo, your selected area will be displayed with a moving dotted line around it (commonly called "marching ants").

If it adds more than you'd like to your selection, you can always un-select these areas later.

In the **Tool Options Bin** below your photo, you'll find the settings for the **Quick Selection Tool**.

The **Brush** settings allow you to set the size of the tool's selection brush. (You can also quickly widen or narrow your brush's size by pressing the [and] keys on your keyboard.)

To add to your selection, select the **+** tool from the **Tool Options Bin** or hold down your **Shift** key as you continue to paint with the **Quick Selection Tool**.

To de-select a selected area, select the **-** tool in the **Tool Options Bin** or hold down the **Alt/Option** key on your keyboard as you paint with the **Quick Selection Tool**.

4 When you're satisfied with your selection, click the **Out of Bounds Effect** button on the **Panel Bin**.

The program will crop your photo per your settings, except for the areas you've selected.

As you can see, there are some additional effects which can be added to your photo effect in this workspace, including a **Drop Shadow** and a **Gradient background**.

1. ☐ Add Frame

2. ✎ Selection Tool

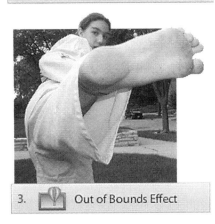

3. ⬇ Out of Bounds Effect

If, after you've clicked **Done,** your results still seem a bit rough, you can return to the Expert Editor and use some of its tools (the **Eraser,** for instance) to clean up and refine the edges of the effect.

If, in **Expert Edit**, you look at the **Layers** panel, you'll see that this simple trick actually involves a number of high-end tools and effects, including **Layer Masks** and multiple copies of your photo on separate layers.

In fact, if you look at one of the bottom-most layers, you'll see that your **Original Image** is still down there, unchanged.

Just in case you want to throw out the whole effect and start again from scratch!

Create a Picture Stack

A fairly automatic effect, the **Picture Stack Guided Edit** breaks your photo into four, eight or twelve pieces, making it look as if it's assembled from a collage of several photos.

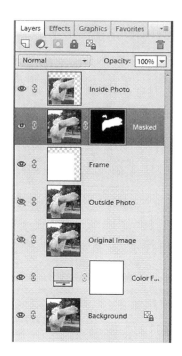

1   With the photo open in the **Guided Edits** workspace, select **Picture Stack** on the option panel.

    The **Panel Bin** will display the **Picture Stack Guided Edits** panel.

2   Customize your effect.

    Select the **Number of Pictures** you would like your photo broken into, the **Border Width** you'd like around each picture and the **Background Color** the photos will be stacked on. Click **Done**.

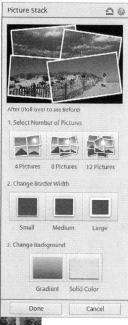

The Photo Stack Guided Edit turns your photo into a photo collage.

The Actions panel

New to Photoshop Elements 11 is the **Actions** panel, a cool new tool borrowed from the professional version of Photoshop.

The **Actions** panel offers a number of pre-recorded, multi-step tasks, tasks that can be applied to a photo open in your editor simply by selecting the **Action** and then clicking the **Play** button on the top right of the panel.

The **Actions** panel can be opened by selecting the option under the **More** button in the lower right of the Photoshop Elements interface or by selecting **Actions** under the program's **Window** menu.

There are four categories of **Actions** included with Photoshop Elements:

Bottom Borders add a border below your photo onto which you can add text.

Lose Weight narrows your photos, distorting it slightly to make your subject look a little taller and thinner.

Resize and Crop automatically crops and resizes your photo to a specific shape and resolution.

Special Effects automatically give your photo the look of being printed with faded ink, add vignetting or a sepia tint, age your photo or make it look like a Polaroid snapshot by resizing it and adding a white border to it.

If you click on the arrow to the left of any **Action**, you can see the individual steps the program will take in the completion of that **Action**. You have the option of applying the entire **Action** to your photo or, by selecting a sub-task, just one of the main task's individual steps.

Adobe Photoshop Elements

Part II
The Expert Editing Workspace

Background/Foreground Colors

Move and View Tools

Selection Tools

Enhance Tools

Draw Tools

Modify Tools

Color Tools

Chapter 5

Get to Know the Photoshop Elements Toolbox

Your main photo editing tool kit

In Expert mode, the most visible tools in the Photoshop Elements Editor workspace are those gathered into the Toolbox, displayed as two columns of little icons along the left side of the Editor workspace.

Understanding these tools, how they work and how to customize them for your particular needs will take you a long way toward mastering this program.

VIEW

SELECT

ENHANCE

DRAW

MODIFY

COLOR

Quick	Guided	**Expert**

The Toolbox

When Photoshop Elements is set to **Expert** mode, the full Photoshop Elements **Toolbox** will appear along the left side of the Editor workspace. The tools in the **Toolbox** are divided into six categories:

View Tools. Tools for zooming into, out of or changing the view of your image files.

Select Tools. Tools for selecting and isolating areas in your image files.

Enhance Tools. Tools for cleaning up and changing your image files. This category includes the tools for blurring, sharpening, dodging and burning, based on techniques long used by professional photographers.

Draw Tools. Tools for drawing, painting, coloring and erasing. Among the **Draw** tools are tools for adding text. Because working with text is a category all its own, we'll discuss these tools in depth in **Chapter 10, Create and Edit Text**.

Modify Tools. Tools for cropping, shaping and straightening your image files.

Color Tools. Tools for setting the colors of the elements you will add to your files.

The Tool Options

Sharing space with the **Photo Bin**, below the **Editor** workspace, the **Tool Options Bin** gives you access to the options for customizing how each tool works. (This space is toggled on by clicking the **Tool Options** button in the lower left of the interface.)

Some of these custom settings are so deep that one tool can actually work as several tools. And a few tools even allow you to *add* custom settings of your own!

Tool Options for some tools, for instance, include drop-down menus that list patterns, brushes or effects and sliders for setting specific brush sizes. We'll discuss specific **Tool Options** for each tool as we discuss each individual tool.

Access many tools under one button

Most buttons in the **Toolbox** will grant you access to more than one tool. When the **Blur** tool button is selected, for instance, buttons in the **Tool Options Bin** allow you to optionally select the **Blur, Sharpen** or **Sponge** tools. As we discuss the individual tools in this chapter, we'll indicate which sets of tools share a single **Toolbox** button.

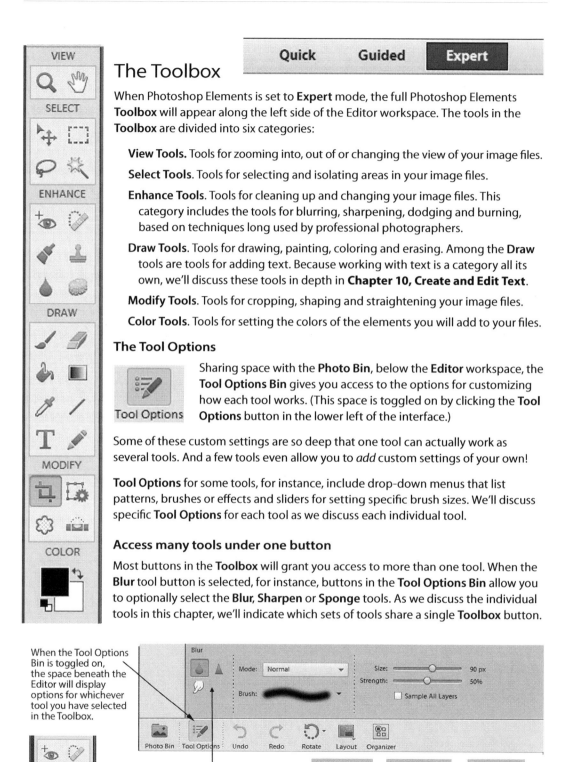

When the Tool Options Bin is toggled on, the space beneath the Editor will display options for whichever tool you have selected in the Toolbox.

A single button on the Toolbox could hide several tool options, each of which appears as a button on the left side of the Tool Options Bin.

Set Foreground and Background Colors

You'll likely refer often to this swatch icon, displayed at the very bottom of the **Toolbox**. The colors that are set here play a role in how a number of your tools function.

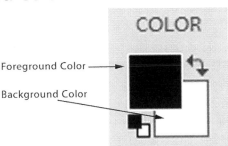

Foreground Color ⟶

Background Color

Generally, the **Foreground Color** will be the default color in which new items you create will appear.

- When a paintbrush, drawing or shape tool is selected, for instance, the brush will paint with or the shape will appear in the **Foreground Color** by default.
- When you use the **Typing Tool,** your text will also appear, by default, in the **Foreground Color.**
- When you use the **Eraser Tool**, the area you erase will be replaced by the **Background Color.** (At least when you're erasing from a background layer or flattened image file. When you're work on a layer, erasing makes that area on the layer transparent.)
- When you use **Fill** or **Stroke**, you will have the option of doing so with the **Foreground** or **Background Color.**
- When you use the **Gradient Tool**, the area will be painted, by default, with a gradation or blend of color from the **Foreground Color** to the **Background Color.**

There are a number of ways to set which colors appear as your **Foreground** and **Background Colors**. The easiest way is to simply click on either the **Foreground** or **Background Color** swatch icon on the **Toolbox**.

This will launch the **Color Picker.**

The Color Picker

The **Color Picker** displays a color sampling screen and a slider bar, representing **hue, saturation** and **brightness**. (Hue is your color's shade or tint; saturation is the amount of that hue in your color; brightness is the amount of lightness in your color.)

Your current color is displayed in the lower half of the box, located in the upper center of the **Color Picker**, as illustrated to the right.

Your new color will appear in the upper half of this box.

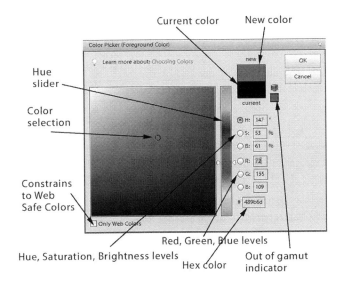

Current color   New color

Hue slider

Color selection

Constrains to Web Safe Colors

Hue, Saturation, Brightness levels

Red, Green, Blue levels

Hex color

Out of gamut indicator

To adjust the hue for your color, move the white triangles up or down on the **Hue slider** that runs down the center of the **Color Picker**. Then to pick your color, click in the big "picker" box, representing the saturation and brightness of that hue.

By checking the **Only Web Colors** box in the lower left corner of the **Color Picker,** you can restrict the available colors in the picker to only those colors that display consistently on Web pages.

Colors can also be set digitally in the **Color Picker** by typing in numbers for **Hue, Saturation** and **Brightness** or for the 256 levels of **Red, Green** and **Blue** in the color mix. The alpha-numeric **Hex** numbers for the color, in the lower right, can also be manually designated.

Once you've selected your color, click **OK**. Your selected color will become your new **Background** or **Foreground Color.**

The Eyedropper/Sampler Tool

Another way to set the **Foreground Color** is by sampling a color from an open photo or image with the **Eyedropper/Sampler** (located among the **Draw** tools) on the **Toolbox.**

To sample a color, select this tool from the **Toolbox** and then click on a color area in an open image file.

The **Tool Options** for this tool includes options for selecting an average color sample from a block of pixels and for selecting colors that appear on either the current layer or all layers of your image file.

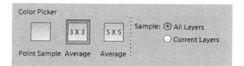

The Color Swatch panel

The **Color Swatch** panel can be opened by selecting it from the Photoshop Elements **Window** menu or by selecting the option from the **More** button in the lower right corner of the interface.

When you click on a swatch in the **Color Swatch** panel, it will become your **Foreground** Color.

The **Color Swatch** panel includes hundreds of color options, categorized in several swatch sets. These various swatch sets can be accessed from the drop-down menu at the top of the panel, as illustrated to the right.

You can even create custom colors for your swatch library.

To do so, set your **Foreground Color** using the **Color Picker,** then click the **New Swatch** icon in the lower right of the **Color Swatches** palette. The color will be permanently added to your swatch library.

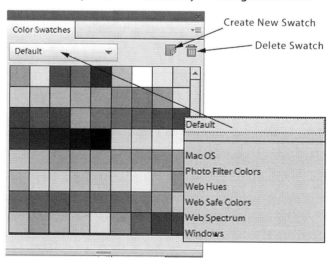

The Foreground and Background Colors can also be set by selecting a chip from the Color Swatches palette. The drop-down menu at the top of this panel offers options for displaying a number of additional color libraries.

The size and number of swatches displayed can be set by clicking the option switch on the upper right of the panel.

Additional Foreground/Background Color options

Swap Foreground and Background Colors. You can quickly switch the **Foreground** and **Background Colors** by clicking on the double-headed arrow to the upper right of the **Foreground/Background Color** swatch icons, or by pressing the **X** key on your keyboard.

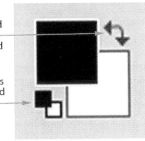

Swap Foreground and Background colors

Reset colors to black and white

Quickly set Foreground/Background Colors to black and white. You can quickly reset the **Foreground** and **Background Colors** to black and white, respectively, by clicking on the black/white icon to the lower left of the **Foreground/Background Color** swatch icon on the **Toolbox**. A keyboard shortcut for setting the colors back to black and white is the **D** key.

Move and View Tools

Three tools in the **Toolbox** are for viewing and positioning your image file.

VIEW

The Zoom Tool

 One of two **View** tools, the **Zoom Tool** is represented by a magnifying glass, this tool is used, naturally, to zoom in and out of your image.

Select this tool and click on your image and you will zoom in. (Or you can use the keyboard shortcut **Ctrl+✛** on a PC or **⌘+✛** on a Mac.)

Hold down the **Alt/Option** key and click on your image and you will zoom out. (Or you can use the keyboard shortcut **Ctrl+−** on a PC or **⌘+−** on a Mac.)

The buttons and checkboxes on the tool's **Tool Options Bin** can be used to 'jump' your view to specific zoom levels.

The Hand Tool

 Represented by a **Hand** icon, this **View** tool is useful if you're zoomed in so closely to an image that sections of your image are outside the file's window. When the **Hand Tool** is selected, you can click and drag the image's view around within the viewable area.

A keyboard shortcut for the **Hand Tool** is the **Spacebar** on your keyboard. No matter what tool you're working with, you can always reposition your view by holding down the **Spacebar,** then clicking and dragging your image around in the viewing area.

The Move Tool

 The top left **Select** tool in the **Toolbox,** and more or less the default tool in Photoshop Elements, **the Move Tool** is used to move or drag the elements, selections, text or layers in your image files to new positions.

The settings in the **Tool Options** for this tool are useful for arranging the positions and order of objects in your image.

The selected area of your image file will appear surrounded by a moving dotted line, commonly called "marching ants."

Toggles in the Tool Options Bin for the Selection Tools set whether the tool adds to or subtracts from the selection.

New Selection

Add to Selection (or hold down Shift key)

Remove from Selection (or hold down Alt key)

Select Intersection of old and new selections

Selection Tools

The tools the **Toolbox's Select** category are used to select areas of your image files.

A selected area can be cut, copied or pasted. But, more so, a selected area is *isolated*, so that any effects you add to your photo or image file will be applied *only* to the selection without affecting the rest of the image. Selecting and isolating is a very powerful function of Photoshop Elements, which is why we spend an entire chapter (**Chapter 6, Select and Isolate Areas in Your Photos**) discussing it in depth.

Your selected areas will be surrounded by little, moving dotted lines – which are traditionally referred to as "marching ants."

Add to and subtract from a selection

When selecting an area in a photo or image file, you don't have to get the selection exactly right the first time:

- Once you've selected an area, you can add to the selection by toggling **Add to Selection** in the **Tool Options Bin** (as illustrated above) or by holding down the **Shift** key as you continue to select.

- To un-select areas from your selected area, toggle **Subtract from Selection** in the **Tool Options Bin** or hold down the **Alt/Option** key as you drag over the area you want to deselect.

- To select only the area overlapped by your current and your new selection, toggle **Intersect with Selection** in the **Tool Options Bin**.

Using these tools to add to or subtract from your selection, you can hone your selection until it is precisely the area you want to work with.

- To turn off, or **deselect**, all of the selected areas for your image file, press **Ctrl+d** on a PC or ⌘**+d** on a Mac.

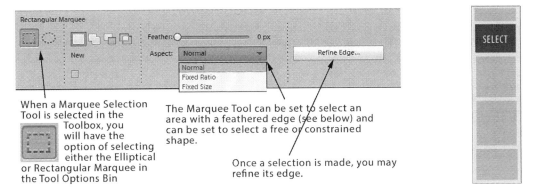

When a Marquee Selection Tool is selected in the Toolbox, you will have the option of selecting either the Elliptical or Rectangular Marquee in the Tool Options Bin

The Marquee Tool can be set to select an area with a feathered edge (see below) and can be set to select a free or constrained shape.

Once a selection is made, you may refine its edge.

The Marquee Selection Tools

The **Rectangular Marquee Tool** and the **Elliptical Marquee Tool** are both available under the same **Toolbox** button. To switch between them, click on the currently selected tool the **Toolbox** button and then select one or the other in the **Tool Options Bin**, illustrated above.

To select an area on your image with either of these tools, click and drag across your image file. As long as that tool remains selected in the **Toolbox**, you can reposition the selected area by dragging it. To deselect the area press **Ctrl+d** on a PC or **⌘+d** on a Mac.

Beyond the **Feathering** (discussed below), the **Tool Options** for this tool include a few functions which can also be activated with keyboard shortcuts.

To constrain the tool to select a perfectly circular or square area, select the **Fixed Ratio** option from the **Aspect** drop-down in the **Tool Options Bin** – or hold down the **Shift** key as you drag to make your selection.

When the **Aspect** is set to **Fixed Size**, you can designate the exact size of the area you will select.

Feathering

Most selection tools include an option to allow **Feathering**. This option is available in the **Tool Options Bin** for the **Marquee Selection Tools** as well as a refinement option under the program's **Select** menu.

Feathering means softening the edge of a selected area so that, rather than a sharp division between the selected and unselected areas, there is a soft gradation of selection.

A "feathered" selection has a softer edge so that, when the selection is removed or an effect is added to it, the distinction between the selected and unselected area of your image is a gradation rather than a solid line.

We look at this feature in more detail in the **Feathering** sidebar on page 73.

The Lasso Tool selects as you draw freehand.

The Polygonal Lasso Tool draws a selection from point to point as you click.

The Magnetic Lasso Tool follows the edge of a color break as you drag or click to create points.

Lasso Selection Tools

SELECT

The three "lasso" tools share the same **Toolbox** button.

To switch between these tools, click the button for whichever tool is displayed in the **Toolbox**, then select the tool you'd like to use in the **Tool Options Bin**.

Lasso Selection Tools define a selected area by drawing a line around it (as if wrapping it in a lasso). There are three **Lasso Tools,** each functioning slightly differently.

The Lasso Tool is a freehand tool for selecting an area. To select an area with the **Lasso,** you just drag and draw. When you release your mouse button, the defined area will be selected.

The Polygonal Lasso Tool works similarly to the **Lasso Tool** except that, to designate an area to be selected, you click and release to create a series of dots, which will be connected by straight lines. To close a **Polygonal Lasso Tool** selection, finish the selection by clicking onto your selection's starting point.

The Magnetic Lasso Tool is also a freehand tool for selecting an area. However, as you draw your selection with this tool, it will try to automate your selection by following the edge of an object, based on its color.

In other words, in the picture above, I dragged around the dog to select it in the photo. As I dragged my mouse around the dog's head, the **Magnetic Lasso** automatically made fine adjustments to my selection (based on the distinction in color between the dog and the background) to more precisely select the dog.

An important **Tool Option** setting for this tool is **Edge Contrast**. This setting defines the tool's tolerance for color contrast between the areas it does and the areas it does not select.

In other words, if the color of the subject you are drawing a selection around is a very different color than that of the background, you can use a high **Edge Contrast** percentage to ensure that the tool finds the edges.

If the subject is not so clearly distinguished from the background, you'll need a much lower **Edge Contrast** percentage. And you'll likely need to be more careful guiding the tool around the selection, or you may need to add to or subtract from the selection to refine it.

The Magic Wand
Tool selects everything
within a color range,
based on the Tolerance
level you've set.

The Selection Brush
Tool draws a selection
as you "paint" an area with
its brush.

The Quick Selection
Tool combines the
the behaviors of both tools,
selecting a similar color
range as you "paint"
across your image file.

Quick Selection Tools

The **Magic Wand, Quick Selection** and **Selection Brush** tools
share the same button in the **Toolbox**. To switch between
these tools, click the button for whichever tool is displayed in
the **Toolbox**, then select the tool you'd like to use in the **Tool
Options Bin**.

The Magic Wand Tool. One of the most useful tools in the **Toolbox**, the
Magic Wand Tool, automatically selects an area on your image based on
color similarities. (We put it to good use in **Chapter 12, Photo Editing
Tricks**.)

When you click or drag on your photo with this tool, adjacent pixels of a
similar color are automatically selected. By holding down the **Shift** key to add
and the **Alt/Option** key to subtract, you can continue to select or de-select areas
of your image file to build your desired selection.

The most important **Tool Options** setting for this tool is **Tolerance**. The lower the
number, the narrower the range of colors the **Magic Wand** will consider similar. A
higher **Tolerance** number widens the range of similar colors the **Magic Wand** will
select as you click.

The Selection Brush Tool works just like it sounds like it would – as you "paint" with
it, you create a selected area. **Tool Options** include settings for defining the size
and hardness of the brush. You'll find more information on brush options in our
discussion of **Brush settings and options** on page 59.

The Quick Selection Tool works like a combination of the **Magic Wand** and the
Selection Brush Tool. As you drag it across your image, it "paints" a selection area,
grabbing nearby areas of similar color along the way. This is a great tool for quickly
paint-selecting a flat-colored background that you'd like to remove or replace. Its
Tool Options include settings for the size, shape and hardness of the brush.

SELECT

Enhance Tools

Enhance Tools are used to change your image file – whether to clean up a photo or to change it or add a special effect. Some of these tools are simple and almost automatic. Others can do some pretty complex effects!

The Red Eye Removal Tool

You know what this tool is for. It's for when you've taken a flash picture in dim lighting and you find that, in the final photo, your best friend or your dog has eyes that glow like those of some evil robot!

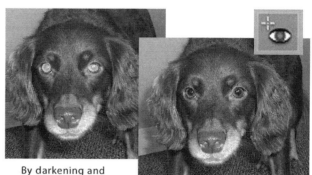

By darkening and desaturating the areas you click on, the Red Eye Removal Tool instantly tames demonic-looking subjects.

To use it, select the tool and then click on the subject's bright, red pupils. The tool essentially strips the color out of the pupil area and darkens it.

Tool Options for this tool allow you to set the **Pupil Size** and **Darken Amount**.

The Spot Healing Brush Tool

Sharing a button with the **Healing Brush Tool**, this tool is great for getting rid of unwanted moles, blemishes or other such flaws in your photos, as illustrated at the top of the next page.

When you click an area or "paint" with it, the tool blends the selected area with color information from the surrounding pixels. **Tool Options** include settings for the brush's size and hardness (For more information on brushes, see **Brush settings and options** on page 59) as well as the option to remove objects using **Content Aware Fill** (see facing page).

What is Anti-Aliasing?

Anti-Aliasing is a method of smoothing or slightly feathering the edges of an object or text so that it looks more natural. When **Anti-Aliasing** is turned off, the object or text will have very sharp edges, usually resulting in a very blocky, unnatural look.

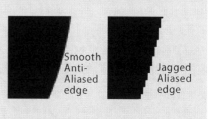

Smooth Anti-Aliased edge

Jagged Aliased edge

The Healing Brush Tool

Similar to the **Clone Stamp Tool** (discussed on the next page), this tool borrows color and texture information from one area of your photo (which you've defined by **Alt-clicking** on it) and uses it to paint over another area.

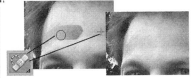

The Healing Brush uses a Content Aware Fill system to replace blemishes, telephone lines and other unwanted elements in your photos with imagery from the surrounding area!

Using a Content Aware Fill system, the Spot Healing Brush uses nearby imagery to replace blemishes and other flaws in your photos virtually invisibly!

The difference between this tool and the **Clone Stamp** is that the **Healing Brush Tool** then blends this borrowed imagery with the colors of the existing pixels to form a natural "healing patch" over the area.

As with the **Spot Healing Brush Tool**, the **Tool Options Bin** includes settings for the brush's size and hardness.

You can see the **Healing Brush** at work in our **Photo Editing Trick** on page 145.

Content Aware Fill

A very exciting enhancement to the **Spot Healing Brush Tool** in Photoshop Elements is something Adobe calls **Content Aware Fill**.

In past versions of the **Healing Brushes**, the tool filled areas that you designated by averaging the colors of the surrounding pixels to create a smooth patch. This was very effective for removing blemishes and small marks in a photo – but it was less so at patching larger areas.

Content Aware Fill essentially looks at the entire area around what you're trying to hide or remove, and it smoothly fills the area you designate with similar, very natural-looking imagery.

This makes it especially effective at removing telephone wires from an otherwise perfect picture of a sunset – or even painting former friends completely out of a scene!

The Content Aware Fill feature in the Healing Brush Tools makes it easy to remove even large objects from many scenes.

The Smart Brush Tools

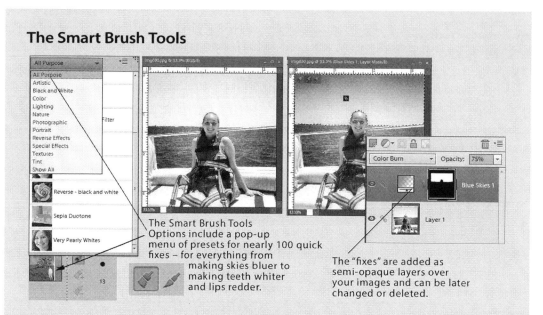

The Smart Brush Tools Options include a pop-up menu of presets for nearly 100 quick fixes – for everything from making skies bluer to making teeth whiter and lips redder.

The "fixes" are added as semi-opaque layers over your images and can be later changed or deleted.

The **Smart Brush Tool** and the **Details Smart Brush Tool** are part of a great **Quick Fix** tool set built into Photoshop Elements. (To toggle between these two tools, select the button on the **Toolbox** representing the currently active tool and then select one of the two **Smart Brushes** in the **Tool Options Bin**.)

Both tools work similarly, the main distinction being that the **Details Smart Brush Tool** affects only the area you "paint" with the brush (like the **Selection Brush** described on page 51), while the **Smart Brush Tool** expands the selected areas of your picture, based on their similarities to the areas you paint (like the **Quick Selection Tool** also described on page 51).

The **Smart Brush Tools** enhance your photos automatically, using presets available under the pop-up menu on the **Tool Options Bin**. These presets will make grass greener, skies bluer, teeth whiter, lipstick redder, etc. – or they can add color or texture effects to your photos.

To apply a **Smart Brush** fix, select the appropriate preset from the **Tool Options Bin's** drop-down menu, as illustrated above, and then paint over the area in your image file that you'd like to add effects to.

When you finish selecting the area of your photo and release your mouse button, the program will make the adjustments to your picture, as in the illustration above.

Using the **+** and **−** brush icons that appear on your image as you work, you can paint to add to or remove from the selected area (or hold down the **Shift** key to add and the **Alt/Option** key to subtract). The program will update the effect automatically.

The true beauty of these adjustments is that they don't permanently change the image itself! If you look at the **Layers** panel, you'll see that these adjustments are actually just masks added as what are called **Adjustment Layers**, as illustrated on the above. By clicking on these **Adjustment Layers**, you can reactivate the **Smart Brush Tools** and make further adjustments, or even delete the **Adjustment Layers** completely. The original image remains unmolested! At least until you flatten the layers or save the file as something other than a PSD file.

A favorite tool for "stunt photo work," the Clone Tool lets you paint over portions of your image file – removing objects or even people – with imagery from another area of your image file (defined by Alt+clicking).

The Clone Stamp Tool

This amazing tool takes imagery from one area of your photo file (an area indicated with an **Alt-click**) and paints it onto another.

The tool is popular for doing special effects, like "erasing" somebody or something from a scene (see pages 146).

In addition to settings for the brush size and hardness, the **Tool Options Bin** includes an **Opacity** setting. Opacity (the opposite of transparency) controls whether the area you paint over is replaced entirely with the new image or whether the new image is blended in semi-transparently with the old to some degree.

The Pattern Stamp Tool

Rather than painting an area in your photo with imagery from another area in your image, the **Pattern Stamp Tool** paints over your image with a pattern, as selected from the pop-up menu in the **Tool Options Bin**.

There are many pages of patterns available for this effect, by the way. And you can see the other categories of patterns by clicking on the flyout menu button in the upper right corner of the option box that appears when you click on the "pattern" drop-down.

An **Impressionist** option turns the pattern into a liquid swirl of paint that intensifies as you hold down on your mouse button.

The Pattern Stamp tool paints over your image with any of dozens of patterns.

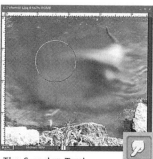

The Blur Tool blurs
the area you drag across

The Smudge Tool
smears your image as
you drag acrosss it

The Sharpen Tool
increases pixel contrast
in the areas you drag across

ENHANCE

Blur, Smudge and Sharpen

These three tools, which share the same button in the **Toolbox**, treat your image file a bit like liquid, allowing you to blur, smear or sharpen it.

To switch between these tools, click the button for whichever tool is displayed in the **Toolbox**, then select the tool you'd like to use in the **Tool Options Bin**.

The three tools share similar settings on the **Tool Options Bin** – Brush size, hardness and **Strength** (amount) of the blur, smudge or sharpening. (For information on brush settings, see **Brush settings and options** on page 59.)

The Blur Tool

Dragging this tool across your image softens the pixel edges of the area you drag across, blurring your picture.

The Smudge Tool

This tool treats your image as if it were wet paint. When you drag across it, you smear it!

The Sharpen Tool

The Sharpen Tool increases the contrast between pixels, giving your image a crisper look as you drag across it.

Unlike the general **Unsharp Mask** (discussed in **Chapter 8, Correct Color and Lighting**) which sharpens your entire photo, the **Sharpen Tool** sharpens only the areas of your picture that you drag across.

The Sponge Tool desaturates, or removes color from, an area

The Dodge Tool lightens the area you drag across

The Burn Tool darkens the area you drag across

The Sponge, Dodge and Burn Tools

These three tools are sometimes referred to as the "darkroom tools" because they're based on techniques photographers used to use in the darkroom to enhance their prints.

To switch between these tools, click the button for whichever tool is displayed in the **Toolbox**, then select the tool you'd like to use from the **Tool Options Bin**.

The three tools share similar **Tool Options** for setting brush hardness and size.

The Sponge Tool

The Sponge Tool desaturates, or removes color from, an area of your image as you drag over it. (The **Tool Options Bin** includes an option for reversing the process, or increasing color saturation.)

The **Flow** setting on the **Tool Options Bin** determines how much color is removed.

The Dodge Tool

The Dodge Tool lightens the area you drag over, as if it were a photographic print which received less exposure in the darkroom. The **Tool Options Bin's Exposure** setting designates how intensely the area is dodged.

The Burn Tool

The Burn Tool darkens the area you drag over, as if it were a photographic print which received more exposure in the darkroom. The **Tool Options Bin's Exposure** setting designates how intensely the area is darkened.

DRAW

Draw Tools

The Brush Tools

The three **Brush Tools** share the same button on the **Toolbox**.

To switch between these tools, click the button for whichever tool is displayed in the **Toolbox**, then select the tool you'd like to use in the **Tool Options Bin**.

The Paint Brush

This tool is your basic paintbrush – similar to the **Pencil Tool** as a line drawing tool, except that the **Brush Tool** includes options for painting soft-edged or even textured lines.

The **Tool Options** for this tool includes settings not only for the size and hardness of the brush and the opacity of the paint but also for switching the brush to **Airbrush** mode – which, as you'd expect, paints a stroke that grows more intense the longer you "spray" it on one spot.

The Brush Tool paints a soft or textured freehand line.

In addition, if you click on the **paintbrush icon** in the **Tool Options Bin**, you'll find an option panel for creating your own brush. (For information on brush settings, see **Brush settings and options** on page 59.)

The Impressionist Brush

The **Impressionist Brush** is a pretty cool special effects tool.

When you click and hold or paint with this brush, it "liquefies" and swirls the colors in your image so that it resembles an impressionist painting.

The Color Replacement Brush

The **Color Replacement Brush** replaces the color of an area you "paint" over in your image file with the **Foreground Color** (although, in **Tool Options**, you can also set it to replace only the hue, saturation or luminosity of your picture).

The Impressionist Brush swirls your image.

Because of the way this brush senses the differences in color ranges within your image, it can, amazingly enough, paint the leaves on a tree but leave the sky behind them alone or even, as illustrated on the right, tint the darker leaves of a tree in the background while leaving the brighter leaves of the tree in the foreground alone!

The **Tolerance** level you have set in the **Tool Options Bin** determines how much distinction there must be between the areas to be re-colored and those left intact.

The Color Replacement Brush overlays color, but only over the range of colors you designate.

Brush settings and options

Many tools behave like brushes. The tool's effects or colors are essentially painted on.

In fact, the size and softness settings in the **Tool Options Bin** for many tools are nearly identical to those of the **Paint Brush Tool**.

There are two basic brush settings: the **Size** of the brush (measured in pixels) and its **Hardness**.

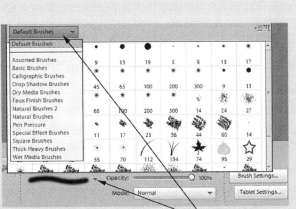

Brush sub-categories, textures and sizes on the Tool Options panel.

Hardness determines sharpness of the edge of the stroke that the brush paints. The softer the edge, the more feathered the area between the brushed area and the unbrushed area. When using the **Clone Tool**, for instance, a softer edged brush may show a more natural, less abrupt line between your old and newly-added image areas.

Some brushes, called **Scatter** brushes, create an effect like painting with steel wool. Their effect is scratchy and hard.

Brushes can also have shapes. These oblong shapes (included among the **Calligraphy** presets) will paint a wider line when you are painting one direction than they will another, as when you are writing with a calligraphy pen.

Brushes can even be set to paint **patterns**. When a pattern is selected for a brush, the pattern's image will appear again and again as you paint. This can be used, for instance, to paint several stars across a sky in a single brush stroke or to paint a trail of footprints.

In addition to the over 300 preset brushes you'll find in Photoshop Elements, you can also save your own personal brush settings. To do this, once you've set your brush to the shape and size you want, click on the ≣ menu on the upper right of the brush preset drop-down menu and select the option to **Save Brush**.

The **Paint Brush** tool also has some cool advanced brush tool settings in the **Tool Options Bin**, which we discuss on page 61.

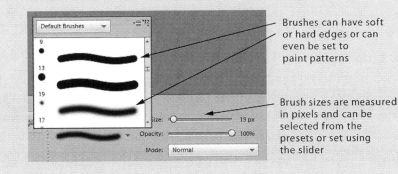

Brushes can have soft or hard edges or can even be set to paint patterns

Brush sizes are measured in pixels and can be selected from the presets or set using the slider

The Eraser Tool removes what you drag across, replacing it with your Background Color or, if a layer, transparency.

The Background Eraser erases up to color breaks, based on the Tolerance level you've set in the Tool Options.

The Magic Eraser instantly removes an area you click on, based on its color range and the Tolerance level you've set.

DRAW

Eraser Tools

Simply put, the **Eraser Tools** remove the image from your file as you drag across it.

The three **Eraser Tools** share the same button on the **Toolbox**. To switch between these tools, click the button for whichever tool is displayed in the **Toolbox**, then select the tool you'd like in the **Tool Options Bin**.

The Eraser

- If you're erasing from a flattened image or a background layer, what you erase will be replaced with your **Background Color** (see page 45).
- Erasing from a layer creates transparency through that layer.

Tool Options for this tool include settings for brush size, hardness and opacity (transparency level).

The Background Eraser Tool

The **Background Eraser** erases one color or color range and ignores dissimilarly colored areas in your image file.

In other words, this tool can be used to erase the background from the photo of a person and yet not erase the person!

The tool determines the color you want erased based on the pixels that are in the tool's crosshairs as you "paint" with it. So, as you erase, if you keep the crosshairs off of what you don't want removed, the tool will erase along the edge of the color break, as in the illustration above, in which it erased the wall but not the dog.

Tool Options include settings for the brush size and hardness as well as **Tolerance** – how much distinction must exist between the area you're erasing and the area you're not in order for the tool to recognize the difference.

The Magic Eraser Tool

Like the **Magic Wand Tool,** this tool selects, and then erases, areas in your image file that fall within a range of colors, based on the pixel you click on or the pixels you drag across.

In other words, using this tool, you could easily remove a consistently green background from an image in a single click or simple click and drag.

The **Tolerance** setting, in the **Tool Options Bin**, designates how wide a range of color is considered similar to your selected pixels, and thus is erased. (The higher the number, the more "tolerant" the tool is of variations in the background color.) The **Opacity** level determines if the image is erased completely or simply softened or made semi-transparent.

Advanced brush tool settings

In version 11, Adobe has introduced a couple of new tools that makes working with the brush tools even more intuitive. When the **Paint Brush** is selected, these tools appear on the far right of the **Tool Options Bin**.

Brush Settings

Brush Settings allow you to create a brush with whatever characteristics you'd like, including **Fade** (How much the opacity of the paint changes along your brush stroke), **Hue Jitter** (How much the stroke wavers between your selected **Foreground** and **Background**

With Brush Settings, you can create a custom brush with hard or soft edges or even with a non-round shape for creating lines as if drawn with a calligraphy pen.

Colors as you paint), **Scatter** (How much the stroke appears as speckles rather than a solid line), **Spacing** (How much the stroke appears as a series of dots rather than a solid line), **Hardness** (How soft the edges of the stroke are) and **Roundness** (the shape of the brush; an oval brush can be used to make the brush draw variable-width strokes, as if drawn with a calligraphy pen).

Tablet Settings

Drawing tablets, such as those made by Wacom, enable you to draw and paint in Photoshop Elements using a very intuitive pad and stylus. The **Tablet Settings** enable you to use your tablet to create custom brushes.

Tablet Settings control how the program interfaces with devices like the Wacom tablet.

The Paint Bucket (Fill) Tool

When you drag the **Paint Bucket** to your canvas, it paints your image file with the current **Foreground Color**. It does this in one big, even flow of paint.

If you have a **Selected** area on your canvas or on your image file, the **Paint Bucket Tool** will fill only the selection.

There are two keyboard shortcuts that also fill with color, by the way:

Alt+Backspace will fill a selected area with your **Foreground Color**.

Ctrl+Backspace (⌘+**Backspace** on a Mac) will fill a selected area with your **Background Color**.

 In the **Tool Options** for the **Paint Bucket**, the tool can be set to fill an area with a pattern rather than a color.

The Gradient Tool

The **Gradient Tool** paints your image or selected area with a gradation or blend of one color to another. By default, this gradation will begin with your **Foreground Color** and blend to your **Background Color**.

Tool Options include a number of patterns for your gradients, from linear gradients to radial gradients to pattern gradients. The gradient they create will be a blend of your **Foreground** and **Background Colors**.

The **Gradient Editor** also includes presets for color blends other than the default. You can access them by clicking the **Edit** button in the **Tool Options Bin**.

Tool Options also include a setting for **Opacity,** so that you can set whether the gradient covers your image file completely or blends semi-transparently to some degree with the existing image.

The Paint Bucket fills your canvas or your selected area.

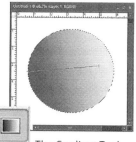

The Gradient Tool fills your canvas or selected area with (by default) a gradation from the Foreground to the Background Colors.

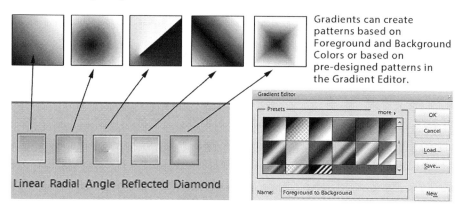

Gradients can create patterns based on Foreground and Background Colors or based on pre-designed patterns in the Gradient Editor.

Linear Radial Angle Reflected Diamond

The Shape Tool includes several common shapes, from lines of varying width to customizable polygons.

The Custom Shape Tool option drop-down menu offers over 550 more, including faces, flowers, plants, animals and funny hairstyles! Each are vector art and can be resized until their shape layer is simplified.

Choose 3D shape style.

Set shape's color.

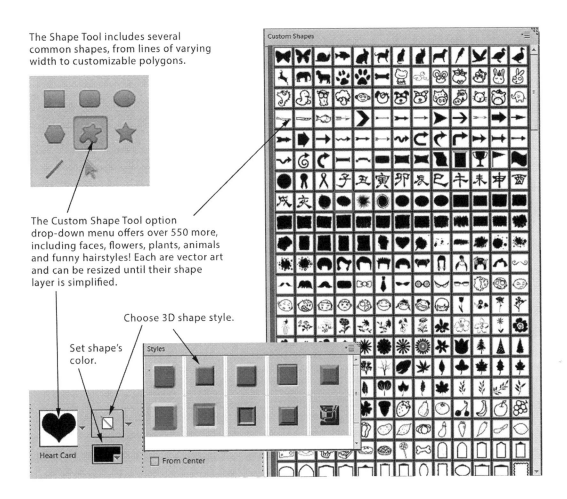

The Shape Tools

The **Shape Tools** draw shapes as you drag across your image file. These shapes appear as a new layer on your file, and remain editable until you simplify the layer or flatten your image. (See **Simplify or flatten layers** on page 110 of **Chapter 9, Work with Photoshop Elements Layers**.)

There are about half a dozen common shapes available under the **Shape Tool** button. To switch between them, click the button for whichever tool is displayed in the **Toolbox**, then select the tool you'd like in the **Tool Options Bin**.

If you select the **Custom Shape Tool** option, you will have access to hundreds of more shapes. These custom shapes are available on the pop-up option panel in the **Tool Options Bin**, and include everything from basic snowflakes and arrows to cartoon talk bubbles, animals, flowers, faces and ornaments. (To access more than the default shapes on this pop-up panel, click on the drop-down menu at the top of the option box and select a category or **All Elements Shapes**.)

When **Add to Shape Area** is selected on the **Tool Options Bin**, you can even combine several shapes to create just about any shape!

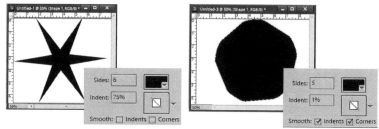

Using custom settings on the Tool Options panel, the same tool can be used to create many different shapes.

Shapes possess some unique characteristics. As you can see, if you look at your **Layers** panel after you've added a shape to your image file, shapes aren't simple raster objects, but are, rather, "masks" with color added to them.

The designers at Adobe have decided to treat shapes this way so that they behave like vector art. In other words, once you've added a shape to your image file, you can resize it and reposition it without any concern for its resolution or pixel depth. You can also re-color a shape just by double-clicking on the shape in the **Layers** panel and then changing its color on the **Color Picker** that pops open.

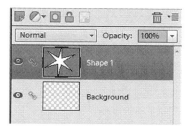

Because shapes are composed of paths rather than pixels, they can be resized and reshaped without concern for their resolution.

Some **Shape Tools** have interesting customization settings available in their **Tool Options**. For instance:

The Rectangle Tool, Ellipse Tool and Rounded Rectangle Tool

These tools include options for constraining their shapes to a perfect square or a circle. Additionally, the **Rounded Rectangle Tool** has an option for setting how round its corners are.

The Polygon Tool

The Polygon Tool (illustrated at the top of this page) has options for setting the number of sides on the polygon you will create, how round its corners are and if the sides make it a flat-sided polygon or a starburst-like shape.

The Line Tool

The Line Tool Options panel includes options for setting the line's width and if it includes arrowheads on its start and/or end points.

Typing Tools

Because working with text is a subject unto itself, we've dedicated an entire chapter to it and the **Typing Tools**. For more information, see **Chapter 10, Create and Edit Text**.

The Pencil Tool

As the name implies, this is a freehand line drawing tool. (Unlike the **Paint Brush**, the **Pencil** always draws lines with a hard edge.)

Tool Options for this tool include settings for the size of the pencil and the opacity of the line. The **Auto-Erase** option allows you to toggle the **Pencil Tool** (with a click of the mouse) between working as a drawing tool and working as an erasing tool.

The Pencil Tool draws a hard-edged freehand line.

Modify Tools

The Crop Tool

The **Crop Tool** is the tool used for cutting both the image and canvas. In other words, this tool changes the canvas size of the actual image file. To use it, click to select the tool, then drag to create a box on your image file.

Once you've created the proposed cropping area, it can be reshaped and even moved, by dragging on its corner handles, until you've isolated the area of the image file you want to keep, as illustrated below.

To finalize and crop your photo, click on the green checkmark or press **Enter** on your keyboard.

The **Custom** pop-up menu in the **Crop Tool's Tool Options** (illustrated on the next page) gives you options for constraining the area that you've cropped to specific shapes, sizes or resolutions.

The Crop Tool resizes your canvas based on your selected area. Once selected, the area can be resized, repositioned or canceled. To finalize your crop, click the green check mark or press Enter on your keyboard.

A dotted line overlay indicates the Rule of Thirds "power alleys" for your photo's composition.

MODIFY

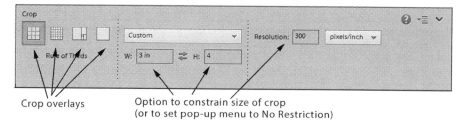

Crop overlays

Option to constrain size of crop
(or to set pop-up menu to No Restriction)

Additionally, if you fill in specifics for **Width, Height** and **Resolution**, you can prefigure the tool to cut your image down to a precise size and resolution!

Crop Tool composition overlays

On the left side of the **Tool Options Bin** for the **Crop Tool**, you will find overlay options for the **Crop Tool**:

The Rule of Thirds

Unless you're trying for a certain effect, centering a subject in your photo can make for a fairly boring picture. As many photographers and graphic artists know, pictures are much more dynamic if the focus of the photo is slightly off-center, as illustrated at the bottom of this page.

To help you create this kind of composition, the **Crop** and **Recompose Tools** display an overlay with dotted lines that indicate your photo's Rule of Thirds "power alleys" (as in the illustration on page 65), guides for assisting you in composing your newly cropped photo.

The Golden Ratio

Ancient Greek mathematicians were the first to discover the **Golden Ratio**, an aesthetically pleasing balance of width and height that works out to approximately 1.618 to 1.

The **Golden Ratio** can be found occurring naturally in plants and animals – and it's often intentionally imposed on many works of art and architecture.

Selecting **Golden Ratio** from the **Tool Options Bin's Overlay** menu (as illustrated above) constrains the shape of your cropped area to these aesthetically pleasing dimensions.

A photo composed with its subject on one of the picture's "thirds" (off-centered) is much more interesting and dynamic than one in which the subject is merely centered (above).

With the Recompose Tool, you can make a photo of people sitting too far apart look much cozier.

The Recompose Tool

The cool and powerful **Recompose Tool** gives you the ability to reshape a photo – re-positioning people or other elements in it nearer together – without distorting these elements in any way.

What's most amazing about this tool is that it does most of what it does automatically (although there are also manual ways to "protect" certain elements in the photo).

When you **Recompose** a photo, you squeeze it, either from top to bottom or from side to side, compressing the elements of the photo so that they become closer together – *but without changing the shapes of any of the key elements in the picture!*

In many cases, when you're using this tool, the **Recompose Tool** will automatically recognize people in your photo and it will protect them, as much as possible from distorting as you resize your photo. It will also try to keep certain major elements in the background of the photo – trees or cars – from distorting. It merely makes these key elements look closer together.

In our experience, however, the program can often use a little help identifying which elements in the photo you want to preserve. Fortunately, this is very simple to do.

1   With your photo file open, click to select the **Recompose Tool**. (The tool will launch a help screen that explains how to use the tool. You can elect not to see this screen again by checking the box in its lower left corner.)

   In **Recompose** mode, you'll see handles on each corner and in the middle of each side of your photo file. Dragging on these corner handles will resize your photo.

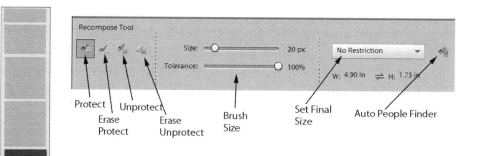

Protect | Unprotect

Erase Protect   Erase Unprotect   Brush Size   Set Final Size   Auto People Finder

MODIFY

2 Drag one side of your photo in to squeeze your photo. In most cases, people and other major elements in the photo will move closer together – though they may very soon begin to distort.

3 To "protect" the elements you don't want to distort, select the green paint brush from the **Recompose Tool Options Bin** and paint over the elements you want to preserve. As with any brush-based tool, you can enlarge or reduce the size of the brush by setting its size on the **Tool Options Bin** or pressing the **[** or **]** buttons on your keyboard.

In my illustration below, I've painted "protection" over the three people and their chairs.

To remove protection from an area, switch to the green eraser tool and drag across a "painted" area.

To designate an object or person as something you *want* to see distorted or removed, paint it with the red "unprotect" brush. To remove this indicator, use the red erase brush.

There is also a green "people finder" tool that can often automatically find and protect the people in your photo. It tends to work best when the photo was shot in ideal lighting conditions.

With key elements in your photo designated as protected, these elements move closer together, undistorted, as you resize the photo by dragging on its side handle.

4 With your designated elements protected, drag the handle on the side of your photo in to compress the photo. As you do, the elements and people you've protected will move closer to each other and yet will not change shape.

(There is, of course, a saturation point at which even protected elements will distort.)

You can also change the dimensions of the photo numerically by typing a width or height in the **Tool Options Bin**.

When you are happy with your new composition, click the green check mark or simply press **Enter**. Photoshop Elements will process and re-render your photo.

Note that, because of the way this tool works, your new photo will be layered. So, in order to save it as something other than a PSD or layered TIF, you will need to flatten the layers by selecting **Flatten Image** under the program's **Layer** menu.

The Cookie Cutter Tool

The **Cookie Cutter Tool** will crop your picture into any of hundreds of custom shapes, from starbursts to butterflies to ragged-edged photos.

(The shaped image will have alpha, or transparency, around it so that, if you save your image file as a PSD, the shaped image will appear with no square background when the file is used in Premiere Elements.)

The Cookie Cutter Tool cuts your image into any of over 550 shapes

Once you've selected the tool, select a shape from the **Cookie Cutter** pop-up menu in the **Tool Options Bin** and then drag to draw the shape onto your image file. Once you click on the green checkmark or press **Enter** on your keyboard, your image file will be cut to that shape.

There are many pages of options for shapes, by the way. And you can access them by clicking on the drop-down menu at the top of the panel that appears when you click on the **Tool Options Bin's Cookie Cutter** pop-up menu, as illustrated.

The Cookie Cookie Tool Options Bin

With the Straighten Tool selected,
drag a line to define an object
you would like to appear perfectly horizontal. The tool will automatically
rotate and straighten your photo accordingly.

Straighten Tool

I love this tool! It's great for straightening a photo whose subject is a bit crooked.

To use it, just select the tool and then drag to draw a line along an element in your image (a rooftop, a mantle, somebody's shoulders) that you would like to appear perfectly horizontal.

As above, when you release your mouse button, the image will instantly rotate and straighten!

Making Selections
Refining Selections
Effects and Selections
Cutting & Pasting Selections
Stroking & Filling Selections

Chapter 6
Select and Isolate Areas in Your Photos
Working with selections

A key function in Photoshop Elements – and one which a number of tools support – is selecting.

Selecting means isolating areas of your image file so that effects can be applied to those areas only, without affecting the rest of the image, or so that those areas can be cut or removed completely.

Selections can have hard edges or soft. They can be changed and refined and even saved.

Selecting and isolating make many of this program's most powerful effects possible.

When an area of your image file is selected (surrounded by a moving dotted line), effects and tools applied will only affect the selected area, leaving the rest of your image unchanged.

Why select and isolate?

There are three main reasons for selecting an area of your image file:

To **apply an effect** or adjust the color or lighting of one area of your image file without affecting the rest of the image;

To **protect areas** of your image file so that, for instance, you can paint or erase one area without affecting another area of your image;

To **cut an area** of your image file – cutting a person from a photo, for instance – so that you can either paste him or her into another image file or remove him or her completely.

In **Chapter 5, Get to Know the Photoshop Elements Toolbox**, we discuss a number of tools that can be used to select and isolate areas of your image file.

The **Marquee Tools**, which include the **Rectangular Marquee** and **Elliptical Marquee Tools,** allow you to select a circular or rectangular area of your image file.

The **Lasso Tools**, which include the **Magnetic Lasso, Polygonal Lasso** and freehand **Lasso Tool**, allow you to draw any shape as a selected area.

The **Magic Wand Tool** automatically selects an area of your image that shares a similar color range, based on the tolerance level you've set.

The **Quick Selection Tool** allows you to select an area by "painting" across it, selecting adjacent pixels of similar color as you paint.

A complicated selection may require several passes with several tools to get it exactly right – using the Add to Selection and Subtract from Selection controls to refine the selected area.

As you select an area, it will appear with a moving, dotted line surrounding it – commonly referred to as "marching ants." As we discuss in the individual descriptions of each tool in **Chapter 5**, the selection tools can be used in combination with each other – while selecting the **Add to Selection** and **Subtract from Selection** options (see page 74) – to create or refine your selection into any shape you'd like.

Feathering

Selection tools usually include an option to "**feather**" your selection. **Feathering** means softening the edges of the selection.

For instance, if you were to use the **Elliptical Marquee Tool** to select an area of your image file, this selection would be, by default, a perfect oval or circle, with a clearly defined, hard edge.

But in a number of situations, you'd like that edge softer.

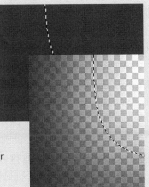

A "feathered" selection has a softer edge so that, when the selection is removed or an effect is added to it, the distinction between the selected and unselected area of your image is a gradation rather than a solid line.

If you're applying an effect to a selected area in a photograph, for instance, you might like the boundary between the affected area and the non-affected area to be softly defined. This can make the effect seem more natural than a hard, abrupt edge might.

Also, when you're cutting a subject from one photo in order to paste him or her into another, a slight feathering around the edge can help blend the pasted image so that it fits more naturally into the new background.

Feathering is measured in pixels. This means that, when working with a low-resolution image, you'll need fewer pixels in your feathering than you will in a higher-resolution image to achieve a similar softened edge effect.

Feathering also plays a role in the **Refine Edge** tool, as discussed on page 75.

The Tool Options for each Selection Tool include settings for adding to or subtracting from your selected areas.

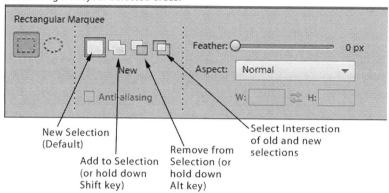

New Selection (Default)

Add to Selection (or hold down Shift key)

Remove from Selection (or hold down Alt key)

Select Intersection of old and new selections

You can add to an already selected area by clicking on the **Add to Selection** button in the **Tool Options Bin,** or by holding down the **Shift** key as you continue to select.

You can remove an area from your selection by clicking the **Subtract from Selection** button in the **Tool Options Bin** or by holding down the **Alt/Option** key as you select.

You can refine your selection so that it includes only the area overlapped by your current and new selections by clicking the **Intersect with Selection** button in the **Tool Options Bin.**

As you build your selected area, two other keyboard shortcuts are worth noting:

To go back a step at any point in the program – even deselecting the most recent area you've selected or removed from your selection – press **Ctrl+z** (⌘+z on a Mac) or click the **Undo** button in the upper right of the interface.

To deselect an area completely, press **Ctrl+d** on a PC or ⌘+d on a Mac.

The Select menu

Once you've selected an area of your image file, the Photoshop Elements **Select** menu (illustrated on the facing page) offers a number of options for refining and changing your selected area.

Select All (**Ctrl+a** on a PC or ⌘+a on a Mac) selects your entire displayed image. If you are working on a layered file, you will select only the image that appears on the active layer. (For more information, see **Chapter 9, Work with Layers.**)

Deselect (**Ctrl+d** or ⌘+d) deselects all of your selections.

Reselect (**Ctrl+Shift+d** or ⌘+Shift+d) re-selects all that you've just deselected – in case you suddenly change your mind.

Inverse (**Ctrl+Shift+i** or ⌘+Shift+i) switches your selection so that the areas you currently have unselected become your selected areas and vice versa.

All Layers and **Selected Layers** expand your current selection to other layers in your image file, if you are working on a layered file.

Grow expands your selected area to similarly colored adjacent pixels in your image file, based on your current selection.

Similar selects all similarly colored pixels throughout your image file, whether they are adjacent to your current selection or not.

Feather (**Ctrl+Alt+d** or **⌘+Option+d**) allows you to apply feathering to soften the edge, after the fact, of your currently selected area.

Refine the edge of your selection

Once you've selected an area in your image file, you can refine the edge of the selection by using the **Refine Edge** tool, accessed under the **Select** menu or by clicking the **Refine Edge** button in the **Tool Options Bin**. Adobe has made some great improvements to this tool, borrowing some amazing features from the professional version of Photoshop.

Select	Filter	View
All		Ctrl+A
Deselect		Ctrl+D
Reselect		Shift+Ctrl+D
Inverse		Shift+Ctrl+I
All Layers		
Deselect Layers		
Similar Layers		
Feather...		Alt+Ctrl+D
Refine Edge...		
Modify		▶
Grow		
Similar		
Transform Selection		
Load Selection...		
Save Selection...		
Delete Selection...		

Edge Detection

The new **Edge Detection/Smart Detection** feature in the **Refine Edge** panel can help you find the edges of a selection that includes very fine details, such as fur or strands of hair. (This is truly an amazing feature!)

Note that you'll get the best results if your subject's background is a smooth color and is distinct in color from the hair, fur or detailed edge of your subject.

1   Using the **Magic Wand, Selection Brush** and/or the **Quick Selection Tool**, select your subject as accurately as possible.

2   Open the **Refine Edge** panel by selecting the option under the **Select** menu or clicking the button in the **Tool Options Bin**.

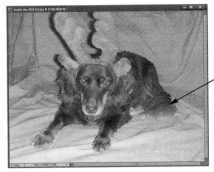
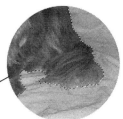

Selecting fine details along the edge of your selection, like fur or strands of hair, can be very challenging.

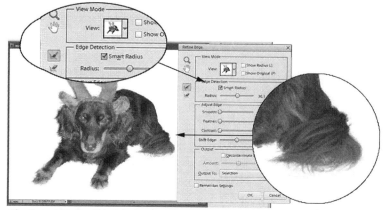

The Smart Radius Edge Detection feature makes selecting even fine details like strands of hair possible!

The **View Mode** pop-up menu at the top of the **Refine Edge** panel allows you to see your selected area in a variety of modes. **On White** is a good mode for this process, since it makes everything outside your selected area appear as white, as seen above.

3   Check the **Smart Detection** box and set **Radius** to about 30 px. (You can adjust it later if you need to.)

4   Select the **Edge Detection Brush** to the left of **Edge Detection/Radius** and drag to "paint" the area of your selection's edge that includes details or stray hair, trying to keep the crosshairs on the brush over the background as much as possible. When you release your mouse, your new selection will be visible, as illustrated above, with some very fine details selected!

You can correct any over-selection with the **Selection Eraser Tool**, below the **Edge Detection Brush**.

Refine Edge Adjustments

Other ways to make adjustments and refine the edge of your selection include:

Radius is how detailed any refinements you make in this panel are. The smaller the radius, the finer the adjustments.

Smooth determines how detailed your selection is. The higher you set **Smooth**, the more the fine details in the edge of your selected area will be rounded out.

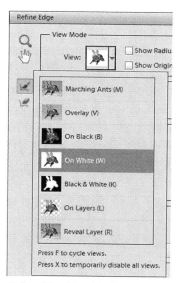

Refine Edge View Modes

Feather. As discussed on page 73, feathering blurs the boundary between the selected and unselected areas, giving a more natural, less abrupt edge to your selection.

Contrast controls how soft or sharp the edge is between your selected and unselected areas.

Shift Edge removes or adds a few extra pixels from around the edge of your selection. This can be helpful if, for instance, you're cutting a person from a background and, in your current selection, some of the background is still showing around the edges. **Shift Edge** and **Feather** are often used in combination to create a very clean, natural edge.

Decontaminate Color replaces any fringe colors that you've selected with colors from surrounding pixels. In other words, if you've selected brown hair and some green background has crept into your selected area, **Decontaminate Color** will tint this green "fringe" brown to match the hair so you don't have any stray color in your selection.

Output gives you options for automatically cutting your selected area into a new layer on your image file, masking your selection on its current layer or copying to a new document.

Checking the **Remember Settings** box will make your current settings your default **Refine Edge** panel settings.

By drawing a selection around the dog, I can isolate him – applying, for instance, color correction to him only, not affecting the background

When I reverse the selection (by selecting Inverse from the Select menu) – my selection becomes everything in the image file *except* the dog. I am now able to apply effects or use brushes – I can even paint a new background with the Clone Tool – affecting everything in the photo *except* the unselected dog!

Use a selection to protect an area

A key reason to select an area of a photo is so that an effect can be applied to the area you've isolated without affecting the rest of your image file.

In the example above, for instance, the dog in the original picture was too yellow for my tastes. However, I preferred that any color corrections I made affected the dog only, and left the rest of the picture as is.

Using a combination of tools – adding to and subtracting from my selection and then refining the edges – I isolated the dog as a selection. I was then able to make color changes to the dog only, without changing the color values of any other part of my image file.

I then inversed the selection (choosing **Inverse** from the **Select** menu) so that the background was selected and the dog was not. Using the **Clone Stamp Tool** (see page 55), I painted in more foliage behind the dog. Because the background was selected and the dog was not, the **Clone Stamp Tool** added these trees and leaves right *around* the dog, as if he were on a whole other layer!

Cut and paste a selection into another photo

As you work with Photoshop Elements, you will likely be doing a lot of cutting and pasting. This is, for instance, a simple way to take a person photographed in front of one background and place him or her in front of another.

Because she was shot against a green screen, the young woman is easily selected by selecting the background with the Magic Wand Tool and then inversing the selection. Once she was selected, I could cut her from one photo and paste her into another.

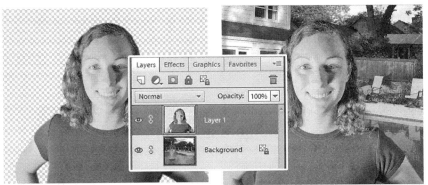

Because pasting places her on a layer, her image can be refined separately – the edges can be softened and she can be tinted to match the background more naturally.

To cut your subject from a background, draw a selection around him or her by using a combinations of tools – adding to and subtracting from your selection as needed. (If your subject is well defined from the background, you may be able to do most of this with the **Magic Wand Tool**, using the other selection tools and the **Add to Selection** or **Subtract from Selection** options.)

Then, to ensure your selection has a slightly softened, natural edge, use **Refine Edge** to **Shift Edge** and **Feather** it. For detailed edges, you can use the **Edge Detection** tool described on page 76.

> To cut your subject from his or her current background, press **Ctrl+c** on a PC or ⌘+**c** on a Mac.

> To paste your subject into a new file or onto a new background, press **Ctrl+v** on a PC or ⌘+**v** on a Mac.

Whenever you paste an image into another image file, it will appear as a new layer in that file, as seen in the illustration above. (In fact, even if you paste the image into the *same* image file you cut it from, it will become a new layer.)

This is to your advantage for a number of reasons:

1   If you need to, you can continue to refine the edge of your pasted-in image so that it fits more naturally with its new background (even using the **Eraser Tool**, if you'd like, to remove more of the image). A very effective feature for adding a more natural edge to your pasted image is the **Defringe Layer** tool, which we discuss on page 99 of **Chapter 8, Correct Color and Lighting**;

2   While it remains a layer, you can resize the pasted-in image separate from the rest of the image file.

Resizing a layer is very easy in Photoshop Elements.

When a layer is selected (by clicking on it to activate it in the **Layers** panel), it appears in your image file outlined by a rectangle, defined on each side and on the corners with a "corner handle." (If your layer image is larger than your current image file, these corner handles may appear outside of the image file, and you may need to **Ctrl+–** on a PC or **⌘+–** on a Mac to see these handles.)

To resize the image on your selected layer, click and drag on these corner handles, as illustrated at the bottom of this page.

As you drag the corner handles, you may notice that the **Tool Options Bin** displays a number of **Transform** options. Using these transform options, you can resize or rotate your layer's image precisely by typing numbers into the spaces in the **Tool Options Bin**.

If **Constrain Proportions** is checked, your image will resize its height and width proportionately – which is usually what you'll prefer. If you uncheck **Constrain Proportions**, you will resize the layer's height and width separately, resulting in a squeezed or disportionate picture.

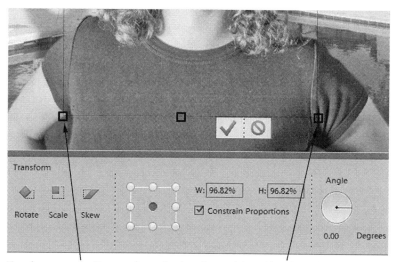

Your layer or selection can be resized and repositioned by dragging on its corner handles or by setting the Transform options in the Tool Options panel.

To finish the resizing, click the green checkmark on your image file or press the **Enter** key.

(While you're in resizing image mode, no other functions in Photoshop Elements will work. So, if you find after resizing your image that no other tool will activate, press **Enter** or click on the green checkmark to complete the resizing.)

If you're enlarging your layer's image by dragging the corner handles, keep in mind the golden rule of raster art: *You can't add pixels where they don't exist.*

You can expand the size of your image only so far before the pixels will begin to break up and your image will appear fuzzy or pixelated. For this reason, it's best to cut and paste between image files that are of similar size and resolution.

Your layer will remain a layer until you flatten your layers or save your file as a file format other than a Photoshop (**PSD**) file. (For information on flattening a layered image see page 110 of **Chapter 9, Work with Photoshop Elements Layers**.)

Fill or stroke a selection

Any area that's selected can also be filled or stroked. In fact, even a selected area on an otherwise blank layer can be filled or stroked.

Filling means painting the selected area with color or a pattern.

A selected area can be filled in any one of a number of ways:

1   Dragging the **Paint Bucket Tool** onto the selected area. The selection will then be filled with the **Foreground Color**.

The Paint Bucket fills your canvas or your selected area.

2   Selecting the **Gradient Tool** and dragging a line across the selection. The selection will be filled with a gradation of the **Foreground** to **Background Color** (or however you've defined your gradient), colored from the beginning to the end of the line you've drawn.

3   Pressing **Alt/Option+Backspace**. The selection will be filled with the **Foreground Color**.

4   Pressing **Ctrl+Backspace** (or ⌘+**Backspace** on a Mac). The selection will be filled with the **Background Color**.

5   Selecting the **Fill Selection** option from the **Edit** drop-down on the Menu Bar.

The **Fill** option panel offers a number of possible ways for filling your selection, including: with the **Foreground Color, Background Color** or a custom color; black, white or gray; or a **Custom Pattern** from the dozens of patterns available in the pattern library.

The Gradient Tool fills your canvas or selected area with (by default) a gradation from the Foreground to the Background Colors.

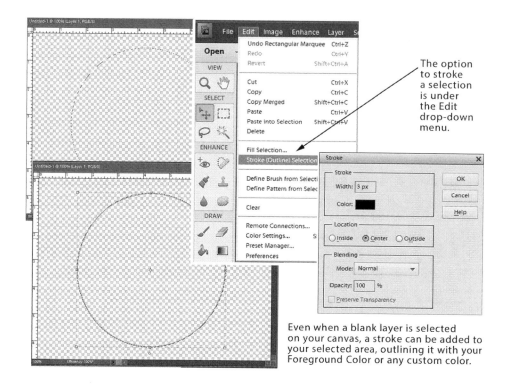

The option to stroke a selection is under the Edit drop-down menu.

Even when a blank layer is selected on your canvas, a stroke can be added to your selected area, outlining it with your Foreground Color or any custom color.

Stroking means outlining a selected area.

A selected area can be stroked by selecting **Stroke (Outline) Selection** from the **Edit** menu.

By default, the stroke color will be the current **Foreground Color**. However, by clicking on the color swatch square on the **Stroke** option panel, you can launch the **Color Picker** (See page 45 of **Chapter 5**), from which you can select any color for your stroke.

The width of the stroke is measured in pixels, by default. And you may set the stroke to appear just outside your selected area (**Outside**), on your selection line (**Center**) or just inside the selection line (**Inside**).

Chapter 7

Resize Your Images

Image and canvas sizes

Resizing can mean a number of different things in Photoshop Elements.

- You may want to enlarge or reduce the overall size of your image file.

- You may want to enlarge or reduce the canvas your image appears on.

- You may want to trim the edges off your image by cropping.

Each of these functions has methods and challenges for getting the best results.

Image Size changes the overall size of the actual image

Canvas Size trims or adds to the size of the canvas the artwork appears on, sometimes cropping the artwork itself

Image Size vs. Canvas Size

As we discussed in **Chapter 1, Things You Need to Know**, there is a key difference between **Image Size** and **Canvas Size**.

Image Size (page 86) is the overall size of your image file. Changing the **Image Size** changes the size of the entire image file without removing or adding to its basic content. In other words, in changing the **Image Size** of your photograph of a city skyline, the content of the picture will remain essentially the same. The entire skyline image will remain. Only the size and/or resolution of the image file will change.

Canvas Size (page 88) refers to the size of the *canvas*, or background, your image appears on. Changing the **Canvas Size** changes the *content* of the image file, either adding to or subtracting from (essentially cropping) the image itself. Reducing the **Canvas Size** of the photograph of the city skyline, for instance, will *chop off* the edges of the image itself without changing the resolution of the image file.

Cropping is a form of changing the **Canvas Size**. When you crop an image, you don't change the size or resolution of the content. You merely trim the canvas. (For more information on cropping, see the **Crop Tool** on page 65 of **Chapter 5, The Photoshop Elements Toolbox**.)

Both **Image Size** and **Canvas Size** are available under the program's **Image** menu, under the **Resize** sub-menu.

You can't create pixels!

This is a principle we repeat several times in this book.

Your image file is made up of pixels – thousands or even millions of little boxes of color. You can't create pixels where none exist. You can't add more resolution to a low resolution image.

Well, *sometimes* you can. But mostly you can't. And it's never a good idea to try.

See, when you add to the **Image Size** of a file – increasing a 640x480 pixel image to 800x600 pixels, for instance – you're essentially telling the program to create more pixels for that image. Photoshop Elements will do its best to oblige – but it can't work miracles. So what the program does is create new pixels by duplicating existing pixels.

This works to a certain extent. (A rule of thumb is that it will work somewhat effectively for up to about a 10% increase in size.) But, since the result will simply be made of *duplicated* pixels, your image will be larger – but you won't get any more detail.

In fact, if you increase your image's size too much, your image will eventually just look fuzzy and pixelated. (Officially, "over-rezzed.")

Remember that those little blocks of color can only get so big before they start to show. And, if you've ever downloaded a photo or a logo from a web site and then tried to enlarge it and print it, you know exactly what I mean. There's no magic way to increase detail where none exists.

However, there may well be times when you need to *cheat* your image resolution just a bit. Force it up in size – maybe 10%. Going from 640x480 to 700x525 pixels, for instance. And when you do, Photoshop Elements allows you to set *how* it creates these new pixels for the best possible results. This process is called **Resample Image**, and we discuss it in **Image Resizing**, on the following page.

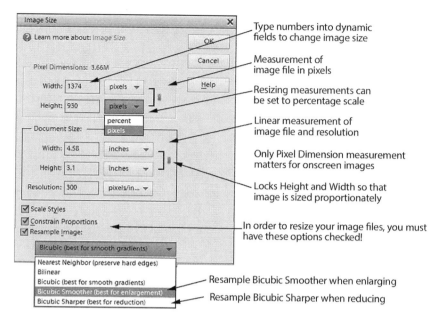

Type numbers into dynamic fields to change image size

Measurement of image file in pixels

Resizing measurements can be set to percentage scale

Linear measurement of image file and resolution

Only Pixel Dimension measurement matters for onscreen images

Locks Height and Width so that image is sized proportionately

In order to resize your image files, you must have these options checked!

Resample Bicubic Smoother when enlarging

Resample Bicubic Sharper when reducing

Image Resizing

The option panel for resizing an image is launched by selecting **Image Size** under the program's **Image** menu, on the **Resize** sub-menu.

Resizing an image means increasing or reducing the size or resolution of the image file itself, usually without substantially changing the photographic content of that image.

In other words, resizing a photograph of a scene from 2048x1536 pixels (the size of an image from a 3 megapixel camera) to 640x480 pixels (the size, in square pixels, of a standard definition video frame) reduces the file size, details and resolution of the photo, but it does not change the essential scene in the photograph itself.

The **Image Size** option screen displays the size of your image file in pixels as well as in linear measurements (inches, centimeters, etc.). It also includes a resolution setting, listed in **Pixels per Inch** (or centimeters, etc.). (For more information on picture resolution, see **Resolution** on page 5 of **Chapter 1**.)

The information listed on the **Image Size** option panel includes:

Pixel Dimensions, a measurement of your image file's size, an actual count of the number of pixels (**Width** and **Height**) that make up your image file.

As we discussed in **Chapter 1, Things You Need to Know**, if you're working on photos or graphics for video or for the Web, these **Pixel Dimensions** are the *only* measurements that you really need to be concerned with. Linear measurements, including resolution, are meaningless in the onscreen image world.

Document Size, a linear measurement of your image file in inches, centimeters, points, picas, etc. (the drop-down menu next to each number allows you to change the measurement method), as well as resolution.

If you are producing photos and graphics for print, these three measurements are very important, since stretching, or "over-rezzing," an image beyond its actual size can produce a poor quality or fuzzy picture. All three numbers are important in the print world because, to produce a relatively clean print image, your photo or graphic will need at least 150-200 pixels per inch and 300 or more p.p.i. for a very high-quality print.

Changing the Image Size changes the size of the photo itself without affecting content.

These measurements are all dynamic fields, and you can change the size of your image by typing new numbers into the boxes. (The **Pixel Dimensions** fields, in fact, can be changed from **pixel** measurements to **percentages** so that you can accurately re-scale your image.)

Note that, as indicated in the illustration on the facing page, **in order to properly change the size or resolution of your photo or image file, you must have the Scale Styles, Constrain Proportions and Resample Image options checked.**

> **Scale Styles.** This checkbox applies to any styles or effects you've added to your image file. (**Drop Shadows**, for instance.) When this box is checked, the size of the **effect** is changed, proportionately, as your image file is resized.

> **Constrain Proportions**. When checked, this feature automatically calculates the **Width** to match whatever **Height** you type in (or vice versa) in order to keep your image file proportionate.

> **Resample Image.** Resampling is a vital function of resizing. Resampling is how Photoshop Elements creates new pixels when you enlarge an image, and how it averages pixel information when you reduce an image's size.

> If this box is unchecked, with the **Nearest Neighbor** option set, you will not be able to dynamically change your **Pixel Dimensions**.

The **Resample Image** drop-down menu offers a number of options for resampling your image's pixels when you resize a file. Only two are really of value for the vast majority of your work.

> **Bicubic Sharper.** When you are **reducing** an image file's size, select this resampling method. This creates the cleanest-looking reduced image.

> **Bicubic Smoother.** When **enlarging** an image file, select this resampling method. As we've said, there are limits to how much you can increase the size of any image file – but the **Bicubic Smoother** will create the smoothest and most natural blends of color among the new pixels it creates.

Photoshop Elements also includes a function for batch-resizing a number of photos or image files at once. For more information on batching processes, see **Process Multiple Files** on page 163 of **Chapter 13, Advanced Photoshop Elements Tools**.

When the Canvas Size is changed, the image file itself will either be cropped or it will have its background area extended.

Canvas Resizing

The option panel for resizing your image's canvas is launched by selecting **Canvas Size** under the **Image** menu, on the **Resize** sub-menu.

The "canvas" is the image file itself, the canvas on which your imagery exists. When you reduce or enlarge the canvas for a photo, you are adding more to the sides or cropping from the size of the image file.

This tool is particularly effective for changing the shape (aspect ratio) of your image file.

The **Canvas Size** option panel displays the dimensions of your image file.

The **New Size** area of this panel contains two dynamic measurement listings, which you can write over. Using the drop-downs, you can set the measurements for these dimensions to any of the standards available in Photoshop Elements. For video, web or other onscreen graphic or photo, you will want to set these measurement standards to **Pixels**.

Though the most common way to resize your canvas is to designate what you want its new **Height** or **Width** to be, you can also simply designate how much you want removed instead. Checking the **Relative** option allows you to designate precisely the amount of your canvas that will be added or removed when it is resized. In other words, if you check **Relative** and set the **Width** to -20 (minus 20) pixels, 20 pixels will be cropped from the width of your canvas.

The **Anchor** area of this panel displays a square with arrows that point up, down, right, left and from each corner of the square. This **Anchor** setting represents how and from where your image canvas will be added to or subtracted from when you resize it – as indicated by the directions its arrows point.

Each of these arrows determines which area of your canvas will be affected by the changes to the **Height** or **Width**.

In other words, if you were to set the **Anchor** so that the arrows point down and to the right and then *decrease* the size of your canvas, your image would be resized by cropping from the *top left* of your image file. (Think of it as cropping toward the bottom right).

Because the Anchor is set to the lower right corner, the reduced Canvas Size crops from the upper left of the image file.

Likewise, if you were to set the **Anchor** so that the arrows point up and to the right, increasing the size of the canvas would add space *above and to the right* of your current image, as illustrated below.

If no arrow is selected, the tool will crop from or add to your canvas equally, around all sides.

By default, any canvas added to your image file will appear in the **Background Color**. However, the **Canvas Extension Color** drop-down menu at the bottom of this option panel allows you to set the added canvas to appear in the **Foreground Color,** black, white, gray or any other custom color.

Because the Anchor is set at the lower left corner of the image, increasing the Canvas Size adds "canvas" to the upper and right side of the file.

Added canvas is, by default, the Background Color, but can be set to any color.

Auto Fixing Your Photos

Adjusting Brightness & Contrast

Adjusting Color

Adjusting Sharpness

Adjustment Layers

Chapter 8

Correct Color and Lighting
Adjust and clean up your images

Under the Enhance drop-down menu, Photoshop Elements includes a number of tools for cleaning up, correcting color and adjusting the lighting of your image files.

Many of these tools are based on advanced tools in the professional version of Photoshop. Others are more simplified "quick fixes."

Whether your goal is to clean up your photos or to change the colors in your image files to produce a special effect, there's likely an adjustment tool for your general or specific need.

Auto Fixes

Under the **Enhance** drop-down on the Menu Bar, there are six automatic fixes for your image files. In many cases, an automatic fix may be the easiest way to correct your photo's lighting and color.

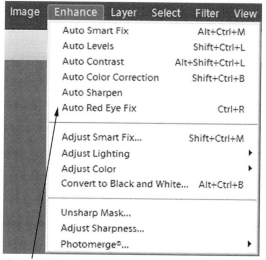

Photoshop Elements includes a number of "auto" fixes under the Enhance drop-down for correcting color and lighting.

But remember that automatic fixes are just math, not magic. Automatic fixes merely look at the lightest spot in your image file and assume it should be pure white, then look at the darkest spot in your image file and assume it should be pure black – and then they calculate the rest of the image's color and light values as a range between them.

So, although in many cases, auto fixes can be very effective – they're still just a best guess. And, depending on the results, you may want to move on to manual adjustments from there or even **Ctrl+z** (⌘+z on a Mac) to undo the fix and do it entirely manually.

Virtually every auto fix has a manual adjustment alternative.

The six automatic fixes are:

Auto Smart Fix. A good, general automatic fix, correcting for poor exposure, contrast problems, color balance and color saturation in a single sweep.

Auto Levels considers the luminance values of red, green and blue in calculating its best color and lighting adjustments.

Auto Contrast considers only the brightness and contrast levels in calculating its best guess settings, without regard to the image file's colors.

Auto Color Correction focuses on the mid-tones in the image, correcting the image file's color by presuming the middle range of colors as gray and balancing the other colors based on that. Unlike **Auto Levels**, **Auto Color Correction** does not look at the individual color channels but judges the colors of the image file as an overall mix.

Auto Sharpen increases the contrast between pixels, which can make a photo appear clearer, sharper or more focused.

Auto Red Eye Fix uses its best guess to locate "red eyes" on the people in your photos and then darken and desaturate them.

Control what gets changed

When an area of your image file is selected (defined by "marching ants"), any changes made to color or lightness will affect *only* the area within the selection.

The color and lighting adjustments you make to your image files may be applied to the entire file or to isolated areas of your file. You may, for instance, want to brighten or adjust the color of a person in the foreground of a photo but not change the color or lighting for the background. Or you may want to make the sky bluer in a picture but keep the grass a rich green.

There are three ways to control how and where your effects are applied in your image files:

1. **Selection**. As we discuss in **Chapter 6, Select and Isolate Areas in Your Photos**, when you select an area in your image file, only that area will be changed by any added effects or adjustments. This is far and away the most common way to control what areas of your image files are affected.

2. **Brush Tools**. As we discuss in **Chapter 5, The Photoshop Elements Toolbox**, the **Smart Brush** tools are designed for applying effects only to certain areas of your image file. With **Smart Brushes**, you "paint" the effect onto only certain, specific areas of your image file.

    Additionally, the **Red Eye Removal Tool** darkens and desaturates only the area you brush – removing the bright red reflections from your subject's eyes. And the **Dodge** and **Burn Tools** allow you to lighten or darken specific spots of your image file.

    Brushes, as we explained in **Chapter 5,** can be large and wide or very small and fine, and may have hard edges or soft, feathered edges.

3. **Layers**. As we discuss in **Chapter 9, Work With Photoshop Elements Layers**, unless you specifically direct Photoshop Elements to affect several layers at once, any changes you make to an active layer in a layered image file will apply *only* to that layer. As we demonstrate in **Cut and paste a selection** on page 78, this is a very useful function as you work to match a person who has been cut and pasted from another document onto a new background.

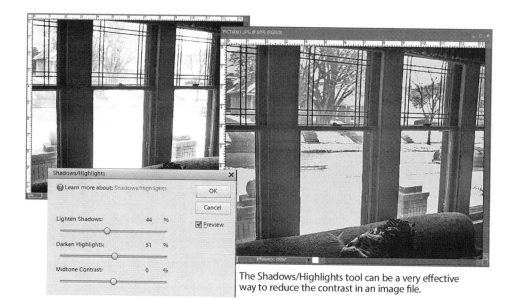

The Shadows/Highlights tool can be a very effective way to reduce the contrast in an image file.

Adjust Lighting

Certainly the most basic adjustments you'll make to your photos will be to adjust their brightness and contrast. As with all adjustments you can make in Photoshop Elements, there are simplified and complex tools for making these adjustments. The more complicated the adjustment, the more control you will have over the results.

These functions are located under the program's **Enhance** menu, on the **Adjust Lighting** sub-menu.

Brightness/Contrast

As basic an adjustment as you'll find in Photoshop Elements, **Brightness** lightens or darkens your photo while **Contrast** determines the difference between the blackest blacks and whitest whites in your image file.

Shadows/Highlights

A personal favorite, this great tool has saved many photos for me. Basically, it decreases the contrast in your image file by enhancing the midtones, as illustrated above. This is helpful if, for instance, you have a photo of a bird in flight, which appears as just a dark silhouette against the bright sky. The tool reduces the contrast between bird and sky and brings out details in the bird that would otherwise be indiscernible. It's great for bringing out details in an image shot on a very sunny or snowy day, a photo with such high contrasts that its lights are too light and its darks are too dark.

Levels

In my opinion, **Levels** really is more of a *color* adjustment than a lighting adjustment. In fact, it's my favorite go-to tool for color correcting an image file.

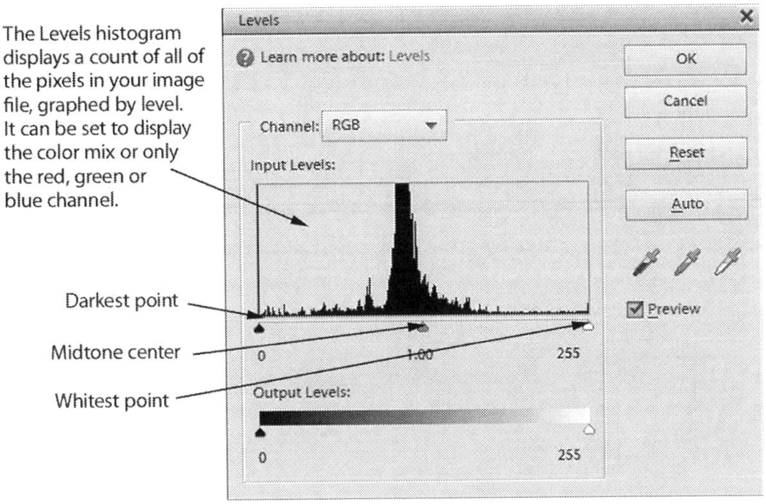

The Levels histogram displays a count of all of the pixels in your image file, graphed by level. It can be set to display the color mix or only the red, green or blue channel.

Darkest point

Midtone center

Whitest point

The histogram on the **Levels** option screen (illustrated above) maps the pixels in your image from darkest to lightest.

By moving the arrows on either end of the histogram in or out, you define the darkest dark and lightest light points in your image file. The middle arrow defines the center midtone. The **Output Levels** widen the distance between dark and light. In essence, then, this is a more precise way to set your brightness and contrast.

But you can go even deeper in your adjustments on this **Levels** screen. If you drop down the **Channel** menu at the top of the panel, you'll see that you can set these levels for each individual color also. This makes this tool one way to, say, lower the amount of red in a photo or increase the amount of blue.

The **Levels** tool also makes a great color correction tool, as we discuss in the sidebar on page 97.

Quick Fixes and Guided Fixes

Quick Fixes are semi-automatic fixes to color and lighting that Photoshop Elements applies to your image file. These include "red eye" fixes, fixes for enriching the color of the sky or whitening teeth and many simplified and automatic fixes for correcting color and light. We discuss them and how to use them in greater detail in **Chapter 3, Quick Fix Your Photos**.

Guided Fixes, as the name implies, are adjustments that are automatically applied to your image file as you work through a list of options. We discuss them and how to use them in greater detail in **Chapter 4, Use Guided Edits**

Preview changes

When Preview is checked on any adjustment panel, you will see a preview of any adjustments to your image file.

When you launch an option screen for any adjustment or effect, you may notice a checkbox labeled **Preview** on the screen. **Previewing** allows you to see, in real time, how your adjustments will affect your final image.

When this function is enabled, your image file will temporarily display any changes or adjustments you make.

Additionally, by checking and unchecking the **Preview** option as you make your adjustments, you can do a before-and-after comparison of your changes.

If you click **OK**, these changes will be permanently applied to your image file. If you click **Cancel**, your changes will not be applied.

Adjust Color

As every photographer knows, there's almost no such thing as perfect lighting. Natural sunlight tends toward blue while indoor lighting tends toward yellow, and even the best cameras can have a problem adjusting their white balance for every situation. Fortunately, Photoshop Elements offers a number of tools for adjusting and correcting color.

These tools are available under **Enhance** menu, on the **Adjust Color** sub-menu.

Remove Color Cast

This tool is a smart fix that bases its color correction calculations on a single point that you define. To use it, click on the eyedropper on the panel and then click on a spot on your image file that you'd like to appear as either pure white, pure black or pure gray. The tool will then automatically adjust all the other colors in the image based on that definition.

Adjust Hue/Saturation

Hue is the *tint* of a color (essentially the color itself), its levels based on the 360 degrees of a color wheel.

Saturation is the *amount* of color. (The opposite of saturation is no color, or black & white.)

Lightness is how *dark or light* the color is.

Adjust Hue/Saturation is probably less effective as a color correction tool than it is as a color *changing* tool. But it does serve as an alternative to adjusting your image's colors based on red, green and blue values.

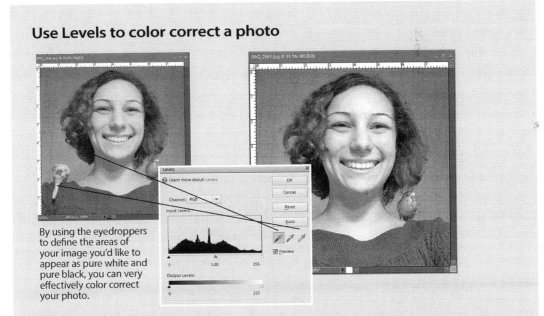

Use Levels to color correct a photo

By using the eyedroppers to define the areas of your image you'd like to appear as pure white and pure black, you can very effectively color correct your photo.

Here's a professional trick that I often use to correct color in a photo using this **Levels** panel.

The three eyedroppers to the right of the histogram can be used to define the black, white and midtone points in your image file.

To correct the colors in a photo, click on the first (**Black Point**) eyedropper, then use that eyedropper to click, or "sample," the blackest spot in your photo (as illustrated above).

Then click on the third eyedropper (**White Point**) and sample the whitest spot in your photo.

If you want to further correct color, you can use the center eyedropper (**Gray Point**) to define a spot on your image file you'd like to appear as central gray.

By defining the blackest and whitest areas of your photo, you can usually neutralize any color hues and set a clear contrast level.

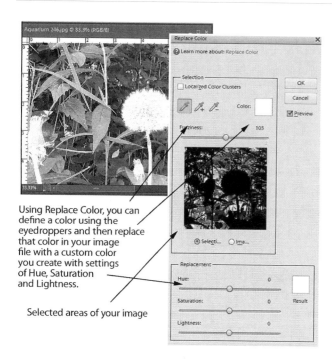

Using Replace Color, you can define a color using the eyedroppers and then replace that color in your image file with a custom color you create with settings of Hue, Saturation and Lightness.

Selected areas of your image

Remove Color

Remove Color desaturates your image file, leaving it as pure grayscale (black & white). But it's probably not the best way to get a quality grayscale image from a color photo.

A better, more powerful alternative for creating a grayscale image from a color photo is **Convert to Black and White**, discussed on the facing page.

Replace Color

Replace Color uses the same color adjustment tools as **Adjust Hue/Saturation**, but it applies these changes to a defined area of your image file only.

To define the area of your photo to be changed, create a **Selection** using the eyedropper in the option panel (as well as the add to/subtract from eyedroppers). Your selected areas will appear as levels of white in the preview window. Once you've defined your selection, the mixture of **Hue, Saturation** and **Lightness** you create in this panel will replace the colors in your selected areas.

Adjust Color Curves

Adjust Color Curves is a very high-level correction tool that allows you to not only adjust the levels of the darkest and lightest areas in your image file but also, by adjusting the points in the curve or by moving the sliders, adjust the intensity for several color level points in your image, as illustrated below.

The **Select a Style** window allows you to select some color curve presets. Once selected, these settings can be further tweaked by moving the sliders.

Curves adjusts the color for your image files from five separate levels of brightness. The styles listed under Select a Style offer preset curves for making some general adjustments.

Adjust Color for Skin Tone

Skin tones are often the single most challenging element in a photo to color correct. With this tool, you focus on skin tones only, assuming the rest of your photo will follow suit. To use it, click to select a sample of skin tone in your photo, then adjust the **Tan**, **Blush** and color **Temperature** sliders until the skin colors look right.

Defringe Layer

Defringe Layer is designed to work with layered image files. It's particularly effective when you're pasting a person or other subject from one image file into another (which automatically places the pasted image on a new layer, as we demonstrate in **Cut and paste a selection** on page 78 of **Chapter 6, Use a selection to protect an area**). Based on the number of pixels you designate, **Defringe Layer** blends the outline of the pasted layer so that it fits more naturally with its new background.

Convert to Black and White

As the name implies, this tool desaturates – or removes the color from – your image file, rendering it as grayscale. But, unlike the simplified **Remove Color** tool discussed earlier in this chapter, **Convert to Black and White** includes options for enhancing the grayscale in your image so that your final black & white image is as vivid as the original color image.

Under **Select a Style**, you'll find half a dozen presets for improving your image. In most cases, one of these presets alone will give you a strong, vivid grayscale. But if you'd prefer, by adjusting the sliders, you can further tweak the image to give you the strongest possible results.

With the proper adjustments (or preset adjustments) a black & white photo can look as vivid as the original color photo.

Adjust Sharpness

A somewhat simplified version of the **Unsharp Mask**, **Adjust Sharpness** uses pixel contrast levels to correct for a certain amount of fuzziness in your photos.

It can't make an out-of-focus picture suddenly look crisp and focused, of course. But, when a photo is just a bit soft or blurred, **Adjust Sharpness** can make it appear crisper and clearer.

As with the **Unsharp Mask**, you can only add so much sharpness to an image before it becomes counter-productive. Too much sharpness can make your photo appear grainy and overly-sharp, its individual pixels too highly contrasted. So remember, the goal with either of these tools is sharpness, not crystal clarity.

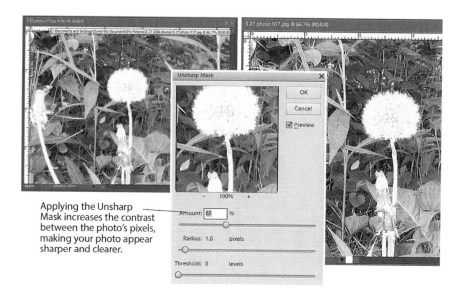

Applying the Unsharp Mask increases the contrast between the photo's pixels, making your photo appear sharper and clearer.

Unsharp Mask

Traditionally, the last adjustment made to any photo is to apply the **Unsharp Mask.**

Although the results for **Unsharp Mask** and **Adjust Sharpness** are similar, **Unsharp Mask** is traditionally considered the more "professional" of the two. **Unsharp Mask** increases the contrast in your pixels (dark pixels become darker, light pixels become lighter), the result being a cleaner, sharper image.

As a general rule, **Amount** should not be set to more than 80%, **Radius** is usually set to 1.0 pixels and **Threshold** is set to 0 levels. Although the best settings will vary depending on the needs and resolution of your photo, too much **Unsharp Mask** can result in an overly sharpened, grainy image.

Work with Adjustment Layers

When working with most adjustment tools in Photoshop Elements, any changes you make to your image file are permanent. The image itself is changed – the pixels are lightened or darkened or colors are shifted. The only way to remove an adjustment is to undo it (by pressing **Ctrl+z** on a PC or ⌘+z on a Mac or using the **Undo** button or the **Undo History** panel) – and then you're also undoing whatever other work you've done since that adjustment.

However, Photoshop Elements also provides a way to keep these changes separate from the original image file. The effect is the same – your adjustments show as changes in the edited image file. But the changes are not permanent until you save the file as something other than a Photoshop (**PSD**) file or you flatten the image.

To launch an **Adjustment Layer** for your image file, go to the program's **Layer** menu and select **New Adjustment Layer** and then, from the sub-menu, whatever adjustment (**Levels, Brightness/Contrast, Hue/Saturation,** etc.) you'd like to make.

As when you make direct adjustments to your image file, your changes will be displayed on your image file if the **Preview** option is checked.

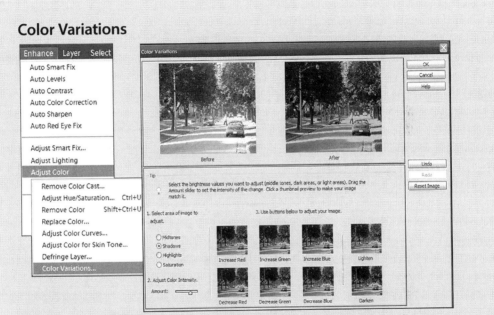

With Color Variations, making adjustments to your photos is as simple as choosing from the adjustment previews – sometimes through several steps – until your picture looks as you'd like.

Color Variations can be a very effective – and very intuitive – way to adjust the color and lightness of an image file.

When you open the **Color Variations** option screen for your image file, you will see a **Before** and **After** comparison of your image.

Color Variations shows you a number of options – previews of what your image will look like when certain adjustments are made to the brightness or color. By simply clicking to select a thumbnail from the preview options, you automatically make your brightness and color adjustments.

As you click on a thumbnail, the adjusted image will appear in your **After** screen, and the option thumbnails will update with new adjustment previews based on your new selection.

Continue to make selections – like following a trail – until your photo is as you'd like it to look, then click **OK** to finalize the changes.

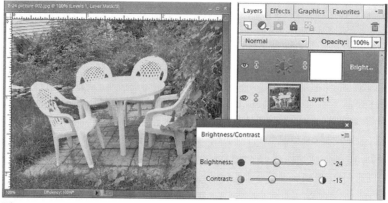

When using an Adjustment Layer, changes to lightness or color appear in your image – but these changes are actually a separate layer and your original image remains unchanged.

The difference is that, when you **OK** your changes, the changes are not applied to the original image. Rather, your adjustments show up as a separate layer – an **Adjustment Layer** – in the **Layers** panel.

There are a number of advantages to using **Adjustment Layers** rather than changing the actual image file:

1 **Your changes do not affect the original file.** Remember, once you change your native file and save it, there's no going back. Once you've closed and re-opened your image file, you can't even undo your changes. Using **Adjustment Layers**, your original, native file remains in its original, unadjusted form.

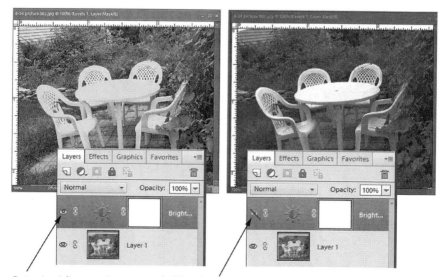

By turning Adjustment Layers on and off (by clicking the eyeball icon), you can do a before-and-after comparision for your adjustments or even compare several adjustments on several Adjustment Layers!

2   **Adjustment Layers can be turned off and on.** By clicking on the eyeball icon to the left of each layer in the **Layers** panel, you can turn that layer on or off. This is also true of **Adjustment Layers**. By turning your **Adjustment Layers** off and on, you can do a before-and-after comparison of your adjustments.

3   **You can create several alternative versions.** There's no limit to the number of **Adjustment Layers** you can add to an image file and, by turning these layers off and on, you can try to compare several different adjustments (**Levels** vs. **Brightness/Contrast** for instance) to see which gives you the best results.

4   **Adjustment Layers can be re-adjusted.** By double-clicking on the adjustment icon on any **Adjustment Layer** on the **Layers** panel, you can re-launch your adjustment screen for that layer, allowing you to further tweak your settings.

When none of your changes are permanent, you're more free to experiment, to try a variety of changes and even make a few easily-undoable mistakes. And, with **Adjustments Layers**, you're also able to compare your options.

Whenever possible – particularly if you're creating proofs for a client – I recommend your using **Adjustment Layers** to create your variations. The ability to turn any changes off or on, or remove them completely, helps prevent you from making changes to the original photo file that are impossible to undo.

The Layers Panel

Simplifying Vector Layers

The Layer Mask

Copying Layers from One File Another

Creating Non-Square Graphics

Chapter 9

Work With Photoshop Elements Layers

Stacks of images

If you're new to Photoshop Elements, layers may seem a bit intimidating – and maybe even a bit superfluous. But, as you work with them, you'll begin to see how powerful a feature they truly are.

It's not uncommon for an advanced Photoshop user to have a dozen or more layers stacked up in his or her image file at once.

Layers also play an important role in the creation and editing of DVD and BluRay templates for Premiere Elements.

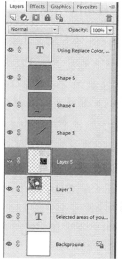
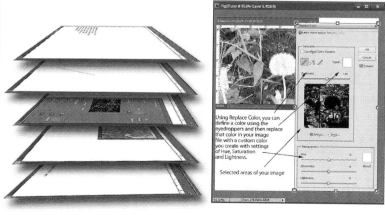

Layers are like a stack of images, with shapes and text on upper layers revealing lower layers through transparent areas.

How layers work

The simplest way to understand how layers work is to imagine them as a stack. The top layer in the stack is completely visible. And, if the top layer is text or does not cover the entire canvas or if there are transparent areas in it, the layers below show around or through it.

One advantage of having elements of your image file on separate layers rather than merged into a single layer is that each layer remains editable, separate from the rest of the image file.

Some other functions of layers include:

- As discussed in **Cut and paste a selection** on page 78 of **Chapter 6, Select and Isolate Areas in Your Photos**, when you cut and paste elements from one image file to another (or even cut from and paste into the same image file) the pasted elements will appear as a new layer. This function allows you to further manipulate and adjust the pasted layer so that it better blends with the background.

- When you add text to an image file (as we discuss in **Chapter 10, Create and Edit Text**) it will appear as a separate layer. The text on this layer remains editable until the layer is simplified or flattened.

- When you create a shape for your image file, it also appears as its own layer (as we discuss on page 63 of **Chapter 5, Get to Know the Photoshop Elements Toolbox**). Like text, shapes remain editable until you simplify or flatten the layer. (See **Simplify or Flatten a Layer** on page 110.)

- As we discuss on page 100 of **Chapter 8, Correct Color and Lighting**, an **Adjustment Layer** allows you to make adjustments to the lighting and color of your image file without actually changing your image file. (The adjustments appear as a separate layer.)

The **Smart Brush Tool** (discussed on page 54 of **Chapter 5, Get to Know the Photoshop Elements Toolbox**) works similarly. The **Smart Brush Tool's** color and lighting adjustments remain separate from the image itself. These adjustments can then be further tweaked – or even removed altogether – without making any permanent changes to your original image file or photo.

Additionally, there are a couple of other functions of layers worth mentioning.

You can duplicate your layers, making several versions of the same layer, each with unique effects or adjustments applied to it. In this way, you can create several versions of your image, comparing them to each other by simply turning the layers on and off.

The easiest way to duplicate a layer is to drag it, in the **Layers** panel, up onto the **Make New Layer** icon at the top left of the panel (as illustrated on the following page).

Layers are the key to creating non-square graphics! Non-square graphics include logos, shapes and text-only graphics files.

By removing the background, using layers and saving your files to the proper format, you can create and export graphics in any shape you want, without the constraints of that pesky rectangular background (as we'll demonstrate in **Create non-square graphics** on page 113).

Select a layer to edit

To select the layer you want to work on, click on it in the **Layers** panel. The selected layer will then be highlighted.

In Photoshop Elements, you can also select a layer simply by clicking on the graphic or text in your image file in the **Editor** workspace. (The layer that the graphic is on will automatically be selected in the **Layers** panel.)

This makes repositioning the layered elements in your image file fairly intuitive.

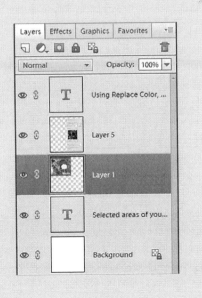

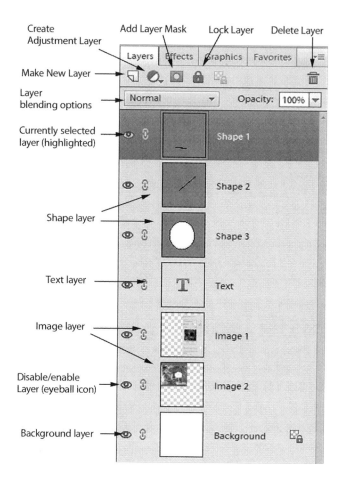

The Layers panel

The layers of your image file will appear stacked in the **Layers** panel. Your image file will usually include, at the bottom of this stack, a **Background** layer (unless you've manually removed it).

With the exception of Photoshop (PSD) files (and some rare TIFs), graphic formats (JPEGs, GIFs, PNGs) are flat. When you open them in Photoshop Elements, the only layer that will appear in the **Layers** panel will be a **Background** layer. (This layer is locked by default, indicated by a padlock icon on it. However, it can be unlocked and turned into a layer simply by double-clicking on it.)

As can be seen in the illustration above, the **Layers** panel includes a number of tools for working with and managing your layers:

> **New layers can be created** by clicking on the **Make New Layer** or **Create Adjustment Layer** buttons at the top left of the panel, as illustrated above. As mentioned earlier, some functions – such as cutting and pasting, creating shapes and adding text – automatically create new layers.

Layers can be re-ordered or re-stacked simply by dragging them
around in the panel. For instance, if you'd like a shape on one layer to
appear *over* rather than *under* the image in another, you can just drag
it above the other in the stack on the **Layers** panel.

Layers can be deleted – singularly or several at once – by selecting
them (or **Shift-clicking** to select several) and pressing the **Delete** or
Backspace key on your keyboard or clicking on the trash can icon.

Layers can be linked. When you select two or more layers at once (by
Ctrl-clicking or ⌘-clicking or **Shift-clicking** to select more than one),
any transformation or positioning changes applied to one will apply
to *all selected layers*. You can "permanently" link two or more layers by
selecting them and then selecting the **Link Layers** option from the
pop-up menu in the upper right corner of the panel.

Layers can be locked. Locking a layer (clicking on the padlock) prevents
that layer from being edited or moved.

Layers can also be temporarily disabled (made invisible) by clicking
on the eyeball icon to the left of each layer. When the eyeball icon is
toggled off, your layer will be invisible. Clicking on the eyeball icon
again will re-enable the layer.

There are two advanced tools on the **Layers** panel– the first of which is
worth knowing well and the other of which is worth merely knowing
about:

Blending options are available through the drop-down menu that
appears at the top left of the panel, as illustrated on the facing page.
By default it reads **Normal** – and it is not available for use with the
Background layer.

Blending affects how a selected layer reacts with the layers below
it. It's a pretty high-level tool, but it can also create some pretty
interesting effects. When the **Overlay** blend option is selected, for
instance, you can paint on one layer and it will "colorize" the image on
the layer below it!

More advanced uses for this feature are beyond the scope of this
book, but are worth experimenting with.

Layer Sets are essentially folders on the **Layers** panel that contain
groups of layers. They can be turned on or off, moved or manipulated
as a group or as individual layers.

Layer Sets can't be created in Photoshop Elements. They're a function
of the professional version of Photoshop.

However, depending on how large the file you're working on is,
you can often open and edit a **Layer Set** in Photoshop Elements – a
key process when using **Edit DVD and BluRay disc templates in
Photoshop Elements** (as discussed on page 164 of **Chapter 13,
Advanced Photoshop Elements Tools**).

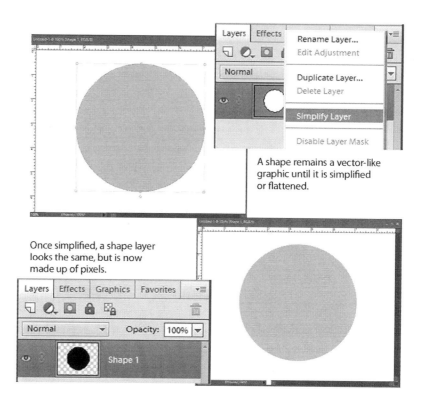

A shape remains a vector-like graphic until it is simplified or flattened.

Once simplified, a shape layer looks the same, but is now made up of pixels.

Simplify or Flatten a Layer

For the most part, the image layers you'll be working on in Photoshop Elements will be raster art. They'll be made up of pixels and, on some layers, may include transparent areas.

Two types of layers, however, are more vector than pixel-based, and include some unique abilities and liabilities.

Shape Layers (as discussed on page 63 of **Chapter 5, Get to Know the Photoshop Elements Toolbox**) are in reality something called "masks." In other words, although a shape may look like a circle, it is actually a colored layer with all the area *except* the circle made transparent. (You can see this if you look at their representation in the **Layers** panel, as in the illustration above.) This gives shapes some unique characteristics – namely that you can manipulate them like vector art, resizing and reshaping them without regard for resolution.

Text, likewise, is not pixel-based art. It is a font, which behaves like vector art. In fact, if you click on a block of text with the **Selection Tool**, you can even resize the text block by dragging on its corner handles, just as if it were a shape! Text also remains editable as long as it remains a separate text layer.

These two types of Photoshop Elements objects float as layers over your other layers until one of two things happens:

The layer is simplified. To simplify a text or shape layer, **right-click** on it in the **Layers** panel and select the **Simplify Layer** option, as illustrated on the facing page. Although the shape or text may not appear different, it has now become raster art. It is now made up of pixels and can no longer be edited as vector art.

The file is flattened or layers are merged. You can flatten all of the layers in your image file onto your background, or you can just merge two layers together. The result is the same: The separate layers become one single collection of pixels.

Layers can be merged onto one another or flattened completely.

To merge one layer onto the layer below it, **right-click** on the layer in the **Layers** panel and select **Merge Down** (or press **Ctrl+e** on a PC or ⌘**+e** on a Mac).

To flatten all of the layers in your image file, **right-click** on the **Layers** panel or select from the program's **Layers** menu the option to **Flatten Image**. All of your layers will flatten into a single, rasterized **Background** layer.

Although TIFs can also be forced to maintain layers, only PSDs maintain all of your layers in an editable format. All other formats are flat. That's why, as you work on an image file, it's best to maintain a native, working PSD of your work file in addition to the JPEGs, TIFs or whatever else you are using for your output.

Although other file formats don't maintain layers, certain graphics formats can save transparency information in the form of something called an "alpha channel." That's an important function we'll explain in **Creating non-square graphics**, on page 113.

Copy layers from one image file to another

Layers can be easily copied from one image file to another.

Although you could certainly use **Copy and Paste** to move elements from one image file to another, you can more easily copy layers, layer sets, shapes and text by simply *dragging* the layers from the **Layers** panel of one image file onto another open image file.

By **Shift-clicking** to select several layers at once, you can copy a whole group of them from one image file to another!

This function becomes very useful when **Editing DVD and BluRay disc templates in Photoshop Elements**, as discussed on page 164 of **Chapter 13, Advanced Photoshop Elements Tools.**

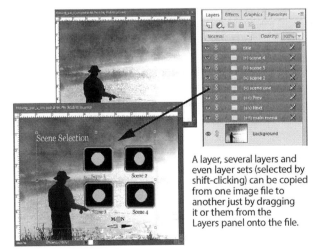

A layer, several layers and even layer sets (selected by shift-clicking) can be copied from one image file to another just by dragging it or them from the Layers panel onto the file.

Add transparency with Layer Masks

A high-level feature in Photoshop Elements is the ability to add **Layer Masks** to your image file layers – a feature previously available only in the professional version of the software.

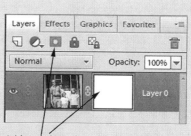

Layer Masks create transparent and semi-transparent areas in your image layers. But, because they do so by *masking* rather than actually removing pixels, they don't actually change or remove any image data from the image itself. The areas are merely *masked*.

Add a mask to a layer by clicking the Add Layer Mask button. The Layer Mask appears as a white box, linked to the side of the layer in the palette.

1 To create a **Layer Mask**, select a layer in one of your graphics files.

   (If you are working with a flat graphic or photo, you can make the **Background** a layer by **double-clicking** on it in the **Layers** panel.)

2 Click the **Add Layer Mask** button at the top of the **Layers** panel.

   A white box will be added to your selected image's layer, as seen above.

   This white box is that layer's **Layer Mask**.

   When you paint black on a **Layer Mask**, the corresponding area on the layer will be masked (made transparent). Shades of gray are read as levels of transparency.

3 Click to select this white box on the **Layers** panel, then select a brush from the Photoshop Elements **Toolbox.** Set the **Foreground Color** to black (by pressing **D** on your keyboard) and paint across your image in the **Editor** workspace. (You are actually painting on the **Layer Mask**.)

The areas of the **Layer Mask** that you paint black will mask, or make transparent, the corresponding areas of that layer's image. If you are using a soft-edged brush, the feathered edges of your brush strokes will appear semi-opaque.

In my example, I took a 640x480 pixel photo and, using a 104 px, rough-edged brush from the **Thick Heavy** brush collection, I painted a ragged black frame around the sides of my **Layer Mask**. The result, as you can see, is a photo with a ragged, grungy edge. However, this ragged edge is only a mask. The actual image has not been changed in any way. And, since this is only a mask, it can be easily revised or even removed completely without affecting the original photo.

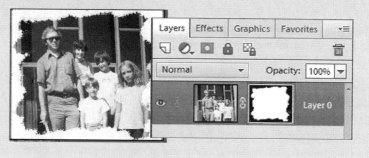

Create non-square graphics

Most commonly-used graphics formats (JPEGs and TIFs, for instance) are rectangular. They are a certain number of pixels wide and a certain number of pixels tall, and they have four sides and four corners.

However, your graphics (logos, titles, etc.) are often not. And when you have a non-square graphic, you'll want to bring it into Premiere Elements in the shape of the graphic itself. Not square, not rectangular. And with any blank area around it – and even some blank areas through it – transparent.

Using layers, you can create graphics for Premiere Elements in shapes other than rectangular.

This is accomplished by utilizing something called an **alpha channel**.

Because of the way graphic files carry their visual data, transparency has to be communicated from program to program with a separate channel of visual information – the same way that the colors red, green and blue are communicated as individual channels. Transparency, then, is essentially a fourth color – commonly referred to as "alpha." Only a few graphics formats have the ability to carry transparency as an alpha channel.

Use graphics that include alpha channels

Not all graphics formats can carry alpha data. JPEGs and BMP files can not. TIFs and PDFs can, but they aren't typically used for partially transparent graphics. There are five commonly-used graphic formats that can include transparency, and all five will work in Premiere Elements. They are:

Graphic formats that include alpha channel information are transparent around the layered graphic or text.

PSDs. This is the native Photoshop and Photoshop Elements format. It's far and away the most common way to deliver a non-square graphic to Premiere Elements. This is because, not only do PSDs communicate alpha information between the programs, but the original files also remain easily re-editable (even the text) in Photoshop Elements.

GIFs and PNGs. GIFs (pronounced "jiffs", according to their inventors) are the graphics you see all over the Internet. They're the ones that include animation (like those annoying, flashing Web banner ads). PNGs (pronounced "pings") were designed to replace GIFs, and they do display color much better. Outputting either of them with their alpha channels intact involves a similar process, which we demonstrate later in this chapter.

EPSs and AIs. These are vector-based file formats created by programs like Adobe Illustrator. Though they technically don't carry alpha as a separate color channel, vector art is created by connecting corner points rather than assembling pixels. Because of this, they have no background layers and therefore often include transparent areas.

Create a backgroundless graphic in Photoshop Elements

To create a partially transparent graphic in Photoshop Elements, you need to remove the background layer from the **Layers** panel.

When you first open a PSD or other graphics or photo file in Photoshop Elements, it will likely consist of one layer, labeled "**Background**" on the **Layers** panel. Even if the file does include layers, there may be a **Background** layer at the bottom of the layers stack.

Double-click on the **Background** layer in the **Layers** panel. The **Background** layer will become a layer.

Layered files behave very differently once they have no **Background**. Layers with no background have transparency behind them.

For instance, if you erase or cut an area on a **Background** layer, that area will be replaced by your **Background Color.** However, if you erase or cut an area from a layer, you cut *through* the layer. It becomes transparent!

If you have converted your **Background** into a layer by double-clicking on it, you can remove areas of it by using the **Eraser Tool** or by selecting non-essential areas of the graphic (selecting the white around your logo, for instance, using the **Magic Wand** or the **Quick Selection Tool**) and pressing your **Delete** key.

That light gray checkerboard you see around your graphic represents alpha. That means there is nothing there. No background. No canvas. Just transparency.

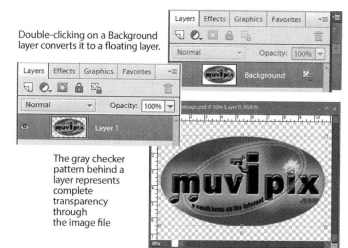

Double-clicking on a Background layer converts it to a floating layer.

The gray checker pattern behind a layer represents complete transparency through the image file

If you'd like to start with a clean slate, you can even remove everything on the layer (press **Ctrl+a** on a PC or ⌘**+a** on a Mac to select all and then press the **Delete** key).

Once you've removed the background, whatever you draw, write or place on a layer – a graphic, a shape, text, a photo of a person with the background cut from behind him – if it does not cover your entire canvas, has transparency around it.

If the area around the graphic, text, shape or image you've added to a layer reveals that checkerboard pattern around or through it, your graphic will include areas of transparency.

And, if you were to save this file without flattening it in a format that supports alpha (ideally a **PSD**), that unused area will remain transparent when you import the file into another Adobe program – such as Premiere Elements.

If you place a graphics file containing transparency on the upper track of a Premiere Elements project, those transparent areas will also be transparent in your video. Only the graphic itself will show – your video on a lower track will be visible behind and around it.

File formats that support alpha

Although **PSDs** are the ideal (and easiest) format for sending non-square graphics to a Premiere Elements project, there are two other file formats you can export from Photoshop Elements that will include alpha. These are the formats you will use if you are creating non-square graphics for the Web or for a non-Adobe program that doesn't support PSD files.

GIFs were invented by Compuserve (remember them?) in the early days of the Internet, and they remain, along with JPEGs, one of the most common file format used on the web.

But GIFs don't handle color very efficiently. **PNGs** were invented to unite the color qualities of a JPEG with the alpha channel abilities of a GIF.

To export a graphic as a GIF or PNG and maintain transparency around the graphic, go to the Photoshop Elements **File** menu and select **Save for Web**. This will open a workspace for resizing, compressing and optimizing your graphics for export as a JPEG, GIF or PNG (as in the illustration on the right).

Select **GIF** or **PNG-24** from the **Preset** drop-down menu.

Once you've done that, a checkbox will appear offering the option of **Transparency**.

Check this option and your graphic will be exported as a flat graphic, but with the same transparency as your original **PSD** file.

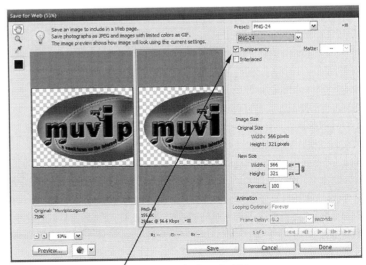

The option to preserve transparency on the Save for Web screen.

Chapter 10

Create and Edit Text
Typing, sizing, coloring and shaping

The text tools in Photoshop Elements run surprisingly deep.

Not only does the program allow you to work with such basic text attributes as font, style and color, but it also includes a variety of tools for shaping and warping text.

Text sizes and shapes can be edited using the text editor, or a block of text can be sized and shaped as if it were an object – all while remaining editable type.

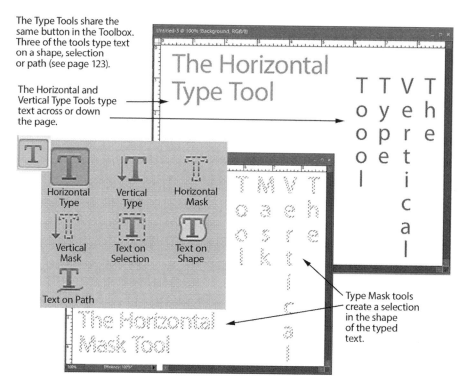

The Type Tools share the same button in the Toolbox. Three of the tools type text on a shape, selection or path (see page 123).

The Horizontal and Vertical Type Tools type text across or down the page.

Horizontal Type
Vertical Type
Horizontal Mask
Vertical Mask
Text on Selection
Text on Shape
Text on Path

Type Mask tools create a selection in the shape of the typed text.

The Type Tools

The seven **Type Tools** are accessed by clicking the **"T"** button in the **Toolbox,** along the left side of the **Editor** workspace, and then selecting the specific **Type Tool** from the **Tool Options Bin**.

Two of these tools add text to your image file as you type.

> **The Horizontal Type Tool**, as the name implies, types your text from left to right, by default in the **Foreground Color** (see page 47).

> **The Vertical Type Tool** types your text from top to bottom, by default in the **Foreground Color.** When you press **Enter** as you type, a new column of text is created *to the left* of the first.

 Horizontal text on your image file can be turned into vertical text, and vice versa, by selecting the text and then clicking the **Change the Text Orientation** button in the **Tool Options Bin**.

Two other **Type Tools** create a "mask" or selection in the shape of the text typed.

> **The Horizontal Type Mask Tool** creates a text-shaped selection mask from left to right as you type.

> **The Vertical Type Mask Tool** creates a text-shaped selection mask from top to bottom as you type.

Though called **Masks**, these type tools actually create **selections**. (**Layer Masks,** discussed on page 112, are very different and have a very different function in the program.)

As you type with a **Type Mask Tool**, your image file will be temporarily covered by a semi-opaque, red mask. Your text will appear to be cut out of this mask. When you click off of your text or select another tool, your typed text area will become a **selection** (surrounded by "marching ants"). (For more information on making and working with selections, see **Chapter 6, Select and Isolate Areas in Your Photos**.)

The selection created by your **Type Mask Tools** can be manipulated in a number of ways:

A selection can be deleted by pressing the **Delete** key, removing the area you've selected from the layer you've selected it on. Or you can select **Inverse** from the program's **Select** menu and, by pressing the **Delete** key, remove all *except* the text-shaped area.

A selection can be cut and pasted into another image file or onto a new layer in the current file.

If you switch to the **Move Tool, your selection can be resized or reshaped** by dragging its corner handles.

A selection can be colored using **Stroke** or **Fill**.

A selection's lighting and color can be adjusted, and your adjustments will affect only the selected area.

For the most part, **selections** made using the **Type Mask Tools** are no different than any other **selections** – except that their shape is defined by the shape of the text you type.

Re-edit a text layer

Your text will remain editable as long as it remains a separate text layer in a PSD file. You'll easily recognize a text layer in the **Layers** panel because the layer will appear as a big, gray "**T**", followed by the layer's name (which, by default, will be the text you typed).

Double-clicking the "T" on a text layer makes the text re-editable.

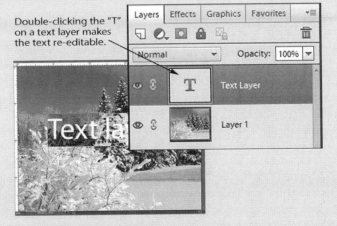

To re-edit a text layer, double-click on the big, gray "**T**" representing the layer on the **Layers** panel. The text layer will be activated and the **Type Tool** will automatically be selected.

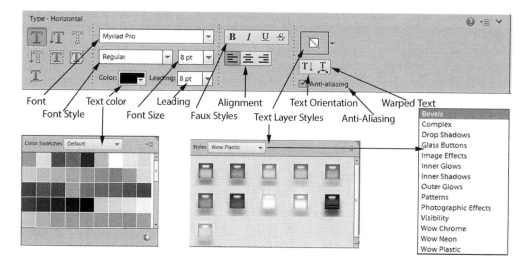

The Type Tool Options Bin

All of the **Type Tools**, whether text tools or mask tools, use a similar **Tool Options Bin**, which runs along the bottom of the **Editor** workspace.

The **Type Tool Options** are primarily used for setting basic fonts, text styles, colors and sizes.

In most cases, the default settings for the **Type Tools** options will be the *last settings you used*. In other words, if you used 8 pt. Myriad Pro Regular to the last time you added text to your image file, the next time you select a **Type Tool**, it will be set to 8 pt. Myriad Pro Regular.

Font. The **Font** drop-down menu lists pretty much every font available on your system. These fonts will vary from computer to computer. Windows includes around 20 basic fonts. Other programs you've installed, including Premiere Elements and Photoshop Elements, may have added a few more.

The symbol to the left of each font in its listing indicates if it is a True Type (**TT**) or an Open Type (**O**) font. Without getting into too deep a discussion of font systems, True Type is the most basic font system. Open Type is the more advanced font system, sometimes including dozens of styles and options within the font. (An Open Type font, for instance, may include the option to use *ligatures* to make an adjacent "f" and "i" into one, combined character with no dot over the "i", as in the word "find.")

A quick way to "call up" a font is to type its name into the **Font** box on the **Tool Options Bin** (without opening the drop-down menu). As you type the name of the font, Photoshop Elements will automatically search and load the font for your **Type Tool**.

Font Style. Most fonts include specific text styles such as **Bold** and **Italic**. Because these styles are designed as part of the font itself, setting them in the **Font Style** drop-down menu is preferred to applying the **Faux Styles** to the right.

Font Size. Measured in "points", font sizes are relative to the pixel density in your image files. In other words, a 14 point font on a low-resolution image will appear much larger than a 14 point font will on a high-resolution image. In addition to setting font sizes numerically, you can size your text as a block, as described in **Shape and Size Your Text** on page 122.

Leading is the space between lines of text. In most cases, the **Auto** setting will give you the best results. However, for aesthetic reasons, you can manually set your leading tighter or looser. The numerical settings correspond to the font's size.

Text Color. By default, your text will be the **Foreground Color (see page 47)** that was set when you selected the **Type Tool**. You can manually change the **Text Color** by selecting it from this drop-down menu or by clicking on a swatch displayed in the **Color Swatches** panel (available under the program's **Window** menu).

Faux Styles are ways to add styling (bold, italic, etc.) to fonts. They're called "faux styles" because they aren't part of the font's original design, but rather the program's *simulation* of the style. In other words, faux bold merely thickens the font, faux italic slants it to one side, etc.

Paragraph Alignment aligns your text to the left, right or center. **Paragraph Alignment** is important if you plan to create Premiere Elements DVD templates (see **Chapter 13, Advanced Photoshop Elements Tools**) because it will determine the direction your custom text will flow when you type in the names of your scenes or chapters.

Anti-Aliasing. Aliasing has to do with how sharp the edges of a font are. With **Anti-Aliasing** turned off, text can look unnaturally sharp and jagged. You'll probably want to keep the **Anti-Aliasing** checkbox checked then. (For an illustration, see **What is Anti-Aliasing?** on page 52 of **Chapter 5, Get to Know the Photoshop Elements Toolbox**.)

Text Layer Styles. There are dozens of styles which can be applied to your text layer, from bevels to drop-shadows to glows to patterns. Click on the **Text Layer Styles** button, as illustrated on the facing page, to open the option panel. To see the various pages of available styles, click on the pop-up menu at the top of this **Layer Styles** panel.

Warped Text. You can choose a **Warp** style before, after or while you are typing your text. The various warps include arcs, bulges, fish-eyes, waves and twists. And, as you select each, your text will preview the warp for you. Also, once you've selected a warp, you can customize it by adjusting the **Bend, Horizontal Distortion** and **Vertical Distortion** to create pretty much any look you want.

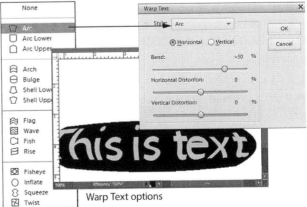

Warp Text options

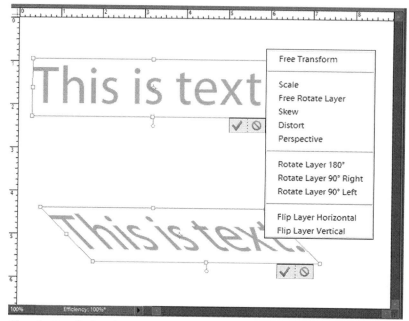

When the Move Tool is selected, text can be resized as if it were vector art by dragging on the corner handles. The right-click (Ctrl-click) option to Skew allows you to angle your text block.

Shape and resize your text

You can resize and reshape a text layer just as you can any other image or shape layer. Because it behaves like vector art, you can enlarge or stretch your text layer without regard to resolution.

 To resize a text layer, select the **Move Tool** in the **Toolbox** and then select the text layer by either clicking directly on it in your image file or clicking on the layer on the **Layers** panel.

Press **Ctrl+t** on a PC or ⌘**+t** on a Mac to put the Editor into **Transform** mode.

The text block will appear with handles on each corner and on the sides. Drag on these corner handles to resize and reposition your text. As long as the **Constrain Proportions** option is selected in the **Tool Options Bin**, the text block will resize proportionately.

Other reshaping options are available by **right-clicking** on the text block (**Ctrl-clicking** on a Mac). These options are:

Free Transform (default). This option allows for both resizing and rotating of the text block.

Scale. You have the option of resizing the block, but rotation is locked out.

Free Rotate Layer. You will be able to rotate the block, but scaling is locked out.

Skew. By dragging the corner handles, you will slant the text block, as in the illustration above.

Lock in any changes by clicking the green checkmark or by pressing **Enter**. Cancel any changes by clicking the red cancel icon or pressing **ESC**.

Other transform options

The **Distort** and **Perspective** transform options are grayed-out of the text block's **right-click** menu. These options are only available for raster art, but can be applied to text if the text layer has been simplified (converted to pixels).

To simplify a text or shape layer, **right-click** on the text layer in the **Layers** panel (**Ctrl-click** on a Mac) and select the **Simplify Layer** option. (Simplifying text turns it into pixels, so it will no longer be editable.)

> **Distort**. By dragging the corner handles of your layer, you will be able to shape it into any four-sided shape you'd like.

> **Perspective**. Dragging the corner handles stretches two sides at once – allowing you to stretch and shape your layer so that it appears to have perspective.

For more information on simplifying layers, see **Simplify or Flatten a Layer** on page 110 of **Chapter 9, Work with Photoshop Elements Layers**.

Type on a Selection, Shape or Path

In addition to standard typing tools, Photoshop Elements includes options for typing your text around the outline of a selection or shape or on a path. To select a **Text On** tool, click on the **Type** button on the Premiere Elements **Toolbox** and then select the tool you want from the **Tool Options Bin** that below the **Editor** workspace.

Type Text on a Selection

When **Text on Selection** is selected, your cursor will become a **Quick Selection Tool** (as described on page 51).

1   Drag over your photo to make a **Quick Selection**.

    As you drag, the program will select adjacent areas of similar color. When you are satisfied with your selection, click the green checkmark or press **Enter**.

To Type on a Selection, first use the Quick Selection Tool to create a selected area. Click the check-mark to finalize it.

2   Hover your mouse over the selection path until your cursor indicates you are on the type path.

    Select your font and text characteristics, then click and type. The text will flow around the outside of the selection, beginning at the point on the selection's outline at which you initially clicked.

Hover your mouse over the path created until your cursor displays as the type icon. Click and type.

Tool Options for the Text on Shape Tool include a number of shape options as well as options for setting the color, size, font and style of your text.

Type Text on a Shape

You can create a shape to type along by selecting a shape from the **Tool Options Bin** or by using the **Shape Tool** (see page 63). (The shapes in the **Tool Options Bin** will create a type path only and not an actual shape.)

1   Create a shape.

   To create a shape using the **Text on Shape Tool**, select one of the shape options in the **Tool Options Bin** (as above), then drag to draw the shape on your photo.

2   Hover your mouse over the outline of the shape until your cursor indicates you are on the type path.

When you use the Text on Shape Tool, your type will flow around whatever shape you provide for it.

   Select your font and text characteristics, then click and type. The text will flow around the outside of the shape, beginning at the point on the selection's outline at which you initially clicked.

Type Text on a Custom Path

The **Text on Custom Path Tool** will align text along any path you create.

1   Create a path.

   When you select the **Text on Custom Path Tool**, your cursor will become a pencil. Draw the path you would like your text to follow over your photo.

2   Hover your mouse over the path until your cursor indicates you are on the type path.

   Select your font and text characteristics, then click and type. The text will flow around the outside of the selection, beginning at the point on the selection's outline at which you initially clicked.

With the Text on Custom Path Tool, your text will follow any path you draw.

Chapter 11
Add Photo Effects and Filters
Use Photoshop Elements' special effects

Photoshop Elements includes hundreds of customizable effects and filters that can be applied to your image files.

Filters can add new elements to your image file or they can make your photo look like an artist's sketch or painting.

Effects can be used to add drop shadows and glows around your layers.

Additional effects can make your new photographs look like they were taken a hundred years ago!

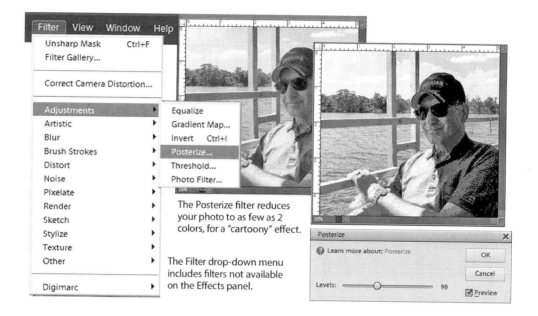

The Posterize filter reduces your photo to as few as 2 colors, for a "cartoony" effect.

The Filter drop-down menu includes filters not available on the Effects panel.

Effects and filters can be used to stylize or create interesting, new looks for your photographs and other image files. You can also just use them to have fun – to make your photo look like a watercolor painting, for instance, or to make a modern photo look like a withered, old snapshot.

Many of Photoshop Elements' filters can be found under the program's **Filter** menu. Except for those listed below, virtually all of these filters can also be found, displayed as intuitive thumbnails, in the **Effects** panel, located by default in the **Panel Bin** to the right of the **Editor** workspace. (If, for some reason, the **Effects** panel has been closed, you can open it by selecting the option under the program's **Window** menu.)

The Filter menu

We'll discuss the bulk of the program's **Filters** in our discussion of the **Effects** panel, beginning on page 130.

But there are six filters under the **Filter** menu that are *not* included in the **Effects** panel set. These are the **Adjustment** filters, and they include:

Equalize. This filter interprets the darkest area of your image file as black and your lightest area as white and then it evenly distributes the levels of colors between. The process often softens the contrast in a photo.

Gradient Map. This filter turns your photo into a grayscale image and then it replaces that grayscale with any set of colors, based on the selections you make by clicking on the pop-up menu (as displayed when you click the grayscale area on the option screen).

Invert. Creates a negative of your image file.

Posterize. This filter reduces the number of colors displayed in your image file, based on your settings.

Threshold. Converts your image file into a high-contrast, black & white image, based on the level you set.

Photo Filter. This filter applies one of 20 **photographic filters** to your image file, as if your camera shot your photo through a tinted lens. It can also be used to "warm" or "cool" the colors in a photograph.

Additionally, the **Filter** menu gives you access to an amazing tool for correcting some distortions caused by certain lenses (or, if you're of the mind to, creating some).

Correct Camera Distortion is a filter which reshapes your photo to compensate for rounding or keystoning – unnatural distortion to a photo which can occur because of the use of a wide-angle lens or because it was shot from an unusual angle. Launching the **Correct Camera Distortion** filter opens a workspace in which you can "un-round" or "round" your photo or even reshape it so that it widens at the top, bottom or side, as in the illustration above. This filter works automatically when you combine several shots in a **Photomerge**, as discussed on page 155 of **Chapter 13, Advanced Photoshop Elements Tools**.

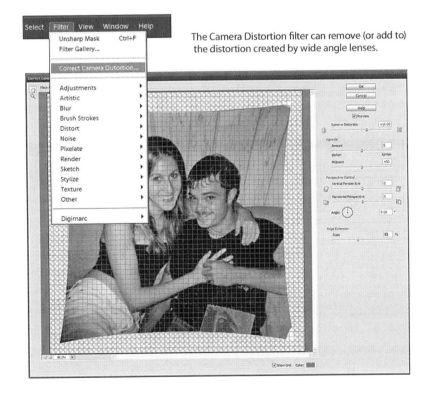

The Camera Distortion filter can remove (or add to) the distortion created by wide angle lenses.

The Filter Gallery

Opened by selecting the option under the **Filter** menu, the **Filter Gallery** is a workspace for applying one or more filters to your image file, setting the filter levels and previewing the results.

It is also a means of quickly browsing a large portion of the **Filter** library, displayed as thumbnails down the center of the panel.

The **Filter Gallery** displays as four panels or work areas.

To the left is the **Preview** window. This window displays your image file as it will appear when the selected filter is applied to it. To the lower left of this display you will find controls for zooming in or out of your image.

The center column of the of the **Filter Gallery** contains a large portion of Photoshop Elements' library of **Filters**, each displayed as a thumbnail representing its effect. These filters are arranged in six categories, which you can open and close by clicking on the little triangles to left of each category's name.

As you click on each filter, a preview of its effect on your image file will be displayed in the **Preview** window. When you select a new filter, the old will automatically be removed when the new is applied.

The Filter Gallery is a workspace for test-driving and multiplying filters applied to an image file.

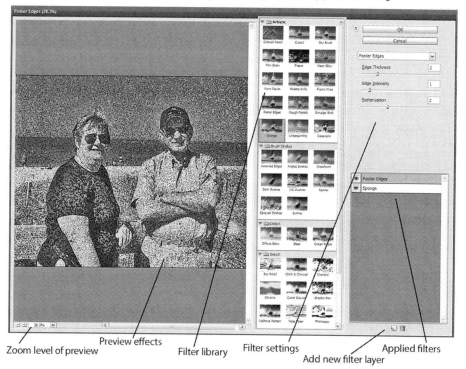

Zoom level of preview · Preview effects · Filter library · Filter settings · Add new filter layer · Applied filters

The **levels** for each filter are set in the upper right of the **Filter Gallery.** (The drop-down menu above these settings is yet another way to switch from filter to filter.)

In the lower right of the **Filter Gallery** is a **properties** panel, which displays a listing of the filters you have applied to your image.

- You can combine and apply as many filters as you'd like to your image file. To add an additional filter, click on the **New Effect Layer** button at the bottom of this properties listing space.

- Your filters can be turned off and on in this area by clicking the eyeball icon to the left of each effect listing. And filters can be removed completely from this listing by selecting the filter from the list and clicking on the trashcan icon.

The Effects panel

There are nearly 300 effects available on the **Effects** panel, which resides, by default, in the **Panel Bin** to the right of the Photoshop Elements Editor workspace. (If this panel is not visible, click the **Effects** button in the lower right of the **Basic Workspace** interface.) Some of the tools on this panel are filters. Many more are effects (such as **Drop Shadows** and **Glows**) that can be applied to layers, text or shapes in layered image files or to create a 3D-like photographic special effect.

These effects and filters are available in different categories, which can be accessed by clicking on one of the three category tabs at the top of the panel (**Filters, Styles, Effects**).

You can get a general idea of how each filter or effect will change your image file by looking at the thumbnails displayed in the **Effects** panel.

The size of these thumbnails can be adjusted by selecting one of the **Thumbnail Views** available under pop-out menu in the upper right of the panel, as illustrated.

The Effects panel

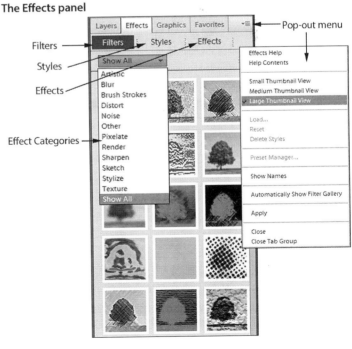

If your program workspace is in **Custom** rather than **Basic** mode (set under the **More** menu in the lower right of the interface) the **Effects** panel, like all of the panels in the **Panel Bin**, can be undocked, if you'd prefer, and placed anywhere on your computer's desktop. To undock a panel, drag on its tab at the top of the panel.

Once you remove it from the bin, it becomes a "floating" panel and you can position it wherever you'd like in your workspace.

To re-dock the panel, just drag it by its tab back into the **Panel Bin** and release your mouse button. The panel will pop back into the bin.

To return the **Panel Bin** to its original array of panels, go to the **Window** menu and select **Reset Panels**.

Filter Effects

Filter Effects

Photoshop Elements divides its **Filters** into 12 general categories. These **Filters** can be found under the **Filter** menu or accessed by clicking the **Filters** tab on the **Effects** panel.

Artistic. These filters give your photo a "painterly" look, as if they were created by an artist's brush or sketch pencil. It includes **Plastic Wrap**, an effect which makes the elements in your photo look as if they were sealed in Saran Wrap!

Blur. These filters soften or blur an image file or selected area. Among the blurs are a **Radial Blur**, which gives your photo a spinning effect, and a **Motion Blur**, which can make your image file or selected area appear to be zipping by your camera.

Brush Strokes. These filters make your photo look as if it were painted with fine arts brushes or drawn with ink.

Distort. This category includes 3D filters for distorting and reshaping your image files. The **Liquify** filter makes your image file behave as if it were made of smearable paint.

Noise. Filters for softening scratches or flaws in a photo – or creating noise as an effect!

Other. A miscellaneous category of filters, like **High-Pass** and **Offset**, for creating customizable image effects.

Pixelate. Filters which clump pixels, creating mosaic-like versions of your images.

Render. We discuss this unique category of effects in detail in the sidebar on page 132.

Sharpen. The **Unsharp Mask** in this category increases the contrast between pixels to sharpen the look of a photo.

Sketch. These filters give your photos a hand-drawn look, with some filters even simulating the look of various drawing papers. **Photocopy** makes your photo look as if it were run through a Xerox machine. **Chrome** makes it look as if it were formed out of metal.

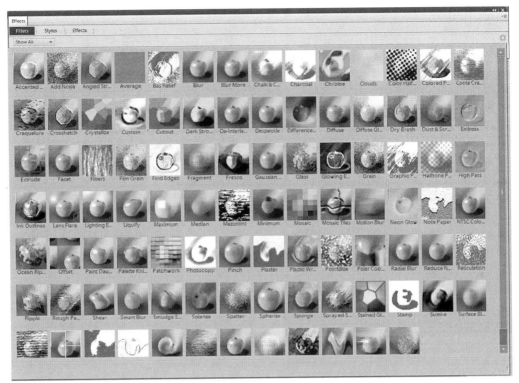

Filters available on the Effects panel

Stylize. These filters create an impressionistic effect or they create very unnatural special effects. **Emboss** makes your image file look as it if were pressed into a piece of paper. **Wind** makes the color look as if it was smeared by a blast of air.

Texture. **Texture** filters add a 3D texture to the image, as if it was printed onto a texturized paper. The **Stained Glass** filter adds a mosaic look, which makes your photo look like a stained glass window!

Style Effects

The **Styles** effects are accessed by clicking the **Styles** tab on the **Effects** panel. The styles are displayed as thumbnails representing their effect. Photoshop Elements includes over 175 **Layer Styles** effects in 15 categories.

Layer Styles are, as you might suppose, effects applied to layers in an image file.

In fact, if you try to apply these effects to a flat image file or a **Background** layer, a message will pop up warning you that these effects will only work on layers.

Render Filters, a close-up

The **Render** set of **Filters** deserves a more detailed discussion, because these filters often don't so much change your image file as add new elements to it. They include:

Clouds. When applied to an image file, layer or selection, this filter draws clouds. These clouds will be a combination of the **Foreground Color** and **Background Color** you currently have set (see page 45).

Difference Clouds. This filter draws clouds over your image file or selected area, producing colors that are complementary to the image file's existing colors.

Fibers. This filter draws a fibrous pattern, based on the settings you provide and the **Foreground Color** and **Background Color** you currently have selected. The option panel that opens when you apply this filter allows you to set the **Variance** and **Strength** of the fibers.

Lens Flare. A popular effect, this filter creates the effect of a bright light shining back into the camera.

On the option screen, you can set both the brightness and type of light and, by dragging the crosshairs, set where in the photo you'd like the flare to appear.

The Lens Flare filter adds a bright sparkle.

Lighting Effects include a number of presets and custom settings.

Lighting Effects. This filter lets you create the effect of bright light and shadow across your photo, based on a variety of settings.

The circular control allows you to set the angle and intensity of the light, while the various style and slider settings allow you to create dozens of different lighting effects.

Some of the more than 175 Styles available on the Effects panel

Many of these effects take advantage of the unique nature of layers. The **Drop-Shadows** and **Outer Glows**, for instance, clearly wouldn't show any effect if they were applied to a **Background** layer. Likewise, the **Visibility** effects, which make your layer semi-transparent, by nature deal with the way layers interact.

Styles can be applied to text layers and shape layers as well as image layers. They can even be applied to layered image files with no **Background** layer.

A **Style** is applied by selecting a layer in the **Layers** panel and then either double-clicking on the style or dragging the style onto the layer.

Many **Styles** can be customized on the **Style Settings** screen. To open **Style Settings**, click the gear icon on the top right of the **Effects** panel, or double-click on the "*fx*" button on a layer to which **Styles** have been applied, as in the illustration on the following page.

Styles can be added to text layers as well as shape and image layers – and more than one style may be applied to a single layer.

Double-clicking the "fx" button on a layer to which Layer Styles have been added launches the Style Settings screen, where the layer effects can be customized or turned off or on.

Style Settings for the **Bevel** effect, for instance, include settings for the depth of the bevel and a toggle for setting whether a selected layer bevels up or down. **Glow** settings affect the size, color and opacity of the glow.

Additionally, by checking or unchecking the styles listed on the **Style Settings** screen, you can toggle your **Styles** off and on.

To undo the effect, either click the **Undo** button or press **Ctrl+z** on a PC or ⌘+z on a Mac. To remove all effects from a layer, click the **Style Setting's** panel's Reset button.

The 15 categories of **Styles** are:

Bevels. Bevels create a 3D effect by making your layer look as if it or its frame bulges out of your image file or is impressed into it.

Complex styles combine **Bevel, Pattern, Texture** and/or **Drop-Shadow** effects to your selected layer.

Drop-Shadow styles cast a shadow from the layer onto lower layers or the **Background**. To change the angle or other characteristics of a **Drop Shadow** once it has been applied, open **Style Settings** by double-clicking on the "*fx*" button on the layer in the **Layers** palette, as discussed earlier.

Glass Buttons styles turn your selected layer into a beveled, glass-like button.

Image Effects add effects like snow, rain, a jigsaw puzzle texture or a night vision look to your layer.

Inner Glows add a glow color inward from the edge of the layer.

Inner Shadows add a drop shadow inward from the edge of the layer, as if the layer were sunken into the image file.

Outer Glows add a glow outward from the edges of your layer.

Patterns replace your layer with a texture like a brick wall, blanket, stone, etc.

Photographic Effects add a tint to your layer or give it a sepia tone.

Strokes create a frame for your layer in a number of line weights and colors.

Visibility makes your layer semi-opaque, showing the other layers or the **Background** through it.

Wow Chrome replaces your layer with a 3D chrome texture.

Wow Neon replaces your layer with a bright, 3D glowing texture.

Wow Plastic replaces your layer with a shiny, 3D plastic texture.

Photo Effects

Photo Effects are special effects which can be applied to make your photographs look aged or have a 3D effect.

All but a few of these **Effects** work by creating a duplicate of the **Background** layer and then applying color or texture effects to it. Because of this, the effects it applies don't change the original artwork. The original photo remains in its unaffected state, hidden behind the layer to which effects have been applied.

The original and the layers to which effects have been applied remain separate as long as you save your file as a layered PSD (Photoshop) file and you do not flatten the layers or save your image file as a format that does not support layers (such as a JPEG or a non-layered TIF).

Photo Effects can make bright, new photos look old and worn.

The layer to which the effect has been applied can then be accepted and kept or deleted (by selecting the layer and clicking on the trashcan icon on the **Layers** panel).

The **Photo Effects** include:

Faded Photo creates an old photo effect by fading areas of your photo from color to black & white.

Frame creates a frame or drop-shadow effect by shrinking your image file so that it is smaller than the canvas.

Misc. Effects apply any of a number of texture or special effects to your photo.

Monotone Color reduces your color photo to tints of monochrome or a single color.

Old Photo adds aging and distressed effects to your photo, as illustrated above.

Vintage Photo is another "old photo" effect, this one making it appear that the paper your photo is printed on is cracked and withered.

Adobe Photoshop Elements

Part III
Advanced Photo Editing

Swapping Out a Face

Swapping Out a Background

Healing Blemishes

Removing Things from Photos

Adding Things to Photos

Chapter 12

Photoshop Elements Tricks
Have fun with your photos

Stunt photography – or trick photography – is the fun side of Photoshop Elements.

It's about swapping out elements in your photos – or adding new things or removing things you don't want.

It's about creating situations that didn't really exist.

But there's a "legitimate side" to Photoshop Elements tricks too. They can be very helpful for cleaning up little messes on your photos.

Stunt photography can be a lot of fun. Swapping a friend's face for the Mona Lisa's, for instance. Or making your child look like she's walking on the Moon. It's fun – and surprisingly easy, using just a few basic tools.

But, of course, these tricks can also be functional. Occasionally you've shot a perfect photo – except for a stray wire hanging in the background or an untimely blemish. And sometimes, for a variety of reasons, you just want to place someone in a location other than where he or she was actually photographed.

It's all good. And it's all based on a couple of simple tricks and the basic Photoshop tools described earlier in this book.

Swap out a face

It's about more than just swapping faces, of course. It can be about placing someone into a scene – or even creating a composite of elements from a couple of photos.

I was challenged once with touching up the photo of a person who had a muscle weakness in one eye that caused his left eye to drift. In the photo I had of him, his eyes seemed to be looking in two different directions. By copying his left eye from another photo, I was able to seamlessly replace the drifting eye with one more in line with the right, creating a much more flattering picture.

The process of swapping in an element from one photo to another is best accomplished when you use two key principles:

- Ensuring that the two photo sources have similar resolution, lighting and color; and
- Blending the edges as smoothly as possible between the two photos

In my illustration below, I've gathered two classic Grisetti photos. The first is of me, at age 8, all fully equipped for a day of playing army with my friends. The second, from about 10 years later, is a real-life photo of me from my army days.

So what would happen if I grafted my somewhat adult face onto my childhood picture?

Well, the resolutions and textures aren't quite the same, and I'm facing a slightly different direction in each photo – but this is just for fun, so let's see how it goes.

1   Dragging the **Elliptical Marquee Selection Tool** over my Basic Training picture, I selected my head (and a little beyond).

    The **Elliptical Selection Tool** is one of the two **Marquee Selection Tools**. If the **Elliptical Tool** doesn't show in your Photoshop Elements **Toolbox**, select the **Rectangular Selection tool** and then switch to the **Elliptical Selection Tool** in the **Tool Options Bin**, as described on page 49.

2   Then, using the **Move Tool**, I (literally) dragged the selected area from my Basic Training photo onto my childhood picture, as illustrated above.

    Although I also could have done this with a cut-and-paste command, dragging from one file to another is the easiest way to copy elements (and even layers) between image files. Because my childhood picture is a black & white photo and my army photo is in color, the area I've copied from one photo to another automatically converts to grayscale.

    Also note that the area I've moved from one photo to the other has become a new layer on the childhood picture.

3   Ensuring that Layer 1 (my face) is selected on the childhood picture, I slid the **Opacity** level on the **Layers** panel to about 60%, as illustrated on page 142. This allowed me to see both the background and layer (as sort of a double-exposure) so that I can scale and position my new face over my old.

4   Dragging the corner handles around my face, I sized and positioned my older face over the younger in the childhood picture, as described on page 142.

    Because I was facing to the right in one picture and a bit more to the left in the other, I flipped the "face" layer horizontally by dragging the side handle for my face completely across and over the to other side, turning it into a mirror image.

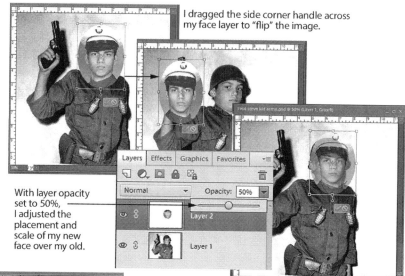

I dragged the side corner handle across my face layer to "flip" the image.

With layer opacity set to 50%, I adjusted the placement and scale of my new face over my old.

With opacity back at 100%, I used the Eraser Tool to remove all but my face from the layer.

The final, rather creepy, result

(I could also have done this, by the way, by going to the **Image** menu and selecting **Flip Horizontal** from the **Rotate** sub-menu.)

I knew the two faces weren't going to match up perfectly but, by stretching, scaling and rotating, I am able to line up the eyes and the mouths.

Once the layer was in position, I pressed **Enter** to lock in the scaling. Then I set the **Opacity** for the layer back to 100%.

5   Selecting the **Eraser Tool** and, setting it to a soft-edged 45 px brush in the **Tool Options Bin**, I erased all the unwanted imagery around my "face" layer.

Because the **Eraser Tool** brush setting had a soft edge to it, the line between the erased and unerased areas on the layer were slightly feathered, creating a softer, more natural edge.

Because my face had changed shape over the years, I can't completely replace my young head with my older head – but, when I erase around the sides of my face, my older face blends in pretty well with my younger head.

The result, at left, is just a bit creepy – but it works!

The first step in pasting Sarah into the Monaco scene was using the Magic Wand Tool to select the green background in her photo.

Swap out a background

Swapping in a background uses essentially the same principles as swapping in a head, except that you're trying to create an entire scene from a composite of images.

In the illustration above, I've decided to take Sarah, who was conveniently shot in front of a green screen, and place her in front of the castle wall, overlooking downtown Monaco.

Green screens and blue screens are, of course, great photographic backgrounds for doing this kind of work – as well as for doing Chroma Key and Videomerge, similar background-swapping tricks performed in video.

This is because not only do green and blue screens give you a nice, even color that's easy to select and delete, but these bright shades of green and blue don't show up in human skin tones. This makes it easier to separate the human from the background.

1   Using the **Magic Wand Tool**, as illustrated above, I selected the green background, behind Sarah.

The **Magic Wand Tool** is one of the three **Quick Selection Tools**. If the **Magic Wand** doesn't show in your Photoshop Elements **Toolbox**, select the **Quick Selection** or **Selection Brush** and then switch to the **Magic Wand** in the **Tool Options Bin**, as described on page 51.

How much gets selected on a single click of this tool depends on how high the **Tolerance** is set in the **Tool Options**. In order to select the entire green area, I set the **Tolerance** to 25 – and even then needed to hold down the **Shift** key and click on a couple of areas to build the selection until I had the entire green screen was selected. (At this point, I won't worry about the green showing between her curls.)

Inverse swaps the selection so that Sarah is now selected rather than the background.

2 From the program's **Select** menu, I selected **Inverse**. This swapped the selection area so that now *Sarah* was selected rather than the green screen background.

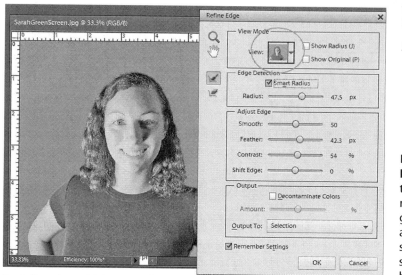

3 From the **Select** drop-down, I then selected the **Refine Edge** tool. This tool allowed me to tweak the edges of my selected area a bit.

By adjusting the **Shift Edge** slider, I ensured that my selection did not include any of the green screen. I also adjusted the **Feather** slider to 3 px so that the selection edge would be softer and more natural.

The Refine Edge tool tightens the edge around the selection and adds some feathering so that the selection blends with its new background. The Overlay View Mode shows unselected areas as overlayed with a red mask.

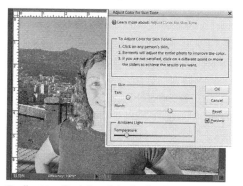

Finally, using the Adjust Color for Skin Tone tool, Sarah's color temperature is adjusted to more closely match her new background.

Stray green spots, particularly around the hair, are removed with a soft-edge Eraser Tool brush.

4 I then dragged the selected area, Sarah, onto the Monaco photo. Because I had ensured that the photos had similar resolution, Sarah fits nicely onto her new background.

5 Using the 45 px soft-edged brush setting, I dragged the **Eraser Tool** to clean up any stray green left around Sarah. Remember, when you are working with a layer, erasing *cuts transparency through* the layer – revealing the background or layers below.

Using different sized **Eraser Tool** brushes, I removed what I could from between the curls in her hair. Depending on how much detail you're trying to clean up, this part of the process can be the most challenging and time consuming. (I could also have saved myself this clean-up by refining my selection's edge using the **Smart Detection** tool, as described on page 76.)

6 Finally, with **Layer 1** (Sarah) selected, I went to the program's **Enhance** menu, selected the **Adjust Color** sub-menu and then **Adjust Color for Skin Tone**. Using the eye-dropper, I sampled a mid-tone of skin on Sarah's face. Then moving the **Ambient Light** slider (and, to a lesser degree, the **Tan** and **Blush** sliders), I fine-tuned Sarah so that she better matched the color tones of someone standing under the Mediterranean sun.

Removing blemishes, spots and other embarassments is easy with the Spot Healing Brush.

Remove warts and blemishes

Nobody's perfect. And neither is any scene. Fortunately, Photoshop Elements makes it easy to dab away the occasional blemish.

In the illustration above, we see Sarah posing with her pet budgies. Unfortunately, Sally, the bird on the left, has left an ugly deposit on Sarah's sweater, marring an otherwise very cute picture.

The **Healing Brush Tool** and **Spot Healing Brush** are both very effective for removing these little flaws and spots.

1 With the photo open in the **Editor,** I selected the **Spot Healing Brush** from the **Toolbox** and, in the **Tool Options Bin,** I set the brush size to 34 px (which is just about the size of the spot I wanted to remove).

2 Dragging the mouse over the area, I "painted" the spot with the **Healing Brush**.

   When I released the mouse button, Photoshop Elements automatically filled in the area with color and texture information borrowed from surrounding pixels.

And we're done! The **Spot Healing Brush** is a terrific, virtually automatic tool that I find all but indispensable.

With the Spot Healing Brush Tool, you merely "paint" over the area you want to remove and, when you release the mouse button, the program blends color and texture information from the surrounding pixels to fill the area and remove the spot!

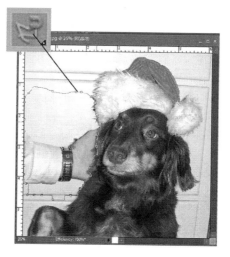

The Magnetic Selection Tool makes it easy to follow the color break along Buddy's fur and hat and create a selection isolating the arm area.

Remove big things from your photos

Sometimes you want to remove something larger than a blemish or spot from your photo. Sometimes you may even want to remove an entire person! This is most easily accomplished by "painting" over the object or person with imagery "cloned" from of another area of your photo – using one of the most powerful and popular Photoshop tools in the program's tool kit.

As illustrated above, my friend Ron dressed up and posed his dog, Buddy, for a photo he plans to use for the cover of his Christmas card. Ron, however, prefers that the final photo not include his arm in the shot so that it looks more like Buddy is standing up on his own.

1 Using the **Magnetic Lasso Selection Tool**, I drew a selection lasso along the edge of Buddy's fur and around the area where Ron's arm appears.

The **Magnetic Lasso** is one of the three **Lasso Selection Tools**. If the **Magnetic Lasso** doesn't show in your Photoshop Elements **Toolbox**, select the **Lasso** or **Polygonal Lasso** and then switch to the **Magnetic Lasso** in the **Tool Options Bin**, as described on page 50.

Selecting an area isolates it so that any changes you make will affect only the selected area, and won't affect Buddy).

The Clone Tool uses imagery from the designated area to paint over the brushed area, while the selection restricts changes to the selected area.

The **Magnetic Selection Tool** made it easy to draw my selection because, as I dragged it along Buddy's outline, it followed the color break between Buddy's dark fur and the much lighter background.

2 Switching to the **Clone Stamp Tool,** I **Alt+clicked** to designate the clone source area of my photo – the area of the photo from which I would "borrow" picture information to paint over Ron's arm.

Since I wanted to replace Ron's arm with the color and texture of the painted wall behind it, I held down the **Alt** key and clicked to select a spot on the white wall, above Ron's arm. This "source" area is designated with crosshairs, as seen in the illustration on the left.

Once my source spot was selected, I released the **Alt** key.

3. With the **Clone Tool** set to a fairly large brush (200 px in this case) with soft edges (to blend the imagery I'd be adding to the background), I "painted" over Ron's arm, replacing it with the area I'd designated as my clone source.

Because I had created a **selection area**, there was no danger of my accidentally painting the background over Buddy – since he was outside my selection. My painted area was restricted to the area within the "marching ants" dotted lines.

Add things to your photos

Just as the **Clone Tool** can be used to paint over and remove images from your photos, it can also be used to paint new imagery onto a photo – even imagery borrowed from another photo!

For instance, the world may never wonder how I'd look with Jeanne's hair – but it can still be fun to find out.

1. With both photos open (I also ensured both photos were of similar resolution and that our heads were in a similar position), I selected the **Clone Stamp Tool**. I then **Alt+clicked** on Jeanne's photo to select her hair, at approximately the top center of her scalp. This defined the area of the image I was going to use as my cloning source.

2. I then clicked on the Steve photo (to activate it) and, dragging the **Clone Tool** across it, I painted Jeanne's hair over mine, starting at approximately the same spot on my head as I'd designated for my source on hers.

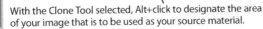
With the Clone Tool selected, Alt+click to designate the area of your image that is to be used as your source material.

147

As you drag the Clone Tool over your destination image file, the destination is "painted" with imagery from your source.

Because I was using such a soft, large brush (100 px, in this case) and because Jeanne has such curly hair, I got a lot of the background from her picture along with the hair.

I could also have created a new layer on the Steve picture and painted the hair onto it – and then used the **Eraser Tool** to clean up the layer, removing the background or other unwanted elements that slipped over from Jeanne's picture.

And, okay. I guess I wouldn't make such an attractive blonde.

Though, if I were, I might have a great career as an aging rock star!

Photomerge: A powerful Photoshop Elements tool

A great, multi-faceted tool that many people don't even realize is in the Photoshop Elements toolset is **Photomerge**, a tool for combining elements from several photos into one great picture!

- **Photomerge** can be used to create panoramic photos, combining several photos of a scene into one, big one.
- Or it can be used to build great photos out of the best bits and pieces of several slightly-flawed ones.
- You can even use it to add a person from one group shot to another!

We discuss a couple of its key features and how to use them beginning on page 155.

Chapter 13

Advanced Photo Editing Tools
Photoshop Elements extras

Have you ever scanned in several photos at once and then found yourself cropping and straightening each one individually?

Or have you ever taken several photos of a scene and wondered if there was an easy way to stitch them all together into one big picture?

Photoshop Elements includes tools for doing these things – plus a few more tools worth knowing about, including the ability to interface with a camera or scanner.

In addition to tools for creating and editing graphics and photos, Photoshop Elements includes a number of tools that don't fit into any neat category. These include tools for interfacing with a scanner or camera and tools for processing photo files before you actually bring them into the program. There are also a couple of the program's preferences that are worth knowing about.

Scan your photos

Built into Photoshop Elements is a tool for interfacing with your scanner.

The scanning itself is done by your scanner's software – and that software does vary just a bit, from device to device and brand to brand. But the basic principles are the same. Through a system called TWAIN, the scanner's software becomes a "plug-in" for Photoshop Elements. You seamlessly launch the scanner from within the program.

You can, in fact, launch your scanner's software in one of two ways, from either Photoshop Elements or the Organizer:

> From the **File** drop-down menu in Photoshop Elements, select **Import**, then the name of your scanner; or

> From the **File** drop-down menu in the Elements Organizer, select **Get Photos and Videos**, then **From Scanner**.

Whichever you choose, the same scanner software is launched.

As I've said, this software can vary from model to model and from brand to brand of scanner. But the principles are still the same:

Launching the scanner tool in the Editor.

Many consumer scanners include an **automatic mode**, which configures the scanner for you and scans your photos at a preset resolution and color setting but which you can customize to some degree. This is the simplest solution – but also produces, of course, the most generic results.

The **professional mode** usually includes options for a number of settings:

> **Reflective vs. Film (or Transparency).** If your scanner includes the ability to scan slides and film, this setting controls whether your scanner scans a reflection of the photo or shines light through it.

> **Photo vs. OCR.** Some scanners include the ability to scan documents with **Optical Character Recognition**. This OCR function scans your document in

as text, which you can later edit in a word processing program. It's not a flawless system, but it *can* save you a lot of retyping.

Resolution. Remember that the size of the document you will get from your scan is a combination of its size and its resolution. In other words, you may only need a 72 dpi image – but if the photo you're scanning is only the size of a postage stamp, you will need to scan it at a much higher resolution to get enough image data to work with.

Your scanner is controlled by the software that came bundled with it. However, most scanners use similar settings.

Scan reflective (photo) or transparent (slide)

Color mode

Size/resolution

Unsharp Mask

Reduce "dotty" look while scanning from newspapers and magazines

Enrich color on old photos

Auto light correction

Soften image to hide dust and scratches

Preview scan

Final scan

My scanner software includes a setting for **Target Size**. If I set this, the software automatically configures the scan to the necessary scan resolution. (Remember, you're always better off having too much resolution and having to rez down than not having enough resolution and needing to force your image larger later.)

Color Mode. There are three main color modes:

24-bit Color is standard **RGB color** – 8-bits per color channel.

Grayscale is monochrome, often called black & white.

But don't confuse it with **Black & White** (also known as **Bitmap**), which reduces all your colors to either 100% black or 100% white. **Black & White** is a color mode that is generally reserved for things like scanning signatures, which generally don't include shades of gray.

Some scanners also include on-the-fly picture adjustments or scan settings. Here are a couple of valuable adjustments.

Unsharp Mask. This will automatically sharpen your scanned images. It's usually best to have it turned on.

Descreening. When scanning photos from newspapers, magazines and low-end print pieces (like high school yearbooks), you may notice your scanned images have a lot of "dotty-ness." Descreening can help soften those low-quality printing artifacts.

Color Restoration. This feature will automatically enrich the color as you scan a faded, old photo.

Dust Removal. This feature adds a slight blur to your scan, sometimes hiding dust or scratches on a photo.

After a Preview Scan, you will have the option of designating the area of the Final Scan (indicated by a "marching ants" dotted line marquee outline).

Scanning is usually done in two steps:

1 **Preview Scan.** A **Preview Scan** gives you a low-resolution preview of everything that's on your scanning table. Your **Preview Scan** will usually include an option for you to define the final scan area by dragging or resizing a marquee, displayed as a moving dotted line outline (the "marching ants").

  The area you designate with this outline will be the only area actually included in your final scan.

2 **Full Scan.** This final scan will be a scan of your *defined area only*, using the color, resolution and adjustment settings you've configured. It will produce an image file that will open in your Photoshop Elements **Editor** for further editing.

A Photoshop Elements feature that is a great supplement to your scanning tools is **Divide Scanned Photos,** discussed on page 154.

Download photos from your digital camera

As with the scanner, the software that interfaces with your camera can vary from model to model and brand to brand. And your computer probably includes a number of ways for you to get photos from your camera – all of which will produce editable photo files for Photoshop Elements.

The chief advantage to using Photoshop Elements to interface with your camera and download your photos is that your photos will also be automatically added to your Organizer catalog in the process.

There are two ways to launch the Photoshop Elements Photo Downloader for your digital camera:

- Unless you've selected the **Always Do This** option, when you plug your camera into your computer and turn the camera on, **Windows will launch a pop-up screen** offering a number of optional functions. One of these will be to use Photoshop Elements to download your photos; or

- From the **File** drop-down in the Organizer, select **Get Photos and Videos,** then **From Camera or Card Reader.**

Both methods launch the same **Adobe Photoshop Elements Photo Downloader.** This option screen allows you to designate where the photos are downloading from, what to name the files and where to save them on your computer.

Connecting your camera to your computer launches an option screen which offers you a selection of all of the photo software installed on your system.

The Adobe Photoshop Elements Photo Downloader includes options for automatically naming your files and for deleting them from your camera after downloading them.

In Advanced Dialog mode, you have the option of selecting which of the photos stored on your camera are downloaded to your computer.

Get Photos From. From this drop-down menu, select your digital camera, smartphone, iPod or other USB-connected picture-taking device.

Import Settings/Location. Click the **Browse** button to browse to a location on your hard drive into which you'd like to save your photos.

Create Subfolder. Automatically creates a new photo storage folder on your hard drive for the photo download, according to the specifications you set in the drop-down menu.

Rename Files. Names your downloaded photos according to the specifications you set in the drop-down menu.

Delete Options. Offers the option of deleting your photos from your camera once you've downloaded them to your computer – an easy way to clean up your camera's photo storage.

Advanced Dialog. Clicking this button opens up an option screen which displays all of the photos in your camera's memory. By checking and unchecking the checkboxes, you can select which photos are included in your download and which will remain on your camera.

The amazing Divide Scanned Pictures tool automatically crops and straightens a scanned "scatter" of photos into individual shots.

Divide Scanned Photos

If you've ever needed to scan a number of photos in one sitting, you've probably tried to save a little time by scanning several pictures at once. This leaves you with a "scatter" of pictures.

Often, however, it's a such a chore to crop, straighten and save each photo that the time you save scanning several photos at once is traded off in the time it takes to separate and straighten the results!

Thankfully, Photoshop Elements now includes a tool for automatically doing the latter chore for you.

To use it:

1 **Scan a group of photos** at once, as described earlier in this chapter. Although the photos don't need to be straight and aligned, they do need to be far enough from each other that Photoshop Elements sees them as separate image files (as illustrated).

2 In Photoshop Elements, go to the program's **Image** menu and select **Divide Scanned Photos**.

The program will automatically separate each photo into a separate image file, cropping and straightening each as needed.

Photomerge

Photomerge is not just one but an entire package of great little tools for combining elements from more than one photo in order to either create an enhanced picture or to create a brand new photo composition. These tools are available on the **Photomerge** sub-menu under Photoshop Elements' **Enhance** menu.

Enhance	Layer	Select	Filter	View	Window	Help
Auto Smart Fix					Alt+Ctrl+M	
Auto Levels					Shift+Ctrl+L	
Auto Contrast					Alt+Shift+Ctrl+L	
Auto Color Correction					Shift+Ctrl+B	
Auto Sharpen						
Auto Red Eye Fix					Ctrl+R	
Adjust Smart Fix...					Shift+Ctrl+M	
Adjust Lighting						▶
Adjust Color						▶
Convert to Black and White...					Alt+Ctrl+B	
Unsharp Mask...						
Adjust Sharpness...						
Photomerge®...						▶

Photomerge© Group Shot...
Photomerge© Faces...
Photomerge© Scene Cleaner...
Photomerge© Panorama...
Photomerge© Exposure...
Photomerge© Style Match...

> **Photomerge Group Shot** is a tool for creating a composite shot in which a person or people who appear in one photo can be painted into another.

> **Photomerge Faces** is a tool for creating a perfect portrait by combining the best elements from several photos of the same face.

> With **Photomerge Scene Cleaner** you can combine elements from two photos of the same scene, borrowing the best elements from each shot, so that you can remove unwanted elements – or even unwanted *people* – from an otherwise perfect shot!

On the pages that follow, we'll show you step-by-step how to use **Photomerge Panorama, Photomerge Exposure** and **Photomerge Style Match.**

Screen captures

In addition to scanning and downloading photos, you can add images to Photoshop Elements by, essentially, "taking a snapshot" of your computer screen. This can be a very helpful function if you're trying to show someone some strange behavior on your computer or if you, like me, are creating software illustrations for a book. This snapshot is called a **Screen Capture**.

Screen Captures are very easy to do on PCs. To do so, you simply press the **Prt Scr** (short for Print Screen) button on your keyboard. (Holding down the **Alt** key as you press this button captures only the current, active window.) On a Mac, press ⌘+**Ctrl+Shift+3**.

The image will be copied to your operating system's Clipboard. You can then paste this image into virtually any program (including Microsoft Word) by using the **Edit/Paste** option or by pressing **Ctrl+v** (⌘+**v** on a Mac).

You can also open the entire captured image as an image file for editing in Photoshop Elements. To do this, go to the program's **File** menu and select **New**, then **Image from Clipboard**.

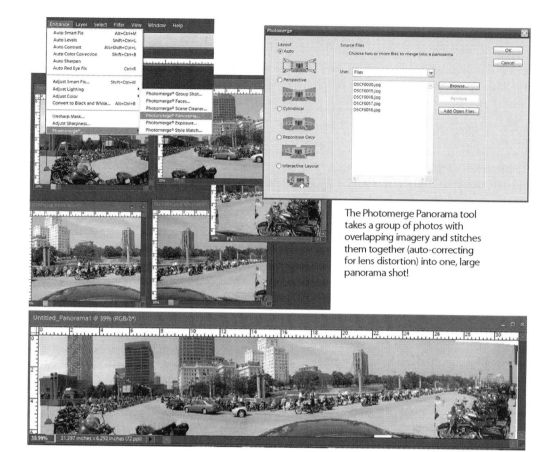

The Photomerge Panorama tool takes a group of photos with overlapping imagery and stitches them together (auto-correcting for lens distortion) into one, large panorama shot!

Combine photos with Photomerge Panorama

Sometimes a single photo doesn't capture the entirety of a scene or landscape. The Grand Canyon, the Golden Gate Bridge, Vatican Square – a single snapshot just can't tell the whole story.

Photoshop Elements' **Photomerge Panorama** tool combines several photos of a scene into one complete photo – producing, for instance, a panoramic image of a wide scene from three or four photos taken of adjacent areas of that scene.

The tool works amazingly well in most cases – even compensating for lens distortion and slight color differences between shots. About the only requirement is that there be a little bit of overlap in the photos' contents so that the program can interpret the scene composition and calculate where to combine the images.

In my illustration above, I gathered a number of photos I'd shot while watching a Harley-Davidson "birthday" parade in downtown Milwaukee.

1   With your photos open, launch the tool by going to the **Enhance** menu and selecting **Photomerge**, then **Photomerge Panorama**.

Why you should clear your camera's memory regularly

Sometimes, when your camera's storage gets full, you may be tempted to delete just a few photos to make room for a few new ones. There are serious liabilities to doing this.

Your photos are typically stored in your camera or on your camera's storage card as JPEGs. These JPEGs vary slightly in size. Removing a photo or two leaves a "hole" of a certain size on your memory card. When you take a new picture, if it is of a slightly larger than this hole, your camera's storage may corrupt and you could lose several pictures!

For this reason alone, it's good, safe housekeeping to regularly clear off your digital camera's storage completely to "clean" or reformat the memory card.

2 In the option screen that appears, browse to select the photo files or photo folder you'd like included in your **Panorama**. (You can also indicate for the tool to use the photos that are currently open in the Editor workspace.)

3 In most cases the **Auto Layout** setting produces very good results. However, should you need to tweak the composition, the **Interactive Layout** option opens a dialog box for manually repositioning your **Photomerge** elements.

As you can see in my example on the facing page, there is a small flaw. In the center of the picture, you can see the front end of a car that appeared in one photo but not the photo adjacent to it. But, otherwise, the results are nearly perfect.

And, at 32 inches long, it might make a very nice poster!

Mix elements from two photos with Photomerge Exposure

Another **Photomerge** tool is **Photomerge Exposure**, a tool for taking the best elements of two or more photos and combining them into one great-looking picture.

This is a terrific tool for combining the best parts of several shots taken with a flash at night or in which the subject is standing in front of a window or other brightly-lit background.

It works similarly to **Photomerge Faces** and **Photomerge Scene Cleaner** in that you select acceptable elements in each photo and the program combines them into a best-of composite photo.

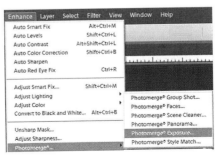

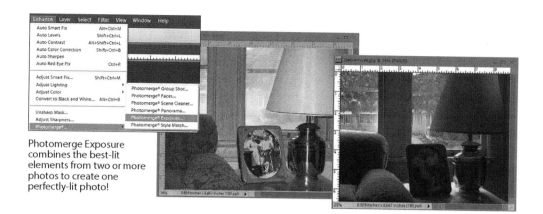

Photomerge Exposure combines the best-lit elements from two or more photos to create one perfectly-lit photo!

Above are two photos. The first was shot with a flash – lighting the foreground but over-lighting the view out the windows. The second photo was shot with natural lighting, the result being that the background (the view through the windows) is perfectly exposed but the furniture in the foreground is too dark.

1 I opened both of my photos in the Editor workspace.

You need at least two photos to create a **Photomerge Exposure** – although you can potentially use several photos, combining the best elements from each to create your **Final** photo.

2 From the **Enhance** menu, I selected **Photomerge**, then **Photomerge Exposure**.

In **Automatic** mode, which the program opens into by default, **Photomerge** will automatically make its best guess at the ideal blending of the two photos. Sometimes **Automatic** mode will give you the results you need – although it may also benefit from some tweaking by moving the sliders in either **Simple Blending** or **Smart Blending Mode**.

I prefer to work in **Manual** mode. It gives me more control of the result. So I clicked on the **Manual** tab on the **Photomerge Exposure** panel.

Manually align your photos for Photomerging

If the program does not automatically align your **Foreground** and **Background** photos, you can manually align them by selecting the **Alignment Tool** under the **Advanced Options** button on the **Photomerge** panel.

When the **Alignment Tool** is selected, three alignment points will appear on your **Background** photo. Place those three alignment points on key reference points in the photo. Then click to select the **Foreground** photo. When three similar alignment points appear on it, move them to the exact same reference points as you did on the **Background** photo and click **Align**.

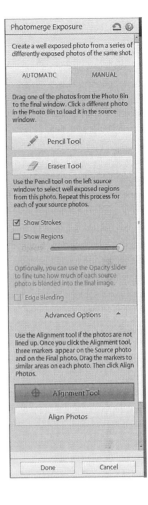

It only took a couple of scribbles drawn through the window area to select these elements for Photomerging onto my Background photo. The second photo shows the results of the Photomerging of elements.

3   The program used the first photo in the **Photo Bin** (below the Editor workspace) as my **Source**. The **Source** is the photo that **Photomerge** will draw its new elements from.

If you'd prefer to use another open photo as your source, drag it to the first position in the **Photo Bin**.

4   I then dragged the photo I wanted to use as my **Final** – the photo that my **Source's** elements will be added to – from the **Photo Bin** to the **Final** window.

Photomerge automatically adjusted the positions of similar photos to line them up as closely as possible.

5   With the panel's **Pencil Tool**, I indicated the elements on my **Source** photo that I'd like to add to my **Final**, as in the illustration above. (I designated that the **Source's** views out the windows be added to my **Final** photo).

You can adjust the **Pencil Tool's** size with the slider.

As illustrated above, you don't need to completely cover the selected elements in the **Source** photo. Drawing over part of an area tells the program to grab all the similarly-colored elements around your drawing.

Use the **Eraser Tool** to de-select selected elements.

To make the combination of elements look more natural, you can select the **Edge Blending** option.

The biggest challenge with the tool is that, because the **Pencil Tool** selects elements in your photos based on pixel color similarity, you sometimes end up taking more from your **Source** photo to your **Final** photo than you'd like. In my example, for instance, when I used the photo with the over-exposed background as my **Final**, every time I selected the lampshade, I also got the whited-out windows!

The solution for me was to swap the photos I was using as my **Source** and **Final**. Remember, just because you plan to use elements which are in the *background* of your photo doesn't necessarily mean that the photo with these elements won't make a better **Final** source image!

159

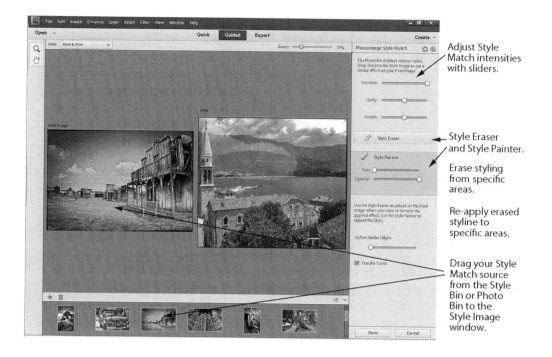

Adjust Style Match intensities with sliders.

Style Eraser and Style Painter.

Erase styling from specific areas.

Re-apply erased styline to specific areas.

Drag your Style Match source from the Style Bin or Photo Bin to the Style Image window.

Stylize your photos with Photomerge Style Match

Photomerge Style Match applies the lighting and tone levels of one photo to another.

Photoshop Elements even comes included with some stylish photos that you can use for your style sources – although you can use any photo as a template.

1   With the photo you want to stylize open in the Photoshop Elements Editor, launch the tool by going to the **Enhance** menu and selecting **Photomerge**, then **Photomerge Style Match**.

   If you'd like to use a style from one of your own photos rather than from one of the Photoshop Elements templates, make sure that this photo is also open in the Editor so that it appears in your **Photo Bin,** along the bottom of the interface.

2   Drag the photo that you are going to use as your style source from the **Style Bin,** along the bottom of the interface, into the **Style Image** box (the box labeled 'Drag Style Image Here').

   If you are using one of your own photos as your style source, select the **Photo Bin** tab at the bottom of the interface, then drag your photo from the **Photo Bin** into the **Style Image** box.

   Once you've provided a style source, your working photo (which appears in the **After** box in the **Style Match** workspace) will show some change.

If you'd like to replace the photo you are using as your style source, just drag a new photo from the **Style Bin** or **Photo Bin** into the **Style Image** box.

3   Using the sliders in the **Photomerge Style Match** control panel, on the right, adjust **Style Intensity, Style Clarity** and **Enhance Details** to your satisfaction.

4   If you'd like to remove applied styles from specific areas of your photo, select the **Style Eraser** and drag it across your photo in the **After** window. By adjusting the **Soften Stroke Edges** slider, you can control how subtle the effect of the **Style Eraser** is.

You can also select different brush textures and sizes for this (as well as for the **Style Painter** tool).

5   To re-apply styles to an area you've erased them from, select the **Style Painter** tool and repaint the style back onto your photo. As with the **Style Eraser**, you can control the subtlety of the re-applied style by adjusting the **Soften Stroke Edges** slider.

6   When you are satisfied with your results, click **Done**.

Edit Camera RAW

Usually, when you take a snapshot with your camera, your photo is delivered to you as a JPEG. This JPEG has been processed by the camera, automatically adjusting its exposure and white balance and packaged in a convenient, moderately compressed photo format.

Professional cameras, as well as many of the more advanced consumer cameras today, however, also include the option for you to access the photo data in its **Camera RAW** state.

Camera RAW photos are, as the name implies, raw photo data. The files are uncompressed and none of the usual automatic adjustments have been applied. (Think of them as your photo's "negatives." In fact, RAW files are sometimes even called DNG or "digital negative" files.) They can't be printed or used in their **RAW** state. However, their format gives you much more flexibility, when it comes to making adjustments to your photos. You're working with the raw camera data, not undoing changes the camera has already made.

Photoshop Elements 11 includes a surprisingly robust **RAW** photo editor.

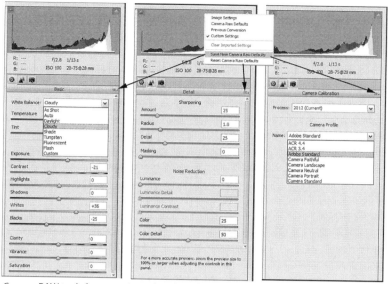

Camera RAW tools for correcting color, sharpening details and selecting a camera profile.

The Photoshop Elements 11 **Camera RAW** adjustments panels, organized under the three tabs to the right of the workspace, include a variety of color correction and sharpening tools.

> **Basic**. Under the **Basic** tab are sliders for adjusting your photo's color temperature, white and black balance, brightness, contrast and color saturation. There are also pre-sets for these settings under the **White Balance** drop-down menu at the top of the panel.

> **Detail**. Under the **Detail** tab are adjustments for setting the sharpness and contrast of your individual pixels.

> **Camera Calibration**. Under this tab, you'll find pre-sets that match a number of standard camera settings.

If you click the pop-up menu button in the upper right of any adjustment panel, you'll find the option to save your current settings as your **Camera RAW** default settings, as illustrated above.

Unlike changes you make in the Photoshop Elements Editor, the changes you make to your **RAW** image do not permanently change your file. Even after you've clicked **Done** and closed your **RAW** file, you can re-open it and make further adjustments – or set the adjustments all back to zero.

Once you're satisfied with your adjustments, you can port a copy of the adjusted file to your Photoshop Elements Editor by clicking on the **Open Image** button in the lower right of the **Camera RAW** adjustments panel.

The photo will open in the Editor and you will be able to print it or save it in any of the standard image file formats.

Your original **Camera RAW** image, however, will remain unchanged.

Process Multiple Files

The **Process Multiple Files** feature is a tool for editing or revising a whole batch of photo files in one action. This means that, for instance, you can apply a **Quick Fix** – like **Auto Levels, Auto Contrast, Auto Color** or **Sharpen** – to an entire folder full of photos with just a few clicks! You can also rename an entire batch at once or convert an entire batch to a new file format.

The Process Multiple Files tool (located under the File menu) will process, rename or resize a batch of files in one action.

Creating a separate Destination folder preserves your original files in their original state and size.

A common use of **Process Multiple Files** is to **resize** an entire batch of photos in one action. By properly configuring this tool, you can even send the resized images to another location, preserving your original photos in their original sizes.

1   To launch **Process Multiple Files**, select the option from the Photoshop Elements' **File** menu.

   Process Multiple Files can be applied to a folder or to all of the photo files you have open at the time the tool is launched.

2   Select the appropriate option from the drop-down menu at **Process Files From** and, if appropriate, browse to the photo folder at **Source**.

3   Set the **Destination** if you'd like your changed photo files saved to a new location.

4   If you'd like to rename your photo batch, check the **Rename Files** option and set your desired naming conventions. Generally, a batch of photos uses a similar front name followed by a sequence of alphabetic or numeric suffixes.

5   If you'd like to change the **Image Size** for your batch of photo files, check the **Resize Images** option and then set the **Width** or **Height** and **Resolution**.

As long as **Constrain Proportions** is checked, there's no need to set *both* the **Width** and **Height** for your photos. The tool will resize your photos proportionately, based on the single dimension you define.

For instance, if you are resizing your photos for video, you need only to set the **Width** to 1000 pixels. As long as **Constrain Proportions** is ticked, each photo will be resized to the 1000 pixels wide and whatever height is necessary to keep the photo in its correct proportions.

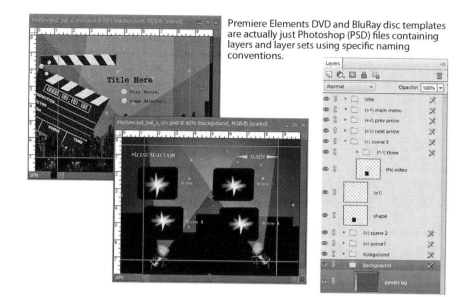

Premiere Elements DVD and BluRay disc templates are actually just Photoshop (PSD) files containing layers and layer sets using specific naming conventions.

Create Premiere Elements Movie Menu templates in Photoshop Elements

You can do a lot of customizing of disc menus right in Premiere Elements (as we discuss in **Chapter 30, Create Movie Menus**). You can customize the text on the buttons, change the fonts, change the locations of the buttons and titles on the menu pages and even swap out an existing template's background.

But, using Photoshop Elements, you can actually *create your own templates* virtually from the ground up! This template can include your own custom background, your custom graphics, your default fonts, your custom buttons and button frames – with each menu page's elements positioned right where you'd like them.

Menu templates are PSD files

Premiere Elements DVD and BluRay disc menu templates are really just PSD (Photoshop) files. They have a specific structure to them – but they are basically PSD files with layers and layer sets laid out in a specific hierarchy.

For a number of reasons, which we'll explain later, we recommend that, when you "create" any new menu template, you begin with an existing menu set.

Just copy and rename **Main Menu** and **Scene Menu** files from an existing template over to a new folder you've created in the DVD TEMPLATES directory.

On a Windows 7 or Windows 8 computer, this directory is located in:

C:/PROGRAM DATA/ADOBE/PREMIERE ELEMENTS/11.0/ONLINE/DVD TEMPLATES/ALL_LANG

If you are running Windows XP, this directory is located in:

C:/DOCUMENTS AND SETTINGS/ALL USERS/APPLICATION DATA/ADOBE/PREMIERE ELEMENTS/ 11.0/ONLINE/DVD TEMPLATES/ALL_LANG

On a Mac, this directory is located in:

MAC HD/LIBRARY/APPLICATION SUPPORT/PREMIERE ELEMENTS/11.0/ONLINE/DVD TEMPLATES/ALL_LANG

Anatomy of a Movie Menu
Template File Set

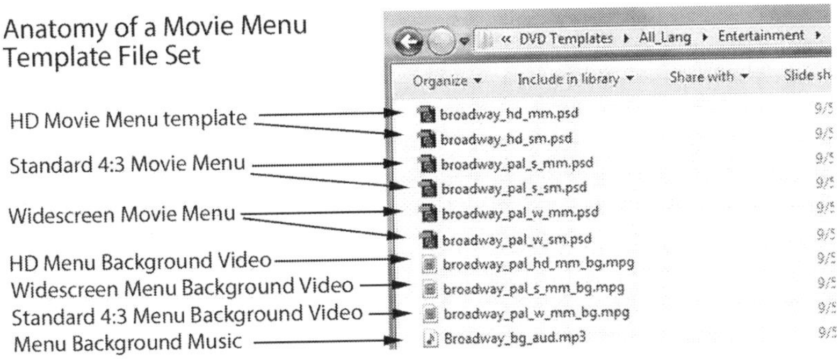

HD Movie Menu template
Standard 4:3 Movie Menu
Widescreen Movie Menu
HD Menu Background Video
Widescreen Menu Background Video
Standard 4:3 Menu Background Video
Menu Background Music

If you see few or no PSD files in these directories, it's because the online content has not been downloaded yet. For more information on downloading additional templates, themes and additional content for Premiere Elements, see page 204.

Studying how these files are named and stored in this folder will help guide you as you create your own.

The illustration above shows the PSD and media files that are combined by Premiere Elements to create a Movie Menu template.

The *names* given to these files are nearly as important as the structure of the files themselves. Each segment of the template file's name has meaning.

In, for instance, **MyTemplate_pal_s_mm.psd**, the "s" means that the file is for standard 4:3 video (as opposed to "w" for widescreen or "**hd**" for high-definition). The "**mm**" means it is a *main menu* template (as opposed, of course, to an "**sm**" *scene menu* template). So we highly recommend you stick with the standard naming conventions when creating your templates.

The "**pal**" designation in the menu templates used to mean that the template was designed for the PAL video system. However, since version 3 of Premiere Elements, both PAL and NTSC have used the same templates. The "**pal**" designation is just an artifact from the days when there were separate templates. *All* current disc templates are "**pal**" templates.

Template folders also include a number .**PNG** files. These files are the thumbnails that appear when you're browsing the Movie Menu templates in Premiere Elements. We'll show you later how to make them for your template.

Create your new template's folder in the sub-folder that best represents the category you'd like your new template to appear under. (GENERAL, for instance. Or ENTERTAINMENT.) **The name you give your folder will be the name that appears as your template's name in Premiere Elements.**

Make sure that any new template folders you add to the ONLINE/DVD TEMPLATES directory include a file called DOWNLOADED.TXT, which you can copy from the folder of another template you've already downloaded. This TXT document tells Premiere Elements not to download a new file to this folder – and, if it's not there, Premiere Elements will erase your new template the first time you try to use it!

Naming and storing the files

Whenever you create a disc menu template, **you will need to create both a main menu and a scene menu template** – whether you actually intend to use both menu pages or not. This is because, in order for Premiere Elements to recognize your files as a template, two things are required:

- There must be both an "**mm**" (main menu) and an "**sm**" (scene menu) version of the template files. (The names of both menus must be identical, except for the "mm" or "sm" element, as we'll explain below.)

- Each menu set, as well as any accompanying media files (background music, motion background, etc.), must be in *their own, separate folder* on your hard drive in the DVD TEMPLATES directory. The name you give this folder will become the name Premiere Elements uses for your template.

The basic template file structure

We highly recommend that even if you are "creating your Movie Menu template from scratch," you start with a copy of an existing menu template. There are several good reasons for basing your new template on an existing template set.

Anatomy of a scene button PSD layer set

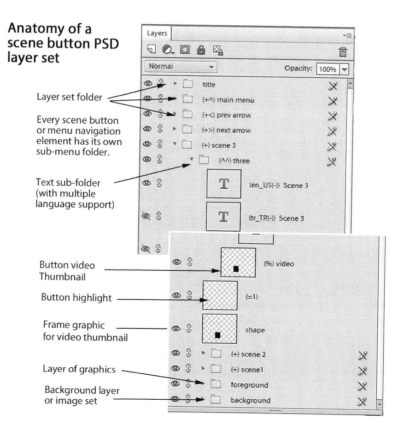

Layer set folder

Every scene button or menu navigation element has its own sub-menu folder.

Text sub-folder (with multiple language support)

Button video Thumbnail

Button highlight

Frame graphic for video thumbnail

Layer of graphics

Background layer or image set

1   Unlike most graphic files you'll create or work with in Photoshop Elements, **disc templates use non-square video pixels**. And, when you work from an existing template, your working files will already be conformed to this video standard.

2   If you use an existing template, **all the necessary layer sets will already be included and named properly**. And it's much easier to discard what you don't want or need (or copy it if you need more) than it is to create a whole tree of layer set folders from scratch.

    And last but not least:

3   **Photoshop Elements can usually *edit* but it can not *create* layer sets!** Layer sets are technically a feature of Photoshop Pro.

Layer sets are sub-folders (and sometimes sub-sub-folders) on the **Layers** panel which contain individual layers, as in the illustration at the bottom of the facing page.

How these sub-folders are set up and how the elements inside each are arranged plays an important role in how your template functions.

If the layer sets aren't set up and named correctly, your template won't work.

Trust us. You'll be way ahead of the game if you start with an existing template set, copied to a new folder.

Replace the background layer of a menu template

Replacing a background of an existing template is relatively easy.

To do this, have both the template you plan to revise and the photo you want to use for your replacement background open.

(If you can not display more than one photo file at once in your Photoshop Elements Editor because they appear as a tabbed set, go to the **Arrange** menu and set it to **Float All Windows**, as described on page 16.

1   Size your new background photo to around 800x600 pixels. (1920x1080 for a high-definition template.)

    Drag this photo from its existing photo file onto the open menu template file that you want to revise, as illustrated on the next page. Your photo will automatically become a layer in your menu template file!

2   The photo will come in with corner handles, which you can drag to size and position the photo until it fits within the menu template.

    Once it's all in place, press **Enter** to lock in the size.

3   To move this new layer into position as a background layer, grab the layer in the **Layers** panel and drag it down into position right above the layer currently named **Background** (the current background layer for your menu template), as in the illustration.

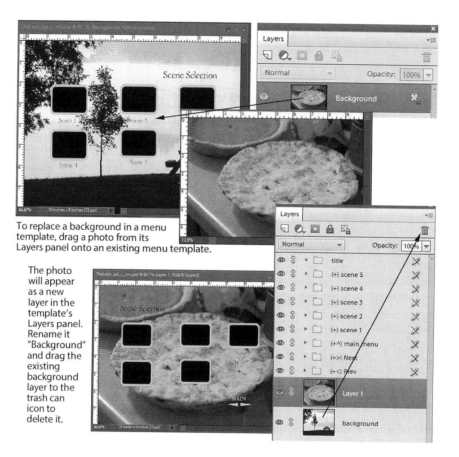

To replace a background in a menu template, drag a photo from its Layers panel onto an existing menu template.

The photo will appear as a new layer in the template's Layers panel. Rename it "Background" and drag the existing background layer to the trash can icon to delete it.

Now drag the old current **Background** to the little trash can icon on the **Layers** panel to get rid of it.

Double-click on the name of the photo layer you have just added so that the name becomes editable and rename it "**Background**".

If there are additional layers or layer sets of graphics, you can delete them also.

Naming this background layer "**Background**" isn't required in order for the template to work, but it is good housekeeping.

It also identifies the layer in the template as a background layer for Premiere Elements – necessary if you decide to replace the background for this template in the **Movie Menus** authoring workspace of Premiere Elements.

Now sit back and admire your work! Even if you do nothing else, you've essentially created your own custom disc menu template!

Scene layer sets

Each of the scene buttons in your disc template file is in a separate folder, or **layer set**, on the **Layers** panel, as illustrated to the right.

Inside each layer set, you'll find graphics for navigation (such as placeholders for the scene menu button thumbnails), a highlight graphic and a sub-folder layer set containing text and named (^^).

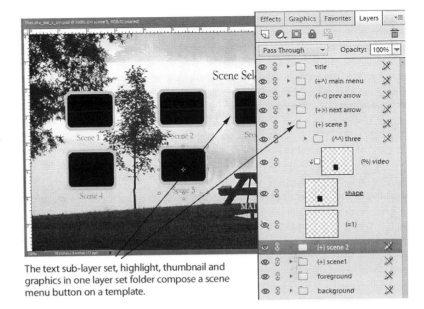

The text sub-layer set, highlight, thumbnail and graphics in one layer set folder compose a scene menu button on a template.

Those little symbols inside parenthesis following a layer's name are key elements in your layer and layer set naming conventions. They identify the function of each layer for Premiere Elements, and it's very important that you use them correctly.

Along with the text (^^) sub-layer set, each of these button layer sets also often contains a layer called **(%) video**. This layer includes a graphic (usually a black square but sometimes the Adobe logo) which serves as a placeholder for the disc navigation scene button, corresponding to your Premiere Elements **Menu Marker**. In other words, the (%) layer is where the menu button's video thumbnail will display.

There is also a layer called (=1). This is your button highlight. The graphic on this layer will serve as the highlight that appears over your scene menu button when someone watching your disc navigates from scene button to scene button on your menu page.

You can customize these layers any way you want, as long as you keep them in their current layer sets and maintain their names – *as well as their accompanying symbols* – so that Premiere Elements can find them when it turns your template into disc menu pages.

1 Although you cannot create a layer set in Photoshop Elements, you can manipulate the individual layers within each layer set or sub-folder by holding down the **Ctrl** key as you click on the layer.

    With the **Ctrl** key held, you can edit, resize and reposition these sub-layers without affecting the other layers in that layer set.

2 You can also swap in any graphic you'd like as your menu highlight, replacing the current one in the layer set. You can even use a hand-drawn image or a photo. Just ensure that it is saved as a layer called (=1).

    We do recommend, however, that you never use white as your highlight graphic's color. White often won't appear as a highlight on the final menu.

Additional graphics

Some menu templates also include a layer or two of graphics between the background and the scene layer set folders. The significance of these layers of graphics is that, if you replace the background (by including a media file background or by selecting a custom background in Premiere Elements' DVD workspace), these graphics layers will remain.

You can use this to your advantage, of course, if you'd like. You can include still images as a "foreground" layer to your animated background, for instance, or you can use them to create a frame graphic within which to play your background video.

3   You can change the font, size, color or paragraph alignment for any (^^) text layer, as discussed below.

4   You can also add, remove or revise graphics used in these layer sets, such as the frames around the video thumbnail placeholders. And you can even remove the thumbnail placeholder itself, if you'd like your template to have text-only scene buttons.

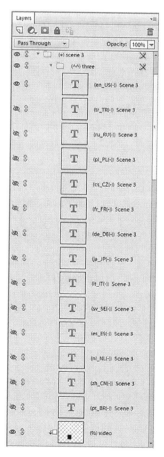

A text layer set includes support for 14 languages. The text can be edited for content or style by double-clicking on the "T" icon on the layer.

Text layer sets

Within each layer set folder is a *sub*-layer set called (^^), which includes the text for that button or text block.

Open this layer set folder and you'll find 14 layers of text for this button, each in a different languages. Each language layer is named with an abbreviation identifying the language and the (-) symbol – as in (en_US (-)) **Scene 5**.

You can change the font, font color, font size and paragraph alignment for any of these layers just by double-clicking on "**T**" icon on the layer.

If your text layer is disabled or turned off, click the eyeball icon to the left of the layer to turn it on. (Which layers are enabled and which are disabled has nothing to do with how the template ultimately functions.)

As with the graphics layers within the layer sets, you can move the individual layers or the entire (^^) text layer set to a new position on your menu page – independent of the rest of the layer set – by holding down the **Ctrl** key as you select it.

Layer sets are scene buttons

Each layer set (folder) on your **Layers** panel – with its text, highlight, scene thumbnail and possibly thumbnail frame – constitutes one menu button.

And, after you're finished customizing the individual elements for each scene button, you can position and scale each button as a single object. To do this, select the layer set in the **Layers** panel or click on the button on the PSD file in the Editor workspace, then drag it into position or drag the corner handles to resize it.

Adding scene menu buttons to a template

Perhaps you've come upon the perfect Premiere Elements template – only to find that it includes only four scene buttons on a menu page, but you want six. Or you find a template that has no main menu scene buttons when you want three or four.

Fortunately, adding scene menu buttons to a template page is as easy as adding a photo or layer to a PSD file.

1   **To create additional scene buttons** on a current menu page, drag an existing scene layer set folder from its position on the **Layers** panel to the **Add Layer** icon at the top of the **Layers** panel. This creates a duplicate of the entire layer set – and thus creates an additional menu button. Update the text and you're set.

The duplicate layer set and its contents will have the same names as the original set and its contents – except that the word "copy" will be added to its name. Double-click on the necessary layer names and rename them as appropriate.

2   **To add new scene buttons** to a main menu template that doesn't have any, drag one of the layer set folders from your scene menu template's **Layers** panel, or drag a scene button directly from the scene menu template, and place it onto the main menu image file, as illustrated below.

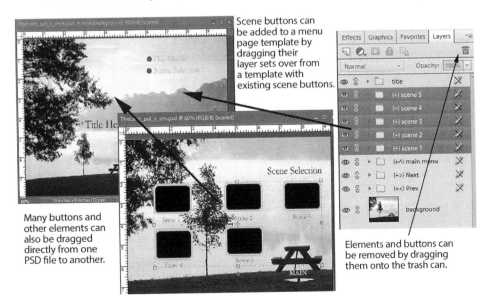

Scene buttons can be added to a menu page template by dragging their layer sets over from a template with existing scene buttons.

Many buttons and other elements can also be dragged directly from one PSD file to another.

Elements and buttons can be removed by dragging them onto the trash can.

A copy of this layer set will appear in the main menu's **Layers** panel and the scene button will appear on your template file, to be customized and positioned as you'd like.

3   By holding down the **Shift** key, you can select several of these layer set folders at once and drag them all onto your main menu, if you'd like to add several scene buttons in one swoop.

Once there, you can position them and/or their internal elements individually. (Scene Menu buttons link to green **Scene Menu Markers** on your Premiere Elements project timeline. Main Menu buttons link to blue **Main Menu Markers**.)

4   Deleting a scene button from a menu template is as simple as dragging the layer set folder from its position on the **Layers** panel onto the little trashcan icon at the top right of the palette.

Menu buttons can not overlap!

Note that, as you hover your mouse over a scene button on a template file, Photoshop Elements will indicate the "live" area of your button by highlighting it with a blue box outline. This is a very important feature because *one thing Premiere Elements will not tolerate in a disc menu template is overlapping navigation*.

So, as a final test drive once you've finished revising your templates and positioning your buttons, be sure to hover your mouse over each of the buttons on your template page to make sure none of your navigation areas invades another's live space!

Adding background video and audio

In addition to the PSD files that make up a basic DVD or BluRay disc template, Premiere Elements can use audio and video files in the template's directory folder to add motion or music to the disc menu.

Your video background (optionally including audio) can be AVIs, MPEGs or SWFs.

Your audio background can be either MP3s or WAV files.

The order of the layers in a Disc Menu Template

It is important to note that the *order* of the layer sets in the **Layers** panel – not the *names* of the layer sets – determines the order that Premiere Elements uses them as scene markers. Your first scene, in other words, must be the *bottom*-most scene layer set in the **Layers** panel and the last scene, the top-most.

In other words, even if you call a layer set "Scene Five", if it is below the other layer sets in the **Layers** panel, it will be used for "Scene One" when Premiere Elements uses the template to create its DVD or BluRay disc menu.

To include audio or video backgrounds as part of your templates, you need only *include them in the same directory folder as your disc menu templates* and then name them exactly the same as the template files – except with the letters "**bg**" at the end.

In other words, a video loop background for the main menu

TemplateName_pal_s_mm.psd

would be called

TemplateName_pal_s_mm_bg.avi

A video background file for the scene menu

TemplateName_pal_s_sm.psd

would be called

Template_pal_s_sm_bg.mpg

To apply the same mpeg video to both the main and scene menus, simply omit the "**mm**" or "**sm**" reference in the name as in:

TemplateName_s_pal_bg.mpg

Any AVI, MPG or SWF video file you include in your template folder and name accordingly will automatically replace the background layer in your menu with video when the template is applied in Premiere Elements.

MP3s and WAV files will play audio or music with your menu.

Each of these will, of course, be over-written if you choose to customize the background video or audio for the template in your Premiere Elements' **Add Movie Menu** workspace.

Naming conventions

Finally, though Premiere Elements is surprisingly forgiving about the names used for its DVD and BluRay menu template files, I recommend you stick with the "traditional" names whenever possible.

More than once I've helped troubleshoot a custom menu for a client, only to find that the heart of the problem was his naming one of the layer sets or template files incorrectly. Using standard names made all the difference.

Stick to these basic naming rules and you should be all set:

1   The template set *must* include both a main menu and a scene menu in order to be recognized by Premiere Elements, even if you ultimately plan to use only a main menu for your DVD or BluRay disc.

This set of menu template files should be in its own folder in a category sub-directory of the DVD TEMPLATES folder. The name you give this folder is what Premiere Elements will use as the name of the menu template.

Anatomy of a Movie Menu
Template File Set

HD Movie Menu template ——— broadway_hd_mm.psd

Standard 4:3 Movie Menu ——— broadway_hd_sm.psd
broadway_pal_s_mm.psd

Widescreen Movie Menu ——— broadway_pal_s_sm.psd
broadway_pal_w_mm.psd

HD Menu Background Video ——— broadway_pal_w_sm.psd
Widescreen Menu Background Video —— broadway_pal_hd_mm_bg.mpg
Standard 4:3 Menu Background Video —— broadway_pal_s_mm_bg.mpg
Menu Background Music ——— broadway_pal_w_mm_bg.mpg
Broadway_bg_aud.mp3

2 The main menu and scene menu template must have identical names, save for the "**mm**" and "**sm**" designation.

"**s**" templates are for standard 4:3 video

"**w**" templates are for widescreen 16:9

"**hd**" templates are for high-definition BluRay discs

Since version 3, all Premiere Elements disc menu templates, whether to be used in a PAL or NTSC video project, are PAL only. All, therefore, include the "**pal**" designation in their names.

That said, the following is the menu template naming convention we recommend you always use, just to stay safe.

> **TemplateName_pal_s_mm.psd**
> **TemplateName_pal_s_sm.psd**

> **TemplateName_pal_w_mm.psd**
> **TemplateName_pal_w_sm.psd**

> **TemplateName_pal_hd_mm.psd**
> **TemplateName_pal_hd_sm.psd**

For background video or audio, tag the letters "**_bg**" onto the ends of the files names.

If the name includes "**sm**" or "**mm**," the media file will function as background for only the scene menu or main menu page, as in:

> **TemplateName_pal_s_mm_bg.avi**
> **TemplateName_pal_s_mm_bg.mp3**

A media file without "**sm**" or "**mm**" in the name will function as background for *both* the main menu and scene menu.

> **TemplateName_pal_s_bg.avi**

Movie Menu Thumbnails

Finally, in every DVD template folder, you will find a number of PNG files. These little files are the thumbnail images that Premiere Elements uses as previews when you select and lay out your **Movie Menus**.

It's not necessary to create a thumbnail for your movie menu – but if you don't, you will see only your template's name and not a thumbnail preview in the **Movie Menus** workspace.

If you look in the directory of a default **Movie Menu** templates, you'll see thumbnail image sets in several languages. You need only create one each for your scene and main menu in whatever language your program is set up for.

To create English thumbnails:

1 With your main menu template open in the Photoshop Elements Editor, select **Save For Web** from the **File** menu.

  A **Save For Web** option panel will open, as illustrated below.

2 Select the **PNG-24** preset in the upper right of the panel

3 Set the **Image Size/New Size** to 160 px **Width**. (The **Height** will auto-fill.)

4 Click **Save**. A browse screen will open.

5 Browse to the directory folder where your new menu templates are saved.

  Name your file **en_US_TemplateName_pal_s_prv_mm.png**.

Repeat this process for your scene menu template, except replace the "**mm**" in the file's name with "**sm**".

When you next start Premiere Elements, the program should recognize the new template and its thumbnails should appear in your **Movie Menu** workspace.

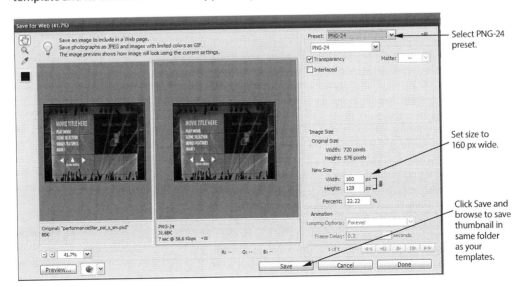

Select PNG-24 preset.

Set size to 160 px wide.

Click Save and browse to save thumbnail in same folder as your templates.

Photoshop Elements Preferences

The Photoshop Elements **Preferences** are accessed under the program's **Edit** menu (or, on a Mac, under the program's name). Many of these settings are pretty self-explanatory. But here are a few that I think are worth noting:

Saving Files. By default, the program is set to **Always Ask** whenever you try to save or overwrite a file. This drives me crazy! When I want to save my work, *I want to save my work!*

Unless you want to save versions of your photos as you work, I recommend setting **On First Save** to **Save Over Current File**.

File Extensions. For most of your work, it won't matter if your **File Extensions** (.jpg, .gif, .psd) are saved in upper case or lower case. However, in some environments – particularly if you're creating images for the Internet, it can make a big difference. HTML sees upper case letters as different names than lower case. There is no right or wrong setting here, but you do want to be aware of how the program is naming your files so that you can maintain some consistency and control.

File Compatibility. I recommend checking the option to **Prefer Adobe Camera Raw for Supported Raw Files**. RAW is a function of higher-end digital cameras that stores images unprocessed and uncompressed, giving you more control over how the imagery is interpreted and adjusted (as discussed on page 161). If your camera supports it, you'll probably want access to it.

Transparency. Transparency in an image file is usually represented in Photoshop and Photoshop Elements by a gray and white checkerboard pattern (as seen in **Create non-square graphics** on page 113 of **Chapter 9, Work With Photoshop Elements Layers**). This preference screen allows you to customize the pattern or turn it off completely.

Units & Rulers. This preference screen sets the default measurements that are displayed on your image files in the Editor workspace. For most online work or for editing graphics and photos for video, you may want to set your **Rulers** to **Pixels**, a more relevant measurement than inches or centimeters.

Type. This one is just a personal preference, a peeve left over from my years as a layout artist. If you're planning to work with type in your image files, select the option to use **Smart Quotes**. **Smart Quotes** are the difference between quotation marks and plain old tick marks. The difference, for instance, between " (which are tick marks, used for measurements) and the slightly curved " (true quotation marks). Using true quotation marks can mean the subtle difference between a layout looking "typewritery" and one looking truly designed.

The Organizer has its own set of **Preferences**, also located under the **Edit** menu. Among them are settings for configuring how the program interfaces with your scanner and camera.

You'll find information for setting up a **Contact Book** in the Organizer preferences on page 449 and information on setting up **E-mail Sharing** on page 446.

The Info Bar

The Status Bar

The Info Panel

Chapter 14

Learn About Your Photoshop Elements File

Important information on your
Photoshop Elements file window

There is a lot more to a PSD, or an
image file, than meets the eye!

In this chapter, we'll take a close look
at an image file, what Photoshop
Elements has to tell us about it and,
ultimately, what it all means.

File Format   Zoom Level (passive)   Active layer   Color Mode   * Color Profile Indicator

File Name

Rulers
(right-click
on ruler
to change
measurement
format)

Rulers are
turned on
by selecting
the option
under the
View menu

Photo size and
resolution

Zoom Level
(dynamic)

The Info Bar

Whenever you open a photo or an image file in Photoshop Elements'
Editor workspace, it appears with a frame around it. This frame includes a
lot of useful information about the file.

Along the top of the frame, you'll see:

File Name. This is the name of the file, of course – including the suffix,
which defines the file's format (PSD, TIF, JPG, etc.).

Zoom Level (Passive). Displayed both after the **File Name**, at the top
of the image frame, and in the lower left corner of the image frame,
this number, a percentage, tells the scale of the image, as currently
displayed in your Editor workspace. You can zoom in or out by pressing
Ctrl++ (the Ctrl and plus key) or **Ctrl+-** (the Ctrl and minus key) on your
keyboard (or, on a Mac, the ⌘++ or ⌘+-) .

This **Zoom Level** number can be a bit misleading, however. This is because
it is measuring the scale of the picture's size in *pixels* rather than in linear
numbers, such as inches or centimeters.

That means that, if you're looking at an image file with a resolution of 300
ppi at 100% zoom, the picture is going to look about *four times larger* on
your computer monitor than it will when it is printed.

But, for most of the images you're working on for video or for the web, at
100% zoom, your image should appear at just about its actual size.

Layer. If you have a layered PSD file open in your **Editor** workspace, the layer that is currently selected will appear in parentheses, following the **Zoom Level**.

Color Mode. Following the **Layer** notation, or alone in the parenthesis, is the **Color Mode** of your image file. In most cases, this mode will be **RGB/8**. However, if you are editing a monochrome (black & white) photo, this mode will read **Gray/8**.

The **RGB** mode means that the pixels in your image are composed of combinations of red, green and blue. Each of these three colors can be set to any of 256 levels (0-255).

Why 256? Well, this seemingly arbitrary number is actually a very *real* number, with its origins in binary code, the base 2 numbering system that is at the heart of all computer programming. Every instruction written into every computer program is based on some base 2 number.

256 is 2^8 (2 to the 8th power, or 2x2x2x2x2x2x2x2). Hence, the red, green and blue color levels are each 8-bit settings (with 256 possibilities) – which is why the number 8 appears after the RGB **Color Mode** listing.

There are other, by the way, even deeper RGB modes. (16-bit color, for instance.) However, 8-bit color is the standard for video and online graphics, and it is the only RGB color mode that Premiere Elements can work with. Besides, the 256 levels of red, green and blue yields 16,777,216 possible combinations of these colors, which is probably more than enough colors for typical photo and video purposes.

Photoshop Elements can work in three additional color modes, which can be selected for your image files under the **Image** drop-down on the Menu Bar.

Grayscale, or black and white, which is actually 256 levels of the single color: black. (White is merely the color black set to the level 0.)

Indexed Color is a system for limiting the number of colors in an image. If you've worked on graphics for the Web, you likely already know how reducing colors on a GIF file can reduce its file size. (Although, because it provides a limited color range, **Indexed Color** is also probably not the best **Color Mode** for working with photos in.)

Bitmap is a **Color Mode** made up of pixels that are only either pure black and pure white – with no shades of gray in between.

Why does a "full-screen" video fill only part of my computer screen?

Remember, a standard NTSC video frame is only the equivalent of a 640x480 pixel image. Most likely your computer monitor is set to a resolution of between 1024x768 pixels and 1280x1024 pixels. That means that a full-screen video image at 100% zoom may take up only one-fourth of your computer screen!

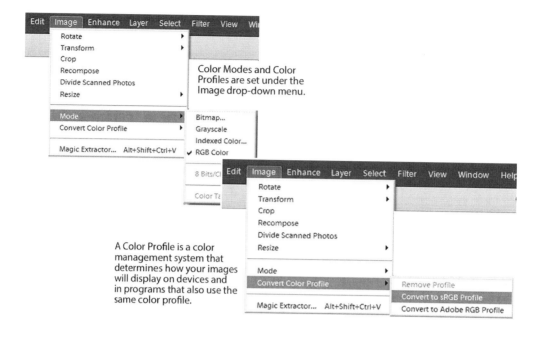

Color Modes and Color Profiles are set under the Image drop-down menu.

A Color Profile is a color management system that determines how your images will display on devices and in programs that also use the same color profile.

The professional version of Photoshop includes additional color modes, which are useful for preparing files, for instance, for production on an offset press. However, for our purposes – and particularly as you produce graphics and imagery for use in Premiere Elements or for the Web – you'll usually be working with **RGB** or **Grayscale** mode only.

* **(Color Profile)**. An asterisk appearing after the Color Mode listing is an indication that a **Color Profile** has been assigned to the image.

A **Color Profile** is a standardization system for color that can be applied across several programs and hardware devices. This ensures that the image's colors appear the same on every device, and in every application, that's using that same profile. The are two color profiles available in Photoshop Elements: **sRGB** and **Adobe RGB**, both of which are standard enough that either one should produce excellent results.

Many graphics cards and monitors will allow you to set a color profile for them. If it is available on your computer, you'll usually find it listed under **Color Management**, under **Settings/Advanced** for your display. (On a PC you can access these settings by right-clicking on your computer's desktop and selecting **Properties**. On a Mac, open your **System Preferences** and click on **Display**.)

Using the same color profile for all of your programs and hardware is the best way to ensure that what you see on your computer is ultimately what you get, image-wise.

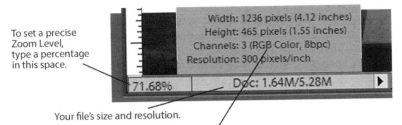

To set a precise Zoom Level, type a percentage in this space.

Width: 1236 pixels (4.12 inches)
Height: 465 pixels (1.55 inches)
Channels: 3 (RGB Color, 8bpc)
Resolution: 300 pixels/inch

71.68%   Doc: 1.64M/5.28M

Your file's size and resolution.

Clicking and holding on the size/resolution bar displays a pop-up info panel.

The Status Bar

There's even more information about your file on the **Status Bar,** which appears at the bottom left of your image frame, as illustrated above.

Zoom Level (Dynamic). Although this number, a percentage, is the same as the information displayed at the top of the panel, the **Zoom Level** displayed at the bottom left of an image frame is *dynamic*. In other words, you can click on it and type any number in this space and, when you press **Enter,** Photoshop Elements will jump to that precise zoom view.

Size/Resolution. Along the bottom of your image panel, to the right of the **Dynamic Zoom Level** indicator, is a display listing, by default, your image file's size and resolution. As illustrated above, when you click and hold on this indicator, a pop-up panel will display additional information about your file.

Additionally, as illustrated below, clicking the black arrow button to the right of the **Status Bar** allows you to set this area to display a number of other facts about your image, including the name of the tool that you currently have selected, the size of your image file and even how long it would take your image file to download from a Web site!

71.68%   Doc: 2.18M/4.95M

The Status Bar can be set to display any category of info on your image that you'd prefer.

✓ Document Sizes
Document Profile
Document Dimensions
Current Selected Layer
Scratch Sizes
Efficiency
Timing
Current Tool

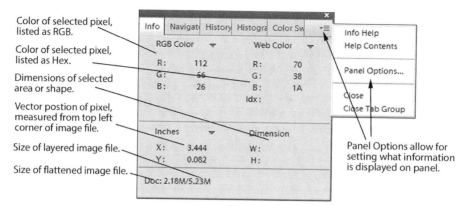

Color of selected pixel, listed as RGB.

Color of selected pixel, listed as Hex.

Dimensions of selected area or shape.

Vector postion of pixel, measured from top left corner of image file.

Size of layered image file.

Size of flattened image file.

Panel Options allow for setting what information is displayed on panel.

The Info panel provides a variety of information about your image file.

The Info panel

Another tool for getting information about your image file is the **Info** panel – which is launched from the program's **Window** menu or by clicking the arrow next to the **More** button in the lower right of the program's interface. As illustrated above, this panel displays color and location information about specific pixels you have selected in your image as well as measurements of selected areas.

Color Info. As you hover your mouse over your image, you'll see numbers appearing next to the R, G and B listings in the upper left panel of this palette. These numbers are the color level settings for the individual pixels your cursor is currently over.

The R, G and B listings on the upper right of the panel display as an alpha-numeric combination.

The six number and letter combinations from these three colors are called the pixel color's **Hex** code, a common system for identifying colors on Web files.

In Hex code, for instance:

Black is 000000
White is ffffff
A medium gray is 808080

If you click on the down arrow next to the **RGB** or **Web Color** listing, you can set that panel to display this information using other color definitions, including **HSB** (hue, saturation and brightness).

Vector Position. The current position of your mouse cursor over your image file is listed in the lower left panel of this palette, as measured in pixels from the top left corner of your photo or image file.

By clicking on the down arrow to the right of the *Inches* listing, you can set this information panel – as well as the information panel on the **Dimensions** panel, to the right – to display these measurements as pixels, inches, metric measurements, percentages or even picas.

Dimensions. If you are working with one of the **Marquee Selection Tools** or one of the **Shape** drawing tools (see **Chapter 5, Get to Know the Photoshop Elements Toolbox**), the lower right panel of this palette will display the dimensions of the area you are selecting or drawing. (Professional designers sometimes use this **Info** palette, along with the **Rectangular Marquee** tool, to select and measure areas of their image files.)

Doc Size. The size of the image file you're currently editing is displayed along the bottom of the Info palette.

If you're working on a layered image file, you'll see two numbers listed. The first is the size of the image file once all of the layers in your image file have been flattened; the second is the size of the image file if saved as a layered PSD file.

Section 2

Adobe
Premiere Elements 11

Get to Know the Workspaces

Basic Editing Moves

What's New in Premiere Elements 11?

Chapter 15

Get to Know Premiere Elements 11

What's what and what it does

The interface for Premiere Elements has been completely re-designed by Adobe to be as simple and as intuitive as possible. It is also remarkably customizable, with a wealth of powerful tools in obvious and, once in a while, not so obvious places.

There are major changes to the interface since the last edition of the program. But you'll quickly find that it makes for a mostly improved editing experience all around – for the newbie as well as for the veteran.

The Add Media panel   Project Assets   Quick View and Expert View   The Monitor Panel   Publish &
                       (Expert View only)   Share tab

The
Adjustments
panel

The Applied
Effects panel

The Timeline

The Action Bar   Pop-Up Panel

Panels, pop-ups and the Action Bar

The Premiere Elements interface has been completely re-designed with efficiency and readability in mind.

The interface is bright and clean with big, easy-to-find buttons and text throughout.

Its tools are tucked out-of-the-way – but easily retrievable with just a click or two.

Many of the tools are hidden away in pop-up panels that snap open with just a click on a tab or button.

The bulk of the tools can be accessed through buttons on the **Action Bar,** which runs along the bottom of the Premiere Elements interface. (Similar **Action Bars** run along the bottoms of the Elements Organizer and Photoshop Elements interfaces.)

The program even includes two fully-separate (though connected) workspaces: Quick View and Expert View – options that allow you to go as deeply into editing your videos as you'd like. (More on them on page 190.)

The Monitor panel

The **Monitor** panel is the big center panel on which you'll preview your movie as your work. It usually rests in the top center of the interface – though it can change position to accommodate the **Adjustments** and **Applied Effects** panels when necessary.

If you **right-click** on it, you'll find options for setting its playback quality and magnification.

The Timeline

Both Quick View and Expert View (discussed on the following page) share a similar workspace for assembling your video: The timeline.

Your timeline is really where the bits and pieces become a movie.

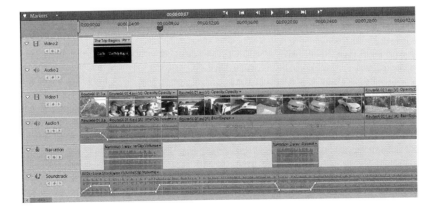

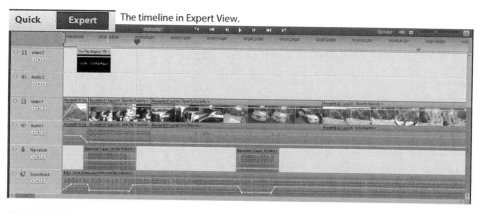

The timeline in Expert View.

The timeline in Quick View.

Quick View and Expert View

Premiere Elements offers you two somewhat different workspaces in which to edit your video project: Quick View and Expert View. In both views, you edit on a timeline. However, the timeline, and its features, vary a bit from view to view.

Quick View and Expert View aren't so much totally different interfaces as they are two different ways to approach the same project. In fact, you can switch between them as you work on your project, taking advantage of the best aspects of each.

Quick View	Expert View
Media clips are added directly to the timeline from your computer, camcorder or recording device.	Media clips are gathered into the **Project Assets** panel before they are added to your timeline.
The timeline consists of four tracks: Titles, Video, Narration and Audio.	The timeline can included up to 99 video and 99 audio tracks.
Only the Video track can include video. Only titles and text can be added to the Title track.	Multiple tracks of video can be combined to create effects, including Videomerge, Chroma Key and Picture-in-Picture
Audio levels can be set using tools available in Smart Mix, on the Audio Mixer and on the Adjustments panel.	Audio levels can be controlled at specific points using keyframes created right on the timeline.
A limited number of effects are readily available in Quick View.	The complete set of effects is available.

Customize your workspace

The sizes and the arrangements of the various panels in the interface are easily customizable. Panels can be resized by dragging on the seams between them.

Feel free to experiment and resize the panels by dragging on the borders between them.

Many of the pop-up panels also allow you to stretch them longer so that you can see more of the assets, effects, templates, etc., at once.

And, if you ever find the program misbehaving or if you just feel like you've lost control of your workspace, you can easily get back to the default look by simply going to the **Window** drop-down menu and selecting **Restore Workspace**.

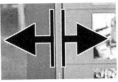

To resize your panels, hover your mouse over the seams between the panels until you see the double arrows – then click and drag.

Minimum screen resolution

Because of the size of the panels and the number of tools that Adobe fits into some rather tight spaces, we recommend that this program not be used on a computer with a monitor with less than 1280x1024 resolution.

There's simply no room for it all to fit otherwise! And you'll waste far too much time scrolling panels around, trying to get to all the tools.

What's a CTI?

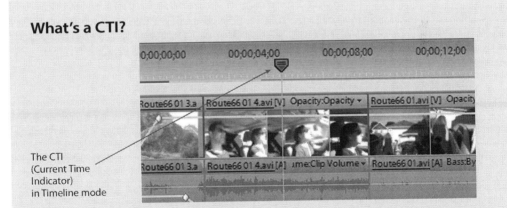

The CTI (Current Time Indicator) in Timeline mode

Vital vocabulary alert! That thin, vertical, red line that moves along the Timeline as you play your video? It's called a **CTI**, which stands for "Current Time Indicator."

That's an all-important vocabulary term that you'll definitely want to know as we continue to work.

Trust us on this. Especially since there's no other word that comes close to describing this thing – and we're going to use the term often throughout this book.

Basic editing moves

No matter what you plan to do with your video and no matter how creatively you plan to do it, the video editing process itself will still fit the same basic structure.

Here's a brief walkthrough of the steps you'll take for creating any video project in Premiere Elements.

1   Gather your media

The assets, or media, you gather to create your movie can come from a variety of sources. It can be video, audio, music, photos or graphics. If you are working in Quick View, any media you gather will go directly to your timeline. If you are working in Expert View, it will go into your **Project Assets** panel.

To import your media into your project, click on the **Add Media** tab on the upper left of the interface.

There are basically three ways to get your media into your project, all accessed by one of the eight buttons on the **Add Media** panel (illustrated below). We show you how and when to use each in **Chapter 18, Add Media to Your Project**.

- **Stream, or capture, your video into your project.**

    The capture function works with tape-based camcorders, like miniDV (the **DV Camcorder** button) or HDV (the **HDV Camcorder** button), which are connected to your computer by a FireWire cable (aka IEEE-1394 or iLink). Video can also be streamed into the program using a DV bridge, like the ADS Pyro AV Link or Canopus ADVC units – although you will not be able to control the playback of these units from the capture screen.

Add Media options

Launches the Elements Organizer — Elements Organizer
Drag videos and photos from Elements Organizer

Launches Video Importer — Videos from Flip or Cameras
Get videos from FLIP, AVCHD cameras or other Memory/Disk devices

Opens Capture screen — DV Camcorder
Capture video from a DV camcorder connected by Firewire or USB 2.0

Opens Capture screen — HDV Camcorder
Capture video from a HDV camcorder connected by Firewire or USB 2.0

Launches Video Importer — DVD camera or computer drive
Get video from a DVD based AVCHD camera or your computer's DVD drive

Opens Capture screen — Webcam or WDM
Capture video from a webcam or WDM compatible device

Opens Photo Downloader — Photos from cameras or devices
Get photos from digital cameras, phones or removable drives

Opens Explorer or Finder — Files and folders
Get videos, photos, and audio files from your computer's hard drive

Add Media ▾ | Project Assets ▾

Video captured from tape-based camcorders is streamed into your Premiere Elements project over a FireWire connection. The camcorder's playback is controlled by the software and you can select which segments to capture.

Video from non-tape-based sources – including hard drive camcorders, Flip and AVCHD camcorders and DVDs – is imported into your Premiere Elements project by the Video Importer, while still photos are downloaded from your digital camera or phone with the Photo Downloader.

Tape-based video, captured over FireWire, by the way, is by far the format that Premiere Elements works with most efficiently. Premiere Elements also includes an option for streaming in and capturing video from a **Webcam or WDM Device**.

- **Download your video from a hard drive camcorder, flash based camcorder or other video recording device.**

  Hard drive camcorders, including high-definition AVCHD and Flip cam units (the **Flip, AVCHD, Cameras and Phones** button), download their video as files rather than stream it into the program. Media can also be downloaded from other sources, including DVDs (the **DVD Camcorder or PC DVD Drive** button) and **Digital Still Cameras & Phones**.

- **Browse to gather media files that are located on your computer's hard drive(s).**

  When you select the **PC Files and Folders** button under **Get Media**, Windows Explorer or the Mac OSX Finder opens, allowing you to browse to video, stills, graphics or music files already on your computer's hard drive. The **Elements Organizer** is a companion file management program that can be used to manage and search media files on your computer.

To add a clip to your timeline in Expert View, simply drag it from the Project Assets panel.

As you add clips, the other clips will "ripple", moving aside if you add the clip in the middle of a project.

To override the ripple effect (as when you're adding music or a video clip to a parallel track) hold down the Ctrl key as you add the clip (or the Command key on a Mac).

Zoom in or out on the timeline by pressing + or - or using the Zoom slider.

2 Assemble the clips on your timeline

Once you've imported your media clips into a project, you can begin the process of assembling your movie. If you are working in Quick View, any media you add will be added automatically to the end of your timeline. If you are working in Expert View, the clips will be added to your **Project Assets** panel. Adding them, then, to your video project is as simple as dragging them from this panel to your timeline.

Once you add your files to your timeline, you'll have a number of options:

- **Trim your clips.** Trimming means removing footage from either the beginning or the end of a clip. To trim a clip, click to select the clip on your timeline and then drag in either the beginning or end to shorten it, as in the illustration on the following page.

- **Split your clips.** Splitting means slicing through your clips so that you can remove footage from the middle or delete one sliced-off segment completely. To split a clip, position the **CTI** (playhead) over your clip at the point at which you'd like the slice to occur and then click on the scissors icon on **CTI**.

- **Place your clip on an upper video or audio track**. An important feature of editing in Expert View is the ability to place your video or audio on tracks other than **Video 1** and **Audio 1**.

  The use of multiple tracks of video is, in fact, key to the creation of many of the more advanced video effects, including **Chroma Key** and **Videomerge**.

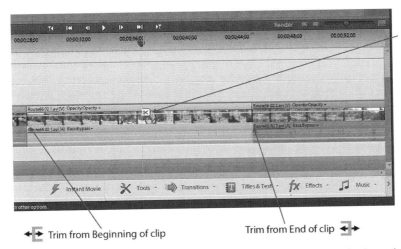

To slice a clip in two, click the scissors icon on the CTI playhead.

If a clip is selected on the timeline, only that clip will be split at the position of the CTI; If no clips are selected, all clips on every track on the timeline will be split at the position of the CTI.

◄┫ Trim from Beginning of clip   Trim from End of clip ┣►

To trim a clip on the timeline, hover your mouse over the beginning or end of a clip until the Trim from Beginning or Trim from End icon appears, then click and drag in or out.

We'll discuss how to assemble your movie in both Quick View and Expert View in **Chapter 16** and **Chapter 20**, respectively. We'll also show you how to use multi-track editing in order to create a a variety of effects and take advantage of a number of key storytelling techniques.

We'll also show you how to use both automatic and manual tools to work with your audio clips.

3   Add and adjust effects

Premiere Elements comes loaded with dozens of video and audio effects as well as hundreds of preset effects for working magic on your movie.

Adding an effect in Premiere Elements is very easy, as we show you in **Chapter 26, Add Video and Audio Effects**.

1   On the **Action Bar**, click the **Effects** button.

This will open the **Effects** pop-up panel, as illustrated on the following page.

2   Locate an effect.

In Expert View, the **Effects** panel displays the **Advanced Adjustments** category of effects by default. But you can select any category of video or audio effects by clicking the title bar on the panel (The bar where the words "**Advanced Adjustments**" appears) and selecting a category from the list that appears.

You can also quickly locate any effect by setting the panel to **Show All** and then clicking the magnifying glass button to do a Quick Search.

3 Apply the effect.

To apply the effect, drag it from the **Effects** panel onto a clip on your timeline.

4 Adjust the effect's settings.

Once you've applied your effect, you may or may not see an immediate change in your video clip. To intensify or fine tune your effect, ensure the clip is selected on your timeline, then open the **Applied Effects** panel by clicking the button on the right side of the interface.

To apply an effect to a clip, simply drag it from the Effects panel onto a clip on your timeline.

The **Applied Effects** panel is a tremendously powerful workspace. Not only can you use it to change the settings for individual effects but also as the main workspace for creating and adjusting **keyframes**, Premiere Elements' tool for creating animations, motion paths and effects that change over the course of the clip's playback.

In the **Applied Effects** panel, locate your effect's listing, then click on it to open the effect's settings.

In **Chapter 27**, we'll show you how to customize and fine tune your effects in the **Applied Effects** panel.

Then, in **Chapter 28**, we'll show you how to use keyframes to animate effects and motion paths.

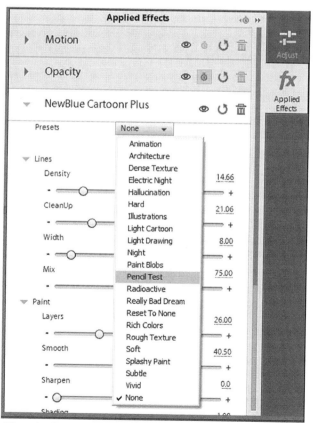

Effects that have been added to a clip appear in that clip's Applied Effects panel, where they can be adusted and customized.

Drag & Drop a Transition Between Clips

3D Motion ▾

Cube Spin | Curtain | Doors | Flip Over
Fold Up | Spin | Spin Away | Swing In
Swing Out | Tumble Away

3D Motion ▾

3D Motion
Dissolve
Iris
Map
NewBlue 3D Explosions Elements
NewBlue 3D Transformations Elements
NewBlue Art Blends Elements
NewBlue Motion Blends Elements
Page Peel
Picture Wipes
Slide
Special Effect
Stretch
Wipe
Zoom
Audio Transitions

Show All

Like Effects, Transitions are arranged in several categories, accessible by clicking the title bar at the top of the panel.

Transitions ▴ | Titles & Text ▴ | *fx* Effects ▴

4 Add and adjust transitions

Transitions are the effects or animations that take your movie from one clip to another. Some are gentle and nearly invisible – others are showy and draw attention to themselves. Most transitions are added to your timeline and adjusted similarly to effects:

1 Click on the **Transitions** button on the **Action Bar**.

The **Transitions** panel will open.

2 Locate a transition.

The **Transitions** panel displays the **3D Motion** category of effects by default. But you can select any category of video or audio effects by clicking the title bar on the panel (The bar where the words "**3D Motion**" appears) and selecting a category from the pop-up list that appears.

You can also quickly locate any effect by setting the panel to **Show All** and then clicking the magnifying glass button to do a Quick Search.

3 Apply the transition.

Apply a transition by dragging it from the **Transitions** panel onto the intersection of two clips on your timeline.

Clicking the More button on the Transition Adjustments panel and scrolling down reveals a number of options for customizing your transition.

Clicking the eyeball button will toggle the panel to display your transition with your actual video clips.

The Custom button will open a screen for customizing the elements of many transitions.

4   Customize your transition.

Nearly all transitions include a number of properties that can be customized, depending on the nature of the transition. Virtually all include options for designating where the transition centers and the duration of the transition as well as an option for setting the transition to reverse its movement (i.e., wiping from right to left rather than left to right).

We'll show you just about everything there is to know about adding and customizing transitions – including why they sometimes seem to behave in very strange ways – in **Chapter 24**. And, as a bonus, we'll even show you how to use the **Gradient Wipe**, a tool for creating your own custom transition effects!

5   Add titles

Titles are text, and sometimes graphics, placed over your clips to provide additional visual information for your video story. In most cases, you'll create your titles in Premiere Elements' **Titles & Text** workspace – a process that automatically places the title on an available video track on your timeline at the position of the **CTI** playhead.

To create a title:

1   Click the **Titles & Text** button on the **Action Bar**.

The **Titles & Text** panel will open.

As with **Effects** and **Transitions**, the panel has several categories of title templates. Among these are text-only stationary titles, titles with graphics and rolling and animated titles

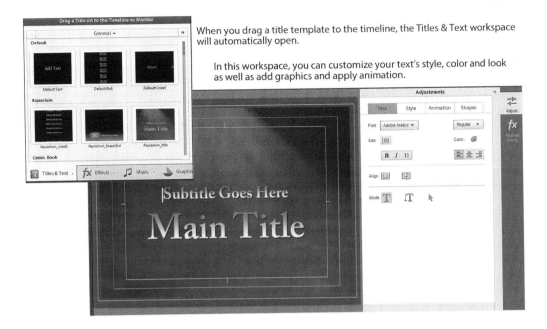

When you drag a title template to the timeline, the Titles & Text workspace will automatically open.

In this workspace, you can customize your text's style, color and look as well as add graphics and apply animation.

2   Add the title to your timeline.

Drag the title from the **Titles & Templates** panel to your timeline. The **Titles & Text** workspace will automatically open.

3   Customize the text.

Type your title over the placeholder text.

With your text selected, you can apply text attributes – including setting the font, size, style and alignment. You can also apply a style to your selected text by clicking on one of the **Text Styles** listed on the panel.

4   Customize your title.

The **Title Adjustments** workspace has tools for customizing the look and style of your text, adding and placing graphics and adding very cool text animations. You can also customize your title template and create rolling and crawling titles.

When you want to return to the regular editing workspace, click on the timeline.

We'll show you pretty much everything you could want to know about using Premiere Elements' tools for creating and customizing your text and titles in **Chapter 25**.

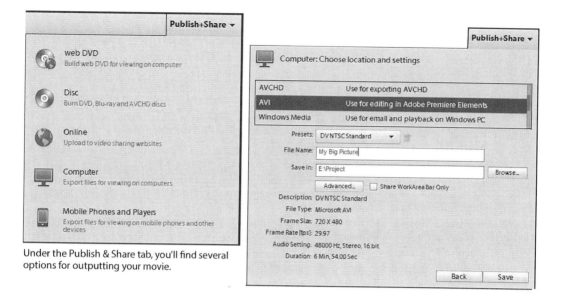

Under the Publish & Share tab, you'll find several options for outputting your movie.

6 Publish your movie

When you're happy with the video project you've created, you'll find a number of options for publishing and sharing it, as we discuss in **Chapter 20**. We'll show you how to publish it to a:

- **Web DVD.** This option allows you to save your DVD files as Web site files that function just like an interactive DVD – complete with menus and scene link buttons – except that they can be posted online!

- **Disc.** Built into Premiere Elements are tools for creating menus and scene markers for creating DVD and BluRay disc projects.

- **Online.** The program comes complete with facilities for loading your finished video to your own personal Web site, YouTube or Facebook.

- **Computer.** The program will save your finished project as an AVI file, MPEG, Quicktime (MOV) file, AVCHD video, Windows Media (WMV) file or a Flash (FLV) file on your computer's hard drive. Once the output is complete, you can then share these files any number of ways, including posting them online or using them as segments in a larger video project.

- **Mobile Phone or Player.** Premiere Elements includes custom presets for creating video for your iPod, iPhone, iPad, smartphone and virtually any other portable video player.

And that's basically it!

You gather your assets; you assemble them on your timeline; you add effects, transitions and titles; then you share your masterpiece with the world.

But between the lines of this simplicity are the countless variations that can elevate your movie project from the realm of a basic structure to something truly amazing!

Expert View

Quick View

What's new in Premiere Elements 11?

In its redesign of Premiere Elements, Adobe has addressed two major issues: the clutter and readability of the interface and the program's overall performance.

In addressing the readability issue, Adobe has stripped back the interface. No longer is it a clutter of hard-to-read, white-text-on-black panels. The new interface is big and bright, with its tools tucked away in pop-up panels that stay hidden until you call them forth.

As for performance, they've tuned up this program in a very big way! It opens a project in seconds rather than minutes (at least after the first activation). And , even working with challenging files, it's stable and snappy. (Though we do recommend some minimal computer specs in **Chapter 32, A Premiere Elements Appendix.**)

In fact, the single most impressive thing about the program is how well it performs with video from just about any recording device – from camcorders to iPads and iPods to smartphones. And what's more, you can even mix video sources in a project with usually terrific results.

Additionally, the program has added 64-bit support to both the Mac OSX and the Windows 7 versions of the program.

Quick View and Expert View

Gone is the old Sceneline view, with all its limitations. In its place is the new Quick View, a simplified workspace for editing your movie. It's not quite as powerful as the Expert View timeline. In fact, it's limited to a video track, a title track and two audio tracks. But because it's a timeline, you can still edit, apply and customize effects – including Time Remapping effects! – and cut and trim video.

Media clips added to the Quick View timeline are added directly from your computer's hard drive or recording device, without a stop at the **Project Assets** panel along the way. So gathering media clips and throwing together a movie is fast and easy.

Best of all, Quick View and Expert View are just two ways to edit the same movie – so you can switch back and forth between the two views as much as you like, taking advantage of the best features of each.

We'll show you how to edit in Quick View in **Part IV** of the book. Then we'll show you how (and why) to edit in Expert View in **Part V**.

Automatic project set-up

Whether you're working in Quick View or Expert View, there's no need to manually set up a project in version 11. Just gather your assets and go to work! The program automatically sets up your project based on the first video clip you add to your timeline.

Of course, there are times when you'll want to manually control your project's specs too. We show you how to do that in **Chapter 17, Start a Premiere Elements Project**.

The Action Bar

Running along the bottom of the Premiere Elements interface (as well as along the bottoms of the Photoshop Elements and Organizer interfaces) is the **Action Bar**, access point for a large number of the program's tools and features.

Clicking buttons along the **Action Bar** opens pop-up panels for the program's **Tools, Transitions, Effects, Titles & Text, Music** and **Graphics**. Within each of these pop-up panels are buttons and search tools for quickly locating the feature you want. Though tucked neatly away, then, most tools and features are only a few clicks away.

We'll show you how to work with the many tools on the **Action Bar** in **Part III** of the book.

Many of Premiere Elements tools and features can be quickly accessed from the Action Bar running along the bottom fo the program's interface.

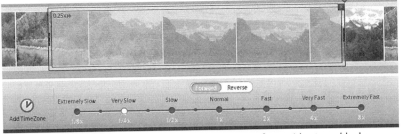

The cool new Time Remapping tool lets you set segments of your video to suddenly slow down or speed up.

Time Remapping

Although the program still includes the **Time Stretch** tool for speeding up or slowing down you clips, Adobe has also added the bigger, better **Time Remapping** tool – which can speed up or slow down specific segments of a video clip. The **Time Remapping** tool combines the effect with tools that render and blend frames so well that you can even slow a video down to one-eighth speed and it will look clean and smooth, as if shot by a high-speed camera.

We'll show you how to use this amazing tool in **Chapter 22**.

The Adjustments panel

Two new pop-up panels are launched by clicking buttons along the interface's right side.

The **Adjustments** panel is loaded with tools for adjusting, correcting and enhancing your clips' color settings and sound levels. Color adjustments in this powerful panel can be made to the overall hue, saturation lightness, contrast and brightness of your video or to the individual red, green and blue color channels using a very intuitive interface. This is professional-quality color correction and enhancement in a simple consumer interface.

We'll introduce you to the tools on this panel in **Chapter 23**.

The Applied Effects panel

Replacing the old Properties panel, the **Applied Effects** panel is now where you edit and adjust your applied effects and where you keyframe motion paths and animations.

Adobe has made this workspace much easier to access and work with in version 11. And we'll show you how to edit effects in this panel in **Chapter 27**.

Then we'll show you how to keyframe animations and motion paths in it in **Chapter 28**.

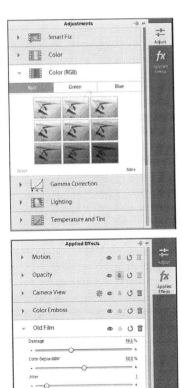

FilmLooks are color templates that can make your movie look like a classic Technicolor Hollywood movie, an old newsreel or a moody film noir.

FilmLooks

A cool, new addition to the **Effects** collection is a set of color adjustments Adobe calls **FilmLooks**. Easily applied, these **FilmLooks** can make your movie look like a washed-out old home movie, a big, bright Hollywood production, a stylish old film noir, a creepy horror film or a sun-drenched day at the beach.

We'll introduce you to these effects in **Chapter 26**.

Increased online sharing options

Premiere Elements now includes tools for uploading your videos directly from the program to Facebook as well as YouTube. Even more if you port them through the **Share** options in the Elements Organizer!

New project presets

Less obvious but extremely welcome are new project settings that support an increased number of video formats. Premiere Elements now supports AVCHD 1080p, a 60 frames per second (50 frames PAL) progressive scan format shot by more and more consumer camcorders.

The program also works very well with video from iPads, iPods and smartphones, formats we're all using increasingly.

We talk more about these formats and how to use them in your Premiere Elements project in **Chapter 17.**

Additional content

Whether you've downloaded the program from Adobe or bought the program in a box, you might be surprised to find that it comes with installation files only. The dozens of additional effects and templates are nowhere to be found.

Once you've installed the program and registered it with Adobe, however, the additional content will suddenly appear.

This is part of Adobe's new strategy for making installation and deployment more efficient. Rather than your having to install all of this additional content on your own, it will download to your computer, automatically, as needed. (This will require, of course, an always-on internet connection.)

Effects and templates indicated with a blue banner over the upper right corner will download to the program automatically when you apply them.

As you work with the program, you may notice that the thumbnails representing a number of effects, transitions and templates have a blue banner over their upper right corners. These banners are indicators that the effect or template is available to you but that it has not yet been installed on your computer.

When you select the effect or template the first time, it will be downloaded and installed on your computer. It will then be available for your unlimited use.

Organizer improvements

Adobe has put at least as much time and effort into improving the Elements Organizer as it has Premiere Elements and Photoshop Elements. Not only does the program perform more efficiently than ever before, but Adobe has also added or expanded its ability to search and manage your media files by the location the video or photos were shot, the people in the picture, the event they recorded and even by their similarity to other video and photo files. Improvements in the **Media Analyzer** tool also mean more and more metadata is created automatically for your files by the program. And the program now includes portals for loading your photos and videos directly to Facebook, YouTube, Flickr, Photoshop Showcase and Adobe Revel.

It's so big we've dedicated the entirety of **Section 3** of the book to it!

Adobe Premiere Elements

Part IV
Editing Video in Quick View

Adding Media to Your Quick View Timeline

Trimming and Slicing Your Video

Adding Transitions

Adding and Adjusting Audio

Adding Titles

Chapter 16

Assemble Your Video in Quick View

The drag-and-drop editing space

Replacing the old Sceneline, Quick View is Premiere Elements' workspace for quickly pulling together a video and applying effects to it.

It combines the simplicity of sceneline editing with the power of a full-fledged Premiere Elements timeline.

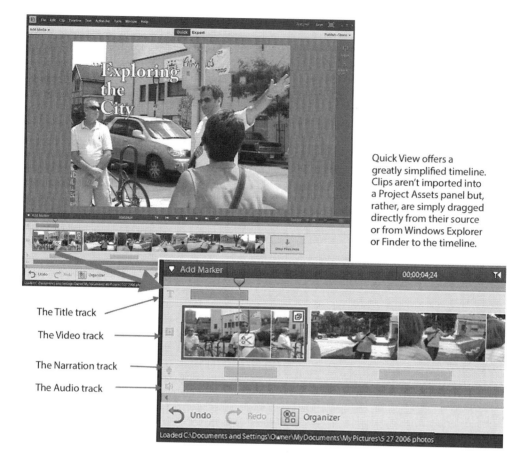

Quick View offers a greatly simplified timeline. Clips aren't imported into a Project Assets panel but, rather, are simply dragged directly from their source or from Windows Explorer or Finder to the timeline.

The Title track

The Video track

The Narration track

The Audio track

Premiere Elements' new Quick View makes assembling your movie as fast and easy as possible. It combines the simplicity of the old Sceneline mode with the power of a full-fledged Timeline.

The Quick View timeline includes four tracks in which you can assemble your movie. They are, from top to bottom:

The Title Track. This is where text or titles that will overlay your video is placed. If you'd prefer your titles with a black background or no background at all, you can also place your titles directly on the **Video Track**. However, only text and titles can be placed on the **Title Track**. Video can not. For more information on adding titles to your movie, see **Chapter 25, Add Titles & Text**.

The Video Track. This is the track on which your movie will be assembled. It will also include your video's accompanying audio track.

The Narration Track. Although any audio may be added to this track, this is the track that any recorded narration (see page 281) will appear on by default.

The Audio Track. Music or any other peripheral audio may be added here. For information on adding music, see **Chapter 29**.

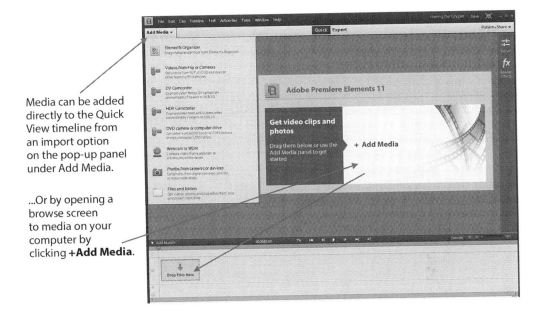

Media can be added directly to the Quick View timeline from an import option on the pop-up panel under Add Media.

...Or by opening a browse screen to media on your computer by clicking **+Add Media**.

Add media to your Quick View timeline

Unlike in Expert View (discussed in **Chapter 20**), in Quick View your video and other media isn't imported into a **Project Assets** area before it is added to your timeline. You simply add your media directly to your timeline and start editing! The program will automatically set up your project by matching its settings to the specs of the first video clip you add.

You can add your media to your project in a number of ways:

- Tape-based video from miniDV and HDV camcorders is captured directly to your project's timeline (as discussed in **Chapter 18,** page 231).
- Video and other media from Flip, AVCHDs, cameras, phones or removable drive devices are imported to your timeline over a USB connection (as discussed in **Chapter 18**, pages 235-237).
- Media that's already on your computer can be browsed to or located and imported through the Elements Organizer.

The tools for importing your media are accessed through the pop-up menu under the **Add Media** button in the upper left of the program's interface. (For more information on **Add Media**, see **Chapter 18**.)Or, when you first start your project, by clicking the **+Add Media** button in the center of the interface, as illustrated above. (Note that the +Add Media button will be replaced by the **Monitor** panel, once you begin to assemble clips on your timeline.)

Your media can also be added directly from your computer's Windows Explorer or Mac Finder screens. Simply drag your audio and video clips directly to your Quick View timeline!

Your view of your timeline can be set using the Zoom Slider or by using the Zoom In/Out buttons.

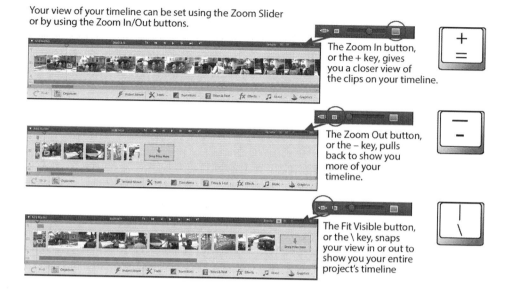

The Zoom In button, or the + key, gives you a closer view of the clips on your timeline.

The Zoom Out button, or the – key, pulls back to show you more of your timeline.

The Fit Visible button, or the \ key, snaps your view in or out to show you your entire project's timeline

Zoom in or out of your timeline

Once you've added media to your timeline, you may want to zoom out to see the entire movie at once, or zoom in to a single moment or frame to make some fine adjustments.

Along the upper right of the Quick View timeline are controls for zooming in and out of your movie. (These controls have the same function on the Expert View timeline.) There are also keyboard shortcuts for settings these views:

The **Fit Visible Timeline** button sets the zoom level so that your entire movie project is visible. You also set this level by pressing the \ key on your keyboard (above the **Enter** key).

The **Zoom Out** button incrementally zooms out of your timeline. You can also zoom in by pressing your keyboard's – key.

The **Zoom In** button incrementally zooms in on your timeline. You can also zoom in by pressing your keyboard's **+** key.

The **Slider** can be used to set your zoom level precisely.

Add transitions

A library of transitions can be browsed by clicking on the **Transitions** button on the **Action Bar** along the bottom of the timeline.

In Quick View, you only have access to a handful of transitions. If you'd like to access the full transitions library, switch over to Expert View, where you can access over 100 video transitions in 15 categories plus 2 audio transitions. To learn more about working with transitions in Expert View, see **Chapter 24, Add and Customize Transitions**.

To apply a transition, simply drag it from the Transitions pop-up panel on the Action Bar to the intersection between two clips (indicated in green).

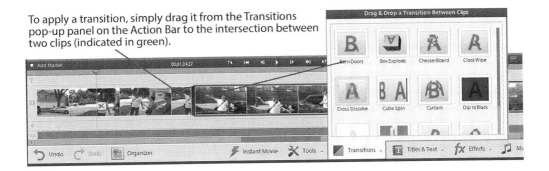

To apply a transition, drag it from the pop-up panel onto a clip on your timeline. A green highlight will indicate where the transition will be applied, based on which end of a clip you are dragging the transition closer to.

When you apply a transition, a pop-up menu (illustrated on the right) will prompt you to choose where you'd like the transition applied in relation to the clips. In most cases, you'll choose **Between Clips**.

This menu also allows you to set the **Duration** of the transition, in seconds. This number can be set by clicking on the up and down arrows or by clicking directly on the number and typing in a custom duration. Increments of seconds (such as .5) can be used.

To re-access this panel and revise these properties at any time, **double-click** on the transition on your timeline.

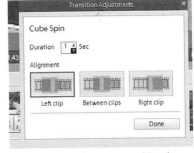

When you apply your transition (or when you double-click on an existing transition, a pop-up menu will appear offering options for how the transition's duration and how the transition rests between tyour clips.

Most transitions also allow for much deeper customization. For more information on customizing your transitions, see page 118.

To replace one transition with another, simply drag the new transition from the **Transitions** panel onto the existing.

To remove a transition, click to select it on the timeline and press **Delete** on your keyboard.

How your transitions behave can be affected by the amount of "head" and "tail" material available on your clips. For more information on this, see **How Transitions Work** on page 308.

Trim or split your video

Video clips, audio clips and even titles can be **Split** or **Trimmed**. To indicate which clips you want to **Split** or **Trim**, click to select the audio or video clip on your timeline so that it is surrounded by a blue highlight, as illustrated on the following page.

To split a clip, click on the Scissors icon on the CTI.

Splitting means dividing a clip into smarller clips at the point of the CTI playhead.

Split clips are indicated with ticker markers.

Ticker markers indicated that there is "hidden" video beyond the clip's end points.

Splitting your video means cutting a larger clip on your timeline into smaller clips.

To Split your video:

1   Position the **CTI** playhead so that the frame that displays in you **Monitor** indicates the exact spot you want to slice your video.

2   Click on the scissors icon on the **CTI**.

Trim left clip.   Trim right clip.

Trimming cuts (or extends) video from the beginning or end of a clip. To trim, hover your mouse over an end of a clip until the trim indicator appears, then click and drag.

A trimmed clip is indicated with a ticker marker.

Trimming means shortening (or lengthening) a clip on your timeline by adjusting the clip's start and end points.

To trim a clip:

1   Hover your mouse over the beginning or end of a clip on your timeline until the **Trim** indicator appears, as illustrated above.

2   Click and drag to the left or right.

A clip that has been split or trimmed is indicated with the ⌊E⌋ icon.

Once a clip has been split, it becomes two smaller clips. Each of these clips can also be trimmed.

Add audio to your Quick View timeline

As you add your camcorder video to your **Video Track**, the accompanying audio will be added automatically, as part of an unseen audio track.

The Quick View timeline offers two additional tracks in which you can add audio, the **Narration Track** and the **Audio Track**.

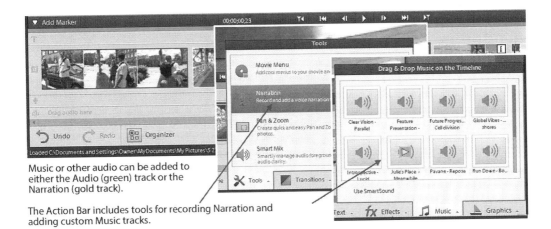

Music or other audio can be added to either the Audio (green) track or the Narration (gold track).

The Action Bar includes tools for recording Narration and adding custom Music tracks.

Although technically you can add audio or music to your movie project on either track, you need to be careful where you place your audio or music if you plan to record narration. Narration gets priority on the **Narration Track**. This means that narration will overwrite any existing audio or music on this track at the position of the **CTI** playhead as your record!

You can place any audio or music clips on the **Audio Track**.

As with your video clips, your audio clips can be **Split** and **Trimmed**, as described on the facing page.

The limitations of Quick View

Although most of the program's features are available in both Quick View and Expert View, a number of features function to a lesser degree or not at all in Quick View. They include:

Multi-track editing. Because the Quick View timeline is limited to one video track, J-Cuts, L-Cuts, split screen and picture-in-picture effects can not be created in Quick View.

Chroma Key and Videomerge. Because **keying** effects, including **Videomerge**, require at least two tracks of video in order to create their composite effects, these effects can not be effectively created on the Quick View timeline.

Audio Keyframing. Audio can not be set to specific levels at specific points in a clip on the Quick View timeline. Audio levels can only be set using the **Smart Mix, Adjustments** and **Audio Mixer** tools.

Fortunately, you can easily switch between Quick View and Expert View as you work on your project so that you can take advantage of the features on each timeline. (However, video and audio added to upper tracks in Expert View will not be visible when you switch to Quick View.)

Adjust your audio levels and mix your audio

The Quick View timeline has a limited number of ways for you to adjust the audio levels or to mix your audio so that one or more audio tracks' levels are lower so that another can dominate.

Smart Mix (discussed on page 284) will automatically mix and adjust your audio levels based on parameters you define.

The Audio Mixer (discussed on page 279) will set audio keyframes for you as you raise and lower levels on the fly as you play your video.

However, each of these methods has its own challenges and limitations. The single best way to precisely control your levels and mix your audio is with audio keyframes (described on page 356), a feature most easily applied on the Expert View timeline.

Add titles

A library of title templates can be browsed by clicking on the **Titles & Text** button on the **Action Bar** along the bottom of the timeline.

The titles library is arranged in categories, and you can browse through the categories of transitions by clicking the backward and forward arrows at the top of the pop-up panel, as illustrated on page 312.

The title templates range from basic text to rolling titles and templates.

Once you've selected a title, drag it to either the **Titles Track** on the Quick View timeline (if you'd like to overlay your video) or to an area on the **Video Track** (if you'd like it to appear with a black or no background).

Once you've placed a title, the **Title Adjustments** workspace will open. In this workspace you'll find options for changing your text's color, style, font or size. You can also add animations and/or graphics to your text.

For more information on working with titles and text, see **Chapter 25, Add Titles & Text.**

Like audio and video clips, titles can be **Split** and **Trimmed**. If your text has animation or a roll or crawl applied to it, the longer you stretch the title on the timeline, the slower the animation and vice versa.

The presence of a title or other video clip on an upper video track is indicated on the Quick Edit timeline with an overlay marker in the upper right corner of the effected clip.

Adobe Premiere Elements

Part V

Editing Video in Expert View

Chapter 17

Start a Premiere Elements Project

Creating and opening your video projects

In earlier versions of Premiere Elements, setting up your project was a vital, and sometimes challenging, part of the process of making your movie.

Much more happens automatically in Premiere Elements 11 – though there is much to be said for making sure your project gets off to a good start.

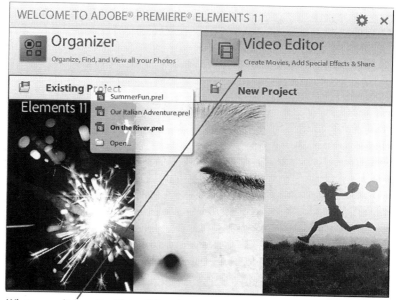

When you click on the Video Editor button, you will see the options to start a new project or open an existing one.

The Welcome Screen

When you first start up Premiere Elements, you'll be greeted by the **Welcome Screen**. Very similar to the **Welcome Screen** in Photoshop Elements, it is a launching point for the workspaces of the program.

From this **Welcome Screen** you can start a new Premiere Elements project, open an old one or launch the Elements Organizer.

Bypass the Welcome Screen

If you'd prefer not to be greeted by the **Welcome Screen**, you'll find options for setting how the program

launches by clicking on the gear icon at the top right of the screen.

Your selection determines if the program opens to the **Welcome Screen**, the Elements Organizer or directly into the Premiere Elements editor.

The Elements Organizer

The Elements Organizer is a powerful media file management program that interfaces with both Premiere Elements and Photoshop Elements.

The Organizer allows you to catalog and search your media files based on a wide variety of criteria. Additionally, the Organizer includes a number of tools for creating and sharing your video and photo projects.

The Organizer reads the EXIF data off your digital photos, adds **Keyword Tags** (both manually and automatically) to your media clips, gives you the ability to sort your files into **Albums** and serves as a launching point for a number of Photoshop Elements and Premiere Elements functions.

We discuss its features and functions in more detail in **Section 3** of this book.

Start a new project

Selecting the **New Project** option from the **Welcome Screen** takes you to the Quick View or Expert View workspace of Premiere Elements. If you open in the Quick View workspace, you can go to work **Adding Media** and assembling it on your timeline (as described in **Chapter 18**).

By clicking on the Expert button at the top of the interface, you can switch the program to Expert View, with its much more powerful timeline and multi-track capabilities. In Expert View, you gather your media into the **Project Assets** panel before assembling it on the timeline.

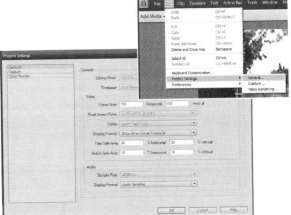

Unlike in earlier versions of the program, you don't need to worry about selecting settings when starting up a Premiere Elements project. The program will set your project up automatically, based on the first clip you add to your timeline. But you do have the option of manually selecting your project settings also.

Meantime, to see which settings your project is currently using, just go to the **Edit** menu and select **Project Properties**.

Starting a new Premiere Elements project

Select the location your project will be saved to.

Name your project.

Most recent project settings.

To start a new Premiere Elements project:

1 Click the **New Project** button on the **Welcome Screen** or select **New Project** from the **File** menu at the top of the interface.

The **New Project** option screen will appear, as illustrated above.

Type the title for your new project in the box displayed at **Name**.

2 Click the **Browse** button to choose a location to save your new project file.

We at Muvipix recommend always selecting the **Browse** option and, wherever you choose to save your file, *creating a new folder* for every new project file.

This little bit of housekeeping keeps all of your new project's files in one neat, little folder. And, when your project is done and you want to clear it from your computer, you can then remove not only the project file but all of the temp, render and scratch disk files Premiere Elements has created for that project simply by deleting that single folder!

This makes post-project clean-up a much easier and neater process.

In most cases, it's not necessary to manually select your project's settings. Whether you're working in Quick View or Expert View the program will automatically set up your project's settings based on the specs of the first video clip you add to your timeline.

And in most cases, that's good enough.

But there are times when you'll want to impose settings on your project. You may want to set up your project for a specific purpose – creating a project for a DVD, for instance – or if you're mixing different formats of video and you don't want the program to automatically switch project settings on you.

In those cases, you can opt to **Force Selected Settings** on your new project.

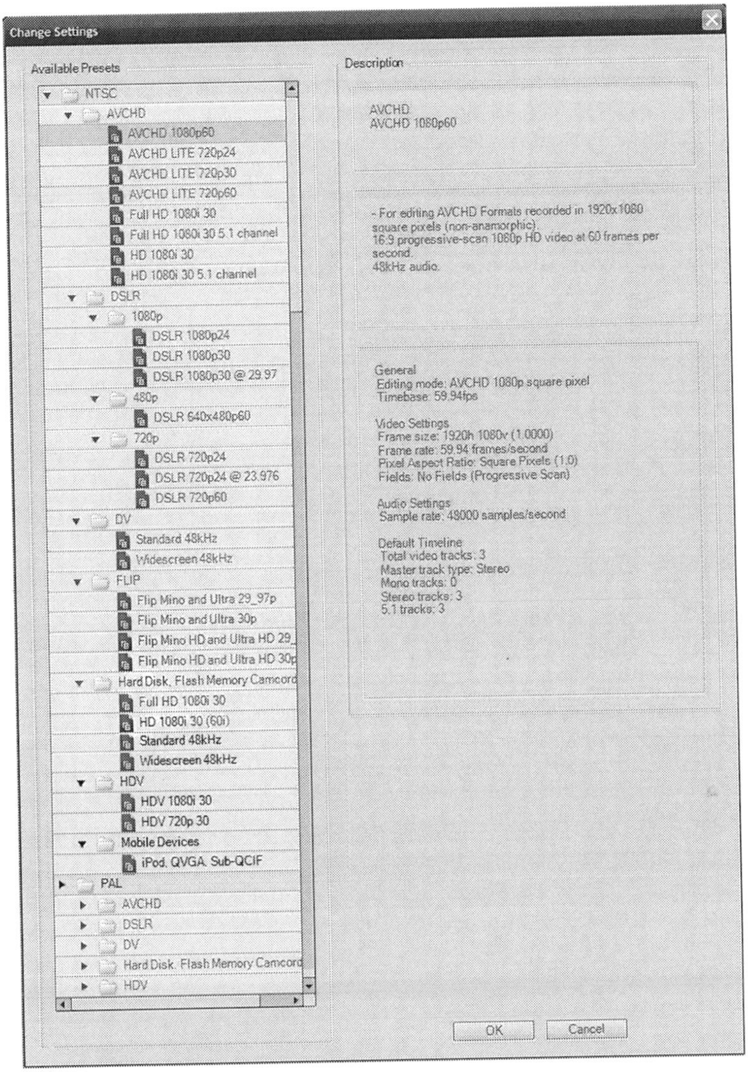

3   Click the **Change Settings** button at the bottom of the **New Project** panel.

This will open the **Project Settings** panel, as illustrated above.

4   Select your project settings (based on the chart on the following pages).

Then click **Okay.**

5   Back at the **New Project** panel, check the box **Force Selected Project Setting on This Project**, as illustrated on the facing page.

Your project's settings will not automatically reset when you add a new clip to your timeline.

Premiere Elements 11 project preset options

Premiere Elements includes a wealth of project setting options for editing your video, including a couple of great, new options. New in version 11 is the much appreciated AVCHD 1080p60 project preset (50p in PAL), which edits AVCHD video shot at 60 (or 50) progressive frames per second. Also much appreciated are new settings for editing video from iPads, iPods and other mobile devices, like smart phones and pocket camcorders.

In most cases – whenever Premiere Elements recognizes the format of the video – the program will automatically select the appropriate project setting, based on the first video clip you load into your project.

AVCHD	AVCHD 1080p60	Full 1920x1080 AVCHD video shooting 60 progressive fps.
	AVCHD Lite 720p24	AVCHD video (1280x720) shooting at 23.976 progressive fps.
	AVCHD Lite 720p30	AVCHD video (1280x720) shooting at 29.97 progressive fps.
	AVCHD Lite 720p60	AVCHD video (1280x720) shooting at progressive 59.94 fps.
	Full HD 1080i 30	AVCHD video (1920x1080 60i/30 fps square pixel, hard drive, high definition) from camcorders that shoot in stereo audio.
	Full HD 1080i 30 5.1 Channel	AVCHD video (1920x1080 60i/30 fps square pixel, hard drive, high-definition) from camcorders that shoot in 5.1 channel audio. *This is the most common format for most newer hard drive, high-definition camcorders.*
	HD 1080 30	AVCHD video (1440x1080 60i/30 fps non-square pixel, hard drive, high definition) from camcorders that shoot in stereo audio.
	HD 1080 30 5.1 Channel	AVCHD video (1440x1080 60i/30 fps non-square pixel, hard drive, high-definition) from camcorders that shoot in 5.1 channel audio. This is the most common format for older hard drive, high-definition camcorders. *Note that, although this format uses less horizontal pixels, it produces the same high-quality, 16:9 image as 1920x1080 video. The pixels are just non-square, or wider than they are tall – as in the traditional television standard.*
DSLR Presets – Use these presets for working with high-quality video from digital still cameras (such as the Canon EOS Movie Full HD series).		
1080p	DSLR 1080p24	1920x1080 16:9 video shooting at 23.976 progressive fps.
	DSLR 1080p30	1920x1080 16:9 video shooting at 30 progressive fps.
	DSLR 1080p 30@29.97	1920x1080 16:9 video shooting at 29.97 progressive fps.
480p	DSLR 640x480p 60	640x480 16:9 video shooting at 59.94 progressive fps.
720p	DSLR 720p24	1280x720 16:9 video shooting at 24 progressive fps.
	DSLR 720p24 @23.976	1280x720 16:9 video shooting at 23.976 progressive fps.
	DSLR 720p60	1280x720 16:9 video shooting at 59.94 progressive fps.
DV	Standard 48 kHz	720x480 4:3 video from a miniDV tape-based camcorders.
	Widescreen 48 kHz	720x480 16:9 video from miniDV tape-based camcorders.

continued on facing page

More Premiere Elements project presets

DV	Standard 48 khz	720x480 4:3 video from miniDV tape-based camcorders.
	Widescreen 48 khz	720x480 16:9 video from miniDV tape-based camcorders.
Flip	Flip Mino or Ultra Flip 29.97	Flip standard definition (640x480) video camcorders shooting at 29.97 fps.
	Flip Mino or Ultra Flip 30	Flip standard definition (640x480) video camcorders shooting at 30 fps.
	Flip Mino HD or Ultra HD 29.97	Flip high definition (1280x720) video camcorders shooting at 29.97 fps.
	Flip Mino HD or Ultra HD 30	Flip high definition (1280x720) video camcorders shooting at 30 fps.
Hard Disk, Flash Memory Camcorder	HD 1080i 30	High-definition video (1920x1080) from non-AVCHD hard drive or flash memory camcorders (such as the JVC GZ-HD7).
	HD 1080i 30 (60i)	High-definition video from (1440x1080) from non-AVCHD hard drive or flash memory camcorders that record in 60i format. (The PAL equivalent is, of course, 50i.)
	Standard 48kHz	Standard-definition (720x480) 4:3 video from hard drive camcorders as well as video from DVDs. *It is very important to use this or the following preset with standard-definition MPEG or VOB sources because it will automatically reverse the field dominance in your video, correcting an interlacing issue that can otherwise cause stuttering in your output videos.*
	Widescreen 48 kHz	Video from standard-definition (720x480) 16:9 hard drive camcorders and video from DVDs.
HDV Presets	HDV 1080i 30	Video from tape-based, high-definition HDV camcorders that shoot full HDV at 1440x1080 pixels.
	HDV 720p 30	Video from tape-based, high-definition HDV camcorders that shoot full HDV at 1280x720 pixels (progressive scan at 30 fps).
Mobile Devices	iPods, QVGA, Sub-QCIF	Video from iPods or other mobile devices shooting 640x480 (progressive scan 15 fps).
		Video shot at 1280x720p using iPads, smartphones or other devices will use the Flip HD 30 fps project settings.

PAL presets

The PAL and NTSC options are identical except that the frame rates for PAL presets are 25 fps rather than 30. Additionally, video listed on this chart as shooting at 60i or 60p would appear as 50i and 50p in the PAL system.

The standard definition video frame (the DV and Hard Disk presets for standard and widescreen) would appear as 720x576 rather than 720x480.

Open an old project from the Welcome Screen

Clicking the **Open Project** button on the **Welcome Screen** will get you access to any work-in-progress or old Premiere Elements projects.

Your most recent projects will appear in the drop-down menu, as illustrated on page 220. Additional Premiere Elements projects on your computer can be accessed by selecting the **Open...** option.

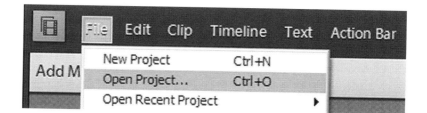

Open a project from within the program

Naturally, you don't have to go all the way out to the **Welcome Screen** to create a new project or to re-open an old one.

Both options are available from the **File** drop-down menu on the top left of the program's interface.

Selecting New **Project** from this menu gives you access to the very same **New Project** settings as are available from the **Welcome Screen**.

Open a project created by a previous version of the program?

Our advice: Don't do it.

It should work. And sometimes it does work. But, for the most part, Premiere Elements goes through such an overhaul from generation to generation, that it usually just leads to trouble. Only open version 11 projects with version 11, version 10 projects with version 10, etc.

Doing otherwise nearly always leads to buggy behavior – audio tracks that mysteriously disappear, clips that behave really strangely. A **Project Assets** panel that seems to have lost its mind.

Your best bet is to finish your Premiere Elements project in the same version of the program you began it in. Trust us on this.

Once it's far enough along that you consider it (or the segment you're working on) to be finished, you can export it – using **Publish & Share/Computer/AVI** (as we discuss in **Chapter 31, Publish & Share Your Video Projects**). You should then be able to import that AVI segment into your version 10 project with no problems, no bugginess and virtually no loss of quality.

But we very much recommend against opening even a version 10 project in version 11.

Capturing Video into Your Project

Downloading Media into Your Project

Adding Media Already on Your Computer

Working with Photos

Working with Music

Chapter 18

Add Media to Your Project

Capturing video and importing
video, audio and photos into your project

Whether you're working in Expert View
or Quick View, before you can edit your
video, you need to get it (along with
your other source media) into your
Premiere Elements project.

This is a relatively simple process,
but unfortunately one that can
occasionally present some challenges.

Before you can begin editing your Premiere Elements movie, you need to gather your video, still photos, music and audio clips into your project. The tools for gathering this media can be found by clicking on the **Add Media** tab at the top left of the interface or by using one of the other options listed in the sidebar at the bottom of this page.

The options that appear on this **Add Media** pop-up panel launch any of a number of built-in utilities for gathering your media clips.

As the chart on the facing page indicates, there are really only three basic ways to get your media files into a Premier Elements project:

Capture your tape-based video over a FireWire connection;

Download your media from a camcorder or other device over a USB connection or from your computer's DVD/CD drive; or

Import media that is already on your computer into your project.

Once you've captured, downloaded or imported your media into your Premiere Elements project, you can either add it directly to your project's timeline (in Quick View) or gather it into your **Project Assets** panel (in Expert View) in preparation for gathering it on your timeline (as we discuss in **Chapter 19**).

In this chapter, we'll look at each of the major media devices and media file sources and show you how to best gather your media from each.

We'll also show you how to work with photos, music and other media.

And, as a bonus, we'll show you how to successfully capture video from analog camcorders and video players, as well as how and when to convert potentially troublesome formats.

We'll even include some troubleshooting steps for when things don't seem to go as they should.

Four ways to Add Media to your project

1 Click on the **Add Media** tab; or

2 **Right-click** on a blank area in the **Project Assets** panel (**Ctrl-click** on a Mac) and select the **Get Media** option; or

3 Select **Get Media From** from the **File** drop-down menu; or

4 Drag media to your project directly from the Elements Organizer's **Media Browser** (see **Chapter 33**).

Methods for adding media

There are three basic ways to get media into your Premiere Elements project:

- **Capture** your tape-based video over a FireWire connection;
- **Download** your video or other media from a hard drive camcorder, camera or other device over a USB connection; or
- **Browse** to import media into your project from your computer's hard drive.

The chart below lists the methods of getting media from a number of devices.

MiniDV tape-based camcorders	**Capture** video over a FireWire connection using the Premiere Elements capture interface.
HDV tape-based hi-def camcorders	**Capture** video over a FireWire connection using the Premiere Elements capture interface.
Webcams	**Capture** video using the Premiere Elements capture interface.
AVCHD and other hard drive hi-def camcorders	**Download** video to computer using the Premiere Elements **Video Importer** over a USB connection.
Flip Mino or Ultra camcorders	**Download** video to computer using the Premiere Elements **Video Importer** over a USB connection.
Flash-based camcorders, such as the JVC-GZ series	**Download** video to computer using the Premiere Elements **Video Importer** over a USB connection.
DVD camcorders or DVDs	With the finalized disc in your computer's DVD drive, rip the video files to your computer using the **Video Importer**.
Analog video	**Capture** through a DV bridge or pass-through set-up using the Premiere Elements capture interface, as discussed on page 43.
Digital still cameras and other portable devices, such as iPads, iPods and phones.	**Download** stills using the Premiere Elements **Photo Downloader** or video using the **Video Importer** over a USB connection.
Music or audio from CDs	Rip music to your hard drive from the CD and then browse to the file(s) using the **Add Media** option **PC Files or Folders**.
Video, music or still photos already on your computer's hard drive	**Import** media into your project by browsing to it using the **Add Media** option **PC Files or Folders** or by dragging it from the Elements Organizer's **Media Browser**.

Also note that some commercial DVD and music formats (including iTunes) include digital rights management, copy protection software that will prohibit their use in Premiere Elements. Information on working around some forms of digital rights management can be found in **Add music files to a Premiere Elements project** on page 242.

FireWire is the common term for an IEEE-1394 connection, also known as iLink.

Add Media options

The tools for bringing your media into your project are most simply launched from the **Add Media** pop-up panel, opened by clicking the tab at the top left of the interface.

On this panel, Premiere Elements offers eight options for bringing your media into your project (as illustrated below).

- The **Elements Organizer** option will launch the Organizer file management program (See **Section 3** of this book).

- The **Videos from Flip or Cameras** option will launch the **Video Importer.**

- The **DV Camcorder** option will launch the program's video capture workspace.

- The **HDV Camcorder** option will launch the program's video capture workspace.

- The **DVD/DVD Camera or Computer Drive** option will launch the **Video Importer.**

- The **Webcam or WDM** option will launch the program's video capture workspace.

- The **Photos from Cameras or Devices** option will launch the Adobe **Photo Downloader.**

- The **Files and Folders** option will open Windows Explorer or the OSX Finder so that you can browse to your media files.

The **Photo Downloader** (illustrated on page 235) is an interface for selecting and downloading still images from a camera or other portable device.

The **Video Importer** (illustrated on page 235) is an interface for selecting and downloading video clips from a camcorder or other video device which stores its video on a hard drive or memory card.

In the **Capture** workspace (illustrated page 232), the program interfaces with the video device. This usually gives you remote control of the device, allowing you to preview the video in real time and select only the segments you want captured into your project.

Add Media options

Launches the Elements Organizer — **Elements Organizer**
Drag videos and photos from Elements Organizer

Launches Video Importer — **Videos from Flip or Cameras**
Get videos from FLIP, AVCHD cameras or other Memory/Disk devices

Opens Capture screen — **DV Camcorder**
Capture video from a DV camcorder connected by Firewire or USB 2.0

Opens Capture screen — **HDV Camcorder**
Capture video from a HDV camcorder connected by Firewire or USB 2.0

Launches Video Importer — **DVD camera or computer drive**
Get video from a DVD based AVCHD camera or your computer's DVD drive

Opens Capture screen — **Webcam or WDM**
Capture video from a webcam or WDM compatible device

Opens Photo Downloader — **Photos from cameras or devices**
Get photos from digital cameras, phones, or removable drives

Opens Explorer or Finder — **Files and folders**
Get videos, photos, and audio files from your computer's hard drive

Add Media ▾ | **Project Assets ▾**

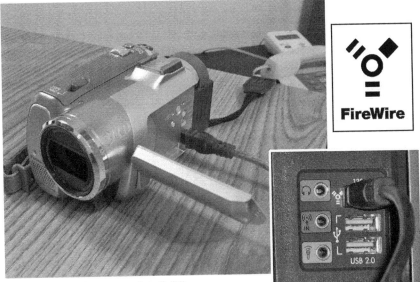

A MiniDV camcorder connected via FireWire.

Capture MiniDV, HDV Video or video from Webcams or WDM Devices

The process of capturing video to Premiere Elements is virtually the same, whether you're capturing from a miniDV camcorder, an HDV (hi-definition) camcorder or even from a DV bridge (see **Capture through DV bridges and pass-throughs** on page 238), as long as these devices are connected to your computer via FireWire (also known as IEEE-1394 and iLink).

You can also capture video from most Webcams.

1. With your camcorder in VTR mode, connect your camcorder to your computer's FireWire port (as illustrated above).

    When your camcorder is properly connected, powered on and set to play, Windows should register the connection (usually with a "bing-bong" sound effect).

Capture over a FireWire connection

All miniDV camcorders have FireWire connectors, even if they also offer a USB connection.

Our advice is to not bother with the USB connection, even if it means you have to buy your own FireWire cable. A few camcorders and some capture software will work with a USB connection, but with FireWire you'll know for sure you're properly connected.

Firewire is the common term for IEEE-1394 or iLink connections.

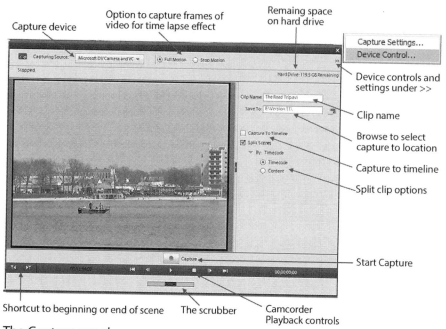

Capture device

Option to capture frames of video for time lapse effect

Remaing space on hard drive

Capture Settings...
Device Control...

Device controls and settings under >>

Clip name

Browse to select capture to location

Capture to timeline

Split clip options

Start Capture

Shortcut to beginning or end of scene   The scrubber   Camcorder Playback controls

The Capture panel   Streaming capture from miniDV, HDV or Webcam

Windows should also launch an option screen offering you a handful of methods for capturing your video, among which Premiere Elements should be listed.

If this is not the case, something is wrong, possibly at a mechanical level, and you'll need to troubleshoot your FireWire connection and camcorder set-up before you proceed. (Troubleshooting steps are listed at the end of this chapter.)

If you have a good connection to your camcorder, cancel out of this Windows option screen and, if you're not already running Premiere Elements, launch the program.

2   In Premiere Elements, click **Add Media**, then select the **DV Camcorder, HDV Camcorder** or **Webcam or WDM** option.

The **Capture** workspace will open, as illustrated above.

If your camcorder (or DV bridge) is properly connected to your computer via FireWire, the panel will show **Capture Device Online** in the upper left corner of the panel and the **Capturing Source** drop-down should list the camcorder or DV bridge you are interfacing with. If not, you may want to try some of the capture troubleshooting steps at the end of this chapter.

With a proper camcorder connection, the playback buttons along the bottom of this panel will remotely control your camcorder. (If you're using a DV bridge or a pass-through, the source device or camcorder isn't connected directly to the computer, so these buttons will have no function.) **Play, Fast Forward, Stop** and **Rewind** you'll recognize immediately. Once you press **Play**, your camcorder's video should display in the panel and the **Play** button should become a **Pause** button.

The ◁ and ▷ buttons to the right of **Rewind** and to the left of **Fast Forward** are incremental advance and rewind buttons. They allow you to advance or back up your camcorder's playback one frame at a time.

The slider under the playback buttons (called a **Scrubber**) allows you to advance or rewind your video at a variety of speeds, depending on how far you push it to the left or right.

At the lower left of the panel are two "shortcut" buttons. Clicking on these buttons will automatically advance or rewind your video to the previous or next scene (the last point at which your camcorder was stopped or paused).

(This shortcut function only works when capturing miniDV, by the way. Not HDV.)

To the right of the screen are the capture options, illustrated above.

Type the name you would like applied to your captured video in the **Clip Name** space. (Premiere Elements will add numbers to the end of this name as it creates new clips during capture.)

You also have the option of designating a location for your captured video for this session. By default, the clips will be saved to the same folder as your project file.

- If the **Capture to Timeline** option is selected, your video will be automatically added directly to your project's timeline as it is captured.

- The **Split Scenes** option allows you to set whether the captured video is broken into clips based on **Timecode** (each time your camcorder was paused or stopped while shooting) or **Content** (when the video content changes significantly). Since, when you're capturing through a DV bridge or pass-through, timecode is not being streamed into your computer from the video device, you cannot split scenes based on timecode while using a DV bridge or pass-through.

  If you select the option to **Split Scenes** in your captured video based on **Content**, the Organizer's **Media Analyzer** will launch automatically once you've finished your capture. Your clips will automatically be **Smart Tagged** and will appear in your **Media** panel as shorter, trimmed clips, based on the changing content of the video.

  For more information on the **Media Analyzer** and its **Smart Tags** function, see page 418 of **Chapter 33, Manage Your Files with the Organizer**.

To capture your tape-based or webcam video:

3   Use the playback controls to locate the segment you want to capture, pause your tape, then click the red **Capture** button.

4   When you want to stop your capture, click the **Stop Capture** button.

When the Stop Motion option is selected at the top of the Capture window and the Time Lapse option is checked at the bottom of the window, and you click the Set Time button, a panel will open in which you can set your capture to either grab frames from your video at regular intervals (Frequency) or change the speed of your video to fit a specific time (Duration).

Finally, at the top center of the **Capture** panel, you'll note that you have the option of capturing your video in **Full Motion** or **Stop Motion**.

The **Stop Motion** option will allow you to set up your capture so that it grabs frames from your video at regular intervals, rather than as a continuous stream – the result being that the video will play very fast, as a "time lapse" sequence when placed on your timeline.

Set your **Stop Motion**, for instance, to capture only one frame every 30 frames, and your captured video will seem to play at *30 times* normal speed.

This is great for showing clouds rolling through the sky or the sun quickly rising and setting, or a flower opening in mere seconds. Great visual effects, even if it does mean you go through a lot of tape to get a very short sequence!

Get standard DV from an HDV Camcorder

Just because you're shooting your tape-based video in high-definition, it does not necessarily mean you'll need to edit it in high-definition.

And, unless you're planning to output your video as a BluRay disc or other high-definition media file, you can achieve excellent results on a standard DVD by *downsampling* your HDV video to standard DV within your camcorder before you capture it into Premiere Elements.

To capture downsampled video from your camcorder, connect your HDV camcorder to your computer via FireWire and set your camcorder to **DV** (called **iLink Conversion** or **DV Lock** on some brands), then capture it into your Premiere Elements project (using standard DV project settings) as if from a miniDV camcorder. The video quality, although no longer in high-definition, will remain excellent, usually much better than you would get from a regular miniDV video.

The overall quality of the results – compared to video captured in HDV and downsampled by Premiere Elements on output – will not be significantly better. However, working with standard DV puts a lot less demand on your system's resources, so you're likely to find it a much faster and more efficient workflow.

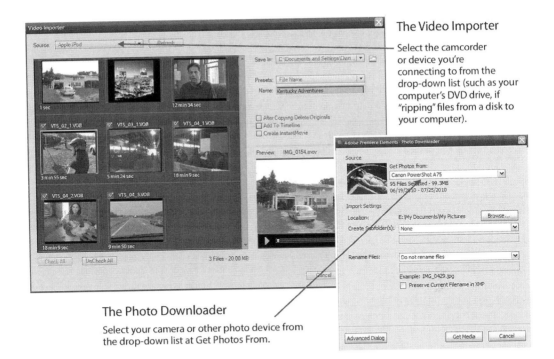

The Video Importer

Select the camcorder or device you're connecting to from the drop-down list (such as your computer's DVD drive, if "ripping" files from a disk to your computer).

The Photo Downloader

Select your camera or other photo device from the drop-down list at Get Photos From.

Add video from DVDs and DVD Camcorders

Video from sources other than miniDV and HDV camcorders – including video from DVD camcorders and hard drive camcorders – is not captured into Premiere Elements the way miniDV is. That is, it's not *streamed* in and captured in real time, as miniDV and HDV video are.

Rather, video from non-tape sources, is *downloaded* into your computer and your Premiere Elements project using Adobe's **Video Importer** or **Photo Downloader** software.

To get video from a DVD or DVD camcorder:

1   Place the DVD into your computer's DVD drive

   Note that discs from DVD camcorders must be *finalized* before Premiere Elements can rip the video from them.

2   Select the **DVD Camera or Computer Drive** option from the **Add Media** panel.

   This will launch the **Video Importer,** as illustrated above.

3   Select your computer's DVD drive from the **Source** drop-down menu at the top of the **Video Importer.**

4   Click the **Browse** button to indicate where on your computer you'd like to save the DVD's files, then click the **Add Media** button at the bottom of the panel to rip the video files to your hard drive.

Add video from Hard Drive and Flash Drive Camcorders

As with video from DVDs and DVD camcorders, the video from hard drive and flash drive camcorders is *downloaded*, rather than captured, into Premiere Elements.

To get video from these types of camcorders

1   Connect your camcorder to your computer with a USB cable.

2   Select the **Videos from Flip or Cameras** option from the **Add Media** panel.

    This will launch the **Video Importer**, as illustrated on page 235.

3   Select your camcorder from the **Source** drop-down menu at the top of the **Video Importer.**

4   Click the **Browse** button to indicate where on your computer you'd like to save the captured files, then click the **Add Media** button at the bottom of the panel to download your video.

Add video from Flip camcorders, iPads, iPods, phones and other portable devices

Flip camcorders plug directly into your computer's USB port. As with hard drive camcorders, the video from Flip camcorders is *downloaded* rather than streamed or captured into Premiere Elements.

1   Connect your Flip camcorder or other video device to your computer's USB port.

2   Select the **Videos from Flip or Cameras** option from the **Add Media** panel.

    This will launch the **Video Importer**, as illustrated on page 235.

3   Select your media recording device (Flip, smartphone, iPod, etc.) from the **Source** drop-down menu at the top of the **Video Importer.**

4   Click the **Browse** button to indicate where on your computer you'd like to save the captured files, then click the **Add Media** button at the bottom of the panel to download your video.

Add video from AVCHD camcorders

As with other hard drive camcorders, the video from AVCHD camcorders is *downloaded* rather than streamed or captured into Premiere Elements.

1   Connect your AVCHD camcorder to your computer's USB port.

2   Select the **Videos from Flip or Cameras** option from the **Add Media** panel.

    This will launch the **Video Importer**, as illustrated on page 235.

3   Select your camcorder from the **Source** drop-down menu at the top of the **Video Importer.**

4   Click the **Browse** button to indicate where on your computer you'd like to save the captured files, then click the **Add Media** button at the bottom of the panel to download your video.

Add video from DSLR still cameras and other devices

Premiere Elements Media Downloader can also download media from other devices, including mobile phones.

1   Connect your device to your computer's USB port.

2   Select the **Videos from Flip or Cameras** option from the **Add Media** panel.
    This will launch the **Video Importer,** as illustrated on page 235.

3   Select your USB-connected device from the **Source** drop-down menu at the top of the **Video Importer.**

4   Click the **Browse** button to indicate where on your computer you'd like to save the captured files, then click the **Add Media** button at the bottom of the panel to download your video.

Add stills from digital cameras and cell phones

1   Connect your still camera to your computer's USB port.

2   Select the **Photos from Cameras or Devices** option from the **Add Media** panel.
    This will launch the **Photo Downloader** as illustrated on page 235.

3   From the **Add Media From** drop-down menu at the top of the **Photo Downloader,** select your camera or other device.

4   Click the **Browse** button to indicate where on your computer you'd like to save the captured files, then click the **Add Media** button at the bottom of the panel to download your video or photos.

As we indicate in **Use photos in your Premiere Elements project** on page 240, for best results your still photos should be resized to an optimal, video resolution size.

Add media from your PC files and folders

To load video, audio or stills already on your computer into your Premiere Elements project:

1   Select the **Files and Folders** option on the **Add Media** panel, or select the **Elements Organizer** option to launch the Elements Organizer program (see **Chapter 33**).

2   Browse to the file(s) you'd like to import on your hard drive.
    Alternatively, you can locate the media in the Organizer's **Media Browser** and simply drag the video, photos, music or audio directly from it to Premiere Elements.

You can also quickly open a browse screen from which to import your media files by **double-clicking** on a blank space (beyond the media listings) in the **Project Assets** panel.

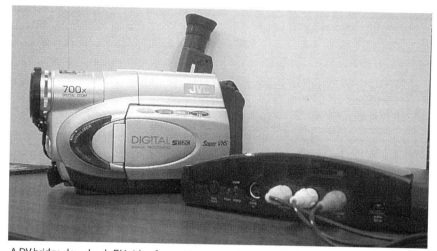

A DV bridge downloads DV video from a VHS camcorder over a FireWire connection.

Capture analog video through DV bridges and pass-throughs

There's a difference between a DV bridge and a plain old capture device or capture card. Capture devices merely digitize your video input to any of a number of video formats. DV bridges, on the other hand, are specifically designed to **convert any video and audio input into DV-AVI files**, the preferred video format for PC-based video editors. (Macs also prefer DV video, although they are saved as DV Quicktime files [MOVs] rather than AVIs. The video data content, however, is identical.)

DV bridges range from relatively inexpensive to high-end professional devices with time base correction and other video optimizers. The best value on the market in DV bridges and a Muvipix recommended "best buy" is the **Canopus ADVC Converter**, a favorite of many videographers.

(Another great DV bridge device that's technically been discontinued but can still be found on the web is the **ADS Pyro AV Link**. Because this device is discontinued, it can be often found for as little as $100 on sites like eBay.)

The **Canopus ADVC** will take any AV input (a camcorder, a DVD player, a VCR or virtually any other video source, including live video) and port it into your computer as a high-quality DV-AVI or, on a Mac, DV-MOV file. This great device can be had for a street price of about $200, a great value if you plan to edit a lot of video from non-DV sources.

Capturing video from a DV bridge is easy. Just plug your camcorder's, DVD player's or VCR's AV cables (RCA jacks) into the DV bridge's inputs and plug the bridge (connected by FireWire) into your computer.

Your computer will recognize the device just as it would a miniDV camcorder connection.

The capture process itself is essentially the same as capture from a miniDV camcorder. The only difference is, since there's no direct connection between your video source device and the computer, you won't be able to control the device with the **Capture Monitor's** playback controls or break scenes by timecode.

But, once you've got the device cued up to the segment you want to capture, you just click the **Capture** button and you're good to go!

By the way, the **Canopus ADVC** can also be used with DVD camcorders and hard drive camcorders, so it's a great way to make any non-miniDV video 100% Premiere Elements compatible.

An alternative to a DV bridge is a set-up called a **pass-through**, which essentially uses a miniDV camcorder as a makeshift DV bridge.

To set up a pass-through connection, attach your non-DV camcorder to your miniDV camcorder via its AV input cables, then link the miniDV to your computer via FireWire.

With the miniDV camcorder in play mode (but without a tape inside) the non-DV camcorder's video flows through the miniDV and into the computer, where it's captured as DV-AVIs.

The biggest challenge to using this method is that fewer and fewer new miniDV camcorders support a pass-through connection. And it's very difficult to learn, from most spec sheets, which camcorders do.

But, if your miniDV camcorder is pass-through capable, this is a simple and effective method of digitizing almost any analog video input.

Convert non-DV-AVI files

For the cleanest results and smoothest operation in Premiere Elements, we recommend that, whenever you are working in standard definition, you use exclusively DV-AVIs as source files for your standard video projects.

If you're not shooting your video on a miniDV or an HDV camcorder, this may present a bit of a challenge. However, there are a number of very easy to use, very *free* programs available for converting almost any file to a DV-AVI, and we've listed a couple in **Chapter 32**.

A favorite program for converting MPEGs and VOB files to DV-AVIs is the free utility **Super Video Converter**, from eRight Software. Instructions for downloading and using this program appear in **Chapter 32, A Premiere Elements Appendix**.

This process of converting may seem a bit inconvenient at first. But the trade-offs in terms of improved performance, trouble-free operation and higher quality outputs from Premiere Elements will very soon convince you that it's well worth the little extra effort.

Premiere Elements will function most efficiently if your photos are no larger than 1000x750 pixels.

Use photos in Premiere Elements

Premiere Elements can work with virtually any of the major photo or graphics formats, including JPEGs, GIFs, TIFs, vector art (EPSs and AI files) and PSDs (native Photoshop and Photoshop Elements files).

The exceptions are images using the CMYK color mode or RGB photo files using other than standard 8-bit color. But, if you are creating your graphics or using photos from a consumer graphics program (such as Photoshop Elements) or from a digital camera, scanner or other device, then you don't need to worry about these exceptions. Virtually all photo and graphics files from these sources are compatible with the program.

Premiere Elements will also support transparency (alpha channels) so that file formats like GIF, PNG, EPS, AI and PSD files with transparent areas will display, when used in a video project, with these areas transparent.

This is particularly useful if you're using one of these graphics file types on an upper video track with a video layer behind it (see **Use L-cuts, J-cuts and multiple tracks** on page 266 of **Chapter 20, Edit Your Movie in Timeline Mode**) or as a graphic added to a title (see **Add a graphic to your title** on page 319 of **Chapter 25, Add Titles & Text**).

Photos make great source files for a Premiere Elements project, but you'll find the highest quality results and the best performance from the program if the sizes of your photos are properly optimized before you bring them into your project.

We urge you to make sure that any photo you use (especially if you use several in a slideshow) has been resized to no larger than 1000x750 pixels before you bring it into your Premiere Elements project to ensure the best quality and optimal program performance. (Photos taken directly from digital cameras can be 20 to 25 times that size!)

At first this may seem to go contrary to common wisdom.

Traditionally, the higher the resolution of your photo, the better the quality of the output. But remember that Premiere Elements is a *video* editing program, and video is a relatively low resolution medium (essentially the equivalent of 640x480 pixels). And, to a point, reducing the resolution of a photo or graphic to be used in a video actually *improves* the quality of the video output. (1000x750 pixels seems to be that point).

The reason for this has to do with a process called downsampling, the system a video program uses to bring high-resolution photos down to video size. Premiere Elements does a fair job of this – but, as any pro knows, nothing that happens automatically will be as clean or as efficient as what you do manually. "Down-rezzing" is definitely one of those things.

There's also a more pressing reason for downsampling your photos yourself. The process of "down-rezzing," like the process of assimilating non-DV-AVI files into a video project, is a very intensive process. So intensive, in fact, that it is *the single biggest reason Premiere Elements crashes*, particularly during the disc burning process.

It also takes a lot longer for the program to down-rez, for instance, a 4000x3000 pixel photo than it does a 1000x750 pixel photo.

Much, much longer. And would you rather wait an hour or two for the program to create your DVD or 10 hours for a process that might end up with the program choking and dying anyway?

Trust us on this. Optimize your photo sizes to 1000x750 pixels before you import them into Premiere Elements. It will save you hours of anguish and misery in the end. (For high-definition video projects, you can go as large as 2000x1500 pixels.)

Graphics and photo formats for Premiere Elements projects

For photos, the most size-efficient file format is the JPEG. As an alternative, PSD files and TIFs use less compression and, though larger, also produce excellent results.

Because JPEGs are highly compressed, they do not make the best format for graphics that include clean, distinct edges, such as logos or graphics that include text. In these cases, PSDs, TIFs, AIs, EPSs and even PNGs produce the crispest lines.

Photoshop Elements, by the way, has a very nice batch resizing feature that can resize a whole folder full of photos in just a few clicks. This feature is called **Process Multiple Files**, and it is located under the Photoshop Elements **File** menu.

Also, *before* you do bring those photos into your video project, go to Premiere Elements' **Preferences/General** (under the program's **Edit** menu on a PC) and uncheck **Default Scale to Frame Size**.

Left checked, **Scale to Frame Size** automatically sizes your photo to fill your video frame, giving a false representation of your photo in the video frame in addition to really getting in the way when you're trying to add motion paths to your photos.

In the event this option was checked when you imported your photos into your project, you can also turn it off for your photos individually by **right-clicking** on each photo on the timeline (**Ctrl-clicking** on the Mac) and unchecking the **Scale to Frame Size** option on the pop-up menu.

For information on applying flicker removal to the photos and still graphics in your Premiere Elements project, see **Add still photos to your project** on page 264 of **Chapter 20, Edit Your Project in Expert View**.

Add music files to a Premiere Elements project

Although Premiere Elements works with a variety of audio file formats, it's probably best to exclusively use **WAVs** as your source files.

They seem to provide the most trouble-free operation.

Also one word of warning, in connection with using music files in your video projects: Many music download sites (iTunes, for instance) employ electronic **Digital Rights Management** (DRM) in their downloaded files.

This DRM system will throw up an error code if you try to load a copy-protected music file into your Premiere Elements project, blocking you from using the file. (Because many music sites, like Amazon.com, don't use such stringent DRM, even iTunes has relaxed theirs more in recent years – so these error codes are becoming less of a problem.)

There is software available on the Web for breaking this DRM. But probably the easiest way to get around this copy protection is to burn the music file to a CD and then use a program like Windows Media Player to rip the CD music file back to your computer as an MP3. The resultant MP3 should load right into Premiere Elements.

This process, of course, doesn't exempt you from respecting the rights of the artist who created the music. So please don't abuse the privilege.

Troubleshoot Windows video capture in Premiere Elements

Video capture from a miniDV or HDV tape-based camcorder seems like it should be easy. And, since you can't do anything in Premiere Elements until you have your video captured into your computer, when capture fails it can be very frustrating!

I wish I could tell you that there was a magic bullet for making all the problems go away, but sometimes there just is no simple fix.

The following, though, can help you troubleshoot your problems. And, if they don't work, the third-party solutions we recommend below will get you through the day (and may ultimately become your preferred workflow!)

1   Before you blame the software, make sure your operating system and its components are optimized and up to date. Following the maintenance regimen on page 395 of **Chapter 32, a Premiere Elements Appendix** – which includes ensuring that your operating system, its firmware and drivers are up to date – is essential to the smooth operation of a process as intensive as video editing!

Remember, you're using a very intensive program on an operating system that's constantly changing, updating and evolving. Like a race car driver who knows that even a few pounds of pressure in one tire can mean the difference between a stable ride and one fraught with problems, you should always make sure your computer's operating system is in perfect working order.

The Windows 7 Legacy Driver Fix

For some reason, the stock drivers for Windows 7's IEEE-1394 connection can be problematic for people trying to capture video. Your camcorder may not even be recognized.

If this is the case for you, there's a pretty simple trick that seems to fix the vast majority of miniDV and HDV connection problems:

1   Click the Windows **Start** orb and type "device manager" into the search box – then select **Device Manager** from the list of programs offered.

2   On the **Device Manager**, swivel open the **IEEE 1394 Bus Host Controllers**.

3   Right-click on your listed 1394 controller and select **Update Driver Software**.

4   Click the **Browse my computer for driver software** button, then **Let me pick from a list**.

5   Select the option that has **(Legacy)** at the end of the name. Click **Next.** The legacy driver will be installed.

6   Close out of the dialog panels and retry your capture.

And always make sure you have the latest version of **Quicktime** and the newest **RealTek drivers** on your system! This may not seem like an obvious solutions to your problems, but more times than not, a simple update makes all the difference.

2   As mentioned earlier in the chapter, if your operating system isn't even registering your camcorder as connected, you're dealing with a more fundamental problem than a Premiere Elements issue.

Check your connections. Make sure your camcorder is set up right for capture (i.e., is in VTR/play mode). Possibly even check the camcorder on another computer to see whether it's the computer, the FireWire cable or even your particular camcorder that's failing.

3   Make sure you're using a FireWire/IEEE-1394/iLink connection for capture. Some miniDV camcorders also offer a USB connection – but, most of the time, they won't work with Premiere Elements. Trust us on this. You want a FireWire connection if it is at all possible.

4   If all connections are working and Windows recognizes your camcorder but Premiere Elements doesn't, note the auto-launch window that Windows opens when you plug your camcorder into your computer.

Which software does it offer to launch to capture your video?

Some software (such as Nero) is less willing to share capture devices with any other software. And sometimes that means, unfortunately, that capturing directly into Premiere Elements may simply not be possible – at least not without way more work than it's worth. In that case, you may want to consider our third-party solutions below.

5   If all seems to be in order and Premiere Elements still isn't recognizing your camcorder, click on the pop-up menu button on the upper right corner of your **Capture** panel.

Select the **Device Control** option and, from the panel that opens, click on the **Options** button.

This button will open another panel in which you can set the program to the exact brand and model of camcorder or DV bridge you're connected to. (There are **Standard** settings also, in the event your camcorder model isn't listed.)

In all honesty, changing these settings rarely revives a dead camcorder connection. However, it can "refine" a connection in which the camcorder is recognized but capture doesn't seem to be going quite right.

Finally, if none of these solutions works, you can use a third-party capture solution. Page 400 of **Chapter 32** lists some great resources for free or low-cost **Capture Utilities** that can help.

Our personal favorite capture software utility for miniDV capture is **WinDV**. This free and fully-loaded capture utility will often work even when nothing else seems to (assuming Windows sees the camcorder connection).

Like Premiere Elements itself, WinDV captures miniDV video in small DV-AVI clips that are perfectly compatible with Premiere Elements and other editors.

Other options include the low-cost **Scenalyzer** and the absolutely free **Windows MovieMaker** (included with your Windows operating system). Both will capture your miniDV files in the DV-AVI format, which you can then import into your Premiere Elements project.

For high-definition video, **HDVSplit** is, like WinDV, free and yet very stable and nicely featured.

Because of the stability, reliability and sometimes extra features included with these free or low-cost utilities, many of our Premiere Elements users actually *prefer* to capture with these third-party applications and save Premiere Elements for what it does best.

Editing video!

The Project Assets Panel

Color Bars and Countdown Leaders

The Clip Monitor

The Create Slideshow Tool

Chapter 19

Explore the Project Assets Panel

The parts that will form your movie

In Expert view, Project Assets is the panel into which you will gather the video, still photos, music and audio that you will use to create your movie.

In the Project Assets panel, you can arrange and categorize your project's media and then pre-trim it prior to adding it to your timeline.

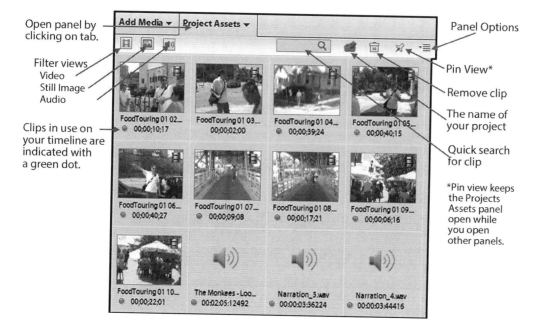

Open panel by clicking on tab.

Filter views
Video
Still Image
Audio

Clips in use on your timeline are indicated with a green dot.

Panel Options

Pin View*

Remove clip

The name of your project

Quick search for clip

*Pin view keeps the Projects Assets panel open while you open other panels.

Only available in Expert view, the **Project Assets** panel is the area where you gather the media you've captured, downloaded or imported into your project.

The **Project Assets** panel is opened by clicking on the **Project Assets** button on the upper left of the program's interface.

But in addition to serving as a holding area for your video project's media, this panel includes a number of great tools for managing, ordering and preparing your clips for your movie's timeline.

Where are my Project Assets in Quick view?

Quick View does not include a **Project Assets** panel.

Because your media is added directly to your timeline in Quick View and the **Project Assets** panel is not visible.

However, Expert and Quick View are actually just two views of the same project. Media files added directly to your timeline in Quick View are added to the Project Assets panel automatically.

So, if you switch from Quick view to Expert view while working on your project, you will find that any media you've added to your Quick View timeline has automatically been added to that project's Expert View **Project Assets** also.

Project Asset views

By default, the media clips in your **Project Assets** panel are displayed in **Grid View**– video and stills displaying as thumbnails and music and other audio displaying as speaker icons. Below the title for each clip is an indicator of the clip's duration (measured in hours, minutes, seconds and frames). Clips used in your movie project are indicated with a little green dot.

To switch your **Project Assets** to **List View**, click on the **Panel Options** button in the upper right of the panel and select **View**, as illustrated to the right.

The Panel Options menu on the top right of the panel allows you to switch views for your assets.

Filters can set to display only video, stills and/or audio.

In **List View**, your media clips appear in a list with columns listing their **Media Type, Frame Rate** and **Duration**. In the **Used** column, a little blue dot indicates that your clip is in use on your timeline and the **Video Usage** column indicates how many times your clip appears in your movie.

The clip listing can be re-ordered by clicking on the column header for any column. For instance, clicking on the **Media Duration** column header will list your clips according to the length of each clip. Clicking on a column header a second time will reverse the order for that column's listing.

In the upper left of the panel are three buttons for toggling on and off which media are displayed in the panel. If you toggle on the **Video** button, for instance, and you toggle off the **Still Image** and **Audio** buttons, you will set the panel to display *only* the video in your project and hide the other two types of media files.

Organize your media files with folders

This is one of my favorite Premiere Elements features, extremely valuable when you're trying to sort through a large number of media files.

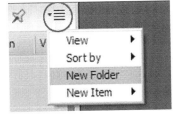

Folders allow you to sort the clips in your **Project Assets** panel into little bundles, like directories on your computer, making it easier to keep all the clips you'll need for a given segment of your project in one neat little place.

To create a folder, select the **New Folder** option under the **Panel Options** menu at the upper right of the panel. (You can also select the option from a context menu when you **right-click** on an empty area of the **Project Asset** panel.)

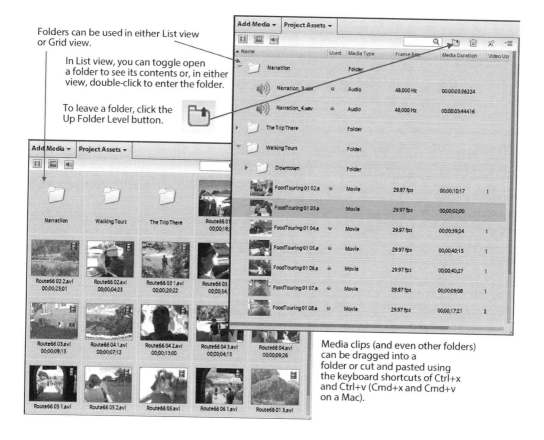

Folders can be used in either List view or Grid view.

In List view, you can toggle open a folder to see its contents or, in either view, double-click to enter the folder.

To leave a folder, click the Up Folder Level button.

Media clips (and even other folders) can be dragged into a folder or cut and pasted using the keyboard shortcuts of Ctrl+x and Ctrl+v (Cmd+x and Cmd+v on a Mac).

Once you have a folder created, you can drag your media files into it – sorting your clips so that all of your files for a particular sequence of your project are in the same folder, for instance.

You can even create sub-folders within your folders – and even sub-sub-folders! – so that it becomes very easy to manage and locate the files you need without having to scroll through a long list of clips.

Even as you're editing, you can drag your media clips around, and in and out, of folders to get them out of your way without affecting their positions or function on your timeline.

Delete clips from your Project Assets panel

There are two ways to remove a clip from your project:

Right-click on the clip in **Project Assets** and select **Clear**; or

Select a clip in **Project Assets** and press your keyboard's **Delete** key.

Either way, the media clip will be removed from your project – though it will *not* be deleted from your computer's hard drive.

Create color mattes, bars and tone and countdown leaders

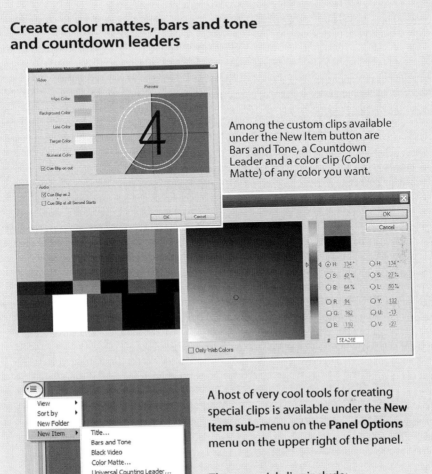

Among the custom clips available under the New Item button are Bars and Tone, a Countdown Leader and a color clip (Color Matte) of any color you want.

A host of very cool tools for creating special clips is available under the **New Item** sub-menu on the **Panel Options** menu on the upper right of the panel.

These special clips include:

Title launches the Premiere Elements **Titles & Text** workspace. We explore this tool in much greater detail in **Chapter 25, Add Titles & Text.**

Bars and Tone creates a clip of bars and audio tone, which broadcasters often require at the beginning of every video in order to calibrate their equipment to your movie's sound levels and color profile.

Black Video and **Color Matte** create blank clips of whatever color you designate. These clips can then be used behind titles or as blank spaces in your video.

Universal Countdown Leader creates a customizable countdown sequence (including an audio "blip" at two seconds) which can be placed at the beginning of your video – another feature broadcasters often require so that they can cue up the beginning of your movie.

Pre-trim your clips in the Clip Monitor

The **Clip Monitor** is a pop-up screen for previewing playback of a clip. It's also a work area in which you can pre-trim a clip prior to adding it to your project's timeline by setting **In** and/or **Out** markers.

The **Clip Monitor** can be used to trim clips in the **Project Assets** panel or clips that have already been added to your timeline.

A clip's **Clip Monitor** is launched either by **right-clicking** on the clip (**Ctrl-clicking** on a Mac) and selecting the **Open in Clip Monitor** option – or by simply **double-clicking** on the clip.

Running along the bottom of the **Clip Monitor** is a little timeline representing the duration of the clip.

As illustrated on the facing page, when you set **In** or **Out** markers in your **Clip Monitor**, only the segment of the clip between those markers will be displayed during the clip's playback in your movie.

In other words, if you have a 5-minute clip, you can set the **In** and **Out** markers so that only a 30-second segment of the clip is actually displayed in your movie – rendering the clip essentially a 30-second clip.

In the **Clip Monitor**, the "live" segment of the clip is indicated with a lighter, blue segment area on the **Clip Monitor's** mini-timeline. You can adjust this live area's length by either dragging the end points in or out, or by playing the clip using the playback controls at the bottom of the **Clip Monitor** and clicking on the **Set In** or **Set Out** buttons to isolate the segment you want to use.

The **In** and **Out** markers in the **Clip Monitor** can be used to isolate segments in audio clips as well as video.

You can not set **In** and **Out** markers on titles and still images, however, because they are stationary elements.

Take a shortcut to "Add Media"

If you want to import additional media from your computer into your Premiere Elements project, or if you want to launch a video capture without leaving the **Project Assets** panel, there is a shortcut to the **Add Media** option menu built right into the panel.

As illustrated at the top of page 254, if you **right-click** on a *blank* area of the **Project Assets** panel (**Ctrl-click** on a Mac), beyond your media listings, you will have access to the same **Add Media** options as are available on the **Add Media** panel.

Additionally, you can quickly open a browse screen so that you can import media already on your computer by simply **double-clicking** on a blank area after your **Project Assets** panel's listings.

The Clip Monitor launches when you double-click on any clip on the timeline or in the Project Assets panel.

Clips can be trimmed in the Clip Monitor either by dragging the in and out points on the mini-timeline or by playing the clip and clicking the Set In and Set Out buttons.

Although the original clip remains its original length, only the "trimmed" segment (the blue highlighted segment in Premiere Elements) will display when the clip is placed on the timeline.

Once the **Clip Monitor** has been launched, it will stay open as long as you keep your project open or until you manually close it.

Because this panel tends to pop up in the middle of the workspace whenever it launches, I usually launch it as soon as I open a project. Then I position it off to the side, out of the way, and leave it open. That way, if I later need to open a clip in this panel for previewing or trimming, the **Clip Monitor** will play this clip where I've positioned it instead of in the middle of my work.

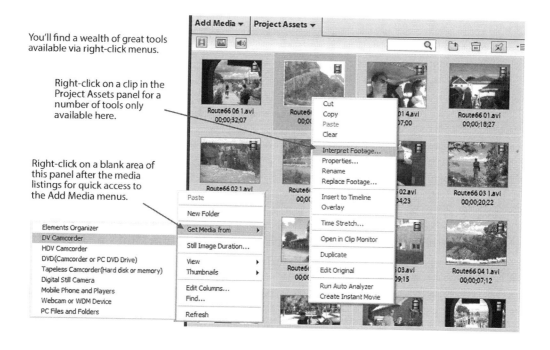

You'll find a wealth of great tools available via right-click menus.

Right-click on a clip in the Project Assets panel for a number of tools only available here.

Right-click on a blank area of this panel after the media listings for quick access to the Add Media menus.

Valuable Project Assets panel right-click tools

There are a number of great tools available throughout Premiere Elements that can be (and sometimes can *only* be) accessed by **right-clicking** on clips or in panels (or **Ctrl-clicking** on a Mac).

I do a thorough discussion of these tools in my *Steve's Tips* article "Powerful Tools in Premiere Elements' Right-Click Menus," available on the Muvipix.com product pages.

Here are a couple of my favorite right-click tools available exclusively in the **Project Assets** panel.

Interpret Footage – Believe it or not, standard 4:3 video and widescreen 16:9 video use exactly the same number of pixels to create a video frame. The difference is that the pixels (the tiny squares of color that combine to create every frame of video) are shaped differently. Widescreen 16:9 pixels are much wider than standard 4:3 video pixels.

Right-clicking on a clip (**Ctrl-clicking** on a Mac) and selecting **Interpret Footage** gives you access to options for conforming a widescreen clip to fit in a standard video or vice versa.

This tool is invaluable if, for some reason, you find yourself with a clip that looks strangely squished, stretched or distorted (as when you add a 16:9 video to a 4:3 project).

Duplicate – This selection makes a duplicate of the clip you've right-clicked on. This is very helpful, for instance, if you've created a title slide with a style you'd like to re-use. You merely **duplicate** it and then revise the duplicate as needed. (Also see **Duplicate a title** on page 320.)

Rename – You can rename a clip by selecting this **right-click** option or by simply double-clicking slowly on the name of the file in the **Project Assets** panel listing so that the name becomes highlighted. Renaming a clip doesn't change the name of the file on your hard drive, by the way. Nor does it affect the clip's position or function on the timeline. But it can make it easier for you to identify the file later.

Create a slideshow in the Project Assets panel

One of my favorite "hidden" features in the Premiere Elements **Project Assets** panel is the **Create Slideshow** tool.

To access this great little tool, select a number of clips or stills from the **Project Assets** panel (by holding down the **Ctrl** or **Shift** key as you select) and then **right-click** on the selected clips (**Ctrl-click** on a Mac) and select **Create Slideshow**.

As you can see below, in the illustration of the **Create Slideshow** option screen, you can set the **Ordering** of your slides in a couple of ways.

> **Sort Order.** In **Sort Order**, the **Slideshow Creator** places your slides in the same order as they appear listed in the **Project Assets** panel.

> **Selection Order.** In **Selection Order**, the **Slideshow Creator** places your slides according to the order you click-selected them in the **Project Assets** panel.

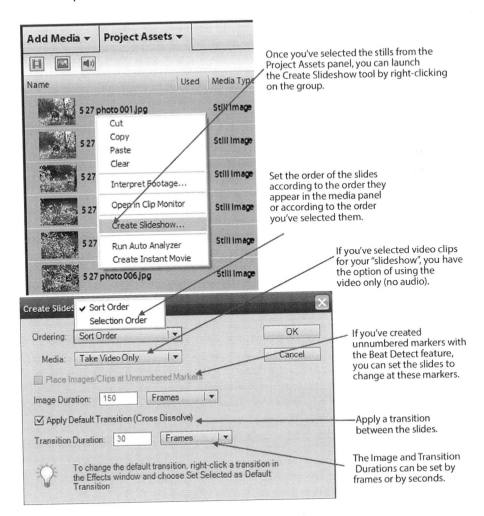

Once you've selected the stills from the Project Assets panel, you can launch the Create Slideshow tool by right-clicking on the group.

Set the order of the slides according to the order they appear in the media panel or according to the order you've selected them.

If you've selected video clips for your "slideshow", you have the option of using the video only (no audio).

If you've created unnumbered markers with the Beat Detect feature, you can set the slides to change at these markers.

Apply a transition between the slides.

The Image and Transition Durations can be set by frames or by seconds.

On the **Create Slideshow** option screen, you also have a number of ways to set the duration of your slides:

Image Duration. You can set your slides to change after a designated interval of time.

Unnumbered Markers. You can set them to change at **Unnumbered Markers** on the **Timeline** (For more information on **Unnumbered Markers**, see **Detect beats in your music** on page 361 of **Chapter 29, Mix Your Audio and Add Music**).

You can use either video or still clips in your slideshow – although only stills can be set to change at a given duration or at the unnumbered markers created by the **Detect Beats** tool.

If you use video clips in your slideshow, the **Create Slideshow** panel includes the option to remove the audio from the clips, as illustrated on the previous page.

You can also select the option to apply a **Default Transition** between your slides. (For information on designating the **Default Transition**, see page 306 of **Chapter 24, Add and Customize Transitions**.)

For information on how to optimize your stills for a slideshow, see **Use photos in Premiere Elements** on page 240 of **Chapter 18, Add Media to Your Project**.

There are actually a number of different ways to create a slideshow in Premiere Elements, including a **Create Slideshow** tool built into the Elements Organizer (see page 436) and **InstantMovie** slideshow themes. (For more information on creating **InstantMovies**, see **Chapter 21**.)

For more information on the tools and other methods of creating slideshows using features in both Premiere Elements, Photoshop Elements and the Elements Organizer – and the advantages of each – see my *Steve's Tips* article "Creating Slideshows with Photoshop Elements and Premiere Elements," available on the products page at Muvipix.com.

Adding Clips to Your Timeline

Auto Enhancing Your Clips

Splitting and Trimming Your Clips

Working with Multiple Tracks of Video

Rendering Your Timeline

Chapter 20

Edit Your Video in Expert View

Where your movie comes together

The Expert View timeline is where your clips are gathered, ordered, trimmed, split, rearranged, and where effects are applied. It's where your movie finally comes together – just as in Quick View.

But Expert View gives you a much more powerful timeline, greater access to your clips and more professional-level tools for working with them.

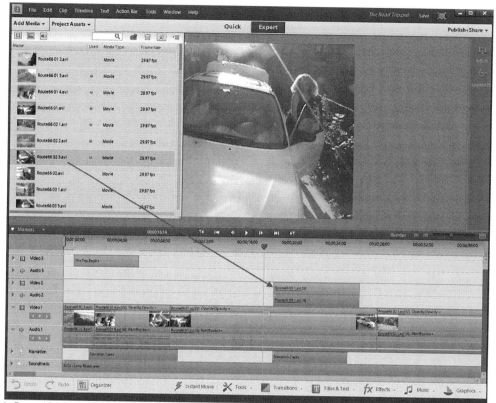

In Expert View, your clips are dragged from the Project Assets panel to any of up to 99 audio and/or video tracks. Transitions are added to points at which clips meet.

Expert View in Premiere Elements is the more professional-style workspace.

There are three main differences between the Quick View and the Expert View timelines:

> In Expert View, media is added to **Project Assets** panel before it is brought to the timeline. In the **Project Assets** panel, your media can be more easily managed and even pre-trimmed before it is added to the timeline. (For more information on the **Project Assets** panel, see **Chapter 19.**)

> While Quick View is limited to four tracks, the Expert View timeline includes the option for up to 99 tracks of video and up to 99 tracks of audio. Multi-track editing allows for some effects that are virtually impossible in Quick View.

> In Expert View, video and audio clips can be manipulated at specific points using keyframing right on the timeline, allowing you to create and control fade ins or outs and, more importantly, allowing you to control and mix audio levels at specific points using keyframing (see page 356).

Nonetheless, Quick View and Expert View are still just two faces of the same project. In other words, you can switch between the two views as needed as you develop your timeline, taking advantage of the benefits of each view as you work.

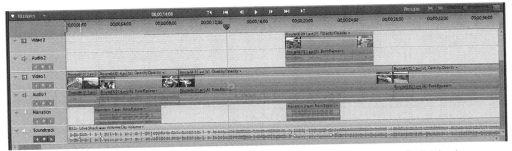

Expert View allows for multiple tracks of audio and video and gives you greater access to each clip's levels.

Override the timeline ripple function

The timeline in Premiere Elements is set, by default, to **"ripple"** as you add and remove clips from your project.

In other words, as you add and remove clips, the other clips on the timeline will move left or right to allow for inserted footage or to fill gaps.

- When you **Delete** a clip from your project, the clips to the right will slide to the left to fill in the gap (unless there is a clip filling this gap on a parallel track).

- When you **Insert** a clip into an assemblage of clips – even if on a parallel video or audio track – the clips to the right of that clip on the timeline will **split** and move further right to accommodate the new clip.

In most cases, rippling will work to your advantage. If you've got an assemblage of audio and video clips in your movie and you decide to reorder it or add a clip to the middle of your project, you'll want the rest of the clips in your movie to stay in relative position, moving as a group to allow for the inserted clip.

But there may also be times when you'll want to override this ripple function – as when you've assembled a movie and you're trying to add background music to it or you want to add a video clip to the middle of your movie without changing the positions of any of its other clips.

Holding down the Ctrl key on a PC or the ⌘ key on a Mac as you add your new clip(s) to your timeline will override this ripple function.

When you override the ripple function, the rest of your clips will remain locked in their positions on your timeline as you add your new clip, and you'll be able to place your music on an audio track – or any clip on any other audio or video track – without disturbing the rest of your movie.

Particularly, if you're doing multi-track editing, holding down this **Ctrl** key on PC or the ⌘ key on a Mac is just about the only way to keep your movie clips in place as you continually add and remove clips on other tracks.

Smart Fix your clips

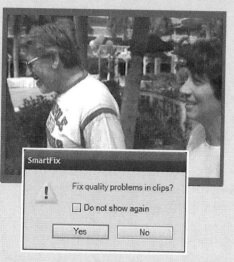

When your clips have been Auto-Analyzed and Smart Tagged, the program will offer to apply a Smart Fix Auto Enhance when you place the clip on your timeline – correcting the contrast and brightness and, if necessary, stabilizing the camera movement.

Premiere Elements includes the option to have the program automatically apply a **Smart Fix** to your clips as you add them to your timeline or sceneline.

When this tool is enabled in the program's **Preferences** (under the **Edit** menu, as discussed below), an option panel will appear each time you add a new clip to your timeline or your sceneline, asking if you would like the program to **"Fix quality problems in your clips?"** (This option panel will only appear if your clips have been **Smart Tagged** prior to your adding them to your project, as discussed on the facing page.)

If you select **Yes**, Premiere Elements will automatically apply the necessary contrast levels to the clip and, if it judges the clip as too shaky, will apply automatic image stabilization!

If the clip is very long and has inconsistent quality issues, the program will even keyframe variations of contrast! (There is no way to set this feature to correct only contrast *or* only stabilization, by the way. Your options are only to have both applied or neither.)

In our experience, the results are usually very good (even if the applied effects mean that the program must then render the clips before they play back smoothly).

This feature can be turned off at any time by checking the **Do Not Show Again** box in the **Smart Fix** pop-up panel, as illustrated above.

To re-activate this feature later, go to **Preferences** (under the program's **Edit** menu on a PC). On the preferences **General** page, check the box that says **Show All Do Not Show Again Messages**.

Smart Fix can also be applied manually to clips that are already on your timeline using the **Smart Fix** tool located on the **Adjustments** panel, as discussed on page 293).

As discussed in the sidebar on the facing page, the automatic **Smart Fix** tool will only be available for clips that have been previously **Smart Tagged**.

Timeline views

Premiere Elements includes a number of features for viewing your timeline, depending on how closely you want to look at your movie.

Using the zoom tool, for instance, you can zoom out to view your entire movie at once – or you can zoom in close enough to see your video's individual frames.

To zoom in or out on your timeline, drag the slider (on the upper right of the **Timeline** panel) left or right – or use the following keyboard shortcuts:

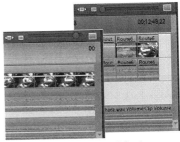

Using the Timeline zoom slider (or your +, – and \ keys) you can zoom out to see your whole project or or zoom in close enough to see individual frames.

 Pressing the **–** key on your keyboard zooms out.

 Pressing the **+** key zooms in.

Pressing the **** key (above the **Enter/Return** key) automatically zooms out to display your entire movie.

To make more efficient use of the panel's vertical space, individual tracks on the Timeline can be toggled between a compressed and an open view.

Open or closed video and audio tracks

In Premiere Elements, you can also toggle the views of the individual tracks on your timeline to display as either open – which allows you to view your video clips as thumbnails and your audio clips as waveforms – or closed, reducing the amount of vertical space the **Timeline** panel requires when you are using multiple tracks of video and audio, as illustrated on the right.

Clips must be Smart Tagged in order to be Smart Fixed

The **Smart Fix** option panel, discussed on the facing page, will appear as you add your clips to your timeline only *if* these clips have been previously **Auto Analyzed**. This is because the **Smart Fix** tool takes its cue from information gathered by the **Media Analyzer/Auto-Analyzer,** an Elements Organizer feature that automatically analyzes and records metadata to your clips based on content and quality issues.

The **Media Analyzer** is set up in the Elements Organizer's **Preferences** (under the program's **Edit** menu on a PC). (For more information, see **The Smart Tags Media Analyzer** on page 418 of **Chapter 33, Manage Your Files with the Elements Organizer.**) In this preference panel, you have the option of setting the **Media Analyzer** to automatically **Smart Tag** every clip in your Organizer catalog, or to only analyze clips meeting specific criteria. On most faster computers, the **Media Analyzer** will work unobtrusively in the background, without interfering with your other editing work, running when you are not working on your computer.

You may, as an alternative to this automatic function, manually prep your clips for **Smart Fix** (or the other Premiere Elements tools that require **Smart Tagging**) by selecting these clips in the Elements Organizer **Media Browser,** either one at a time or several at once, **right-clicking (Ctrl-clicking** on a Mac) and selecting the option to **Run Auto Analyzer** from the context menu.

To add a clip to your timeline, simply drag it from the Project Assets panel.

As you add new clips, the other clips will "ripple", moving aside if you add the clip in the middle of a project.

To override the ripple effect (as when you're adding music or a video clip to a parallel track) hold down the Ctrl key (or the Cmd key on a Mac) as you add the clip to your timeline.

Zoom in or out on the timeline by pressing + or - or using the Zoom slider.

Add clips to your timeline

Adding clips to your project's timeline in Expert View is about as intuitive as it can be. You simply drag the clips from the **Project Assets** panel to a video or audio track.

You can reorder the clips on the timeline by dragging them around. Placing a clip to the left of another clip will cause it to slide it aside ("ripple" it) to accommodate the move. (See page 259 for information on overriding this feature.)

To delete a clip from your timeline, click to select it and press the **Delete** button on your keyboard or **right-click** on it (**Ctrl-click** on a Mac) and select **Delete and Close Gap**. Unless there are clips on parallel video or audio tracks, the timeline will ripple to fill in the gap.

To remove a clip *without* causing the other clips to ripple or fill in the gap, **right-click** on the clip (**Ctrl-click** on a Mac) and select **Delete** instead.

Once your clips are assembled, you can apply transitions between them. More information on this feature can be found in **Chapter 24, Add and Customize Transitions**.

Trim or split your clips

Once a clip is on your timeline, you can edit it to remove unwanted portions by **trimming** and/or **splitting** it.

Trimming removes footage from the beginning or end of a clip.

Splitting divides your clip into smaller segments, which you can then remove or rearrange.

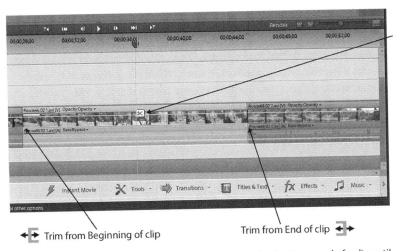

To slice a clip in two, click the scissors icon on the CTI playhead.

If a clip is selected on the timeline, only that clip will be split at the position of the CTI; If no clips are selected, all clips on every track on the timeline will be split at the position of the CTI.

Trim from Beginning of clip

Trim from End of clip

To trim a clip on the timeline, hover your mouse over the beginning or end of a clip until the Trim from Beginning or Trim from End icon appears, then click and drag in or out.

Trim a clip on your timeline

To **trim a clip**, click to select the clip on your timeline and hover your mouse over the clip's beginning or end.

As you hover your mouse over either end of a clip, it will switch to trim mode (becoming a ⬌or a ⬌ cursor). Click and drag the end of the clip to trim it – removing footage from or adding footage to the clip's beginning or end.

The **Monitor** will preview the new in or out point as you drag. (For information on pre-trimming your clip before you drag it to the timeline, see **Pre-trim your clips in the Clip Monitor** on page 252 of **Chapter 19, Explore the Project Assets Panel**.)

If you find, after removing a segment, that you've removed too much of a clip – or not enough – you can simply re-drag the end of the clip to replace or remove the extra frames. (In non-linear editing, nothing is ever permanently removed from a clip.)

Split a clip on your timeline

To **split a clip** – either to remove a portion of it or to isolate a segment so that you can move, or add an effect to, it – position the **CTI** (Current Time Indicator) at the point on your timeline you'd like to slice and then click the **Split Clip** (scissors icon) button on the **CTI**, as illustrated above.

If you have a clip *selected* on your timeline, this tool will slice only that clip; if you have no clips selected, the tool will slice through *all* of the clips on all tracks at the **CTI's** current position.

If you then want to delete the segment you've sliced (or sliced on either side of), click to select the segment, **right-click** (**Ctrl-click** on a Mac) and choose **Delete** or **Delete and Close Gap**, depending on whether or not you'd like the timeline to ripple to fill the gap.

Remove audio or video from your clip

As you can see on page 269, **right-clicking** on a clip on your timeline (**Ctrl-clicking** on a Mac) gives you access to a number of helpful features, tools and options.

> To make a clip on your timeline video only, **right-click** on the clip and select **Delete Audio**.

> To make a clip on your timeline audio only, **right-click** on the clip and select **Delete Video**.

Fade in and out of your clip

The simplest way to fade into or out of a clip is to **right-click** on it and select **Fade In** or **Fade Out** from the right-click menu. (Separate options are offered for fading in or out of your video, your audio or both, if your clip includes both, as illustrated on page 269.)

By default, your fades will last one second. You can, however, adjust the keyframe positions to lengthen or shorten that time.

To do this, look for the white dots that Premiere Elements has placed to create the fade on the thin, horizontal, yellow line that runs through your clip.

Add still photos to your project

Still photos are dragged to the timeline or sceneline just as video clips are. By default, the duration of a still photo in a Premiere Elements project is **five seconds**. (This default can be changed in **Preferences** (under the **Edit** menu on a PC) – although changing it will only affect photos brought into the program *after* the preference has been changed.)

You can increase or decrease how long the photo displays on the timeline by dragging to trim or extend it, just as you would to trim or extend any video clip, as described in **Trimming and Splitting**.

As explained in **Use Photos in Premiere Elements** (page 240) in **Chapter 18, Add Media to Your Project**, you'll get the best performance from stills in a standard video project if they are sized to no larger than 1000x750 pixels.

Additionally, once you've placed a photo on your timeline, you can eliminate a somewhat common problem (related to interlacing) by **right-clicking** on the still on the timeline (**Ctrl-clicking** on a Mac) and selecting **Field Options** and then selecting the **Flicker Removal** option.

Applying this setting will preempt a fluttering problem that sometimes manifests itself in video outputs when highly detailed or high contrast photos are used in Premiere Elements projects.

These dots are called **keyframes**, and we discuss them in much greater detail in **Chapter 28, Keyframing**.

By default, this yellow line represents the **Opacity** (or transparency) of your video clip. On an audio clip, the line, by default, represents its **Volume** level.

See how the line slants down before or after that keyframe? That's your fade in or fade out of the clip's **Opacity** or **Volume** levels.

Adjusting those dots' positions relative to the end of the clip, by clicking on them and dragging them to new positions, extends or shortens the duration of your fade in or fade out.

To find out more about adjusting your audio's volume and how to control it at specific points in your movie, see **Adjust audio levels at specific points on your timeline** on page 356.

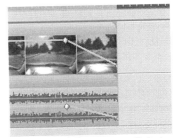

Fade ins and fade outs are really just keyframed Opacity and Volume properties. You can change the length of the fade by changing the positions of the keyframe points on the timeline.

Output a segment of your video using the Work Area Bar

 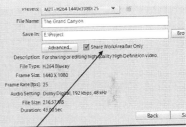

The Work Area Bar can be set to designate only a portion of your video project. Most Share options allow you to output the Work Area Bar segment only.

The **Work Area Bar** is the lighter gray area that runs along the ticker at the top of the timeline, defined by a silver marker on either end. By default, this bar covers your entire video project and grows and shrinks automatically with your project as you edit.

But, by dragging its beginning and end handles, you can manually set the **Work Area Bar** to cover only a portion of your video editing project, as illustrated above. In this way, you can designate only a portion of your project for output.

Nearly all of the output options under the **Publish & Share** tab include a checkbox option for **Export Work Area Bar Only**, as in the illustration. Checking this option directs the program to output *only* the segment of your project you've defined with the **Work Area Bar**. For more information on this function, see the discussions under each output option in **Chapter 31, Publish & Share Your Video Projects**.

To reset the **Work Area Bar** to cover your entire project, **double-click** on its top edge.

Use L-cuts, J-cuts and multiple tracks

The ability to compose your video using several audio and video tracks greatly expands your ability to use interesting and professional-style editing techniques in your video projects.

Multiple tracks of audio, of course, merely mix into a single soundtrack for your movie. (See **Mix Audio** in **Chapter 29, Mix Your Audio and Add Music**.)

But, with multiple tracks of video you can combine elements from several video clips at once to create a number of interesting visual effects.

Think of multiple tracks of video as a stack, like a stack of photos. In most cases, only the uppermost photo in the stack will be visible.

However, if you change the size and position of the photos on the top of the stack, you can see several photos at once. (One example of this, the **Picture-in-Picture** effect, can be achieved using **Presets**, as discussed on page 329 of **Chapter 26, Add Video and Audio Effects**, or by adjusting their **Scale** and **Position**.)

You can also reveal portions of clips on lower tracks by using effects such as **Chroma Key** (as discussed on page 330 of **Chapter 26, Add Video and Audio Effects**), any of the **Matte** effects or even the **Crop** effect to make areas of some clips transparent.

By keyframing the effects in the **Applied Effects** panel, you can also make these positions, sizings or other settings change over the duration of the clip, creating an animated effect. (For more information, see **Chapter 28, Keyframing**.)

Using multiple tracks of video and then scaling and positioning your clips on each, you can have any number of video images in your video frame at the same time. (Think of the grid of faces in the opening credits of *The Brady Bunch* – or see my multiple-panel illustration below.) The products page at Muvipix.com offers a wealth of tutorials describing techniques for achieving these effects using a number of video tracks and effects.

Additionally, two popular techniques that use multiple tracks of video are the **L-cut** and the **J-cut** – so named because, back in the days of single-track editing, when a segment of video had to be removed and the audio left in place to allow for the placement of alternate video, the primary video and audio clip resembled an "L" or a "J" (depending on which segment was removed).

Using Scaling and Position settings with multiple tracks of video allows for Picture-in-Picture effects as well as the opportunity to do split screens, showing several video clips on screen at once

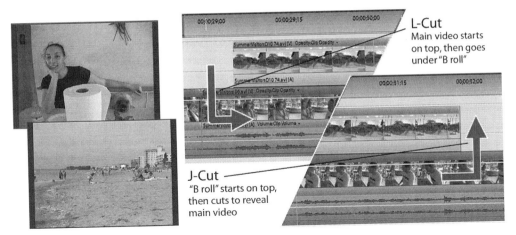

L-Cut
Main video starts
on top, then goes
under "B roll"

J-Cut
"B roll" starts on top,
then cuts to reveal
main video

As audio from main clip continues, video cuts to or from "B roll" footage.

Consider a TV news report that features video of a reporter shown standing in front of a burned-out building, describing the fire that destroyed it.

As he continues speaking, the video cuts away to footage shot earlier of the fire itself. That's an **L-cut**. (A **J-cut**, on the other hand, begins with the cut-away video and the reporter's voice, then cuts to the video of the reporter finishing his report.)

Creating an **L-cut** is easy with multi-track editing.

1   Put the main video, the clip of the reporter speaking to the camera (we'll call it **Clip A**), on Video track 1.

2   Holding the **Ctrl** key (to override the timeline's ripple function), place the second video – the footage of the fire (**Clip B**) – on Video track 2.

3   Overlap the latter part of **Clip A** with **Clip B**, as seen in the illustration on the previous page.

4   **Right-click** on **Clip B** (**Ctrl-click** on a Mac) and select **Delete Audio**, if you need to remove its audio track.

Voila! Tweak **Clip B**'s position for maximum effect and you're done! We begin with the reporter speaking to the camera and, as he continues to speak, we cut away to the footage of the fire.

L-cuts and **J-cuts** are very effective for news-style reports as well as for interviews, in which you cut away from the person speaking to separately shot footage of what he or she is describing. It's a great way to reinforce, with images, what's being presented verbally.

By the way, here's some professional vocabulary to impress your friends with. That secondary footage that plays as the main video's audio continues? It's commonly called **"B-roll footage"**, a relic from the days when this kind of editing actually did involve pasting in footage from a separate roll of film or video.

Render your timeline

As you are working in Expert View, as you add effects and transitions to your project or you add other video sources to your project (including photos), you will see orange lines appear above the clips, as illustrated on the right.

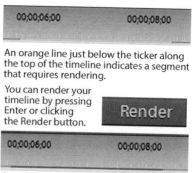

An orange line just below the ticker along the top of the timeline indicates a segment that requires rendering.

You can render your timeline by pressing Enter or clicking the Render button.

Once the sequence is rendered, the orange line will turn green.

These orange lines are indications that these segments of your timeline need to be rendered – converted to the workflow video format. As more and more of your project requires rendering, your computer will begin to operate more sluggishly and the program may even notify you that your system is running low on memory. Your preview video will also suffer a reduction in quality.

This is because, until you manually render these segments, the program is continually creating "soft renders" of them –"on the fly" previews of your unrendered files. And that puts a lot of strain on your system.

In Quick View, there is no orange line on the timeline to indicate the need to render. The only indication will be little pop-ups suggesting that it might be a good idea to render to improve your performance.

To **Render** your video projects' timeline, click the **Render** button on the top right of the timeline.

Alternatively, you can just press the **Enter** key on your keyboard – or select **Render Work Area** from the **Timeline** drop-down at the top of the interface. (Note that only the area of your timeline covered by the **Work Area Bar** – see the sidebar on page 79 – will be rendered.)

Manually rendering your project will create temporary video segments that the program can use to create a clean, clear preview playback of your project – while greatly reducing the strain on your system's resources.

Once your clip has been rendered, the orange lines above the clip will turn green and your playback will be much cleaner and smoother.

You can render your clips continually as you're working. Or you can wait until your playback performance starts to lag. It's up to you.

But do be aware that, if you're having playback problems and your timeline has a lot of orange lines running across the top, a few seconds of rendering can usually do a lot to improve the program's performance.

Cut
Copy
Paste Effects and Adjustments
Delete ◄ ——————————————— Delete clip and do not ripple gap closed
Delete and Close Gap ◄ —————————— Delete clip and ripple gap closed
Delete Audio ◄
Delete Video ◄ ——————————————— Remove audio from your clip
Replace Clip From Project Assets
—————————————————————————— Remove video from your clip
Effects Mask ▸
Remove Effects ▸ ——————————————— Unlink audio and video
✔ Enable
Unlink Audio and Video ◄ —————————— Fade In/Out options for your clips
Group
Ungroup ——————————————————— Set Audio Gain level
Fade ▸

Right-click options for clips on your timeline
(available via Ctrl click on a Mac)

Fade In Audio
Fade In Video
Fade In Audio and Video
Fade Out Audio
Fade Out Video
Fade Out Audio and Video

Apply Videomerge
Smart Fix
Apply Default Transition
Apply Default Transition Along CTI ▸
Time Stretch...
Rotate 90 Left
Rotate 90 Right
Field Options...
Frame Blend
✔ Scale to Frame Size

Audio Gain...
Beat Detect...
Rename...
Reveal in Project
Edit Original
Break Apart Elements Organizer Slideshow
Break Apart InstantMovie
Show Properties
Undo Smart Trim
Show Clip Keyframes ▸

Valuable right-click tools on the timeline

Right-clicking on a clip on your timeline gives you access to a number of valuable tools.

To delete a clip without changing the position of any other clip on your timeline, select **Delete**.

To delete a clip and "ripple" the timeline to fill in the gap, select **Delete and Close Gap**. (The gap will only close, however, if there are no clips on parallel video or audio tracks preventing it from being a true gap!)

To remove the audio or video portion of a clip, select **Delete Audio** or **Delete Video**, as discussed on page 264.

To break apart the audio and video tracks of a clip so that each can be positioned separately, select **Unlink Audio and Video**.

To fade in or out the audio, video or both, select a **Fade** option, as discussed on page 264.

To change the gain level of an audio clip, select **Audio Gain**, as discussed on page 357.

Adobe Premiere Elements

Part VI
The Premiere Elements Action Bar

Chapter 21
Make an InstantMovie Using Movie Themes
The easy way to create movies

Themes are tools in Premiere Elements that can be used for creating automatic or "InstantMovies".

Themes include a combination of titles, music and special effects that can be customized in a variety of ways and then applied to a set of clips you've gathered on your timeline.

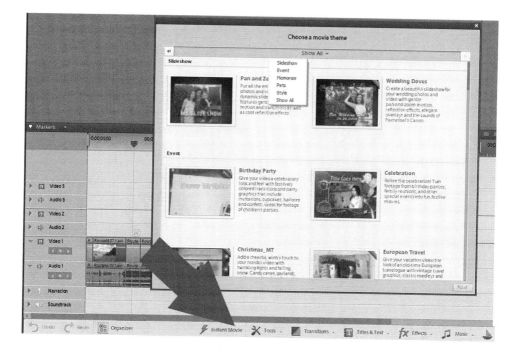

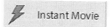

InstantMovie Themes are packets of effects, transitions and music which can be applied to your raw footage to create an exciting movie automatically. To create an **InstantMovie**, you merely provide the raw footage and select a **Theme**, and Premiere Elements does the rest!

To create an **InstantMovie:**

1 Gather your clips on the timeline.

InstantMovies can be used in either Quick View or Expert View.

In Quick View, use **Add Media** to bring your video or still photos to your project's timeline. In Expert View, gather your video or stills from your **Project Assets** panel and drag them to your timeline.

Ideally you'll want at least 2-3 minutes of footage.

InstantMovie will use – *and then replace* – all of the footage on this video track.

2 Click the **InstantMovie** button on the **Action Bar.**

The pop-up panel will display a library of movie **Themes.**

The title bar at the top of the panel is set to **Show All** by default. To filter your view of these **Themes**, click on this title bar and select from the **InstantMovie** categories.

You can see an animated preview of any **Theme** by selecting its thumbnail and then clicking on the play button that appears.

3 Once you've selected a **Theme** for your **InstantMovie**, click the **Next** button in the lower right of the panel.

4 The panel will display a list of the optional elements that make up your **Theme's** template, as illustrated on the right.

Type the titles you'd like included in the boxes provided, then select or deselect the elements you'd like applied to your movie.

You can even swap out music by selecting the **My Music** option and browsing to a music file on your computer.

(You may need to scroll down to see the entire list of optional elements, then click on the little triangles to the left of the listed categories of options to see the entire options list.)

Once you've selected and customized the elements you'd like included, click the **Apply** button in the lower right corner of the panel.

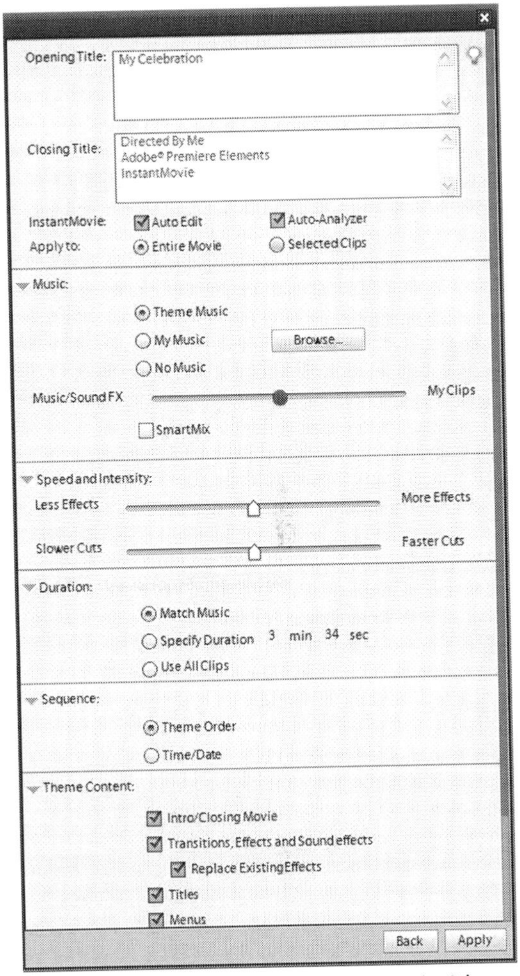

Premiere Elements will **Auto-Analyze** the clips on your timeline (see page 418), process all of the options and then apply the **Theme** elements you've selected.

After your automatically-generated movie appears on your timeline, the program will offer to render it for you.

Once you've selected a Theme, you can customize it by including your own text and selecting which elements will be applied.

It's a good idea to accept this offer, as your movie will likely need to be rendered before it will play at full quality. The rendered video will provide you with a much cleaner representation of what your final video output will look like.

For more information on the rendering process, see **Render your timeline** on page 268 of **Chapter 20, Edit Your Video in Expert View**.

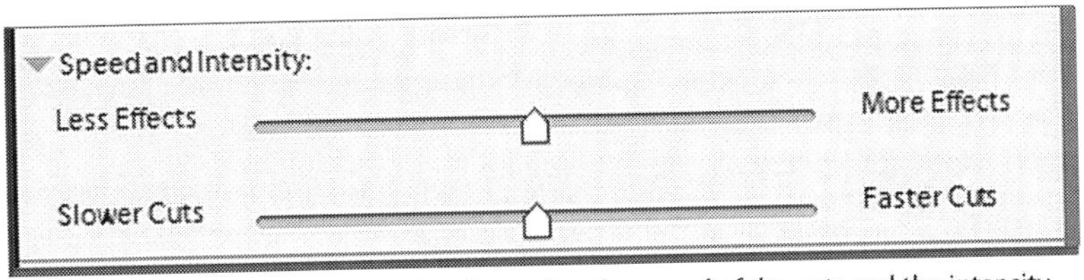

Instant Movie Themes include sliders for setting the speed of the cuts and the intensity of the effects.

Chapter 22

Use the Premiere Elements Toolkit
Powerful tools on the Action Bar

The Action Bar that runs along the
bottom of the Premiere Elements
interface offers quick access to dozens
of tools for applying transitions and
effects, making titles, adding clip
art, adding music and narration and
creating menus for your DVDs and
BluRay discs.

Through the Action Bar, most of the
program's coolest tools are only a few
clicks away!

Running along the bottom of the program's interface is the **Action Bar**. From this **Action Bar,** you have easy access to dozens of tools, effects, transitions and graphics with just the click of a button!

Clicking the **Tools** button launches a pop-up menu with several very cool tools. In this chapter, we'll look at how all but one of them works. (We'll save **Make Menu** for **Chapter 30**.) This pop-up **Tool** kit includes:

Adjustments, which opens the **Adjustments** panel (see **Chapter 23**).

Audio Mixer (available only in Expert View), a tool for monitoring and setting the volume levels of your movie's audio.

Freeze Frame, a tool for grabbing a still photo from your movie.

Movie Menu, which opens a workspace for building a menu system for your DVDs, BluRay discs and WebDVDs.

Narration, a tool for recording a live narration track as your movie plays.

Pan & Zoom, which opens a very intuitive workspace for creating pan and zoom motion paths for your slideshows.

Smart Mix, a tool which automatically mixes the audio levels for your movie, based on criteria you define.

Smart Trim, a tool for automatically removing poor quality video from your project.

Time Remapping, an amazing new workspace for creating fast-motion and slow-motion segments in your movie.

Time Stretch (available only in Expert View), a tool for slowing down or speeding up your clips.

Mix and monitor your audio levels

The **Audio Mixer** can be used to monitor your audio levels as well as adjust them.

The Audio Mixer will display separate controls for each audio track. If adjustments are made while playback is stopped, adjustments will affect the entire clip. If made during playback, audio keyframes will be created.

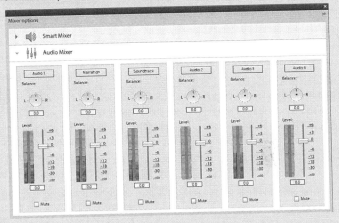

To open this tool, click on the **Tools** button on the **Action Bar** and select **Audio Mixer**. (Note that this tool is available in Expert View only.)

The **Audio Mixer** displays the audio levels for each of your active audio tracks and offers controls for raising and lowering these audio volume levels.

The **Audio Mixer** is a great panel to keep open as much as possible while you work so that you can monitor your movie's audio levels, particularly as you begin the final phases of editing your project. For best results, never let your audio levels peak in the red. Overmodulated audio can sound distorted and fuzzy.

The **Audio Mixer** can also be used to adjust the levels for your individual audio clips:

- When you're not playing your video project, click to select a clip on the timeline at the position of the **CTI** (Current Time Indicator). Raising or lowering the **Audio Mixer** slider for that track will raise and lower the volume level for that clip.

- If you adjust the sliders as your video is playing, on the other hand, keyframe points will be added to your clips so that the audio is raised or lowered in real time at the points at which you adjusted the slider.

As you play your project, watch the meters for each track, adjusting the sound levels as necessary to keep these levels as much as possible in the green, with the bulk of the audio peaking at zero.

In our opinion, this tool serves much more effectively as an audio meter than an audio level adjustment tool.

If used to adjust volume levels while the video is playing, it simply places too many hard-to-adjust audio keyframes on the timeline. You'll get much neater and much more effective results if you use the technique we describe in **Adjust audio levels at specific points in your video** on page 356.

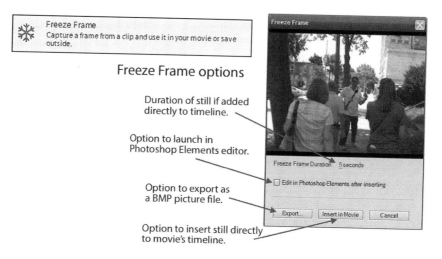

Freeze Frame
Capture a frame from a clip and use it in your movie or save outside.

Freeze Frame options

Duration of still if added directly to timeline.

Option to launch in Photoshop Elements editor.

Option to export as a BMP picture file.

Option to insert still directly to movie's timeline.

Grab a Freeze Frame

Freeze Frame is found on the **Tools** panel, launched by clicking the **Tools** button on the **Action Bar**. (Although it might more accurately be called a "frame grab" tool, since it doesn't so much *freeze* a frame of your movie as much as it *grabs* a frame from it.)

Selecting this tool brings up an option screen which displays the grabbed frame from your video (based on the position of the **CTI** on your timeline) as well as a number of options for saving it, as illustrated above.

- You can choose to simply **insert** the still in your movie. The inserted still will display in your video project at whatever duration you've indicated in **Freeze Frame Duration**.

- Selecting the option to **Edit In Photoshop Elements After Inserting** loads the still into your movie and simultaneously launches it in the edit space of Photoshop Elements.

  Once you've made any adjustments to the photo in Photoshop Elements and saved the file, the updates will automatically appear in the photo in Premiere Elements.

- Whether or not you choose to insert the still into your movie, your **Freeze Frame** will be saved to your hard drive as a Bitmap (BMP) file and will appear in your current **Project Assets** panel.

One thing to note is the many video formats (DV-AVIs, for instance) store picture data in non-square pixels. So, if your video is, for instance, 720x480 anamorphic pixels in size, your **Freeze Frame** may look a bit squished or stretched when you print it or open it in Photoshop Elements.

If you'd like to save a **Freeze Frame** of your movie as a JPEG or TIF for use in either another video, Web or print project, use the **Publish & Share** output option that we discuss in **Output a still of your current video frame** on page 388 of **Chapter 31, Publish & Share Your Video Projects.**

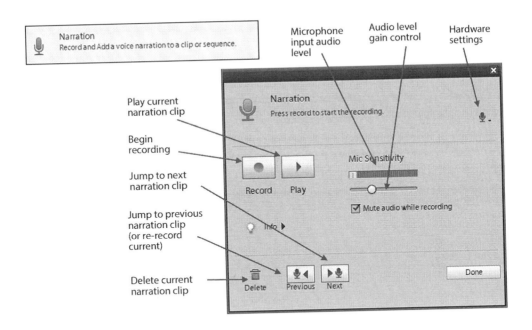

Add Narration

With this tool, you can add narration to your project – and even record it as you watch your video playing.

1 To launch the **Record Voice Narration** tool, click on the **Tools** button on the **Action Bar** and select **Narration**.

The **Record Voice Narration** panel will open.

The microphone recording level displays on the VU meter in the center of the panel.

You'll want to keep it green and full, adjusting the slider as necessary for optimal sound.

Turn down your computer's speakers or select the option to **Mute Audio While Recording** so that you don't get feedback from your speakers as you record.

2 To record your narration, click the red **Record** button.

The panel will display a three-second countdown and then will begin recording as your movie plays.

Click the same button again to stop the recording.

The program will place the narration clip that you've recorded on the **Narration** audio track, at the current position of your **CTI** (Current Time Indicator).

The two shortcut buttons on the panel will jump you back to the beginning of the clip you've just recorded (or to the next or previous narration clip). You can then click the play button to hear the results.

3   If you're unhappy with the results, click the shortcut button to jump back to the beginning of your clip and record new narration. (Your new narration will replace the old automatically.) By clicking the trashcan icon, you can delete the current narration clip completely.

A good microphone and good, quality sound card are essential to getting a good strong narration recording.

If Premiere Elements isn't recognizing your microphone, click the **Hardware Settings** button (the little microphone icon) on the upper right corner of the **Narration** panel) and ensure your microphone input is properly configured.

If it is and you're still not able to record, go to Premiere Elements' **Edit** drop-down menu and select **Preferences/Audio Hardware**. Click the **ASIO Settings** button, and adjust whatever settings are necessary there.

Create a Pan & Zoom motion path

Pan & Zoom
Create quick and easy Pan and Zoom effects in videos and photos.

The **Pan & Zoom Tool** allows you to create motion paths – pans and zooms across your photos – using a very intuitive interface. (It's, of course, not the only way to create motion paths. For more information on using keyframes to create custom motion paths, see **Chapter 28, Keyframing**.)

Although this tool can also be used on video, the effect will create the best results when used on photos that have a slightly higher resolution than the video project. As we explain in **Use photos in Premiere Elements** on page 240, you'll get the best balance of photo quality and system performance if your photos are no larger than 1000x750 pixels in size. (For high-definition video, you can go as large as 2000x1500 pixels.)

To demonstrate this tool, we'll create a simple motion path over a photo.

1   Click to select a still photo on your timeline.

2   Click on the **Tools** button on the **Action Bar** and select **Pan & Zoom.**

The **Pan & Zoom** workspace will open, as illustrated at the top of the facing page.

The concept behind this workspace is a simple one: You indicate the views you'd like for the beginning and end of your motion path and Premiere Elements will create the path of motion between them.

3   Create an initial motion path keyframe.

Ensure that the **CTI** is at the beginning of the timeline that runs along the bottom of the workspace. (You should see a little, diamond-shaped keyframe on the timeline at the **CTI's** position.)

With the CTI at the beginning of the timeline, drag the corner handles to size and position Frame 1 to create the initial composition for your motion path.

Move the CTI to the end of the timeline and then drag the corner handles of Frame 2 to create the composition you'd like your motion path to end on.

Place the CTI at other positions on the timeline and click the New Frame button to create as many additional motion path keyframes as you need (including hold motion frames) to build your motion path.

Drag on **Frame 1** (the green box) and on its corner handles to size and position the frame to create the initial composition you'd like for your motion path. (To quickly build a motion path to the faces in your picture, click the **Face Frames** button in the upper left of the workspace.)

4   Move the **CTI** to the end of the timeline.

There will be another diamond-shaped keyframe at this position on the timeline. When you move the **CTI** over this keyframe, **Frame 2** (a second green box) will become highlighted.

Size and position **Frame 2** to create the composition you'd like to end your motion path with. (A little blue line will indicate the duration (in seconds) of your motion.)

Click the **Play Output** button along the bottom of the panel to preview your motion path.

You may add additional keyframes to create additional movements if you'd like. To do this, move the **CTI** to other positions on the timeline and click the **New Frame** button in the upper left of the workspace, as illustrated above.

5   When you are finished, click **Done** to return to the regular editing workspace.

If you'd like to further customize this motion path, you can do so by opening the clip's **Motion** properties, as described in **Chapter 28, Keyframing.**

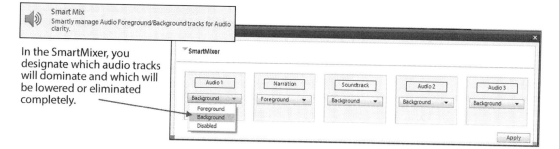

In the SmartMixer, you designate which audio tracks will dominate and which will be lowered or eliminated completely.

Smart Mix your audio

Premiere Elements' **Smart Mix** tool will automatically adjust the levels of several audio tracks to allow one track to dominate over the others.

In other words, if you've got a sequence that includes music, narration and the original audio from a video clip, **Smart Mix** can be set to automatically lower the music and other audio levels whenever there is a narration clip.

1   To set the criteria for your audio clip adjustments, click the **Tools** button on the **Action Bar** and select **Smart Mix** from the pop-up menu.

The **Smart Mixer Options** panel displays each audio track in your Premiere Elements project and allows you to indicate, with drop-down menus, which tracks will serve as your audio **Foreground**, which will serve as **Background** and which will be **Disabled** completely. (As illustrated above.)

2   Once you've set your preferences for the tool, activate the **Smart Mix** feature by clicking on the **Apply** button.

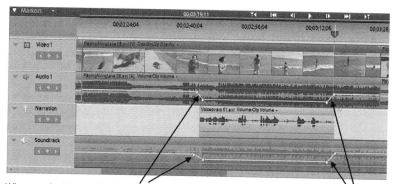

When applied, Smart Trim automatically creates the necessary keyframes to lower the audio on the tracks you've designated as Background.

The **Smart Mixer** will create the necessary audio keyframes – which appear as little white diamonds on your audio clip(s) – to lower the volume of the audio clip(s) that you've designated as **Background** audio.

Further, if you move or change a clip you've indicated as your **Foreground** and re-apply **Smart Mix**, the **Smart Mixer** will automatically remove or revise the audio keyframes!

To set preferences for the **Smart Mixer** – including how much the **Background** audio is reduced in volume and if the **Foreground** audio is automatically **Normalized** – go to the Premiere Elements **Preferences** panel (under **Edit)** and select the **Audio** page.

Smart Trim your video

✂ Smart Trim
    Let Premiere Elements edit your footage for a crisper video.

The **Smart Trim** tool analyzes clips you've added to your movie's timeline, indicating which sequences do not meet quality standards, then recommends trims to remove segments from your clips (or automatically trims the sequences for you).

1. To **Smart Trim** your video, click the **Tools** button on the **Action Bar** and select **Smart Trim** from the pop-up menu.

    If your video has not already been analyzed in the Element Organizer, the **Auto-Analyzer** will automatically search all of the videos on your timeline and indicate in which segments the lighting is bad, the picture is blurry or the camcorder was not held steady.

    These indicated areas – called **Suggested Trimmings** – will appear with blue diagonal lines over them, as in the illustration below.

    If you hover your mouse over these areas, the program will indicate why it recommends they be removed.

    You may then opt to either remove any or all of the **Suggested Trimming** segments or to override the program's suggestion.

If you hover your mouse over a Smart Trim Suggested Trimmimg, Premiere Elements will explain why the segment should be removed.

Right-click on a selected Suggested Trimming area to select whether to cut it or to override the recommendation.

2 Click on a **Suggested Trimming** to select it.

The diagonal shading will highlight in light blue.

By dragging on either end of this selected segment, you can trim or extend the length of this **Suggested Trimming** area.

3 Once you've tweaked your **Suggested Trimming** area, **right-click** on this area and select the option to:

Trim, or remove the **Suggested Trimming** segment from your video.

Keep, or opt not to remove the **Suggested Trimming** segment.

Select All of the **Suggested Trimmings** and remove them.

Additionally, this context menu includes access to the **Smart Trim Options** panel.

A pair of sliders on the **Smart Trim Options** panel allows you to set a **Quality Level** and an **Interest Level** for any new clips you add.

Quality automatically checks your clips for issues like blurriness, shakiness, brightness and contrast.

Interest examines the segments recommended for deletion based on your **Quality** setting and re-evaluates their content to see if they're actually worth saving, based on your **Interest** level.

In other words, the **Interest Level** and **Quality Level** balance each other out, according to the levels you set.

On this **Options** panel, you can also set **Smart Trim** to **Automatic** mode, in which case it will automatically remove any **Suggested Trimming** areas from your video timeline as it detects them.

Create cool Time Remapping effects

Time Remapping is one of the newest and most sophisticated tools in the Premiere Elements tool kit.

With **Time Remapping**, you designate a section of a clip on your timeline and the tool will suddenly speed it up or slow it to a crawl – then just as suddenly, bring it back to real time – like it's some Guy Ritchie film.

You can slow you video to nearly a standstill with this tool, by the way. The **Remapping** feature of this tool does an excellent job of smoothing the motion in between frames so that your slowed action (up to one-eighth speed) looks even and natural.

The workspace for this effect is very simple, yet also surprisingly powerful.

1 Click to select a clip on your timeline.

2 Click the **Tools** button on the **Action Bar** and select **Time Remapping** from the pop-up menu.

The **Time Remapping** workspace will open. Your clip will be displayed on a timeline along the bottom of the interface.

Clicking on the **+** on the CTI or clicking the Add Time Zone button...

Add Time Zone

...creates a Time Zone on your timeline which you can lengthen, shorten or slide to a new position.

3   Create a **Time Zone** by moving the **CTI** to the approximate location of the clip you'd like to remap and either clicking the **Add Time Zone** button in the lower left of the interface or clicking the **+** sign on the **CTI**.

A yellow-green box will indicate the location of the designated **Time Zone** on your clip. The speed of your playback for this **Time Zone** is indicated by a number in the upper left of this box– which by default reads 1.0x (normal speed).

4   Tweak your **Time Zone's** location by dragging on either end of this green box. The duration of your **Time Zone** segment is indicated in the lower right of the workspace interface.

5   Select a **Time Remapping** speed using the big slider.

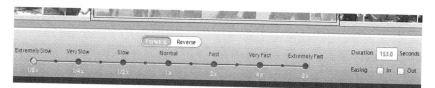

The **X** indicator on the upper left of the green box will indicate the new playback speed of your **Time Zone**, while the **Duration** indicator will list its adjusting playback time. In other words, a 10-second **Time Zone** set to play at 2.0x will have a duration of 5 seconds. Pretty simple, right?

Your **Time Zone** can be remapped to play in forward or reverse, by clicking on either button above the slider.

You can add several **Time Zones** of varying speeds to a single clip, by the way. Although they can't overlap or double-up on each other.

Your audio will be sped up or slowed down right along with your video. If the sped-up/slowed-down audio doesn't fit with your vision, you can remove the audio by clicking the **Remove Audio** button in the lower left of the interface. This will, however, remove the audio from the entire clip, not just the **Time Zone** segment. So if that's not your intention, you may want to leave the audio alone at this point and keyframe it to no volume during the **Time Remapping** segment (as we show you on page 356).

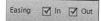

Finally, if the shift to high or low speed and back again seems too abrupt, you can select the option to **Ease In** or **Ease Out** of the **Time Remapping** segment.

Remove Audio

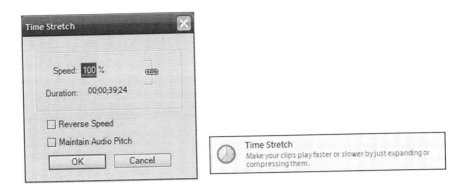

Time Stretch your scenes

Time Stretch (available only in Expert View) isn't nearly as sophisticated a tool as **Time Remapping** – but it gets the job done.

Unlike **Time Remapping, Time Stretch** is applied to an entire clip on your timeline at once rather than applied to a designated segment.

To **Time Stretch** a clip:

1. Click to select a clip on your timeline.

2. Click the **Tools** button on the **Action Bar** and select **Time Stretch** from the pop-up menu. (The tool can also be launched by **right-clicking** on a clip and selecting the **Time Stretch** option.)

   The **Time Stretch** option screen will open, as illustrated above.

3. Set the amount your clip will be **Time Stretched** by either designating the percentage of playback **Speed** or by setting the **Duration** you'd like the clip to extend or contract to. (The shorter the **Duration**, the faster the **Speed**, and vice versa.)

To play a clip in reverse, check the **Reverse** option box.

To keep the clip's audio from being distorted by the change in playback speed, click the **Maintain Audio Pitch** button.

Add a graphic to your movie

A cool little extra feature that Adobe includes with Premiere Elements is a library of over 350 video graphics in 13 categories, including cartoon characters, food, musical instruments, wigs and costumes and themed graphics for birthdays and holidays, new babies and sports.

And most interesting of all, a number of these graphics are even animated!

These animated graphics include cartoon faces that move, a fluttering butterfly, a storm cloud, fire, steam and a circle of stars.

These graphics are transparent, so you can place them right over your video.

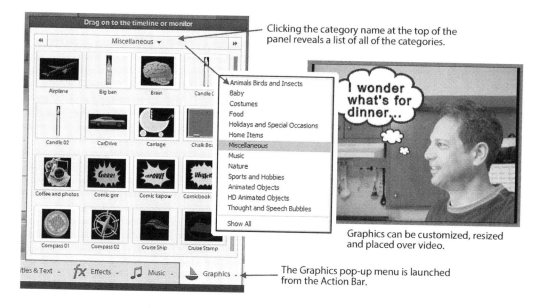

Clicking the category name at the top of the panel reveals a list of all of the categories.

Graphics can be customized, resized and placed over video.

The Graphics pop-up menu is launched from the Action Bar.

Adding them to your movie is as easy as dragging them to your timeline from the pop-up panel, opened by clicking the **Graphics** button on the **Action Bar**.

Among my favorite graphics are the **Thought and Speech Bubbles**.

Functioning essentially like title templates (see **Chapter 25**), a thought bubble or speech bubble is dragged to your timeline on a video track above existing video. (You can then size it by selecting the clip in your **Monitor** and dragging in or out on its corner handles.)

To edit the text, just **double-click** on the graphic clip on your timeline. The graphic and text will open in the **Title Adjustments** workspace (discussed on page 314).

Smart Fixing Your Video

Color, Gamma and Lighting Adjustments

Adjusting Color Temperature and Tint

Adjusting Volume, Balance, Bass and Treble

Keyframing Adjustments

Chapter 23

Make Adjustments to Your Video and Audio
Correct and customize your clips' levels

New to version 11, Premiere Elements now includes a whole panel of adjustment tools for correcting your videos' colors, lighting and color temperature and for setting your audio's volume and balance.

Even better, thanks to Adobe's simple Quick Fix interface, making these adjustments couldn't be more intuitive!

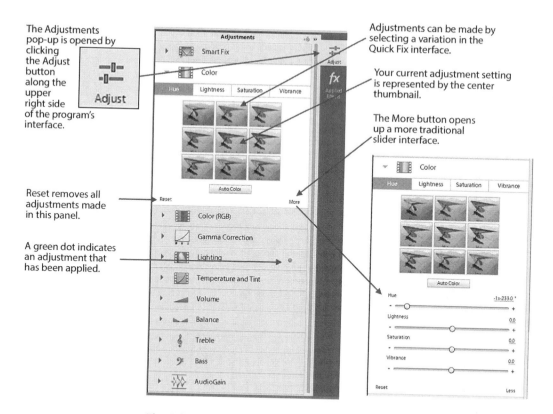

The Adjustments pop-up is opened by clicking the Adjust button along the upper right side of the program's interface.

Adjustments can be made by selecting a variation in the Quick Fix interface.

Your current adjustment setting is represented by the center thumbnail.

The More button opens up a more traditional slider interface.

Reset removes all adjustments made in this panel.

A green dot indicates an adjustment that has been applied.

The **Adjustments** panel includes six powerful video tools and five helpful audio tools for fine tuning the color, lighting, sound and balance levels of your video and audio clips. Which adjustment tools are available depends, of course, on whether the clip you've selected on your timeline includes audio, video or both.

The **Adjustments** pop-up panel is launched by clicking the **Adjust** button in the upper right of the Premiere Elements interface.

Applying an **Adjustment** to a clip is as simple as selecting an audio or video clip on your timeline and selecting an option from the listing in the pop-up menu.

Each video **Adjustment** tool (except **Smart Fix**) includes an intuitive, picture-based interface as well as a slider-based adjustment tool set (opened by clicking the **More** button, as illustrated above).

In the picture-based Tic Tac Toe-style tool (called the **Quick Fix** interface), your un-adjusted image is represented by the center square thumbnail. Adjustments are applied to your video as you click on one of the surrounding squares. To return to your unadjusted image, click the center square.

Any adjustments can also be undone by clicking the **Reset** button in the lower left of the tool panel (or by, of course, pressing **Ctrl+z** on your keyboard (⌘+z on a Mac) to undo the last adjustment applied).

Most of the video **Adjustment** tools include options also for adjusting several individual lighting and color elements. For instance, the **Color Adjustment** tool includes options for fine-tuning **Hue, Lightness, Saturation** and **Vibrance** (as discussed below).

A number of tools also include the option to apply **Auto Levels** or **Auto Fixes**. Once you've applied an **Auto Fix**, you can, of course, further tweak your levels using the **Quick Fix** interface or sliders.

Once any **Adjustments** have been applied to a clip, a green dot will appear on the right end of the **Adjustments** panel next to the applied effect's listing, as illustrated on the facing page.

Smart Fix

Smart Fix is a tool which automatically adjusts the lighting and color in your video and, if necessary, adds the **Stabilizer** effect (see page 260) to reduce movement in handheld shots.

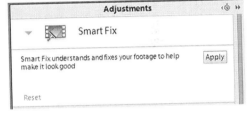

(Note that, if your clip has not yet been analyzed and **Smart Tagged** by the Elements Organizer's **Media Analyzer** (see page 418), the program may need to **Auto-Analyze** the clip before a **Smart Fix** adjustment can be applied.)

When a simple tweak is needed, **Smart Fix** often does a very good job.

Color

The **Color Adjustments** tool has separate adjustment panels for **Hue, Lightness, Saturation** and **Vibrance.**

> **Hue** is the color mix itself, as imagined on a color wheel with violet in the upper left, magenta in the upper right, cyan in the lower right and green in the lower left. Changing this effect will shift the color hue values of all of the colors in your clip.
>
> **Lightness** is the amount of white or black mixed with the color.
>
> **Saturation** is the amount of hue applied (more blue or less blue, for instance).
>
> **Vibrance**, similar to saturation, is the overall richness or intensity of the colors.

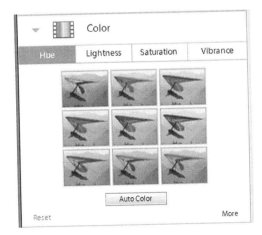

The panel includes an **Auto Color** button for a quick color correction.

Color (RGB)

In contrast to the **Color Adjustments**, the **Color (RGB) Adjustments** are concerned only with the levels of **Red**, **Green** and **Blue**, the three primary colors of video.

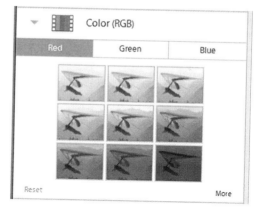

Selecting one of the squares on each of the color's **Quick Fix** interfaces or adjusting the corresponding slider sets an intensity level for that particular color only (on a scale of 0% to 200%) without affecting either of the other two colors' levels.

Gamma

Gamma is basically how bright or dark a picture is. Unlike **Lighting** (below), which bases its changes on the whitest white point and the blackest black point in an image, **Gamma** brightens or darkens an image based on its mid-tones. In other words, **Brightness** and **Contrast** deal with how white or black an image is, while changing the **Gamma** level brightens or dims the image.

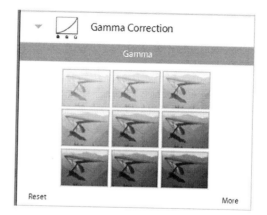

It's a subtle difference, to be sure. But the important thing to understand is that sometimes a video needs its **Lightness** adjusted – and sometimes it needs its **Gamma** adjusted. So, if one doesn't work, try the other. Eventually you'll come to recognize the difference.

Lighting

Lighting sets the level of the whitest white and the blackest black in your video and/or adjusts the contrast between them. This **Adjustment** includes five separate adjustment panels: **Brightness, Contrast, Exposure, Black** and **White**.

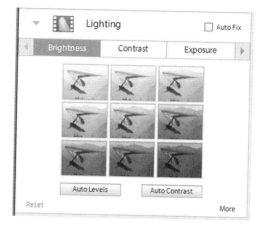

    Brightness sets the levels for the blackest black or whitest white point in your video image. The higher the black level, the darker your image will look; the higher the white level, the lighter.

Contrast increases or reduces the difference between the lighter and darker elements in your image.

Exposure simulates lighting adjustments usually made automatically in your camera or camcorder as it takes a picture or shoots your video. This can be a great tool for fixing a picture shot, for instance, in shade with a brighter background, in which your subject came out too dark.

Black increases or decreases the amount of black in your video image.

White increases or decreases the amount of white in your video image.

(If the **Black** and **White** options aren't visible on your panel, you can scroll to see them by clicking the arrow to the right of the **Exposure** tab along the top of the panel.)

In addition to the **Auto Levels** and **Auto Contrast** buttons, this **Adjustment** tool includes an **Auto Fix** checkbox along the top right of the panel. Checking this box applies a **Lighting Auto Fix** to your video image – however, it also locks out the other tools on this panel from further adjustment.

Temperature and Tint

Temperature and **Tint** are color correction tools for compensating for video shot in less-than-ideal lighting conditions – or, of course, for intentionally applying a cooling or warming effect.

Color Temperature refers to the frequency or temperature of light applied to a given scene. Sunlight and outdoor lighting, for instance, has a color temperature of about 6,500 K, which gives pictures shot outdoors a slightly blue tone. Indoor incandescent lights are around 3,000 K, giving your pictures a redder or yellower tone.

Color temp set too low.

In most cases, you don't notice the difference in color temperatures because your eyes – and camcorders – automatically adjust for it. However, if you've ever shot a video or taken a picture in which a person is lit by indoor lighting while standing in front of a window or an open door, you've seen the difference. The camera adjusts to one or the other color temperature, and you end up with either the person looking orange or the outdoor background looking blue. This can also happen if you've been shooting indoors and then run outdoors and start shooting before your camcorder has a chance to reset. The leaves on the trees come out all green-blue!

Proper color temp setting.

Color temp set too high.

Temperature adjusts the color temperature of your video image so that the unwanted blue or red/yellow tones are corrected.

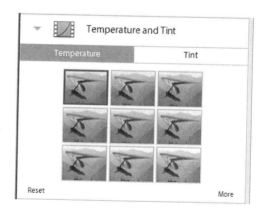

Tint, a more primitive way of correcting color, shifts the hue of your video to various levels of red, green and blue.

You can also use these **Adjustments** to intentionally change the tint of your video to create, for instance, a spookier, gloomier tone. However, to achieve these visual effects, you may find Premiere Elements' **FilmLooks** much more effective. For more information on these **Effects**, see page 326.

Volume

Pretty simply, **Volume** increases or decreases the loudness of your audio clips. This adjustment, by the way, can also be made by raising and lowering the yellow horizontal line running through the audio clips on the Expert View timeline. These levels can also be adjusted higher or lower at specific points on your timeline using keyframing, as we discuss on page 170.

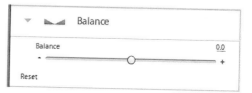

Balance

Balance adjusts the levels of your right and left stereo audio channels with respect to each other.

By the way, if you've recorded with a monaural device and you have audio on only one channel, you spread it across both channels equally using the **Fill Left** or **Fill Right Audio Effects**, as discussed on page 336.

Treble and Bass

These **Adjustment** tools decrease or increase the levels of specific frequencies on your audio clips.

Treble adjusts the levels of the higher frequency sounds in your audio.

Bass adjusts the lower.

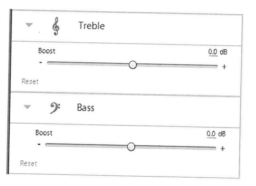

Audio Gain

While the **Volume** sets how loudly your audio clip plays, **Audio Gain** increases or decreases the loudness of the *original audio* on the clip. The difference is subtle but worth knowing.

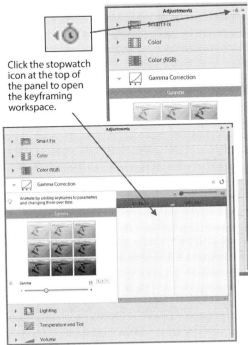

When I've got audio that I've recorded at too low a level and I want to make it louder, **Audio Gain** is my preferred tool for doing so. Increasing the gain tends to make the audio sound richer and fuller in addition to simply louder. At least to my ears.

When you click the **Apply** button on this tool panel, the **Audio Gain** tool launches. For more information on using this tool, see page 357.

Keyframe your Adjustments

By default, changes made in the **Adjustments** panel are applied to your entire clip. In other words, if you change the **Temperature** of a clip, you change it for the entire clip. If you raise the **Volume**, you raise the volume level overall for the entire clip.

However, sometimes you want these **Adjustments** to vary over the course of a clip – if, for instance, your clip includes both video that needs color correction and video that does not, or your audio includes both loud and quiet moments that you want to even out.

To set up your **Adjustments** to vary their levels over the course of a clip you use a process called **keyframing**. (**Adjustments keyframing** is only available in Expert View.)

To create keyframes that vary the levels of your **Adjustments**:

Click the stopwatch icon at the top of the panel to open the keyframing workspace.

1   Open the keyframing workspace.

   With the panel open for the **Adjustments** tool you want to keyframe, click the stopwatch icon at the top right of the **Adjustments** panel.

   The **Adjustments** panel will stretch wide – sliding your **Monitor** way off to the left of the interface – and a mini-timeline will appear to the right of your selected **Adjustments** tool. (By nature of their effects, **Smart Fix** and **Audio Gain** do not have keyframing workspaces.)

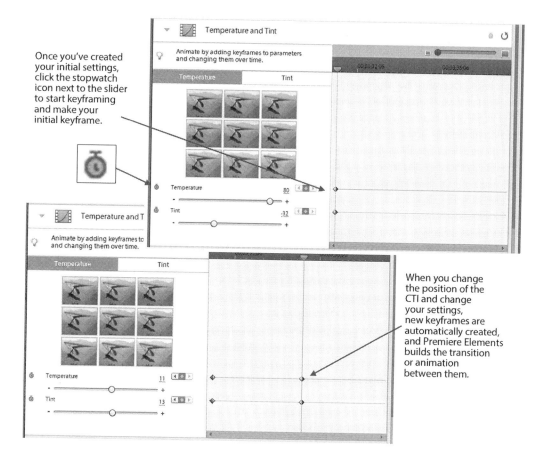

Once you've created your initial settings, click the stopwatch icon next to the slider to start keyframing and make your initial keyframe.

When you change the position of the CTI and change your settings, new keyframes are automatically created, and Premiere Elements builds the transition or animation between them.

The mini-timeline in this keyframing workspace represents the duration of the clip you have selected on your timeline.

2   Set your adjustment level.

Drag the **CTI** in the keyframe workspace to the point on your clip's mini-timeline that you'd like your first setting to be applied.

Click the **More** button at the bottom right of your **Adjustment** tool's panel to open the slider interface and make your adjustment. (Although you can make your adjustments using the sliders or the **Quick Fix** interface, you'll need to have the sliders visible to create your initial keyframe.)

3   Create an initial keyframe.

Click the stopwatch icon to the left of the slider or the sliders you've adjusted (as illustrated above) to begin keyframing.

A horizontal line will appear to the right of your adjustment and little diamond keyframe at the **CTI's** position will indicate your current adjustment setting.

4 Create a second keyframe.

Move the **CTI** in the keyframe workspace to a new position and change your adjustment(s) setting.

A new keyframe will automatically be created, and the program will automatically create the animation or transition between the two.

You can create as many keyframes as you need to create the effect you want. And you can change, move and remove your keyframes as needed. (Or, by clicking the stopwatch again, remove all keyframes completely.)

Keyframes have many applications in Premiere Elements, from creating motion paths over photos and creating animations and special effects to precisely mixing audio tracks. For more information on this powerful tool, see **Chapter 28, Keyframing.**

For information on using keyframes to precisely control the Volume levels on your audio clips, see **Adjust your audio levels at specific points in your video** on page 356.

Chapter 24

Add and Customize Transitions
Cool ways to get from one scene to the next

Transitions in Premiere Elements are very easy to use.

However, like most of Premiere Elements' features, there is also a surprising amount you can do to customize them, if you know where to look.

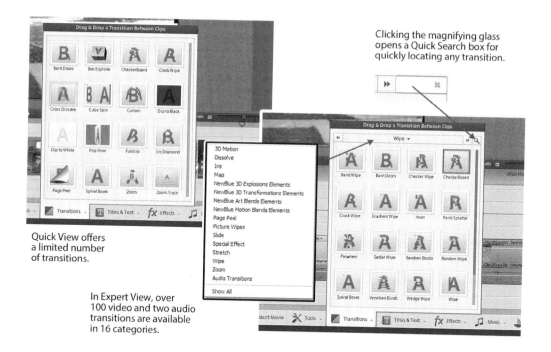

Clicking the magnifying glass opens a Quick Search box for quickly locating any transition.

Quick View offers a limited number of transitions.

In Expert View, over 100 video and two audio transitions are available in 16 categories.

Transitions are added between clips from the **Transitions** pop-up panel, launched from the **Action Bar** along the bottom of the interface.

Whether you're working in Quick View or Expert View, transitions are added to your project essentially the same way. However, Expert View offers a much wider selection of transitions and transition categories.

To apply a transition:

1   Click the **Transitions** button on the **Action Bar** along the bottom of the interface.

The **Transitions** pop-up panel will open.

Once the panel is open, you can enlarge it by dragging on the black bar at the top of the panel.

2   Browse to a transition.

In Quick View, Premiere Elements offers you about a dozen basic video transitions.

In Expert View, you will find over 100 video transitions in 15 categories, plus 2 audio transitions. To select a category and browse to a transition either:

  • Click on the category title bar (which says **3D Motion** by default) at the top of the panel, as illustrated above. A complete list of transition categories will appear and you can click to select and jump to the category; or

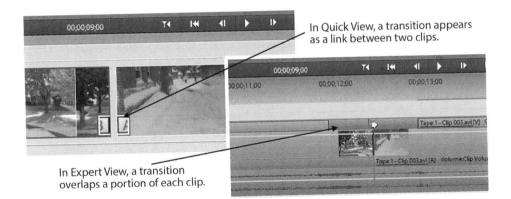

In Quick View, a transition appears
as a link between two clips.

In Expert View, a transition
overlaps a portion of each clip.

- Click on the black double-arrow to the right or left of the
  category title bar to scroll through the various categories.

You can also Quick Search directly to any transition by clicking on
the magnifying glass in the upper right of the **Transitions** pop-up
panel (as illustrated on the facing page) and then typing in the
transition's name.

3 Apply the transition.

Drag your selected transition onto the intersection of two clips.

A **Transition Adjustments** option panel will open.

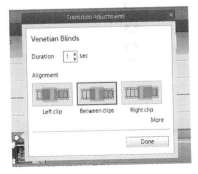

4 Set your transition's **Duration** and **Alignment**.

Your transition will last 1 second by default. You can
change the duration by clicking the up or down
arrows to the right of the current **Duration** length
or you can simply type over the current **Duration**.
To set your transition's **Duration** to fractions of
a second, use decimal points. For instance, a
transition will last two and one-half seconds if you
set its **Duration** to 2.5 sec.

Your transition's **Alignment** is, by default, centered between your
two clips. However, if you'd prefer (or if you lack adequate "head"
or "tail" material [see page 308] on one or the other clip) you can
manually set its **Alignment** over the left or the right clip.

Mac transitions: A limited edition

The Mac version of Premiere Elements 11 does not include all of the transitions available
in the PC version. For a list of the omitted effects, see page 394 of our **Appendix**.

The **Transitions** panel includes a **Default Transition**, which is used to transition between clips when you use the **Project Assets' Slideshow Creator** (page 255) as well as by the **Add Transition Along the CTI** tool (see **Add a transition automatically** on page 307). By default, the **Default Transition** is **Dissolve**. However, you can manually set any transition as your **Default Transition**, as discussed on page 306.

Transitions can also be applied to several clips at once. For more information, see page 307.

Customize your transition

Most transitions include a number of options for customizing their look, animation, borders, colors and other transitional elements.

These options are set in the **Transition Adjustments** panel that appears when you first add the transition to your timeline – or whenever you **double-click** on an existing transition. Click the **More** button on the lower right corner of this panel to access the deeper transitions properties settings, as illustrated below.

At the very least, you'll have a couple of basic customization options available to customize, depending on the complexity of the transition itself. Some transitions have several customizable features. You may need to scroll down in the panel to see all of the options available.

An option available for nearly every transition is **Reverse**. Reversing changes the direction of a transition so that, for instance, it replaces the old clip with the new in a movement from left to right, rather than from right to left.

When you have finished customizing your transition, click **Done**.

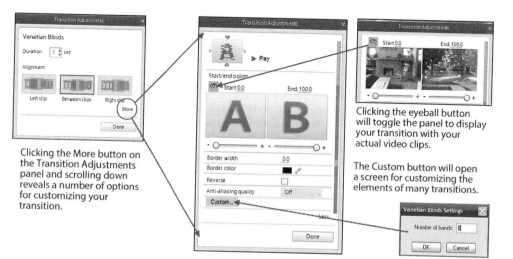

Clicking the More button on the Transition Adjustments panel and scrolling down reveals a number of options for customizing your transition.

Clicking the eyeball button will toggle the panel to display your transition with your actual video clips.

The Custom button will open a screen for customizing the elements of many transitions.

Fade in or out of a clip

Fades, in and out of a clip, are most easily achieved by **right-clicking** on a clip on your timeline (**Ctrl-clicking** on a Mac) and selecting a **Fade In** or **Fade Out** or, in Quick View, the **Fade In and Out** option.

If you've selected a clip that includes both audio and video in Expert View, you'll find separate fade options for the audio and the video. In Quick View, the fade in or fade out is always applied to the both the audio and video.

Video transitions

Video Transitions are displayed in the **Transitions** panel as thumbnails representing their effect. If you click or hover your mouse over any thumbnail, you will see an animated representation of the **Transition** in action.

The categories of **Video Transitions** are:

3-D Motion. These transitions give the illusion that your video clips are transitioning by turning around or flipping over in three-dimensional space.

Dissolve. Cross-Dissolve is the most basic transition, a dissolve from one clip to the next.

The **Dip to Black** transition fades the first clip to black before fading the next clip in from black.

Iris. Iris transitions change from one clip to another through a shape.

Map. These transitions map their transitional phase to your clip's luminance values.

NewBlue 3D Explosions, NewBlue 3D Transformations, NewBlue Art Blends, NewBlue Motion Blends. These categories contain very cool effects created by NewBlue, one of the world's top video effects companies.

Page Peel. These transitions give the illusion of a page peeling or rolling away between clips.

Picture Wipes. These transitions use graphics (such as stars, travel signs or wedding dress lace) to transition from one clip to another.

Slide. Slide transitions push one clip out of the way so that another is revealed or they transition between clips through sliding boxes or swirls.

Special Effects. A hodge podge of very showy transitions.

Stretch. These transitions seem to twist or stretch one clip away to reveal another.

Wipe. A variety of transitions that replace one clip with another with a clear line of movement. (See **Create custom transitions with the Gradient Wipe** on page 309 for information on the unique features of this transition.)

Zoom. High energy transitions that suddenly shrink or enlarge one clip to reveal another.

Audio transitions

To access the **Audio Transitions**, open the **Transitions** panel, click on the category title bar at the top of the panel and select **Audio Transitions** from the drop-down menu. (Audio transitions are only available in Expert View.)

There are only two **Audio Transitions** – **Constant Gain** and **Constant Power** – both variations of an audio cross-fade.

The difference between the two is minor, having to do with whether the effect transitions from one audio clip to another in a linear fashion or by varying the audio levels as they crossfade.

Of the two, **Constant Power** is generally considered to provide the smoother transitional sound – though, in reality, most people can't really tell the difference.

Set the Default Transition

If you use the **Create Slideshow** feature in Premiere Elements (see **Create Slideshow** on page 255 of **Chapter 19, Explore the Project Assets Panel**), you'll note that it offers you the option of applying the **Default Transition** between all of your slides.

By default, that transition is a **Cross-Dissolve**. However, you can designate any transition in the **Transitions** panel as the **Default Transition**.

To designate a transition as your default, **right-click** on the selected transition in the **Transitions** panel (**Ctrl-click** on a Mac) and select the **Set Selected as Default Transition** option.

Set Selected as Default Transition

Push   Slash Slide   Slide

Apply a transition to several clips at once

In Premiere Elements you can add a transition between several clips in one move.

To apply the **Default Transition** to several clips at once:

1 Select your clips, either by holding the **Shift** or **Ctrl** key (⌘ key on a Mac) as you click to select clips on your timeline, or by dragging across your timeline from beyond your clips to "lasso" the clips you would like to select. (You can also use **Ctrl+a** – ⌘+a on a Mac – to select all of the clips on the timeline.)

2 Once the clips are selected, **right-click** (**Ctrl-click** on a Mac) on the group and select **Apply Default Transition** from the context menu.

You may get a warning that your selected clips include "Insufficient media. This transition will contain repeated frames."

This means that one or more of your clips lacks enough "head" or "tail" material and that, if you proceed, some of your transitions will be composed of freeze frames. (For more information on why this happens and what you can do about it, see the discussion of **How transitions work** on page 308.) The only alternative to letting the program generate freeze frames is to trim back your clips so that at least one second of transitional material exists beyond the in and out points on each clip.

There is currently no way to add a transition other than the **Default Transition** (or to add random transitions) to multiple clips in one move.

Add a transition automatically

You can quickly apply the **Default Transition** at the position of the **CTI**. To do so, position the **CTI** playhead over the intersection of two clips and select the option to **Add Default Transition Along the CTI**.

Using the Page Up and Page Down keys on your keyboard, you can quickly jump from intersection to intersection of clips on your timeline, adding transitions along the way.

How transitions work

To create the transitional sequence, the transition must "borrow" extra footage – from beyond the out point of clip 1 and from beyond the in point of clip 2, sometimes resulting in the transition showing frames you've trimmed away.

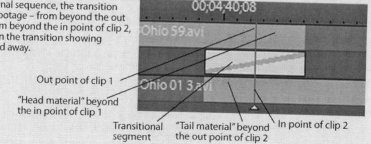

Out point of clip 1

"Head material" beyond the in point of clip 1

Transitional segment

"Tail material" beyond the out point of clip 2

In point of clip 2

Sometimes transitions seem to behave in mysterious ways. They may show frames of video you've trimmed away – or they may show a freeze frame of your video during the transition. However, once you understand what's actually going on, you may find it easier to work with the process to resolve these issues.

1   In order to create the transitional segment – the segment during which both clips are displayed – the transition that you've added needs *a few extra frames*, beyond one clip's end and the next clip's beginning, as illustrated above.

   Officially these extra frames are called "**head**" and "**tail**" material.

   Unfortunately, this sometimes means that frames you've trimmed away from the end or beginning of a clip will appear during this transitional segment!

   If this happens, you may need to trim a few more frames from the beginning or end of the clip so that, even amidst the transition, these unwanted frames are not displayed.

2   If there are no extra frames beyond the beginning or end of your clips for the program to use to create its transition, the program will create a **freeze frame** of the last available video frame for the clip and use that for the transitional material.

   This, too, can be a bit annoying if you're not aware of why it's happening. Once again, the solution is to trim back the clip so that the transition has at least a second of "head" or "tail" material to work with.

3   You may also find, sometimes, that the transition will not sit evenly between two clips on your timeline but, rather, seems to be entirely over one or the other clip.

   This is because the transition was not able to find the necessary head or tail material on at least one of the clips – so it has positioned itself over the clip which offers the most available transitional footage.

   If this is not what you want, you can go to **Transition Adjustments**, as described on page 117, and set the transition's **Alignment** so that it sits evenly over both clips. However, you may find that this also creates an undesirable effect (such as a freeze frame in the head or tail material of one clip).

   So weigh your options carefully. The default point at which the transition lands is usually the best available position for it.

4   If you're using transitions between several photos (as in a slideshow) or even titles, you may find that the transition regularly rests over one or the other clip entirely. In this case, it's best not to bother to tweak its position since, with a still image, head, tail and freeze frames all look the same.

The Gradient Wipe transition creates a wipe a pattern from black to white.

Click the More button on the Transitions Adjustments panel to view the transition's properties.

To load a custom pattern, click the Custom button in the Transition Properties panel, then click Select Image in the Gradient Wipe Settings and browse to your image.

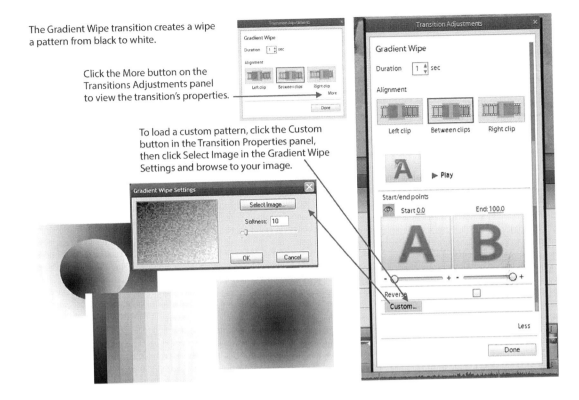

Create custom transitions with the Gradient Wipe

One of the most versatile **Video Transitions** available in Premiere Elements is the **Gradient Wipe** (available in the Wipe category).

The **Gradient Wipe** will create a *custom pattern* wipe from one clip to another based on any gradient (black to gray to white) pattern you provide!

When you first drag the **Gradient Wipe** transition onto a point between two clips, the **Gradient Wipe** Settings panel will open.

You can also re-open this panel at any time by **double-clicking** on the transition on your timeline, selecting **More** and then again clicking on the **Custom** button on the **Transitions Adjustments** panel, as illustrated above.

The **Gradient Wipe Settings** panel will display a default gradient pattern along with a slider to adjust its level of softness.

To use any black and white pattern to create your custom wipe, click on the **Select Image** button. A browse screen will open allowing you to locate and apply any image file on your computer.

The **Gradient Wipe** will base its wipe shape and animation on a movement from the blackest area to the whitest area in the graphics file or pattern you've provided.

In other words, by using a grayscale image you've created in Photoshop Elements, you can design virtually any transitional wipe pattern you can imagine!

For more information on the **Gradient Wipe** and how to use it – plus a free pack of several gradient patterns – see my *Steve's Tips* article "The Gradient Wipe" and the free "Gradient Wipe Pack" on the products page at Muvipix.com.

Titles and Title Templates

Editing Your Titles

Applying Styles, Graphics and Animations

Rolling/Crawling Options

Adding Graphics to Your Titles

Chapter 25

Add Titles & Text
Using title templates and text

With Titles, you can create opening or closing credits for your movie.

Or you can use them to add subtitles or captions to your videos.

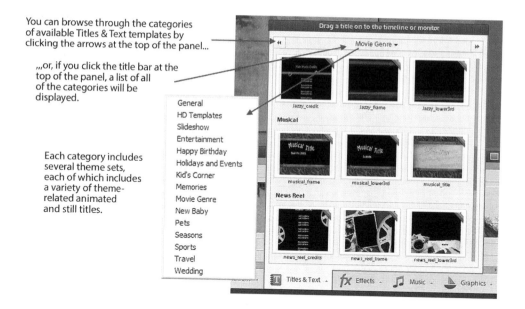

You can browse through the categories of available Titles & Text templates by clicking the arrows at the top of the panel...

...or, if you click the title bar at the top of the panel, a list of all of the categories will be displayed.

Each category includes several theme sets, each of which includes a variety of theme-related animated and still titles.

Titles and other text help to tell your video's story – and to give credit where credit is due.

Premiere Elements comes loaded with hundreds of title templates in 15 different categories.

Within each category are sets or themes. Each theme includes at least four template styles:

A still title, usually with stylized text and often accompanied by theme graphics.

A rolling title with a template for a list of names.

A crawling title (moving left to right or right to left across the screen).

A lower third title, in which the text is positioned in the lower one-third of the video frame.

Many of these templates include custom graphics – which you can reposition or remove in the **Titles Editor**. And most of the templates which include graphics also include transparent areas (which appear as black on the thumbnails in the **Titles & Text** panel) through which any video placed on a video track below the title will show through.

To add a title or text template to your movie:

1   Click on the **Titles & Text** button on the **Action Bar** that runs along the bottom of the program's interface.

The **Titles & Text** pop-up panel will open.

Once the panel is open, you can enlarge it by dragging on the black bar at the top of the panel.

2   Browse to a title.

To browse through the title template theme sets.

- Click on the category title bar (which displays the name of the title category at the top of the panel, as illustrated on the facing page). A complete list of title template categories will appear. Click to select a specific category; or

- Click on the black double-arrow to the right and left of the category title bar to scroll through the various categories.

Once you've selected a category, scroll down the panel to select a title theme and a specific title.

3   Add your title.

Drag your selected title template onto your timeline.

You can add your template to the **Video 1** track, in which case any transparent areas will appear as black in your video, or you can add it to an upper video track, in which case any transparent areas in the title template will show the video on the track or tracks below it.

Once you've placed your title, the program will open up in the **Title Adjustments** workspace, where you can further customize the look and content of your text and accompanying graphics.

Safe Margins

When your title opens in the **Title Adjustments** workspace, you'll notice two concentric rectangles overlaying the **Monitor** panel. These rectangular overlays are called **Safe Margins** – and they are guides for placing important information in your video frame so that they don't become victim's of overscan, television's terrible habit of cutting off up to 10% of the area around the edge of a video frame.

The inner rectangle is called the **Title Safe Margin.**

Keeping all of your onscreen text within the bounds of this inner **Title Safe Margin** ensures that it will always be displayed completely, with no chance of any accidental cut-off.

Customize your title in Title Adjustments

When you first add a title or template to your timeline – or any time you **double-click** on an existing title – the program will open into the **Title Adjustments** workspace.

In this workspace, you can customize and color your text, add additional text, draw, add and remove graphics and add a variety of animations.

The **Adjustments** panel in this workspace (illustrated above) is your tool kit for creating and customizing your titles. Its tools are organized under four tabs, as detailed on the next pages:

Text, where you'll find tools for setting your text's font, style and color.

Style, a catalog of more than 80 text styles that automatically apply fonts, colors, strokes and drop-shadows to your text and graphics.

Animation, a catalog of nearly 50 pre-created text animations.

Shapes, a tool kit for creating and coloring basic shapes and selecting and positioning text boxes and graphics in your video frame.

Create a quick title

If you want to just add a plain vanilla text title to your movie – or maybe a basic roll or crawl – without rooting through dozens of templates, you can do so simply by selecting the **New Text** option under Premiere Elements' **Text** menu.

A title, in the default color and font, will be added to your project at the position of the **CTI** and you'll be launched into the **Title Adjustments** workspace, where you can customize your text's font, size and color and/or add animation and graphics.

Edit your title's Text

The **Text** tab contains tools for creating, customizing and positioning your text.

The top half of this panel include tools for setting your text's **Font, Size, Style, Color** and **Left, Center** and **Right** paragraph alignment within its text box. (For more information on coloring your text, see the **Color your shape or text** on page 317.)

The **Align** tools will automatically center any selected text boxes or graphics horizontally or vertically in your video frame.

The three **Mode** buttons determine the mode of your cursor.

> In the default **Horizontal Type** mode, you can edit existing text or create a new text box by clicking and typing outside of an existing text box.

> In **Vertical Type** mode, any text you type will be written down rather than across.

> In **Selection mode**, you can use your cursor to select a text box or a graphic, resize it by dragging on its corner handles or drag it to a new position on your title area.

Give your title Style

Under the **Styles** tab in the **Title Adjustments** workspace you'll find over 100 **Text Styles** – combinations of fonts, font styles, colors and, in some cases, drop shadows and glows that can be applied to selected text simply by clicking on it.

If you **right-click** on any of these **Text Styles** (**Ctrl-click** on a Mac), you will find the option to set that particular style as your **Default Style**. This style will then automatically be applied whenever you open a new title.

One other thing worth noting: In order for you to color your text's stroke (its outline) using the tool on either the **Text** or **Shapes** tab, you must first have a **Text Style** applied to it that includes a stroke or outline. Otherwise, the **Stroke** color option will not be available.

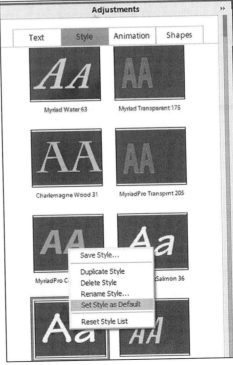

Add a Text Animation

Under the **Animation** tab in the **Title Adjustments** workspace you'll find over three dozen **Text Animations** – very cool pre-programmed movements for getting your text on and off screen. Some juggle entire words, others dance your titles around one letter at a time.

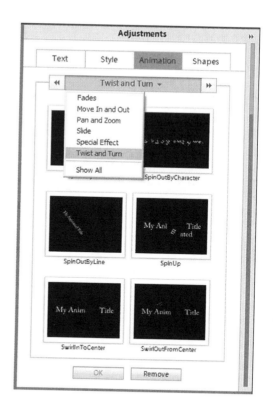

These **Text Animations** are in several categories, and you can browse the various categories by clicking the title bar at the top of the panel or by using the arrow buttons on either side of the title bar.

Fades bring your text in or out with a fade to or from transparency.

Move In and Out animate your text one letter at a time.

Pan and Zoom animations reveal your text through a slow zoom in or out.

Slide animations slide your text in from off-screen all at once or one letter at a time.

Special Effect is a collection of very interesting ways to reveal your text.

Twist and Turn animations spin and twist in or out your text or individual letters.

To see a preview of how an animation looks when applied, hover your mouse over the animation thumbnail until a **Play** button appears, then click on this **Play** button.

To apply a **Text Animation** to your title:

- Your text or text block must be selected on the **Monitor**;
- Your text block must *not* be more than one line long; and
- A **Text Animation** must be selected.

To apply a **Text Animation** to your text:

1   Select your text on the **Monitor** in the **Title Adjustments** workspace.

2   Click to select a **Text Animation.**

3   Click the **Apply** button at the bottom of the **Animation** panel.

4   To undo a **Text Animation**, select the text again and click the **Remove** button.

The speed of your animation is based on the length of your title. To slow your title's animation, stretch it longer on your timeline. To speed it up, trim it shorter.

Animations are applied, by the way, to individual text boxes – not to entire titles (which can include several text boxes). So a single title could conceivably include several animated blocks of text!

Add Shapes to your title

The tools under the **Shapes** tab in the **Title Adjustments** workspace are similar to those under the **Text** tab – except, of course, that the tools under this tab are for drawing basic shapes onto your title.

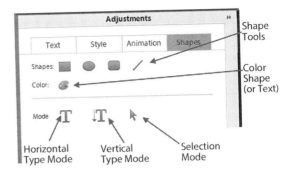

As on the **Text** tab, the three **Mode** buttons determine the mode of your cursor.

In the default **Horizontal Type** mode, you can edit existing text – or create a new text box by clicking and typing outside an existing box.

In **Vertical Type** mode, any text you type will be written down rather than across.

In **Selection mode**, you can use your cursor to select a text box or a graphic, resize it by dragging on its corner handles or drag it to a new position on your title area.

Color your shape or text

Clicking the **Color** button (the painter's palette) on either the **Text** or **Shapes** tabs opens a **Color Properties** panel for setting the color of whatever text or graphic you have selected.

To color your selected graphic or text, click the **Fill** button on the panel and then select a color using the **Color Mixer** at the top of the panel.

A **Stroke** is an outline around your text or graphic. A strange quirk in the program is that you can not add or color your text's **Stroke** in this panel unless a **Text Style** has first been applied to it that includes a stroke (see page 315). Even stranger, this applies to shapes as well as text: To color a stroke around a shape, you must first apply a **Text Style** that includes a stroke around it to your shape!

The **Gradient** drop-down menu allows you to color your **Fill** or **Stroke** with either a solid color or any of a number of gradient mixes. (Or, using the **Ghost** option, to make your text or graphic invisible except for its **Stroke** or **Drop Shadow**.)

A **Drop Shadow** can be added to any text or graphic.

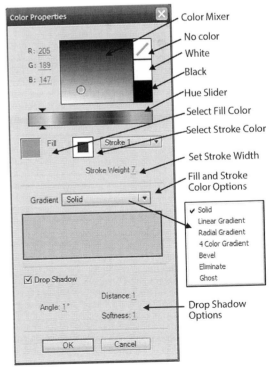

Crawls move horizontally across the screen;
Rolls move up from the bottom of the screen.

Options for starting or ending the title off the screen.

Ease In and Ease Out slow the title at the beginning or end of the roll or crawl.

Create rolling or crawling titles

In addition to **Text Animations**, you can use more traditional ways to move your titles on and off the screen. Premiere Elements includes a tool for making any title you create **roll** (move up over a video frame) or **crawl** (move left to right, or right to left) across your video frame.

The **Roll/Crawl Options** panel is launched from the Premiere Elements **Text** menu (as illustrated above) – and, of course, it's only available while you're in the **Title Adjustments** workspace.

The options you select in this panel will apply to the entire title you are currently editing. In other words, whatever else you've got on your title – text animations, graphics, etc. – setting options in the **Roll/Crawl** panel will make it all roll or crawl across your screen. (If you've selected a title template that is already set to roll or crawl, you'll find that, when you open this panel, some of the options on this panel have already been set.)

The settings on the **Roll/Crawl Options** panel are fairly intuitive. If you select **Crawl**, for instance, you have the option of setting it to either **Crawl Left** or **Crawl Right** across the video frame.

The **Timing** options allow you to set if and how your roll or crawl starts and/or ends off screen.

- You have the options of setting your title to **Start Off Screen** and/or **End Off Screen**. Alternatively, you can manually set the **Preroll** or **Postroll** time for how long the title is off the screen before or after it rolls or crawls.

- The **Ease In** and **Ease Out** options allow you to change the rolling or crawling movement from a steady speed to one that begins slowly and then speeds up (**Ease In**), or vice versa (**Ease Out**).

The speed at which the title rolls or crawls is determined by how long the title is on your timeline. Extending (by dragging one end to lengthen) the title on your timeline will **increase its duration and thus slow the speed** of the roll or crawl; dragging in one end of the title to **decrease its duration will increase the speed** of the roll or crawl.

As an alternative to using these automatic roll and crawl options, you can manually keyframe the movement of your title so that it is revealed through any movement, effect or animation you can imagine. To learn more about using keyframing to create animations, see **Chapter 28.**

Add a graphic to your title

To add a graphic, photo or any image on your computer to your title, select the option to add an **Add Image** from the Premiere Elements **Text** menu or **right-click** on the **Monitor** and select the **Image** option there. (This option is only available while you're in the **Title Adjustments** workspace.)

Once you've added the graphic, use the **Selection Tool** to size and position it in your video frame (as discussed in **Add Shapes to your title** on page 317).

You can grab an image from the Premiere Elements **Graphics** collection (see page 289) by browsing to C:/Program Files/Adobe/Premiere Elements 11/Clip Arts/Common on a PC – or, on a Mac, by browsing to Library/Application Support/Adobe/Premiere Elements/11.0/Online/Clip Arts/All_Lang.

To add a graphic, photo or image to your title in the Title Editor workspace, select the option from under the Text menu or right-click on the Monitor and select the option from the context menu.

Finish your title

Once you've completed your title, click on the timeline to leave the **Title Adjustments** workspace and return to regular video editing mode. Your new title will appear as a clip on your timeline.

Re-edit a title

If, after you've created a title, you'd like to re-edit it, you can re-open it in the **Title Adjustments** workspace by **double-clicking** it on your project's timeline or by simply clicking to select the title on your timeline and then clicking the **Adjustments** tab on the right side of the interface.

Duplicate a title

If you like how your title looks and you want to re-use the look and style for another title, you can duplicate it and then edit the duplicate.

To duplicate a title, **right-click** on it in the **Project Assets** panel (**Ctrl-click** on a Mac) and select **Duplicate**. You can then drag the duplicate title to your timeline and **double-click** on it to re-open its **Title Adjustments** workspace for editing.

It's important that you *duplicate* your title in the **Project Assets** panel rather than merely copying it or doing a copy-and-paste on the timeline.

If you create a *copy* of your title rather than a duplicate, you've merely created a "clone" – and any changes you make to *one* title will be made to *both*.

And that's likely not how you intend to use the title's copy.

Duplicating creates an *independent* and editable copy of your title.

Duplicating a title creates a copy of it, which you can use as a template for a new title. Copying a title, on the other hand, creates a "clone" of your title, such that any changes you make to the original are made to both titles.

Render your title

Your title will likely look a bit rough when you first play it back from your timeline. To see a cleaner playback of your title sequence, press **Enter** on your keyboard or click on the **Render** button along the top right of the timeline. Rendering creates a preview video of the segment that smooths your playback and gives you a much better idea of what your final video output will look like. (For more information, see **Render your timeline** on page 268.)

Video Effects

Color Correction Tools

Chroma Key

Videomerge

Preset Video Effects

Audio Effects

Chapter 26

Add Audio and Video Effects

Bringing excitement to your movie

There is an amazing number of effects
available in Premiere Elements –
too many, in fact, to display on a
single panel.

The program includes nearly 90 video
and 19 audio effects as well as nearly 275
automatic, or "Preset" effects, that include
applied effects as well as keyframed
animations – all of which are infinitely
customizable.

You can browse through the categories of available Effects and Presets by clicking the arrows at the top of the panel...

...or, if you click the title bar at the top of the panel, a list of all of the categories will be displayed.

Each category includes a number of effects.

Clicking the magnifying glass button opens a Quick Search tool that quickly locates any effect as you type its name in the box.

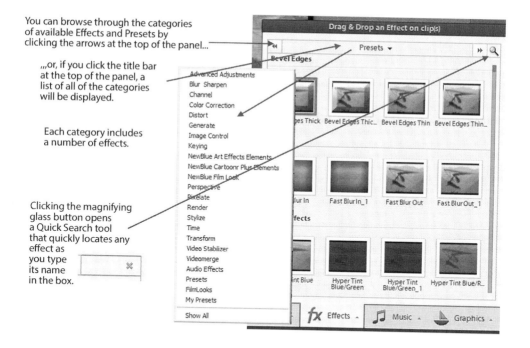

Premiere Elements' **Video Effects** and **Audio Effects** catalogs are accessed by clicking the **Effects** button on the **Action Bar**, along the bottom of the interface.

In addition to its huge catalog of **Video Effects** and **Audio Effects**, the **Effects** panel includes **Presets**, pre-programmed effects (many of them animated), and a **My Presets** folder where you keep your own custom-created effects and animations.

Presets and **Video Effects** display in the panel as thumbnails, demonstrating their effect. Animated **Preset** effects can be previewed by clicking on the thumbnail image. **Audio Effects** appear as speaker thumbnails.

As indicated in the illustration above, you can also quickly call up an effect simply by clicking on the magnifying glass button on the upper right of the panel and typing its name in the search box. As you type, the program will search in real time.

Applying an effect or preset is as simple as dragging the effect from this panel onto a clip on your timeline.

Once an effect has been added to a clip, its settings can be modified, customized and even be animated. (In fact, some effects won't even change your clip much at the default settings.) For more information on customizing these settings – or removing an applied effect completely – see **Chapter 27, Adjust Applied Effects**.

You can apply any number of effects to a clip. In fact, you can even double-up the same effect on the same clip (such as **Channel Volume** on an audio clip) to increase its intensity. Sometimes the way effects interact with each other on a clip can create a new effect all its own.

Apply an effect to several clips at once

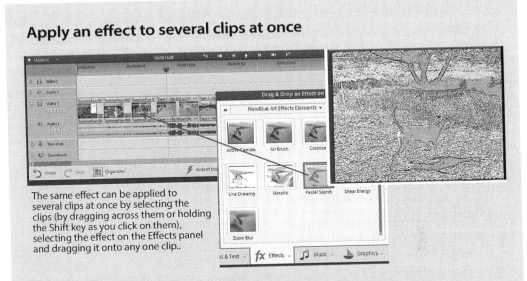

The same effect can be applied to several clips at once by selecting the clips (by dragging across them or holding the Shift key as you click on them), selecting the effect on the Effects panel and dragging it onto any one clip..

Premiere Elements includes the ability to apply an effect to several clips at once.

To apply an effect to several clips in one move:

1 Select your clips, either by holding the **Shift** or **Ctrl** key (⌘ key on a Mac) as you click to select clips on your timeline or by dragging across your timeline from beyond your clips to "lasso" the clips you'd like to apply the effect to. (You can also use **Ctrl+a** on a PC or ⌘+a on a Mac to select all of the clips on the timeline.)

2 Once several clips are selected, go to the **Effects** panel and locate the effect you want to apply.

Drag the effect onto any one of your selected clips.

The effect will be applied to all of your selected clips.

You can fine-tune the effects in the **Applied Effects** panel (one clip at a time). For more information on adjusting effects settings, see **Chapter 27, Adjust Applied Effects.**

To create and customize an effect on one clip and then apply the same effect and settings to several other clips, use the **Paste Effects and Adjustments** feature, as we also discuss on page 346.

Mac video effects: A limited edition

The Mac version of Premiere Elements 11 does not include all of the effects available in the PC version. For a list of the omitted effects, see page 394 of **Chapter 32, A Premiere Elements Appendix**.

Premiere Elements' video effects

Premiere Elements' video effects are arranged in categories. To jump to a category, click on the category title bar at the top of the panel, as illustrated on page 322, and select your category from the drop-down menu. To browse the categories, use the arrow buttons to the right and left of the category title bar.

Here are the various categories as well as brief descriptions of how some of the key effects in that category work.

Advanced Adjustments. The **Advanced Adjustment** effects work primarily with color. These are the effects you'll use if you want to change or correct color in your clip.

Additionally, **Lighting Effects** imposes a spotlight-like effect on your clip.

Posterize reduces the number of colors in your clip, making it appear more cartoon-like.

And the **Shadow/Highlight** effect is a great way to decrease contrast in a clip (e.g., the sky is too bright and the shade is too dark). Also available in Photoshop Elements is **Shadow/Highlight,** one of my personal favorite picture-saving effects!

New in this category is the **Vignetting** effect, illustrated below, which makes your video lighter toward the center and darker around the sides.

Blur Sharpen. These effects soften or sharpen your picture.

The **Ghosting** effects leaves a very cool trail behind objects that are moving in your clip.

Channel. Invert, the single **Channel** effect, turns your video's picture into its negative.

Color Correction. The effects in this set – **HSL Tuner, Split Tone** and the **Three-Way Color Corrector** – are advanced tools for enhancing and correcting the color in your video. We discuss the **Three-Way Color Corrector** in detail on page 327.

Distort. The **Distort** effects warp, twist and/or bend your video image.

Generate. The **Lens Flare** effect in this category adds a bright, white flare to a spot on your video picture, as if a light is being shone back at the camcorder.

Image Control. These effects offer tools for color, contrast and light adjustments. Among this set are tools for tinting, replacing and even removing the color completely from your video.

The Vignette effect.

Keying. Keying effects remove or make transparent a portion of your video's picture.

A powerful tool in this category is the **Chroma Key** effect, which we discuss in detail on page 330.

Other effects in this category are essentially the **Chroma Key** preset applied to certain colors (**Green Screen Key, Blue Screen Key**). The **Non Red Key** can be used to remove some of the "fringe" around the edge of a keyed area on a clip to which **Chroma Key** has been applied. (Yes, you can add more than one **Key** effect to a clip to fine tune the effect!)

Others, like the **Garbage Mattes**, create transparent areas in a clip that can be shaped with user-defined corner handles.

NewBlue Art Effects, NewBlue Film Look, NewBlue Motion Effects. These effects categories include high-level image effects created by NewBlue, one of the world's top video effects companies.

One of the most popular of these is the **Old Film** effect, a highly customizable effect which makes your video look like a damaged, worn, old movie.

The very cool, new NewBlue Cartoonr effect.

NewBlue Cartoonr Plus Elements. This effect makes your videos look cartoon-like, as in the illustration above right!

Perspective. These effects can be used to make your video image look as if it is floating or rotating into space.

Pixelate. The **Facet** effect in this category reduces your video picture to a group of large color blocks.

Render. The **Lightning** effect is great fun, although it takes a lot of computer power to create and customize it!

The **Ramp** effect fades your video out across the screen in a gradiated pattern.

Stylize. The effects in this category, as the category name implies, can be used to create a highly stylized video.

Time. Effects in this category change how your video displays motion by reducing or affecting the look of the frame rate.

Note that this is *not* the place to go if you want to slow down or speed up a clip. That's the **Time Stretch** effect (see page 267), available in the tool kit launched from the **Tools** button on the **Action Bar**.

Transform. A real hodgepodge of effects, this category includes some stylized effects, some 3D transformations and, for some reason, **Clip** and **Crop**, two effects for trimming off the sides of your video picture.

(For the record, **Clip** trims away the sides of your video and replaces them with color while **Crop** trims away the sides and replaces them with transparency – a significant difference, if you're using your cropped clip on an upper video track with another clip on a track below it).

To learn more about using the **Crop** tool (or **Clip** tool, since you use the same method to adjust both) see **Types of effects settings** in **Chapter 27, Adjust Applied Effects.**

Video Stabilizer. The **Stabilizer** effect can be used to take some of the shake out of a handheld camera shot.

Videomerge. This effect is essentially a more automatic version of the **Chroma Key** effect. When applied to a clip, it removes what it interprets to be the background in a single step. We show you how to use it on page 332.

For information on changing settings for effects, see **Adjust settings for effects and properties** in **Chapter 27, Adjust Applied Effects.** For information on animating effects to change over time, see **Chapter 28, Keyframing**.

Apply a FilmLook to your video

Brand new to Premiere Elements are **FilmLooks**, a collection of 12 very cool color presets that automatically give your video the moody look of an artsy Hollywood production (or of a cheap home movie).

Included in this set are effects for shifting colors, tinting your videos, brightening them or making your videos look dark and creepy.

They include:

Crushed Color washes out the color in your video. Great for doing *Cold Case*-style flashbacks.

Deep Copper makes your video black & white with a cold, coppery tone.

Dreamy applies a **Gaussian Blur** effect.

Hollywood Movie increases the blue levels of your video to give it a more filmic look. **Horror** desaturates the color to give your video a dull, deadly look.

Old Film and **Newsreel** lower or remove your color levels and "damage" the video to make it look older.

Pandora turns everyone's skin blue (like the Na'vi characters in *Avatar*).

Red Noir desaturates all of the colors except for a few spots of red.

Sparta gives your video a surreal, golden look.

Summer Day washes out your video's color with yellow "sunshine".

Vintage makes your video look like an old home movie.

Close Up: The Three-Way Color Corrector

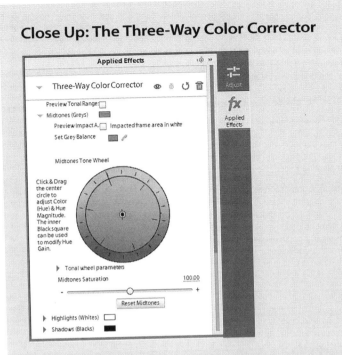

Premiere Elements includes exciting, professional-style effects for correcting and enhancing the colors in your videos (located in the **Color Correction** category of **Effects**).

One of the most advanced is the **Three-Way Color Corrector**. Modeled after color correctors in professional video editing software, this effect allows you to adjust the hue, saturation and lightness for your video's individual **Shadows (Blacks), Midtones (Grays)** and **Highlights (Whites)**.

To adjust the effect's levels, open the **Applied Effects** panel (as discussed in **Chapter 13**).

Locate the **Color Corrector** listing on the **Applied Effects** panel. Under each of the effect's three tonal levels, you will find a color wheel.

To adjust that tonal level's hue and lightness, drag the center circle point around within the color wheel. To adjust the hue's saturation, move the slider below the wheel.

To see which areas of your video image are being affected with each adjustment, check the **Preview Impact Area** checkbox.

For best results, we recommend you adjust **Shadows (Blacks)** first, then **Highlights (Whites)**, then **Midtones (Grays)**.

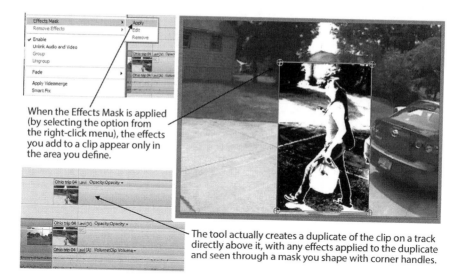

When the Effects Mask is applied (by selecting the option from the right-click menu), the effects you add to a clip appear only in the area you define.

The tool actually creates a duplicate of the clip on a track directly above it, with any effects applied to the duplicate and seen through a mask you shape with corner handles.

Isolate an effect area with the Effects Mask

The **Effects Mask** enables you to isolate an area of your video and apply an effect to it without affecting the other areas of the clip. (This effect is only available in Expert View.)

For example, with the **Effects Mask**, you can define a rectangular area any place in your video frame and apply the **Black & White** effect to it. The area within the defined rectangle will be black & white while everything in the video frame outside this rectangle will remain in color.

To create an **Effects Mask**:

1   **Right-click** on a clip on your timeline (**Ctrl-click** on a Mac) and select **Effects Mask** and then **Apply** from the context menu, as illustrated above.

   A duplicate of your clip will appear on the Video 2 track and a rectangle, with four active corner handles, will appear in your **Monitor.**

2   Click and drag the corner handles to define the mask area.

   This area can be moved and re-shaped later, if you'd like.

3   Click on the **Effects** button on the **Action Bar,** then select and apply an effect to the clip on Video 2 (or simply drag it to the **Monitor**).

   The effect will be applied only to the area defined by the rectangular mask only.

To fine tune the effect, select the clip(s) (they'll be grouped, and when you select one, you'll select both) and open the **Applied Properties** panel, as described in **Chapter 27, Adjust Applied Effects**.

Adjust your added effect as described in **Adjust an effect or property** on page 342.

- To re-edit the position and shape of the **Effects Mask, right-click** again on the clips and select **Effects Mask** then **Edit** from the context menu. The corner handles will again become active and you will be able to drag them, or the mask box, to any new position on the **Monitor** display.

- To remove the **Effects Mask, right-click** on the clip group on your timeline and select **Effects Mask** then **Remove**. The duplicate clip will be removed from the Video 2 track and any effects you've added will be applied to the entire original clip.

  The effect(s) can then be removed from the original clip by **right-clicking** on the clip and selecting the **Remove Effects** option.

Preset Effects

Although they appear as a separate category of effects on the **Effects** panel, **Presets** are, actually, effects to which settings have already been applied. Some of these presets change the size or texture of your video clip, or create a **Picture-in-Picture** effect. Others include animated effects so that your video image moves or changes size or an effect's settings change over the course of the clip. (For more information on motion paths and animated effects, see the **Chapter 28, Keyframing**.)

Presets are represented as thumbnails on the panel and, if you hover your mouse over those that are animated, a preview of the animation will play.

Once you apply a **Preset** to a video clip, you can open the clip's **Applied Effects** panel and customize the settings or animations. (For information on making these adjustments, see **Adjust settings for effects and properties** on page 342.)

To apply a preset effect to a clip, just drag the preset from the **Presets** panel to your clip on the timeline or onto the **Monitor** panel.

The nearly 275 **Presets** fall into a number of categories.

Bevel Edges. These presets create the illusion of a raised edge along the sides of your video clip.

Blurs. Animated **Blur** presets go from blurry to clear or clear to blurry, and can be applied to the beginning or end of a clip.

When using multi-track editing (See **Use L-Cuts, J-Cuts and multiple tracks** in **Chapter 20, Edit Your Video in Expert View**), you can use these keyframed blurs as transitions between video tracks.

Color Effects. These presets can be used to tint your clip or to increase the color saturation.

Close-Up: Chroma Key

Whether you're aware of it or not, you've encountered **Chroma Key** (and its variations in **Green Screen** and **Blue Screen**) countless times.

Every time you've watch a televised weather report – the weather person apparently standing in front of satellite video and moving maps – you've actually seen a **Chroma Key** effect. That weather person is, in reality, standing in front of a plain green screen, electronics removing this green background and replacing it with the weather graphics for the broadcast.

Place your foreground clip on the Video 2.

Place your new background on the Video 1 track, directly below the Video 2 clip.

Chroma Key

Apply the Chroma Key effect to the clip on Video 2.

Virtually every movie that includes scenes of live actors interacting with special effects is using some form of **Chroma Key** – as those actors, like the weather person, perform in front of a green or blue background, which is later swapped out with some new background or effect.

Creating the effect is fairly simple. And once you understand how it works (and maybe how to combine it with keyframed motion), you'll be able to create many of these same big-screen Hollywood effects at home. (Sadly, this effect is not available on the Mac version of the program. However, the **Videomerge** effect [page 332] serves nearly the same function.)

Here's how it works: You shoot your subject standing in front of an evenly-colored screen – usually bright green or blue (colors that are not present in human skin tones). This clip is placed on an upper video track. Your new background is placed on a lower video track, directly below it on your timeline.

The **Chroma Key** effect is then applied to the clip on the upper track and its "key" color is set to the color of the background. **Chroma Key** then renders that "key" color transparent, revealing through it the video on the track below – making it appear that your subject is standing in front of whatever video you've placed on the lower video track!

The **Chroma Key** effect actually appears in a couple of forms in the **Keying** category of Premiere Elements' **Effects**. Also known as the **Blue Screen Key** and the **Green Screen Key**, though the function of the effect is essentially the same – a designated color, or range of colors, on a clip is made transparent. The **Green Screen** and **Blue Screen Keys** are merely preset to the two most commonly used "key" colors.

To create a **Chroma Key** effect, you'll need two things: A video clip that has been shot with a subject standing in front of an evenly-colored, evenly-lit green or blue background and a second clip with a background you'd like to swap in.

By the way, you can only effectively do a **Chroma Key** effect in Expert View, because it requires two video tracks, as shown in the illustration.

Continued on facing page

Chroma Key (continued)

1   Place the video you shot in front of a green or blue screen (we'll call it your **Key Clip**) on the Video 2 track, as illustrated on the facing page.

Place the video or still of the background you want to swap in on the Video 1 track, directly below the **Key Clip.**

2   Apply the **Chroma Key** effect to your **Key Clip.**

3   With the **Key Clip** selected on your timeline, click the **Applied Effects** button to open the **Applied Effects** panel.

4   In the **Applied Effects** panel, click the **Chroma Key** listing to open its properties, as illustrated.

5   On the **Applied Effects** panel, click to select the little **eye dropper** icon next to the color swatch (technically called the **Color Sampler**). Your cursor will become an **eye dropper.**

On the Applied Effects panel, locate the Chroma Key effect listing. Click to select the Sampler (eye dropper) and use it to sample the green background on the clip in your Monitor. It will become transparent – revealing the new background on Video 1.

Use this eyedropper to click on the green or blue colored background in your **Key Clip** in the **Monitor.**

6   Once you've selected your **key color**, most of the **Key Clip**'s background will become transparent, revealing the background clip you've placed on Video 1.

You'll likely need to do some fine tuning with the sliders in the **Chroma Key** properties to remove the **Key Clip**'s background completely and smooth the edges between the keyed area and the subject in the foreground.

One very effective way to fine tune your **Chroma Key** is to check the **Mask Only** option in the **Chroma Key** properties.

This will display your keyed foreground as a white silhouette so that you can focus on removing the keyed area while maintaining the integrity of your foreground subject.

It's usually best to adjust only the **Similarity** and **Blend** levels in **Mask Only** mode. Once you've got these properties adjusted as well as possible, uncheck the **Mask Only** box to return to regular view before adjusting the other properties.

You may also find that the **Green Screen Key, Blue Screen Key** or even **Videomerge** (page 332) will work more effectively for your particular needs or situation than the **Chroma Key** effect.

Don't be afraid to experiment and see which **Keying** effect works best for your situation!

Close-up: Videomerge

As with **Chroma Key**, **Videomerge** works by making areas on a clip transparent – and it tends to do this fairly automatically.

Videomerge can be applied by right-clicking on the clip on your timeline.

You'll find access to the **Videomerge** effect in several places throughout the program:

- **When you drag a potential "key" clip to your timeline** – If you drag to your timeline a clip that includes a flat, evenly-colored background, the program will launch a pop-up panel asking if you'd like **Videomerge** to be applied to the clip.

- **On the Effects panel** – Like **Chroma Key**, **Videomerge** can be applied to a clip by dragging the effect from the **Effects** panel (from the **Vidoemerge** category) onto a clip.

- **Right-click on a clip** – Right-click (**Ctrl-click** on a Mac) on any clip on the timeline and you'll find the option to **Apply Videomerge** in the context menu.

- **On the Monitor** – If you drag a clip onto the **Monitor** while holding down the **Shift** key, the pop-up menu will offer you the option of adding the clip to the track directly above the currently-displayed video clip and applying the **Videomerge** effect to it.

The settings for Videomerge are much simpler than those for Chroma Key.

Once applied to a clip, the **Videomerge** effect has a greatly simplified "key" adjustment tool.

Click the **Applied Effects** tab on the right side of the interface to open the **Applied Effects** panel for the clip. Click on the **Videomerge** listing to open its settings control panel.

The **Videomerge** effect's control panel includes only a few simple adjustments:

- An **eyedropper** for designating the color to be keyed. (Check the **Select Color** box to use the eyedropper to sample your clip's background color on the **Monitor.**)

- A drop-down **Preset list** for controlling how detailed the **Videomerge** key is.

- A **Tolerance** slider for setting the range of colors to be keyed.

- The option to **Invert Selection**, which makes the clip transparent *except for* the designated key area.

In our experience, **Videomerge** is easy to use and surprisingly effective. In many situations, it's a great alternative to the **Chroma Key, Blue Screen** and **Green Screen Key** effects.

And, as the Mac version of the program does not include **Chroma Key, Green Screen Key** or **Blue Screen Key,** it is the only way to create this type of effect on the OSX platform.

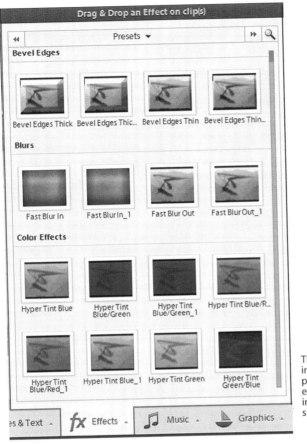

The Preset category includes hundreds of pre-set up effects and effect animations in a dozen sub-categories.

Drop Shadows. These presets reduce your clip's scale and create a shadow effect so that your clip appears to be floating – an effect that's most effective when applied to a clip on the Video 2 track, casting a shadow over a clip on the Video 1 track.

Some of these presets use motion paths so that the shadow moves around over the course of your clip.

Horizontal Image Pans, Horizontal Image Zooms, Vertical Image Pans, Vertical Image Zooms. These presets are pre-programmed motion paths for panning and zooming around your photos – their names describe which size photo they are preset to pan or zoom across.

They'll do the job in a pinch, but you'll have much more control over the process if you use keyframing to create your own motion paths, as explained in **Chapter 28, Keyframing**.

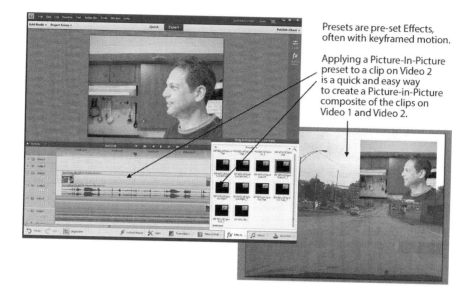

Presets are pre-set Effects, often with keyframed motion.

Applying a Picture-In-Picture preset to a clip on Video 2 is a quick and easy way to create a Picture-in-Picture composite of the clips on Video 1 and Video 2.

The biggest challenge to using these preset pans and zooms is that they are designed for specific sizes of photos (as indicated in each preset's name). If the photo you are panning and zooming around is smaller than the effect, for instance, the effect may pan right off the edge of your photo!

With **keyframing** – and even the **Pan & Zoom Tool** (page 96) – you have the ability to control *precisely* how your motion path behaves.

Mosaics. These animated presets go to or from a mosaic pattern and can be applied to the beginning or end of your clip.

Picture-in-Picture (PiP). The **PiP** presets, when applied to a clip on the Video 2 track with another clip on the Video 1 track under it, automatically reduce the scale of the clip on the Video 2 track and reposition it in the video frame, such that both it and the clip under it are on screen at the same time (as illustrated above).

Some **Picture-in-picture** presets will even add motion, changing the scale or position of **PiP** over the course of the clip – sometimes even incorporating an elaborate animation effect, such as spinning.

Solarizes. These animated presets go to or from a bright **Solarize** effect, and can be applied to the beginning or end of a clip.

Twirls. These animated twirling effects can be applied to the beginning or end of a clip.

Create a custom preset

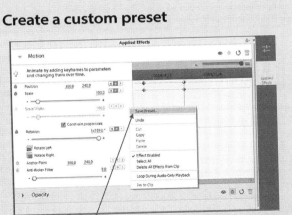

Once you've created settings for an effect or created a keyframed effect or motion path, you can save it as a custom preset effect by right-clicking on it (Ctrl-clicking on a Mac) in the Applied Effects panel and selecting the option to Save Preset.

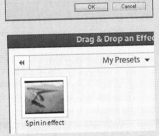

When you Save Preset, you can name it, set it to apply to the beginning or end of a clip and give it a description.

Once saved, your preset will appear in My Presets in the Effects panel for all of your Premiere Elements projects.

You can easily create your own presets, saving your custom effects settings, animations or motion paths for future use.

To create a custom preset, **right-click** on the effect it represents in your clip's **Applied Effects** panel (**Ctrl-click** on a Mac) and select the **Save Preset** option, as illustrated above.

Once you have saved the preset, it will be available in the **My Presets** category on the **Effects** panel.

Applying a custom preset to a clip is just like applying a default preset.

Click to select the clip on your timeline and then drag the preset onto it from the **My Presets** category on the **Effects** panel.

Audio effects

Premiere Elements includes 19 effects in its **Audio Effects** category. (The Mac version includes a slightly reduced set, as discussed on page 394.)

These effects are designed for adding special effects to your audio files or for filtering the sounds in your movie. (More basic audio effects, such as **Volume, Bass** and **Treble** are found on the **Adjustments** panel, as described on page 296.)

A number of these effects (**DeNoiser, Highpass, Lowpass** and **Notch**) are filters for removing sounds at certain frequencies.

The **DeNoiser** effect reduces noise in your audio clip. The **DeNoiser** is primarily designed to clean up tape hiss that may have crept into your audio.

Dynamics and **Invert** are processors for "sweetening" your movie's sound.

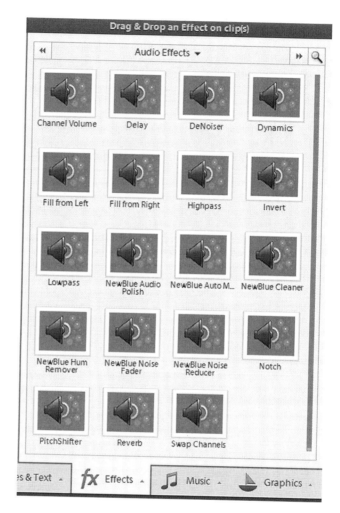

The **Dynamics** effect can be used to compress the sound of your audio by reducing the difference between the highest and lowest levels in a clip. **Dynamics** also lets you "sweeten" the sound by removing some background noise, reducing distortion or otherwise balancing the dynamic range. Well tuned dynamics can give your video a richer, more professional, more big-screen movie-like sound.

Premiere Elements also includes six audio enhancement effects from NewBlue – high-end, professional-style tools for reducing noise and sweetening your audio: **NewBlue Audio Polish, NewBlue Auto Mute, NewBlue Cleaner, NewBlue Hum Remover, NewBlue Noise Fader** and **NewBlue Noise Reducer.**

Fill Left and **Fill Right** are very helpful effects for those times when you have audio on only one of your stereo channels (as when you record with a monaural microphone). Applying **Fill Left** or **Fill Right** to the clip takes the mono audio from one channel and uses it for both the right and left stereo channels.

Delay and **Reverb** create echo effects.

And just for fun, there's the **PitchShifter**, which changes the pitch of an audio track, usually in very unnatural and often comic ways, as indicated by some of the names of some of its presets: **Female Becomes Secret Agent, Cartoon Mouse, Boo!, Sore Throat, A Third Higher, Breathless, Slightly Detuned, A Quint Up** and **A Quint Down**.

As with video effects, audio effects can be applied constantly, for the entire duration of a clip or, by using keyframing, you can vary the intensity or settings for your effects over the course of the clip – adding an echo to one portion of a clip but not another, for instance.

For more information on changing settings for effects, see **Adjust an Effect or Property** on page 342 of **Chapter 27, Adjust Applied Effects.**

For information on keyframing effects to specific settings at specific points in your movie, see **Chapter 28, Keyframing**.

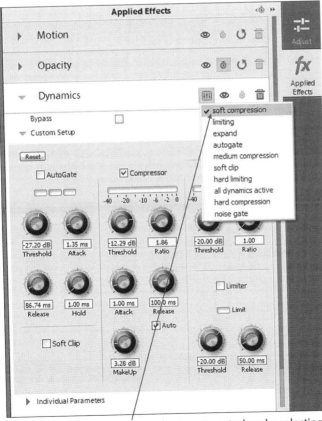

Many effects can be set using adjustment controls or by selecting a preset from the drop-down menu

Cool Tricks & Hot Tips for Adobe Premiere Elements

There is practically no limit to the special video and audio effects you can create with Premiere Elements.

If you'd like to learn some advanced tricks – like creating explosions in the sky or making a person appear to confront his identical twin, making your photos look three-dimensional or creating amazing titling effects – check out our *Cool Tricks & Hot Tips for Adobe Premiere Elements*.

Full of bright, colorful illustrations and step-by-step instructions for creating 50 very cool special effects, with dozens of helpful "Hot Tips" thrown in for good measure, it's a book that will show you the amazing potential of this simple, inexpensive program.

The book is available through major online book stores as well as at the Muvipix.com store.

For more information as well as examples of some of the effects you can learn to create, see Muvipix.com/CoolTricks.

Chapter 27

Adjust Applied Effects

Customizing your effects' settings

The Applied Effects panel is second only to the timeline as the most powerful and important workspace in Premiere Elements.

The timeline may be where you assemble, trim and order your clips, but the Applied Effects panel is where you make the movie magic happen!

It's where the effects are customized and sometimes even animated. It's where motion paths and many special effects are created.

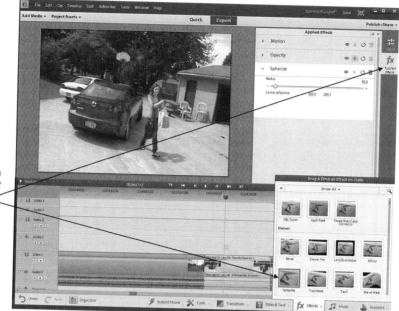

Once an effect has been applied to a clip on your timeline, the settings for that effect can be adjusted in the Applied Effects panel.

After you've applied a video or audio effect to a clip on your timeline, you'll want to tweak its settings to customize how it affects your clip.

This customization is done in the **Applied Effects** panel.

The **Applied Effects** panel will list all of the effects added to your clips (as well as a number of default properties, as discussed on the facing page). These effects and properties each include individual settings for customizing the way the effect behaves.

These custom settings can be made overall, affecting the look or sound of an entire clip, or they can be keyframed, creating an animated effect.

Keyframing is the process of creating motion paths or effects that change settings over time (such as a **Crop** effect in which the cropped area changes shape or a **Ripple** effect that shows actual, moving ripples across your clip). For a more detailed discussion of created animated effects, see **Chapter 28, Keyframing**.

Open the Applied Effects panel

Click to select a clip on your timeline and then click on the **Applied Effects** tab on the right side of the program's interface, as illustrated above.

The **Applied Effects** panel will display a list of any effects applied to your selected clip as well as a couple of default video properties, as illustrated at the top of the facing page.

To access the individual settings for any applied effect, click on that effect's listing.

The Applied Effects panel is opened by clicking the Applied Effects button.

The panel will list any effects you've added to your selected clip. If your selected clip is a video clip, it will also list the default properties of Motion and Opacity.

To open or to close the effect's properties settings, click on the effect's name listing.

Clip effects and properties

The **Applied Effects** panel lists any effects you've added to a selected audio or video clip.

In addition, there are two properties that will appear on this panel for every video clip – **Motion** and **Opacity**.

Click on the **Motion** or **Opacity** listing to open that property's individual settings, illustrated below right.

Motion. Includes individual settings for **Position, Scale** and **Rotation** – the settings used to keyframe pan & zoom motion paths over photos. (See **Chapter 28, Keyframing** for detailed information on how to create motion paths using these properties.)

Position is the location of a clip in your video frame, based on its center point, measured in pixels. For a 720x480 video frame, default center is 360, 240.

Scale is the size of your clip, listed as a percentage, 100 being default.

Rotation is a measure of degrees of angle imposed on your video image.

The settings for a clip's **Motion** properties can be changed in this panel or, more intuitively, by clicking on the video image in the **Monitor** panel and dragging it or its corner angles to change its position, resize the clip or rotate it (as discussed on page 343).

Opacity. Opacity is the transparency level of a clip. (Well, technically "opacity" is the *non-transparency* level of a clip.)

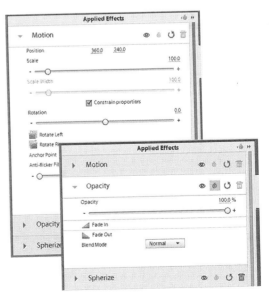

341

A **Fade In** or **Fade Out** transition is, technically, a function of the clip's **Opacity** property. Because of that, a **Fade In** or **Fade Out** can be added to a selected video clip by selecting the option here in the panel as well as by selecting the option from the **right-click** menu, as discussed on page 264. (A **Fade In** or **Fade Out** uses **Opacity** keyframed animation to bring the clip from transparency/black to 100% opaque or vice versa.)

The **Opacity** property settings also include an option for setting the clip's **Blend Mode**. **Blend Modes** are a bit beyond the scope of this book, but basically they're a high-level way of setting how a selected clip reacts with the video tracks below it on your timeline. In the vast majority of your work, you'll likely leave it set to **Normal**. But if you'd like to explore this advanced "bonus" tool Adobe has included, you can place a video on a track below your selected video and experiment with the interesting effects the different **Blend Modes** produce.

Many effects can be added to a single clip, and you can even add multiple instances of the *same* effect to increase its intensity.

Adjust an effect or property

Once you've opened the **Applied Effects** panel for a clip, you'll see a list of all of the effects added to that clip as well as the default properties of **Motion** and **Opacity,** as applicable.

To open up the individual settings for an effect listed in the panel, click on the effect's listing.

A few effects, such as the **Black & White** effect, have no settings at all. They are either on or off.

Some effects (such as **Lightning**) offer dozens of settings for customizing the effect. Others (such as **Posterize**) may offer only a few – or even a single "intensity adjustment" slider.

A number of effects (**Spherize**, for instance), when first applied to a clip, may not show a significant change at their default settings. You need to adjust the effect's settings in the **Applied Effects** panel to see any real change.

There are always several ways to adjust the settings for an effect.

Numbers – The numbers that represent an effect can, depending on the effect, represent the effect's **Position** (measured in pixels across the frame), percentage (as in **Opacity**) or intensity. To change a number, click on it and type in a new amount.

Alternatively, you can click and drag right and left over a number to increase or decrease its level.

Adjusting Applied Effects

Effects settings can be adjusted by moving the sliders or by typing over the numbers.

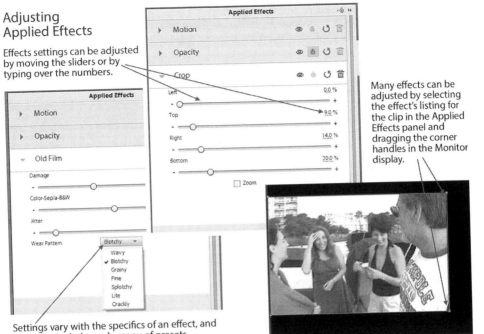

Many effects can be adjusted by selecting the effect's listing for the clip in the Applied Effects panel and dragging the corner handles in the Monitor display.

Settings vary with the specifics of an effect, and may even include a sub-menu of presets.

Sliders – The intensity or percentage settings for a large number of effects settings can be increased or decreased by moving its sliders back and forth.

On the Monitor – For a number of effects, the most intuitive way to change the effect's settings is to click and drag right on the video displayed in the **Monitor**.

When the effect's listing is selected in the **Applied Effects** panel, a position marker or corner handles will appear on the clip in the **Monitor**, as illustrated above. You can then click on this marker or corner handle and drag them into your desired positions.

For effects that involve motion (such as repositioning, rotating or resizing the video image) dragging a corner handle in the **Monitor** will move, rotate or resize the image.

For effects that involve shaping or sizing (such as scaling, cropping or using one of the garbage mattes) dragging the corner handles will reshape the image or affected area.

Once you change your effect's settings, the changes will be immediately displayed in your **Monitor** panel. (If they're not, it's because the **CTI** playhead isn't positioned over the clip you're adjusting on your timeline.) The exception is the **Lightning** effect, which is so intensive and erratic that you'll need to play back the clip to see how your adjusted settings have affected the clip.

Disable or remove an effect

Once you've adjusted the settings for an effect, you can do a before-and-after comparison by temporarily turning off – or disabling – the effect.

Effect enabled

Effect disabled

To temporarily turn off the effect, click on the eyeball icon to the right of the effect listing in the **Applied Effects** panel.

When you disable the effect, the eyeball icon will appear with a slash through it, and the effect's change on your video image will disappear.

To re-enable the effect, click on the same spot. The eyeball icon will return and the effect will once again be applied to your clip.

To remove an effect from a clip, click on the trashcan icon on the right end of the effect's listing. (The **Motion** and **Opacity** properties can not be removed.)

Types of effects settings

Because effects change your clips in different ways (some that shift colors, some that create transparency [see **Chroma Key** and **Videomerge** in **Chapter 26, Add Audio and Video Effects**], some that reshape or distort your video image), each effect has its own unique settings.

Some settings increase the intensity of an effect. Some add optional elements to the effect. Other settings, depending on the effect, may shift color or define which areas on your video image are affected.

The **Crop** effect is an example. The settings for the crop effect define the percentage of the video image that will be cropped from each side. Dragging a slider representing any side will crop away that side of the clip.

Additionally, an effect's settings can be set to vary as the clip plays, creating an animated change, as illustrated on page 353.

- The **Basic 3D** effect, for instance, can be keyframed to create the illusion that your video image is tumbling back into space.

- The **Crop** effect can be animated using keyframes so that the amount of the video image that is cut away changes, opening or closing the cropped area over the course of the clip.

- **Fast Blur** and **Gaussian Blur** can be set to blur and then come back into focus.

For more information on how to create these types of motion paths and animated effects, see **Chapter 28, Keyframing** .

Save a custom Preset

Once you've adjusted, or even keyframed an effect or property, you can save its custom settings as a **Preset** so that you can use it on another clip at any time, even in another project.

To save your customized effect or keyframed animation as a **Preset**, **right-click** on the effect's listing in the **Applied Effects** panel (**Ctrl-click** on a Mac) and select **Save Preset...**

An option screen will then prompt you to name your preset, as illustrated below.

If your effect includes an animation, the screen will ask you if you'd like to set this animation to be applied to the beginning or end of the clip it is applied to.

You can also include a description of the effect, if you'd like.

Click **OK** to save the **Preset**.

The new **Preset** will be available in the **My Presets** category on the **Effects** panel. You can then apply this preset to a clip just as you would apply any effects, by selecting the clip on your timeline and dragging your **Preset** onto it.

When a **Preset** is applied to a clip, it adds the effect, your settings and any animations you included with it.

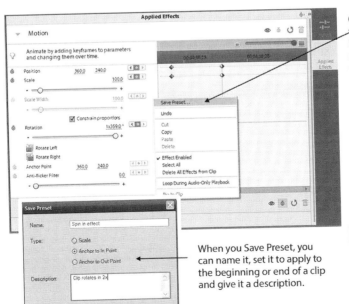

Once you've created settings for an effect or created a keyframed effect or motion path, you can save it as a custom preset effect by right-clicking on it (Ctrl-clicking on a Mac) in the Applied Effects panel and selecting the option to Save Preset.

Once saved, your preset will appear in My Presets in the Effects panel for all of your Premiere Elements projects.

When you Save Preset, you can name it, set it to apply to the beginning or end of a clip and give it a description.

Paste Effects and Adjustments

If you've customized the settings for an effect – or created a keyframed animation – for one clip, you can easily apply it to another or even several other clips with just a few clicks using the **Paste Effects and Adjustments** feature.

Right-click on a clip on your timeline to which you've added your effect or keyframes (**Ctrl-click** on a Mac) and select **Copy** from the context menu.

Then select another clip – or even a group of clips – **right-click** (or **Ctrl-click**) again and select **Paste Effects and Adjustments.**

All of the original clip's effects, adjustments and keyframed actions will automatically be applied to your selected clips!

Chapter 28

Keyframing
Animating effects and creating motion paths

Keyframing is the system that Premiere Elements uses to create motion paths, and to create and control effects that animate or change their settings over time.

With keyframing, you can control the level of an effect or the scale and/or position of a clip at precise points throughout the duration of the clip.

You can raise and lower the audio level at precise points; you can create panning and zooming around a photo; you can even animate, at precise points in any clip, the intensity or movement of a video or audio effect.

The principle is a simple one: You indicate which two or more points (**keyframes**) on your clip represent settings for a position, scale, effect or level of an effect and the program automatically generates the transitional animation between them. (Note that keyframing in the **Applied Effects** panel is only available in Expert View.)

You can, for instance, set **Scale** and **Position** settings in the **Motion** property to create one keyframe point displaying a close-up of one corner of a still photo, and then set the **Scale** and **Position** settings of a second keyframe point so that the entire photo is displayed. Premiere Elements will automatically create the smooth animation between those two positions, seeming to zoom out from the corner to a view of the entire picture.

With Premiere Elements, you can add any number of keyframes to a clip, creating as much motion or as many variations in your effects' settings as you'd like.

But the real power of this tool is in how easy it is to revise and adjust those positions and settings, giving you, the user, the ability to fine tune your motion path or animation until it is precisely the effect you want to achieve.

Although there are other workspaces in which you can create and edit keyframes (See **Adjust the audio levels at specific points in your video**, on page 170), most of your high level keyframing animation will likely be done on the **Applied Effects** panel.

The Pan and Zoom Tool

In addition to its traditional keyframing workspace, Premiere Elements includes a very intuitive workspace for creating pan and zoom motion paths over your photos, accessible by way of the **Tools** button on the **Action Bar**.

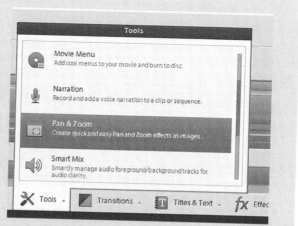

For more information on this new **Pan and Zoom** workspace, see **Create a Pan & Zoom motion path** on page 282 of **Chapter 22, Use the Premiere Elements Toolkit.**

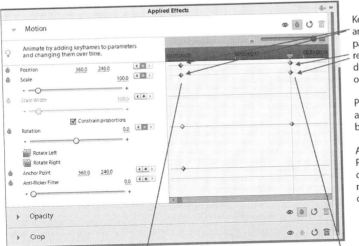

Keyframing is about creating animated effects or motion paths using points representing different position or effect settings.

Premiere Elements creates a smooth, animated transition between these "keyframes."

A motion path between Position and Scale settings on a photograph is called a motion path or a Pan & Zoom – or, commonly, a Ken Burns effect.

Keyframing vs. adjusting an effect's settings overall

Until you begin a keyframing session (by clicking the **Toggle Animation** button, as described below), any positioning, scaling or settings you make for an effect or property in the **Applied Effects** panel will apply to your *entire* clip.

In other words, if you change the **Scale** to 50% in the **Motion** properties, your entire clip will appear at 50% of its size.

 However, once you click **Toggle Animation** (the little stopwatch icon) and turn on keyframing, every change to the effect or property you make will generate a **keyframe point** at the position of the **CTI** (Current Time Indicator) on your timeline.

It becomes a sort of "waypoint" for your effect or motion path.

When you create another keyframe point later in the clip and apply new settings to the effect or property, the program will create a path of motion, animation or transition between the two points.

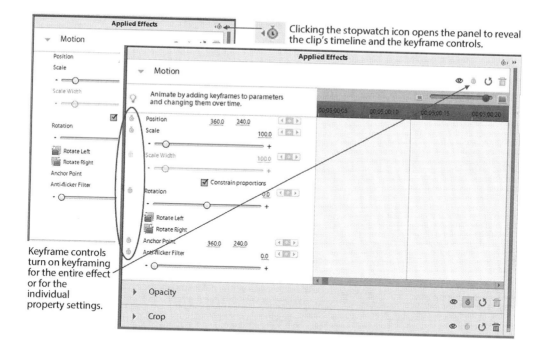

Clicking the stopwatch icon opens the panel to reveal the clip's timeline and the keyframe controls.

Keyframe controls turn on keyframing for the entire effect or for the individual property settings.

Open a keyframing session

When you first open the **Applied Effects** panel for a clip, the keyframing workspace is hidden.

To reveal this workspace (the **keyframing timeline**), click on the **Show Keyframes** button (the stopwatch icon with the arrow pointing left) in the upper right of the panel, as illustrated above. (Expert View only.)

The **keyframing timeline**, which appears to the right of your settings, is your workspace for creating, adjusting and editing your keyframes.

The time positions on this timeline represent positions, in time, on the clip itself. In fact, if you're editing in timeline mode, you'll notice that, as you move the **CTI** on the **keyframing timeline**, the **CTI** on your project's main timeline will move in sync with it.

Create a simple motion path using keyframes

To demonstrate how to use keyframes, we'll create a simple motion path – a pan and zoom across a photo.

1   With the **Applied Effects** panel open and a still photo clip selected on your timeline, click on the **Motion** property listing to reveal the settings for **Motion – Position, Scale, Rotation** and **Anchor Point.**

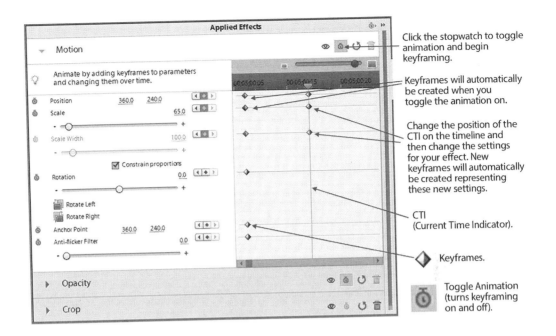

Click the stopwatch to toggle animation and begin keyframing.

Keyframes will automatically be created when you toggle the animation on.

Change the position of the CTI on the timeline and then change the settings for your effect. New keyframes will automatically be created representing these new settings.

CTI (Current Time Indicator).

Keyframes.

Toggle Animation (turns keyframing on and off).

2 Turn on keyframing for the **Motion** property by clicking on the **Toggle Animation** button (the stopwatch at the top right end of the **Motion** property listing, as illustrated above).

When you click the **Toggle Animation** button, a keyframe point – or set of keyframe points – will automatically be created at the position of the **CTI** representing the current settings for that effect.

3 Move the **CTI** to a new position, a few seconds to the right, on the clip's **keyframing timeline**. Then change the **Position** and **Scale** settings, by changing the setting numbers or by clicking on the clip in the **Monitor** panel and either dragging the screen image to a new position or dragging on its corner handles to resize it.

As you change the settings at this new **CTI** position, new keyframe points will automatically be generated on the **keyframing timeline**. (You can also manually create new keyframes by clicking on the diamond-shaped **Make Keyframe** buttons to the right of each effect's setting, as detailed on the following page.)

You have just created a simple motion path!

If you play back the clip, you will see how the program creates an animated movement between your two sets of keyframe points, using your keyframed settings to define the path.

A Simple Motion Path Created with Keyframes

Clicking Toggle Animation creates keyframe points for all settings for the Motion property.

CTI at the beginning of the clip.

When the CTI is in a new position, any changes to any setting automatically creates new keyframes.

A line on the Monitor represents the path of motion in the pan & zoom.

Details of the Motion properties settings

Toggle Animation buttons for individual settings.

Position is the location of the clip's Anchor Point relative to the center of the frame, measured in pixels.

Scale is the percentage the clip has been increased or decreased in size.

Jump to next keyframe point on timeline.

Create new keyframe point at CTI's current position.

Jump CTI to previous keyframe point on timeline.

As with most effects, Motion's Position and Scale settings can be changed numerically here, or by clicking on the image in the Monitor and either dragging it to a new position or resizing it by dragging on the corner points.

Edit your keyframes

The beauty of the keyframing tool is that any motion path or effects animation you create with it is infinitely adjustable.

By dragging the keyframe points closer together or further apart on the **keyframing timeline**, you can control the speed at which the motion occurs. (The closer the keyframes are to each other, the faster the animation.)

You can add more keyframe points and/or delete the ones you don't want. And, if you really want to go deep, **right-clicking** on any keyframe point (**Ctrl-clicking** on a Mac) accesses you the option to **interpolate** the animation movement or use **Bezier** control handles to change the shape of the motion path or vary the speed of the motion.

Many applications for keyframing

Keyframing has many applications in Premiere Elements. (It's also a feature of Premiere Pro, After Effects and virtually every professional video editing system.) It can turn pretty much any effect into an animation. And it can be used to vary audio effects and levels as well as video.

Using Keyframes to create animated effects

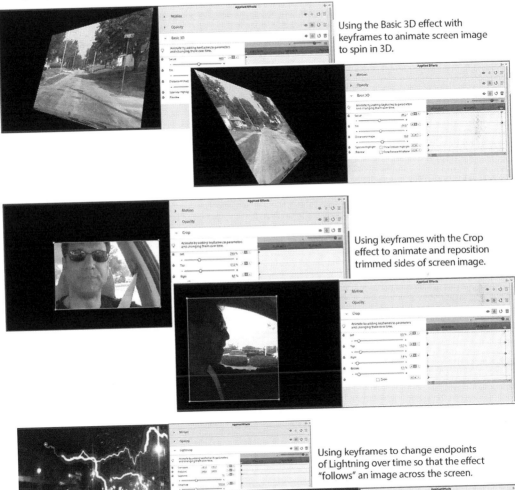

Using the Basic 3D effect with keyframes to animate screen image to spin in 3D.

Using keyframes with the Crop effect to animate and reposition trimmed sides of screen image.

Using keyframes to change endpoints of Lightning over time so that the effect "follows" an image across the screen.

The Adjustment panel (Chapter 9) also includes a keyframe control timeline so you can, for instance, keyframe your Saturation level to make your video shift from color to black & white.

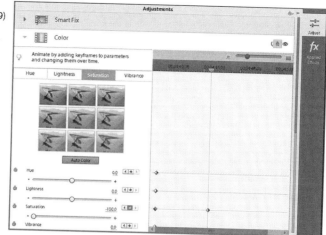

Keyframing can be used to control audio volume levels at precise points in your video project. (For more on controlling audio levels with keyframes, see **Adjust the audio levels at specific points in your video** on page 356 of **Chapter 29, Mix Your Audio and Add Music**.) You can also keyframe audio and video **Adjustments**, as we show you on page 297.

With keyframing, you can control effects, such as **Crop**, so that the area of your image that's cropped widens, narrows or changes position as the clip plays, as illustrated on page 353.

Or you can very precisely increase or decrease the intensity of an effect on a clip or animate a **Picture-in-Picture** effect. (See **Use L-cuts, J-cuts and multiple tracks** on page 266.)

You can even use keyframes to create an animated 3D movement for your video image using the **Camera View** or **Basic 3D** effect so that your video images seems to tumble head over heels in space.

Indeed, mastering the keyframing tool is the key to getting to the deeper aspects of Premiere Elements (or Adobe After Effects, Premiere Pro and even Apple's Final Cut programs).

It may not seem intuitive at first. But, once you develop a feel for how it works, you'll soon find yourself able to see all kinds of applications for it in creating and refining all manner of visual and audio effects.

For more information on some of the deeper aspects of keyframing and their applications, see my *Steve's Tips* articles "Advanced Keyframing: Editing on the Properties Panel Timeline" and "Advanced Keyframing 2: Keyframing Effects," available for our subscribers on the products page at Muvipix.com.

There is practically no limit to the special video and audio effects you can create with Premiere Elements.

Adjusting Audio Levels with Keyframes

Normalizing Your Audio Gain

Creating Music Tracks with SmartSound Express Track

Detecting Beats in Your Music

Chapter 29

Mix Your Audio and Add Music

Working with sounds and music

Great sound is as important as great visuals in your video project. And Premiere Elements includes a number of tools for adding and enhancing your audio and music files.

Premiere Elements even includes SmartSound Express Track, an amazing tool for creating musical tracks – based on your custom specifications– for your movies!

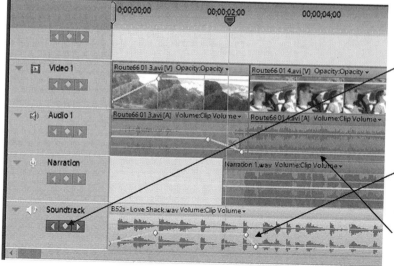

Audio keyframes adjust audio levels at specific points

When a clip is selected (clicked on), audio keyframes can be added with the timeline's Add/Remove Keyframe button.

Keyframes are added at the position of the CTI, but can be dragged to any position.

Dragging the keyframes higher raises the clip's audio level; dragging them lower reduces the audio level.

Dragging the yellow line with no keyframes applied raises or lowers the audio level for the entire clip.

Your audio is as at least as important to your movie as your video. And Premiere Elements includes a number of powerful tools for creating custom music tracks, monitoring and adjusting your audio levels and mixing the levels of your various audio sources.

Adjust your audio levels at specific points in your video

In Expert View, with your audio tracks toggled open (see page 261), yellow lines running horizontally through your clips represent the clips' volume levels, as illustrated above. Raising or lowering a clip's volume level is as easy as dragging this yellow line up or down. (Also see **Monitor and mix your audio levels** on page 279.)

But what about if you want to raise and lower the audio levels for a clip at specific points?

Say you want to fade your music down for a few seconds so that your narration track can dominate? Or you have a conversation recorded in which one person speaks very quietly and you need to raise the audio level for his part of your clip, while leaving the audio level for the rest of the clip as is?

That's when you use audio keyframes.

Create audio volume keyframes on your timeline

To create **keyframes** for your audio clips:

1 Click to select an audio or audio/video clip on your Expert View timeline and position the **CTI** (Current Time Indicator) over the approximate spot where you want to add a keyframe.

   (A clip must be selected and the **CTI** positioned over it in order to create a keyframe on the timeline.)

2 Click on the little, diamond-shaped **Make Keyframe** button on the track header, left of the video or audio track, as illustrated on the facing page.

This will create a keyframe point, which will appear as a white dot on your audio clip at the position of the **CTI**.

You can drag this dot to any position on the clip, or change or delete it at any time.

3 Adjust the keyframe point's position to adjust the clip's volume levels.

- Positioning the keyframe higher on the clip increases the audio volume level at that point.

- Lowering it decreases the audio volume level.

In the illustration, the music on the Soundtrack has been temporarily lowered so that the narration can be heard.

You can create as many keyframes as you need, using several to set the audio levels higher for some segments, and lower for other segments, on your clips.

To delete an audio keyframe, **right-click** on the white diamond keyframe point (**Ctrl-click** on a Mac) and select **Delete** from the context menu.

Audio **Volume** keyframes can also be created and adjusted in the **Adjustments** panel (as discussed on page 297 of **Chapter 23**).

Normalizing and raising your audio's gain

There's a slight but significant difference between raising your audio's volume and raising it's gain. Volume is the amplification applied to your clip's audio. It makes whatever sound is on the clip louder.

Gain, on the other hand, refers to the level of audio on the clip itself. Raising a clip's gain makes its waveform on your timeline bigger and thicker. And increasing the gain can add a richness and fullness to the increased sound level that raising the volume doesn't. Well, at least to my ears anyway.

The **Normalize** tool is designed to automatically raise whatever sound is on your clip to a good, full level.

To use the **Normalizer, right-click** on your audio clip (**Ctrl-click** on a Mac), select **Audio Gain** from the right-click menu. Then, on the **Clip Gain** panel that opens, click the **Normalize** button.

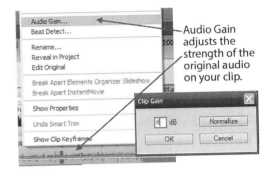

Audio Gain adjusts the strength of the original audio on your clip.

If the **Normalize** tool doesn't automatically raise your clip's gain level enough, you can also manually raise the sound level yourself by typing a **db** number in the **Gain** box. I've rescued some very low level audio by applying a **Gain** of 10 db or more to it.

Create custom music clips with Smartsound Express Track

Premiere Elements includes a powerful tool for creating custom music tracks. In fact, it is installed automatically on your computer when you install Premiere Elements.

This music making bundle includes a free, limited edition of a program called **Sonicfire Pro** – a professional tool for creating and mixing music on your computer – and an easy-to-use companion program called **Smartsound Express Track**.

Working from a library of musical themes, **Smartsound Express Track** will create custom, professional-style music tracks, based on criteria you select, in whatever time duration you designate.

1   To launch **Smartsound Express Track**, click the **Music** button on the **Action Bar**.

The panel will display the **SmartSound** musical themes in your library. You can use these clips as-is by simply dragging them to your timeline. But to enjoy the real power of the **Smartsound Express Track** tool, click the **Use SmartSound** button on the lower left of the panel.

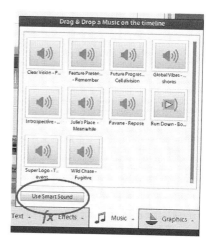

The first time you launch **SmartSound Express Tracks**, you will need to activate **Sonic Fire Pro**. To do so, click on the **Request Free Serial Number** button on the screen that appears when you launch the program and follow the prompts to the SmartSound Web site. Once you sign into the site, there will be some back-and-forth between the site and your e-mail, and eventually you will be sent your serial number. Copy and paste it from your e-mail into the program.

Most likely, once you activate the program, it will also need to apply some updates. Be patient. This can take a couple of minutes. Once it finishes deploying, you'll have both the **Sonicfire Pro** and the **SmartSound Express Tracks** programs open.

2   On the **SmartSound Express Track** option screen (illustrated on the facing page) ensure that **Owned Titles** is selected. (Ten sample **Titles** are included free with the program.)

3   Select a **Title** or filter your **Titles** by selecting a **Style** or **Keyword** in the panels along the top of the program's interface. You can sample any **Title** by selecting it in the **Titles** window and then clicking the blue button **Play** on the lower right of the panel, as illustrated.

4   Once you've selected a **Title**, select a **Variation** and **Mood** from the drop-down menus (most **Titles** include several variations and moods based on the main theme) – then set a custom **Length** for it.

You can be very precise with your length. **SmartSound Express Track** will create the musical clip to your exact specifications – from a short bumper or brief musical clip to an entire movie soundtrack.

Register and request a serial number for Sonicfire Pro ————

Select an
Express Track ————
music title.

Select a ————
Variation.

Preview your ————
music.

Select a Mood. ————

Set a custom Length for your clip.

Click the Send button to send your
custom musical clip to your project.

5 Click the **Send** button to send your custom musical clip to your Premiere
Elements project

If you click the arrow to the right of the **Send** button, you'll also find the
option to send the music track directly to your project's timeline.

Once it's been created, you can further enhance the track in **SonicFire Pro's**
workspace before you import it into your Premiere Elements project.

The program will custom-create a rich, professional-style musical track,
precisely to your specifications. And, best of all, the track is royalty-free, so
you can use it in any of your productions without restriction!

Purchase more music

In addition to the clips included free with the program, **SmartSound.com**
offers hundreds of high-quality, professional-style musical clips, themes and
styles and even sound effects for purchase.

The Beat Detect Tool

Adjust settings as needed for your music

Click to select your musical clip on the timeline, then select Beat Detect from the right-click menu (or the Tools menu at the top of the interface).

Once the program has analyzed your audio clip, markers will appear along a newly-created Beats track along the top of your timeline.

Detect beats in your music

This cool tool can be used as part of the process of creating a slideshow so that your slides change in rhythm with your music. (Note that the **Beat Detect** tool is only available in Expert View.)

To use the **Beat Detect** tool:

1   Click to select a music clip on your timeline or sceneline.

When a clip is detected on your timeline, it will be highlighted.

2   Click on the **Tools** menu at the top of the program's interface or **right-click** on the clip and select the **Beat Detect** option.

The **Beat Detect Settings** option screen will open, as illustrated above.

3   Set the sensitivity and limitations of your beat detection.

4   Click **OK**.

The tool will then analyze your music clip and create a series of markers, representing your music clip's rhythm, on a newly-created **Beats** track along the top of the timeline.

Once these markers have been created, you can use them as indicators for the **Create Slideshow** tool in the **Project Assets** panel so that your slides will change in rhythm with the music.

For information on using the **Create Slideshow** tool, see page 255 of **Chapter 19, Explore the Project Assets Panel**.

Additional Audio Tools

Premiere Elements offers several other tools for adding to and mixing your movie's audio, some of which are discussed in greater detail in **Chapter 22, Use the Premiere Elements Toolkit**:

- The **Audio Mixer** is a tool for monitoring your movie's audio levels and for mixing your volume levels on the fly, as your movie timeline plays. For more information on using it, see **Mix and monitor your audio levels** on page 279.

- **Smart Mix** will automatically mix your movie's audio, based on the criteria you select. In other words, you can set **Smart Mix** to make narration your foreground audio and your music your background. The program will automatically set the music on your timeline to play at regular volume, then lower the music's volume automatically whenever it encounters a narration clip. For more information on this tool, see **Smart Mix your audio** on page 284.

- The **Narration** tool lets you record a narration track right into your movie, even while watching the movie play! For more information on this tool, see **Narration** on page 281.

- The **Adjustments** panel includes tools for raising and lowering your clips' **Volume**, adjusting the **Balance** of your stereo channels and raising and lowering the levels of **Bass** and **Treble**. For more information on these tools, see page 296 of **Chapter 23, Make Adjustments to Your Video**.

- And, finally, the program includes several great **Audio Effects** for sweetening your audio, reducing noise, adding echo effects and filtering certain frequencies to clean your audio or creating special audio effects. You'll find out all about them on page 336 of **Chapter 26, Add Audio and Video Effects**.

Adobe Premiere Elements

Part VII
Publish & Share
Your Videos

Adding Menu Markers

Selecting a Menu Template

Customizing Your Menu's Background and Music

Customizing Your Menu's Text

Adding Media to a Menu's "Drop Zone"

Chapter 30
Create Movie Menus
Authoring your DVDs and BluRay discs

Once you've finished your Premiere Elements video project, you'll want to share it in the most attractive package possible.

Premiere Elements includes over 70 templates for creating DVD and BluRay disc menus for your videos. And it includes tools for customizing them in a variety of ways!

Although the DVD and BluRay menu authoring system in Premiere Elements isn't as advanced as it is in many standalone disc menu authoring programs, you can do a surprising amount to personalize your disc menus just by using Premiere Elements' library of disc menu templates and its fairly powerful menu customization features.

Once you've applied and customized your disc menus, you can then create a DVD or BluRay disc using the options under the **Publish & Share** tab, as described in **Chapter 31, Publish & Share Your Video Projects.**

Add Menu Markers to your movie project

The **Set Menu Marker** tool is a very important part of the DVD and BluRay disc authoring process in Premiere Elements.

The **Menu Markers** you place on your timeline will link to buttons on your disc's main menu and scene menu pages.

To create a **Menu Marker,** position the **CTI** (Current Time Indicator) on your timeline at the approximate position you'd like your marker to appear. (You don't have to be precise. You can drag it to a new position later.) Then click **Markers** at the top left of the timeline and, from the drop-down menu, select **Menu Marker,** then **Set Menu Marker,** as illustrated above.

When you select this option, a **Menu Marker** option panel will open. (You can reopen this panel at any time by **double-clicking** on an existing menu marker on your timeline.) This panel allows you to name your marker as well as determine the role the marker will play in your disc.

As indicated by the **Marker Type** drop-down menu (and detailed along the bottom of the panel), there are three different types of **Menu Markers** you can create, each with its own unique function.

Name of scene as you'd like it to appear on your menu.

Marker Type options.

Scene thumbnail that will appear as your menu button.

Option to set another frame in your video as your scene thumbnail.

Option to make your thumbnail a video loop.

Green **Scene Menu Markers** will be linked to buttons on your DVD or BluRay disc's Scene Menu page(s).

Blue **Main Menu Markers** will be linked to buttons on your DVD or BluRay disc's **Main Menu** page(s).

Red **Stop Markers** stop your movie's playback and return your viewer to your disc's **Main Menu** page. By using these **Stop Markers**, you can create a disc with a number of short movies on it, your viewer returning to the main menu at the end of each.

1   Type a name for your marker in the space provided. This name will automatically appear as the name of the linked button on your disc's main or scene menu.

2   The image from your movie displayed in the **Thumbnail Offset** window is what will appear as your menu button thumbnail on your menu page.

Changing the timecode that appears to the right of this thumbnail – either by typing in new numbers or by clicking and dragging across the numbers – will change which frame from your video is displayed as the button link. (Although changing this thumbnail image will *not* affect the location of the marker itself on your project's timeline.)

Clicking and dragging over the timecode for the Thumbnail Offset numbers changes the thumbnail image that is displayed for the Menu Marker on your disc menu without changing the marker's position.

3   Checking the **Motion Menu Button** checkbox will cause your button to appear as a short video loop rather than a freeze frame from your video.

For more information on how to create and use **Menu Markers**, see my *Steve's Tips* article "DVD Markers," available on the products page at Muvipix.com.

Add Menu Markers automatically

When you select the **Movie Menu** option on the **Tools** pop-up panel on the **Action Bar**, you'll find an additional option, in the lower left corner of the panel, for adding menu markers automatically to your timeline.

If you check this option and click **Settings**, you'll find options to:

- Add menu markers at each scene.
- Designate regular time intervals at which markers will be added; or
- Designate the total number of markers you'd like added to your movie and let the program set them at even paces throughout your movie.

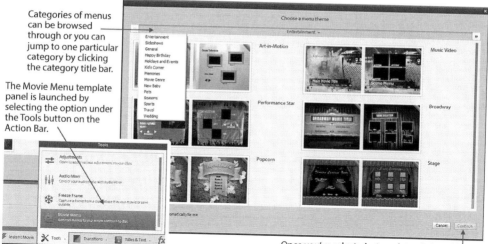

Categories of menus can be browsed through or you can jump to one particular category by clicking the category title bar.

The Movie Menu template panel is launched by selecting the option under the Tools button on the Action Bar.

Once you've selected a template, click Continue.

Create a Movie Menu

After you've added menu markers to your timeline, your next step is to apply a **Movie Menu** template to your movie.

Premiere Elements comes bundled with over 70 standard and hi-def disc templates, in 14 categories, ranging from Entertainment to Travel to Sports to Kids to Birthdays and Weddings – from playful to serious to silly to artistic.

Many of these templates come complete with audio and/or video background loops that add life to your menu pages. These animated templates are indicated with a little media icon on the upper right corner.

Also, many of these templates include a "drop zone," a designated area on the menu page into which you can place a video clip or still. (More about that on page 373.)

Apply a DVD or BluRay movie menu template

To add a Movie Menu template to your project:

1   Click the **Tools** button on the **Action Bar** along the bottom of the interface and select **Movie Menus**.

    The **Movie Menus** templates option panel will open.

2   Select a template.

    The templates are in 14 different categories. You can browse each category by clicking the forward and backward arrows on either side of the **Category** title bar at the top of the panel (which opens to "Entertainment"). Alternatively, you can click on the **Category** title bar and a pop-up menu will list all of the templates categories. Click to select the category you'd like to jump to.

    When you've selected a template, click the **Continue** button at the lower right corner of the panel, as illustrated above.

In the Movie Menus Adjustments workspace you can customize the way your menu pages and scene buttons look and function.

Click Preview Disc to test drive your menus.

Add a different disc template.

The **Movie Menus** workspace will open. The **Main Menu** page of your movie's disc menu will be displayed in the big **Movie Menus Layout** window and thumbnails of each page of your **Main** and **Scene Menus** will appear along the bottom.

Your movie will always have a **Main Menu**. If you've added scene menu markers, it will also include a **Scene Menu**. The program will add as many extra pages as necessary to accommodate all of your scene and main menu markers.

Clicking on any of the thumbnail menu pages along the bottom of the preview window will bring that menu page up in the **Movie Menus Layout** window so that you can customize its individual elements.

As mentioned in **Add Menu Markers**, on page 366, the names you give to your main and scene menu markers will appear as the names of the scene menu links and main menu links on your disc menus. (To change these names, **double-click** on a scene button, as described at the bottom of page 371.)

To see your menu system in action and test drive the links embedded in it, click the **Preview Disc** button at the top right of the workspace.

An important note about **Preview Disc**: The purpose of the preview is to allow you to see a *representation* of how your menu elements will come together and to allow you to test the navigation buttons.

*It is not meant to be a representation of the **quality** of your final menu template*. And, in fact, you'll probably be a bit disappointed with the quality of the picture onscreen. **Preview** is merely an opportunity for you test your navigation buttons.

So don't panic. Once your project is rendered and encoded as a disc, the quality will be up to DVD or BluRay standards.

Click on the background in Movie Menus Layout window to open the background replacement options.

Click to replace background of menu with your own still or video loop.

Set at which point in the clip to begin video loop.

Click to replace or add your own audio loop.

Set at which point in the clip to begin audio loop.

Menu previews.

Set the duration for your video/audio loop (max of 30 seconds).

Customize your menus

Adobe has made it very easy to customize your menu pages right in this **Movie Menus** workspace. As a matter of fact, once you've applied a template, as described on the previous pages, the **Adjustments** panel will open to the right of the **Movie Menus Layout** panel and will display options for customizing your menu pages and scene buttons, as illustrated above.

Which customization options are available in this panel depends on which elements you have selected on the **Movie Menus Layout** window.

- **If you have the menu background selected** in the **Movie Menus Layout** panel, the **Adjustments** panel will display options for replacing the menu background with a still, video and/or audio clip, as discussed in **Customize a menu background** below.

- **If you have a block of text selected** in the **Movie Menus Layout** panel, the **Adjustments** panel will display options for customizing the text's font, style and color, as discussed on page 372.

- **If you have a menu button selected** in the **Movie Menus Layout** window that includes a thumbnail image, the **Adjustments** panel will display options for replacing or customizing the thumbnail image as well as options for customizing the accompanying text's font, style and color, as discussed on page 372.

Customize a menu background

When you have the menu page background selected in the **Movie Menus Layout** window, the **Adjustments** panel will display options for replacing the background with a still or video, and/or replacing or adding a music or audio clip, as illustrated above.

Some **Movie Menu** templates allow you to replace the entire background of the menu page. (The **Elegant** template, illustrated above, in the **Wedding** category is an example.)

If your template has a **Drop Zone** in it – indicated with an **Add Media Here** emblem – replacing the background will add your video or photo in a way that integrates it with the menu template, as discussed on page 373.

If you're using a video clip as your menu background:

- You can use the **In Point** timecode (either by dragging your mouse across the numbers or by playing to a particular point and then pausing) to set your video loop to begin at a specific point in the clip.

- You can set the **Duration** of the video loop for any length up to 30 seconds.

You can also add or swap in audio or music loops that play as your menus are displayed. And, likewise, you can set the **In Point** for your audio clip such that the audio loop begins playing at any point in the song or clip.

To revert back to your menu's default background, music or sound, click on the appropriate **Reset** button.

Above is the same menu seen on the facing page, but with a new background image swapped in.

When a text block is selected in the Layout window, the Adjustment displays options for changing the font, style and text color. (Double-click on a text block to change its content.)

Customize your text

Double-click on a text block or menu button to edit or replace the text.

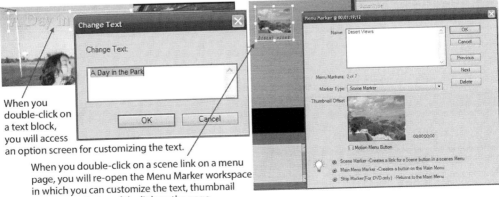

When you double-click on a text block, you will access an option screen for customizing the text.

When you double-click on a scene link on a menu page, you will re-open the Menu Marker workspace in which you can customize the text, thumbnail or other attributes of the link on the page.

When a scene button or text block is selected, the Adjustments panel will display options for customizing the text font, style and color as well as for customizing the button thumbnail with a still or video loop (motion menu).

Customize your text styles

When you click to select a text block in the **Movie Menus Layout** window, the text customization workspace will display in the **Adjustments** panel.

Using this menu, you can change the font, font size and even color of the text.

The **Apply to All Text Items** button will apply your current font and text style to all of the text that appears on this menu page.

Once you've customized the look of your text, you can also customize its position on the menu page.

Click on the text block or button on the **Movie Menus Layout** window and drag it to where you'd like it to appear.

Two Main Menu pages customized from the same Movie Menu template.

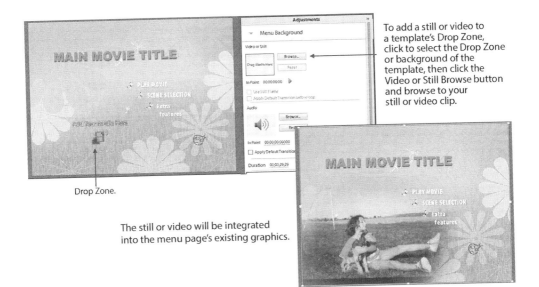

To add a still or video to a template's Drop Zone, click to select the Drop Zone or background of the template, then click the Video or Still Browse button and browse to your still or video clip.

Drop Zone.

The still or video will be integrated into the menu page's existing graphics.

Add your media to a menu page "Drop Zone"

A number of **Movie Menu** templates include a "**Drop Zone**" – a designated area on the template into which you can place your own pictures or videos.

Templates that include **Drop Zones** (and most of them do) will be indicated with the **Add Media Here** graphic.

Adding a still or video file to a **Drop Zone** is essentially the same process as replacing a menu background with a still or video: You select the **Drop Zone** or background in the **Movie Menu** Layout window and then click the **Video or Still Replace** button on the **Adjustments** panel and browse to your clip.

The difference is that, rather than replacing the entire background, your photo or video will be integrated into the existing design of the menu page's graphics, as illustrated above.

A number of templates (the **Entertainment** category's **Art-in-Motion**, and the **Memories** category's **Yearbook** and **Family Memories**, for instance) will drop your still or photos into an existing design so that it appears to be a painting on the wall or a photo in a photo album.

Overlapping scene buttons

If, in the process of arranging your scene buttons on your menu (or, occasionally, if you've added lots of text), your buttons display with a red frame around them, this is an indication that you have two buttons sharing the same space or overlapping.

If you move the buttons apart (or even resize the buttons by dragging in on their corner handles), the red frames should disappear.

Overlapping buttons are not a big deal, if you're playing your disc on a DVD or BluRay player. The player reads each button individually. But, if you play your disc on a computer, overlapping buttons can makes it difficult to select one button or the other since their hyperlinks share the same space. Because of this, the program will not let you create a DVD, BluRay or WebDVD if any scene buttons are overlapping.

Sharing Your Movie as a WebDVD

Sharing to a DVD or BluRay Disc

Sharing Your Movie Online

Sharing Your Movie as a Computer File

Sharing Your Movie to a Portable Device

Chapter 31

Publish & Share Your Video Projects

Outputting from Premiere Elements 11

Once you've finished your video masterpiece, you're ready to output your video and share it with the world.

There are a wide variety of ways to output from Premiere Elements, and a surprisingly large number of formats you can output to.

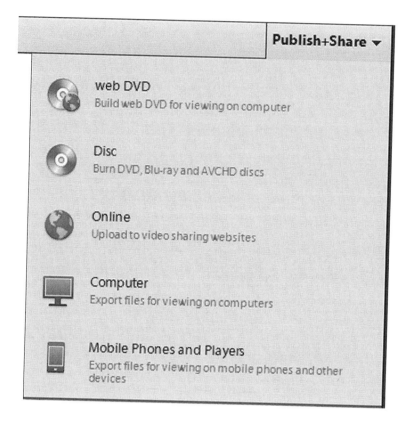

A click on the **Publish & Share** tab on the upper right of the interface reveals a list of five output options for your video, each of which offers formats and settings for each specific output as well as customizable settings for more advanced users.

Your **Publish & Share** options are:

Web DVD – Build a Web DVD for Viewing Online or on a Computer (as discussed on page 378)

Disc – Burn DVD, BluRay and AVCHD Discs (as discussed on page 379)

Online – Upload to Video Sharing Websites (as discussed on page 382)

Computer – Export Files for Viewing on Computers (as discussed on page 384)

Mobile Phones and Players – Export Files for Viewing on Mobile Phones and Other Devices (as discussed on page 390)

Amongst these options you'll find dozens of presets for outputting video for web sites, iPods, iPads and other portable devices, and for creating podcasts and for outputting video that can be used in other Premiere Elements projects.

In this chapter we'll not only show you the stock output methods, but we'll throw in a couple of custom tweaks you may find useful along the way.

The file-sharing interfaces

No matter which destination and format you choose, there are basically four ways to share your files:

- Burn to a disc.
- Upload directly to a Web site.
- Output your file to your computer's hard drive.
- Output your video to an external device, like a phone or portable media player.

The **Publish & Share/Online** option panels use a similar interface:

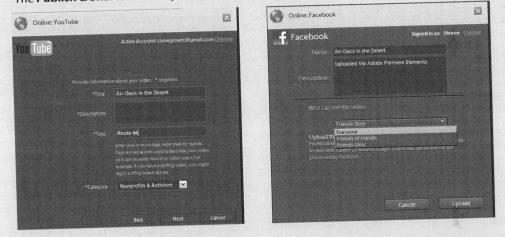

Likewise, the options to **Publish & Share/Computer** and to **Publish & Share/Mobile Phones and Players** use similar interfaces:

Select a preset, name your file and browse to a location. Your media files can be ported directly to a portable device or saved to your computer's hard drive.

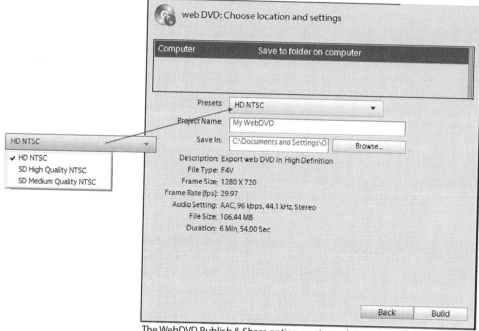

The WebDVD Publish & Share option creates an interactive Web site that functions just like a DVD – complete with menus!

Publish a Web DVD

When you publish your movie project as a **Web DVD,** your create a combination of FLV and HTML files that can be posted to a Web site or saved to a computer, but which function like conventional DVDs – complete with main menus, scene menus and scene buttons!

Web DVD menus are created using **Menu Markers** and **Movie Menu** templates, as we describe in **Chapter 30, Create Movie Menus**. However, because of the way they are produced, **Web DVD** files play on a Web browser (Internet Explorer, Safari, etc.) rather than on a traditional DVD or BluRay disc player.

To create a **Web DVD**:

1   Under the **Publish & Share** tab, select **Web DVD**.

2   Name your file and browse to select a **Save In** location on your computer.

4   Click the **Build** button.

A folder of files will be saved to the location you've selected.

Post this entire set of files to a Web site. The **Web DVD** is launched when a viewer goes to the site, connecting to the **Play_webDVD.html** file.

To play the **Web DVD** on a computer, launch the **Play_webDVD.html** file with your Internet browser.

When you select the option to Publish & Share to Disc, you will have the choice of burning your files directly to a disc or saving them to a folder on your computer's hard drive.

Output to a DVD or BluRay Disc

Probably the most common way to output a movie from your Premiere Elements project is to burn it as a DVD or high-definition BluRay disc.

Premiere Elements will burn to both single-layer and dual-layer discs and to both DVD and BluRay formats. (The program automatically scans your system to see which disc burner hardware you have and if you have a disc in the drive.) It can also burn AVCHD discs, as discussed on page 381.

1   Under the **Publish & Share** tab, select **Disc.** On the **Disc** option screen, select the type of disc you want to burn.

2   If you are burning a DVD or AVCHD, the **Burn To** drop-down menu will allow you to select the option to burn directly to a disc or to burn your files to a folder on your hard drive for either a single-layer or dual-layer disk.

3   Type the name for your project in the space provided. (This is more important if you plan to burn your disc files to a folder on your hard drive for later burning to a disc, as described on page 380.)

4   Click the **Burn** button.

As a rule of thumb, you can fit about 70 minutes of full-quality video onto a standard (4.7 gigabyte) DVD at full video quality and about double that on a dual layer disc.

A BluRay disc (which can store 25 gigabytes of data) can hold about two hours of high-definition video, while a dual-layer BluRay disc can hold about twice that.

If you put more than these recommended capacities on a disc, Premiere Elements will automatically reduce the quality of the video as needed if you have the **Fit Contents** option checked. (This reduced quality may not be noticeable unless you try to squeeze considerably more content onto the disc than the optimal capacity.)

Increase the odds for disc creation success

In a perfect world, outputting a disc from Premiere Elements would be as simple as selecting the options at this screen and hitting the **Burn** button.

Unfortunately, your computer's operating system is something of a living, continually evolving environment, with programs constantly at war for control over your hardware. And failures to burn directly to a disc with this program are somewhat common – which can be quite frustrating if you've waited hours for the program to encode your disc files, only to have it suddenly throw up an error code at the last minute.

If this is a problem for you (and you'll know because the operation will fail in its very last stages), the simplest solution is to go to the **Burn To** drop-down menu and select the option to burn your files to a **Folder** on your hard drive rather than directly to a disc.

Once these DVD or BluRay files are created, you can then easily use your computer's disc burning software (Nero, ImgBurn, etc.) to burn the VIDEO_TS folder that the program creates to a DVD or BluRay disk. This process is detailed in **The "Burn Disc" Workaround** on page 402 of our **Appendix**.

This may seem like an unnecessary workaround at first, but there are a number advantages to using this two-step method for creating discs and very few liabilities. (It certainly doesn't take any more time, and it only adds a few clicks to the process.)

If nothing else, it makes outputting several copies of your disc easier, since creating each copy will be a simple matter of burning this same VIDEO_TS folder to another disc (a process which takes only a few minutes).

The challenge with home-burned DVDs and BluRays

Although this is becoming less of an issue as home-burned DVDs and BluRay discs have grown in popularity, it's important to realize that not all DVD and BluRay players can play home-burned discs. This is because the process used to create commercial discs (pressing) is very different than the process you use to create discs on your computer (a chemical process).

Manufacturers have recognized the growing popularity of creating home-burned DVDs and BluRay discs and have been making their players more and more compatible with them. But be prepared for the occasional friend or client who simply can't play a disc you've created!

And, if for no other reason than because direct burns to disc can so commonly fail, we at Muvipix recommend regularly creating your DVDs with this two-step process. It really is worth the minimal extra effort to ensure the job gets done.

You can also increase the odds your disc burn will go smoothly and that your disc will be compatible with every possible DVD or BluRay player by using high-quality media.

Verbatim and Taiyo Yuden are two very reliable disc brands. Store brands, and even other popular name brands, can be a bit iffier. In our not-so-humble opinion, the little extra expense you'll incur by using one of these two quality brands will be more than offset by the knowledge that you'll get the best possible results and compatibility from them.

Also, *NEVER* stick a label onto your DVD or BluRay disc!

Labels can throw the spin and balance off when the discs are loaded into a player and the glue and label can damage the media itself. If you'd like to customize your discs, we recommend that you buy printable discs and use a good inkjet printer with disc printing capabilities. Epson and HP make very nice printers with this feature for under $100.

Burn an AVCHD disc

The **Publish & Share** to **Disc** panel includes the option to burn AVCHD discs.

AVCHD is an advanced compression format for high-definition video. Premiere Elements includes options for burning both 1920x1080 and 1440x1080 AVCHD formats. (As discussed on page 392, these two formats are essentially the same resolution – one using square and the other using anamorphic pixels to create their video images.)

Many current BluRay disc players are capable of playing AVCHD video. However, before you distribute this format of disc, you should ensure your audience's disc players are AVCHD compatible.

For more AVCHD output options see the sidebar on page 385.

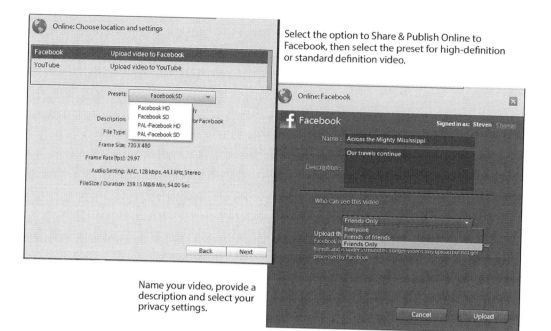

Select the option to Share & Publish Online to Facebook, then select the preset for high-definition or standard definition video.

Name your video, provide a description and select your privacy settings.

Upload your video to Facebook

Under its **Publish & Share/Online** option, Premiere Elements has tools for uploading your movie project directly to Facebook and YouTube.

To upload your video to Facebook:

1   Under the **Publish & Share** tab, select **Online.**

2   On the **Online** option panel, select **Facebook**.

3   From the pop-up menu, select high-definition (**HD**) or standard definition (**SD**) output preset.

   Click the **Next** button.

If this is the first time uploading to Facebook from the program, an option screen will ask you to **Authorize** the upload.

Click the **Authorize** button. Your web browser will open to your Facebook page. If you are already logged into Facebook, you're done with the authorization. You can close your web browser and return to the program to finish the authorization. Otherwise, log in to Facebook and, when prompted, close your browser and return to Premiere Elements.

4   On the **Facebook** option panel, name your video, add a description (if you'd like) and select whether you want it to be available to **Friends Only, Friends of Friends** or **Everyone**.

   Click **Upload**.

Your video will be rendered and uploaded to the site.

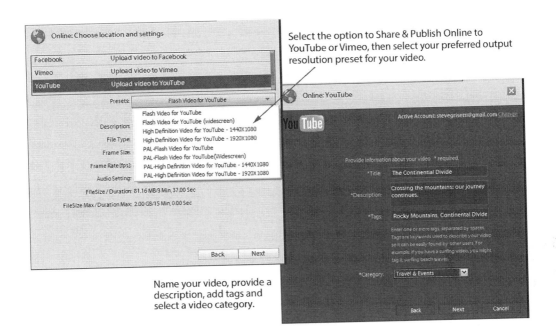

Select the option to Share & Publish Online to YouTube or Vimeo, then select your preferred output resolution preset for your video.

Name your video, provide a description, add tags and select a video category.

Upload your video to YouTube or Vimeo

To upload your video to YouTube or Vimeo:

1   Under the **Publish & Share** tab, select **Online**.

2   On the **Online** option panel, select **YouTube** or **Vimeo**.

3   From the pop-up menu, select a preferred resolution for your video.

    Click the **Next** button.

If this is the first time uploading to YouTube from the program, an option screen will ask you to **Authorize** the upload.

Click the **Authorize** button. Your web browser will open to your YouTube or Vimeo page. If you are already logged into the site, you're done with the authorization. You can close your web browser and return to the program to finish the authorization. Otherwise, log in to the site and, when prompted, close your browser and return to Premiere Elements.

4   On the **YouTube** or **Vimeo** option panel, name your video, add a description (if you'd like), add tags and select a category.

    Click **Next**.

5   On the final **Share** option screen, indicate whether you would like your video to be available to the public or available only to those you invite.

    Click **Share**.

Your video will be rendered and uploaded to the site.

Computer: Choose location and settings

Adobe Flash Video	Use for posting on web pages
MPEG	Use for playback on this computer or burning to DVD
AVCHD	Use for exporting AVCHD
AVI	Use for editing in Adobe Premiere Elements
Windows Media	Use for email and playback on Windows PC
QuickTime	Use for email and playback on Mac
Image	Use for exporting still image
Audio	Use for exporting audio

Presets: DV NTSC Standard

File Name: My Movie

Save in: E:\Project   Browse...

Advanced...   ☐ Share WorkArea Bar Only

Description: DV NTSC Standard

File Type: Microsoft AVI

Frame Size: 720 X 480

Frame Rate [fps]: 29.97

Audio Setting: 48000 Hz, Stereo, 16 bit

Duration: 6 Min, 54.00 Sec

Back   Save

Output a file to your computer

The **Publish & Share** to **Computer** output category is far and away the most powerful for exporting media from your movie projects. Under this panel you'll find options for saving your videos to your computer, creating videos for web sites, outputting still photos from frames in your movie and outputting audio only files.

Also, this is where you'll find the option to output the all-important **DV-AVI** (full quality video) file (for PCs) and **DV-MOV** (on Macs), as explained in **Output video to be used in another video project** on page 386.

Next to each file format listing in this **Publish & Share** category is a descriptor explaining the best use for that particular file format. You'll find a detailed discussion of each file format in **Video output formats** on page 391. Once you've selected your output option, click the **Browse** button to select a location on your computer for your file to be saved.

To export only a segment of your project, indicate that segment with the **Work Area Bar** and check the **Share Work Area Bar Only** option. (For more information, see **Output a segment of your video using the Work Area Bar** on page 265 of **Chapter 20, Edit Your Video in Expert View**.)

AVCHD outputs

Under it's **Publish & Share/Computer** tab, Premiere Elements includes a surprising number of output options for publishing your video with the **AVC** codec.

AVC is a specific form of H.264 compression, the same codec used to create **MP4** video files. In other words, **AVCs** are MP4s (however, not all MP4s are specifically AVC files.)

Among the categories for output as AVC are:

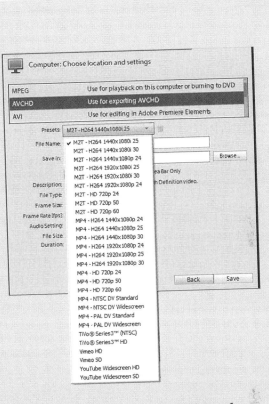

M2T – M2Ts are very similar to the video format produced by AVCHD camcorders. Use this format if you're outputting video that you plan to add to a project made up of AVCHD camcorder footage.

MP4 – MP4s are efficiently compressed delivery format that provides excellent quality-to-size ratios. "Delivery format" video is video that's produced predominantly for viewing online or on a computer or portable device. It's usually not considered a format used as a source for an editing project.

TiVo Series 3 – Video optimized for viewing on TiVo digital video recorders.

Vimeo – These presets will produce video optimized for uploading to the Vimeo web site. It comes in both SD (640x480) and HD (1280x720) flavors.

YouTube – These presets, obviously enough, will produce SD (640x360) and HD (1280x720) video optimized for uploading to YouTube. Many people prefer the results of outputting their video as AVCHD and then uploading it to YouTube over the results of using the **Upload Your Video to YouTube** option discussed on page 383.

AVCHD video can also be burned to a disc and played in AVCHD-compatible BluRay disc players, as discussed on page 381.

Output video for use in another video project

For standard video

If you'd like to export your video project – or even a portion of your project – so that you can import it into another Premiere Elements standard definition video project on a Windows computer, your best **Publish & Share** format is the **DV-AVI,** available as a **Computer** output option.

The Macintosh equivalent to the **DV-AVI** file is the **DV-MOV.** To output a **DV-MOV** file from your project, go to the **Publish & Share** tab and select the **Computer** destination. From the options listed, select **MOV** and, from the preset drop-down menu, select **DV.**

The file you output will have a **.mov** suffix.

For high-definition video

If you'd like to export your video project – or a portion of your project – from a high-definition project for use in another high-definition project, your best **Publish & Share** option is an **MPEG** file using the **MPEG2 1920x1080i 30** preset (1920x1080i 25 PAL). Alternatively, if you're editing video from an AVCHD camcorder, video output as an **AVCHD/M2T** file using the same frame rate (see page 245) will mix in seamlessly!

When loaded into a Premiere Elements project, the program will use a modified version of its **HDV project preset** to edit your file.

Why these are the ideal Share options

The ideal standard definition source file for Premiere Elements, and the universal language for PC-based video editors, is the **DV-AVIs. DV-AVIs** maintain virtually all of the quality of your original source footage. Further, when used in a project using the **DV project preset**, your video will not need rendering until you apply an effect or transition to it.

For Premiere Elements, the ideal source format for high-definition video is the **HDV** format (an MPEG2). As with standard def video, when a project is set up to match this format, this video will not need rendering until you apply an effect or transition to it.

Working on a long project in short pieces

You'll often find a longer project much easier to work with if you work on it in shorter pieces.

Doing this can minimize system lugging and maximize program responsiveness as well as reduce the likelihood that you'll run into problems when you try to export your video as a DVD or BluRay disc.

Once your segments are completed and output to the appropriate format, open a new project and combine the segments into a final mix.

To export only a segment of your project, indicate that segment with the **Work Area Bar** and check the **Share Work Area Bar Only** option. (For more information, see **Output a segment of your video using the Work Area Bar** on page 256 of **Chapter 20, Edit Your Video in Expert View.**)

Create Web video presets for WMVs and MOVs

For some strange reason, Adobe elected not to include output presets for creating Web quality versions of Windows Media and Quicktime files in Premiere Elements 11. Fortunately, if you need WMV or MOV files for use on your Web site or to stream over your company's intranet, creating your own Web quality presets is not terribly hard.

Video created using this method can be uploaded using FileZilla, as described on page 401 of our **Premiere Elements Appendix**.

Create a Web-ready WMV file

1 Go to **Publish & Share/Computer** and select the **Windows Media** output option with the **HD 720p 30** setting.

2 Click the **Advanced** button on the output option panel.

3 On the **Export Setting** screen that opens, set the following options:

On the Video tab:
Codec: Windows Media Video 9
Encoding Passes: One   **Bitrate Mode:** Constant
Frame Width: 320 pixels   **Frame Height:** 240 pixels

You may need to click on the chain link button to un-constrain the proportions. For widescreen video, set **Frame Height** and **Frame Width** to 425x240.

Frame Rate: 30 fps   **Pixel Aspect Ratio:** Square Pixels (1.0)
Maximum Bitrate: 500 Kbps   **Image Quality:** 50%   **Keyframe Interval:** 3 seconds

When you click **OK**, you'll be prompted to name your project preset. Type in "Video for Web." These project settings will then be permanently available as a preset under the WMV presets.

Create a Web-ready MOV file

1 Go to **Publish & Share/Computer** and select the **QuickTime** output option with the **NTSC DV** setting.

2 Click the **Advanced** button on the option panel.

3 On the **Export Setting** screen that opens, set the following options:

On the Video tab:
Video Codec: H.264   **Quality:** 65%
Frame Width: 320   **Frame Height:** 240

You may need to click on the chain link button to un-constrain the proportions. For widescreen video, set **Frame Height** and **Frame Width** to 425x240.

Frame Rate: 15 fps   **Field Type:** Progressive   **Aspect:** Square Pixels (1.0)
Key frame every 15 frames   **Limit Data Rate** to 550 Kbps

On the Audio tab:
Audio Codec: AAC

When you click **OK**, you'll be prompted to name your project preset. Type in "Video for Web." These project settings will then be permanently available as a preset under the MOV presets.

The option to Publish & Share an Image includes a number of JPEG presets.

Output a still of your current video frame

The **Computer Publish & Share** category includes the option to output **a frame of** your video as an **Image**. This **Image** option includes presets for saving the current frame of your video as a **JPEG**.

The **JPEG** output option here makes a great alternative to the **Freeze Frame** option available in the program's **Tools** (discussed on page 280 of **Chapter 22, Use the Premiere Elements Toolkit**) since this tool includes more options for customizing the settings of your output.

One challenge with the default presets, however, is that they are all anamorphic. In other words, they all produce stills with non-square pixels. And this is fine if you're outputting a still that you will use in a video, since video frames are constructed of non-square pixels.

However, in many cases, you'll want to output a still that can be printed out or used on a Web page. And, if you were to use one of these anamorphic output presets, your printed photo would appear distorted or stretched unnaturally tall or wide.

The sidebar on the facing page shows you how to create your own preset for outputting an image that uses square rather than non-square pixels.

Create a custom JPEG output preset

To create a custom square pixel preset, click the Advanced settings button on the Share option screen for outputting an Image.

Uncheck the Constrain Proportions link and change Width and Height to 640 and 480.

Set Aspect Ratio to Square Pixels.

Name the new preset on the pop-up screen.

The **Image** output presets included with Premiere Elements are designed to produce a still photo that can be used in a video. Because of this, these options will produce a still that is composed of anamorphic – or *non-square* – video pixels. This means that, if you use one of these stills on a Web site or in a print project, your photo will be oddly distorted. (For more information on non-square pixels, see the sidebar on page 392.)

For this reason, we recommend that, in addition to the pre-loaded presets, you create an additional, *square pixel* output preset for your general-purpose JPEG frame grabs.

1   Go to the **Publish & Share** tab and select the **Computer** destination option.

    From the list of options that appear on the options page, select **Image**.

2   Set the **Preset** drop-down to **JPEG - NTSC SD**.

    Click the **Advanced** button.

3   On the **Export Settings** options panel, under the **Video** tab, set the **Aspect** drop-down to **Square Pixels (1.0)**.

    Click the chain link button to turn off **Constrain Proportions** and then set the **Width** to 640 and the **Height** to 480.

    Click **Okay**.

4   In the **Choose Name** screen, type the name "**Square Pixels**," then click **Okay** to save it.

This **Square Pixels** option will now be available on the **Presets** drop-down menu whenever you use **Publish & Share** to create a JPEG still of your current video frame.

Output options to mobile devices include a variety of presets for many popular devices, including H.264/MP4s for both video and audio and WMVs for Pocket PCs.

Output to a mobile phone or portable video player

Selecting the option to share to **Mobile Phones and Players** takes you to a screen on which appear all of the major mobile devices for viewing video – from iPods, iPads and Pocket PCs to Smartphones and even Sony PSPs. (You may need to scroll down to see the entire list.)

Whichever you choose, the program will provide the optimal format for that device.

You can, of course, select other options from the **Preset** drop-down menus (as illustrated above) or click the **Advanced** button for even deeper, customized settings. You'll find a detailed discussion of each file format in **Video output options** on the facing page.

Type your file's name in the space provided and click the **Browse** button to select the location on your computer in which you'd like to save your file. Once your file is saved to your hard drive, you can copy it over to your device using iTunes (if it is an Apple device) or the file management software included with your device.

To export only a segment of your project, indicate that segment with the **Work Area Bar** and check the **Share Work Area Bar Only** option. (For more information, see **Output a segment of your video using the Work Area Bar** on page 256 of **Chapter 20, Edit Your Video in Expert View**.)

When you've selected all of the appropriate output options, click the **Save** button in the lower right corner of the panel.

Video output formats

The main video output formats available under the **Publish & Share** tab are **DV-AVI**s (Windows only), **MPEG**s, **WMV**s (Windows Media Video – available on Windows computers only), **FLV**s (Flash video), **MOV**s (Quicktime video – including **DV-MOV** files) and **MP4**s. You'll find at least one of these options offered on each of the **Publish & Share** output panels.

Here is a brief discussion of the best uses for each:

DV-AVIs are the "purest" and highest quality standard definition video output format available on a Windows PC, though the files are considerably larger than the other options. (It's the file format that a miniDV camcorder produces when its video is captured to a PC.) This format is also your best output choice for creating an editable video output if, for example if you are outputting your project, or a segment of your project, for use as part of another video editing project, as discussed on page 386. **DV-AVIs** are the universal language of PC-based video editors, the perfect balance of compression and file size for working with on a computer. They are created by selecting **Publish & Share/Computer/AVI** with a **DV** preset. (This option is not available in the Macintosh version of Premiere Elements. However, the **DV-MOV**, discussed below, is virtually identical.)

DV-MOVs are the Macintosh equivalent of the **DV-AVIs**. This is the format that is created when miniDV footage is captured to a Macintosh computer. Like the **DV-AVI** on a Windows machine, the **DV-MOV** file will load into a standard-definition Premiere Elements project without needing to be rendered. **DV-MOVs** are created by Premiere Elements when you select **Publish & Share/Computer/QuickTime** with a **DV** preset.

MPEGs are a high quality video delivery format that comes in a number of forms. This means that they play at nearly the quality of your original footage. (A form of **MPEG**, called a VOB file, is the format used to store the video on DVDs.) For standard definition video, you should think of **MPEGs** primarily as a delivery format rather than an editing or re-editing format. For high-definition video editing, however, a form of **MPEG** called the **M2T** is the ideal video source format, as discussed below.

M2T videos are high-definition MPEG files. This is the format that is created when you capture video from an HDV camcorder or download video from an AVCHD camcorder, as discussed in **Chapter 18, Add Media to Your Project**. To output an **MTS** video from Premiere Elements, select **Publish & Share/Computer/MPEG** with the MPEG2 1920x1080 preset. This is the ideal format to output if you plan to use your output in another high-def project, as discussed on page 386.

AVCHD is an advanced format for outputting your video. Its H.264 codec delivers high-quality video in a highly-compressed file. To output an AVC file, select **Publish & Share/Computer/AVCHD**. At this output option you'll find presets for creating **M2Ts** and **MP4s** in a variety of resolutions as well as video formatted for playback on Tivo, Vimeo and YouTube. A number of the output options for **Mobile Phones and Players** are also **MP4s**.

Windows Media (WMVs), QuickTime (MOVs) and **Adobe Flash Video (FLVs)** are generally considered to be Web formats. This is because they are highly compressed and often have reduced frame rates and frame sizes (most often 320x240 pixels – about one-fourth the size of a standard video frame) in order to produce the smallest, most efficient file sizes.

Currently, **WMVs** (Windows Media Video) are considered the Internet standard for web-based video. This is because Microsoft's ubiquitous presence means that virtually every computer in the world has the necessary software to play them.

MOVs (Apple's Quicktime format) are also fairly ubiquitous (though PC users must load the Quicktime player manually the first time they play one). Apple's efforts to continually improve the format means that often they can produce a higher quality video than **WMVs**.

FLVs (Flash video files) are gaining tremendous popularity on the internet, thanks to video sharing sites, like YouTube, which appreciate the fact that **FLVs** produce excellent video quality while using minimal Internet bandwith. The biggest challenge with **FLV** files is that they require a special player to view them – a player most people don't have on their computers. In order for **FLVs**, then, to be playable on your Web site, your Web page must have a Flash player embedded in it (as YouTube does).

WMVs, MOVs and **FLVs** can be created by selecting a **Publish & Share/Computer** option. These formats are also present in a number of other **Publish & Share** destination. **FLVs**, for instance, will automatically be your output for video shared to YouTube, while forms of **MOV** and **WMV** will be your automatic **Publish & Share** outputs for some portable devices.

These formats are available in various forms through each of the other **Publish & Share** options, including both the **Online** and **Mobile Phones and Players** destinations.

In fact, if you are having problems uploading directly to a **YouTube** or **Facebook,** or if you're unhappy with the results using the **Publish & Share/Online** tools in Premiere Elements, you can manually produce your own high-quality videos and then manually upload them using the **AVCHD/YouTube** preset output, as discussed in the sidebar on page 385.

A number of the output options under **Publish & Share/Mobile Phones and Players** include presets for creating video files at various resolutions and quality levels. If you select the **Apple iPod, iPad and iPhone** option, you will find presets ranging from **iPhone/iPod Low Quality** (which produces a 400x300 pixel video with a .34 Mbps bit rate) to **iPad Widescreen High Quality** (640x360 pixel video with a 1.1 Mbps bit rate).

Understand non-square pixels

Pixels are the tiny blocks of color that make up your digital photos and video.

For reasons that date back to the early days of television, the vast majority of television video is made up of **non-square pixels**. This is true for PAL as well as NTSC video.

In standard NTSC video, these pixels are approximately 90% as wide as they are tall. Thus a 720x480 pixel video image becomes a 4:3 aspect ratio video (the equivalent of a 640x480 *square-pixel* video). A widescreen video is made up of the *same number of pixels* – however, because these pixels are 120% as wide as they are tall, a 720x480 pixel widescreen video has a 16:9 aspect ratio.

Many high-definition camcorders shoot their video in 1440x1080 *non-square* pixels. This produces exactly the same size video as a cam that shoots in 1920x1080 *square* pixels.

Chapter 32

A Premiere Elements Appendix
More things worth knowing

Recommended "Real World" computer specs

The rule of thumb for figuring out the minimum computer specs to run a program is to take the minimums recommended by the manufacturer and double them.

That's certainly true in the case of Premiere Elements, for which Adobe vastly understates the power needed to run this program effectively.

Virtually any computer made in the last couple of years should run Premiere Elements just fine – although laptops, which tend to be built for portability rather than power, often cost about 50% more for the same power as a desktop equivalent. They also tend to have limited hard drive space and smaller monitors than desktops. So, if you do decide to edit on a laptop, be ready and willing to put down the extra cash for the necessary power and hardware.

Here are our recommended *minimum* specs for running Premiere Elements as you edit standard DV and HDV footage.

- A dual-core processor running at at least 2.6 ghz per core
- 2-4 gigabytes of RAM
- 128 mb video card, ideally ATI or nVidia technology
- 100 gigabytes of free hard drive (This allows plenty of room for captured footage and scratch disk space)
- An ASIO (Audio Stream Input/Output) supported sound card
- DVD burner
- 19" monitor set to at least a 1280x1024 display (dual-monitors are even better)
- IEEE-1394/FireWire/iLink connection

AVCHD video editing specs

AVCHD, a highly compressed high-definition format, requires considerably more power to work with successfully.

For that reason, we recommend these minimums for AVCHD video editing.

- A fast quad-core or i7 processor
- 4 gigabytes of RAM
- 128 mb video card, ideally ATI or nVidia technology
- A DVD or, better, BluRay DVD burner
- 19" monitor set to at least a 1280x1024 display
  (a 22" widescreen or dual 19" monitors are even better)
- IEEE-1394/FireWire/iLink connection

The addition of a second hard drive (either internal or external) – one dedicated to your video projects and source files – can give your workflow a tremendous boost.

Not only does it often make the process go more smoothly, since it keeps the video data flow and scratch disk files separate from your operating system's paging files, but it also reduces fragmentation of your video files.

If you install an internal second hard drive for video editing, make sure to set it up in your BIOS (the set-up that displays before the operating system launches, when you first start up your computer) as well as in your operating system.

And, if you're working in Windows, whether you use an internal or external drive, make sure that the drive is formatted NTFS rather than FAT32 (which all drives are factory formatted as by default) in order to avoid FAT32's file size limitations.

Converting a drive from FAT32 to NTFS is easy and you won't lose any data already on the drive in the process. The instructions for doing so are available all over the Web, including on the Microsoft site.

Features not included in the Mac version

Although the Mac and the Window versions of Premiere Elements function virtually identically, there are a number of features available on the PC that are not available on the Mac.

The Windows version includes 87 video effects and 23 audio effects. The Mac version includes 72 video effects and 19 audio effects. The following **Video Effects** are not included in the Mac version:

Blur & Sharpen: Anti-Alias, Ghosting

Distort: Bend, Lens Distortion

Image Control: Color Pass, Color Replace

Keying: Blue Screen Key, Green Screen Key, Chroma Key, RGB Difference Key

Transform: Camera View, Clip, Horizontal Hold, Vertical Hold

The following **Audio Effects** are not included in the Mac version:

Denoiser, Dynamics, Pitch Shifter, Reverb

The Windows version includes 107 video transitions. The Mac version includes 50 video transitions.

The following **Video Transitions** are not included in the Mac version:

3D Motion: Curtain, Doors, Fold-Up, Spin, Spin Away, Swing In, Swing Out, Tumble Away

Dissolve: Dither Dissolve, Non-Additive Dissolve, Random Invert

Iris: Iris Points, Iris Shapes, Iris Star

Map: Channel Map, Luminance Map

Page Peel: Center Peel, Peel Back, Roll Away

Slide: Band Slide, Center Merge, MultiSpin, Slash Slide, Sliding Bands, Sliding Boxes, Swap, Swirl

Special Effect: Direct, Displace, Image Mask, Take, Texturize, Three-D

Stretch: Cross Stretch, Funnel, Stretch, Stretch In, Stretch Over

Wipe: Band Wipe, Checker Wipe, CheckerBoard, Clock Wipe, Paint Splatter, Pinwheel, Radial Wipe, Random Blocks, Random Wipe, Spiral Boxes, Venetian Blinds, Wedge Wipe, Zig Zag Blocks

Zoom: Cross Zoom, Zoom, Zoom Boxes, Zoom Trails

Maintain your Windows computer

Your computer doesn't just *seem* to run slower as it ages, it often *does* run slower. This is due to the accumulation of data 'sludge' on your hard drive – temp files and bits and pieces of programs you've installed and/or removed from your system. Additionally, any time spent on the Internet loads your hard drive with cache files, cookies and, often, spyware.

The regimen below will help keep your computer running like new. Think of it as cleaning the dust bunnies out of your system.

And, at the very least, keep Windows updated and check the Apple site regularly to **ensure you have the latest version of Quicktime**!

Quicktime plays an important role in Premiere Elements' functions, and a surprising number of problems (such as video not displaying in the monitor while capturing) can be cured simply by loading the newest version.

Do this weekly:

1 Go to **Microsoft Update** and make sure Windows is updated. In fact, don't just check for priority updates. Also look for the non-critical updates (like RealTek drivers and updated hardware drivers) that may not update automatically. (In Vista and Windows 7 and 8, select the option to **Restore Hidden Updates**.)

   You may not need everything offered, but it certainly doesn't hurt to have them.

2 Make sure your **virus software** is updated. (If your virus software isn't set to run in the middle of the night, waking your computer from sleep for a virus scan, you also may want to do a regular virus scan.)

And, every once in a while, go to the Web site for your virus software and make sure you have the latest *VERSION* of the anti-virus software. You may have the latest virus definitions added automatically – but, if you're still using last year's version of the software, you could still be vulnerable.

Microsoft's Security Essentials is an excellent, free antivirus program that is virtually self-maintaining. It's available for download from the Microsoft site.

3   Install the excellent (and free!) **Spybot Search & Destroy** and **Spyware Blaster** to clear off and block spyware. (Update them before you use them, and regularly check their Web sites to make sure you're using the latest versions before you run them.)

You can pick both up from the links on this page:
http://savemybutt.com/downloads.php

4   Run **Disk Cleanup** (located in Start/All Programs/Accessories/System Tools) on all of your hard drives.

Once the program finishes analyzing your drive, it will list your **Disk Cleanup** options. Check all of the boxes and then click **OK**.

5   Run the **Defragmenter** on all of your hard drives.

6   And don't forget to back up your files (at least the **Documents** folder) regularly!

The one piece of hardware on your computer that absolutely *WILL* eventually fail is your hard drive. If you're lucky, you'll have replaced your computer before then. But if not – *please* remember to back up your files regularly.

Do this monthly:

1   Check your graphics card's manufacturer's site, your sound card's manufacturer's site and, if applicable, the **RealTek** site to make sure your drivers and firmware are up to date. Also, double-check the Apple site to ensure you have the latest version of **Quicktime**.

2   Secunia offers a free (for personal use) application that will automatically keep all of your computer's software updated – or remind you when it needs to be done.

To download it, go to **http://secunia.com/**

From the **Products** menu, select **Personal Software Inspector (PSI)**.

3   Go to your web browser and clear the cache.

In Internet Explorer, you'll find the option for doing this right under the **Tools** drop-down.

Older versions and other browsers (including Firefox) keep them under **Tools** and in **Internet Options**.

You can leave the cookies – but do delete the **Temporary Internet Files**. Accumulate enough of them and they will slow down your entire computer system.

Valuable free or low cost tools and utilities

Windows video conversion tools

All video may look the same and sound the same, but it actually comes in many flavors, formats and compression systems (codecs).

Premiere Elements, on Windows computers, is built around a DV-AVI workflow. (DV-AVIs are AVI files that use the DV codec.) This means that DV-AVIs flow easily through it and place the least strain on the program and, ultimately, your system. Not all AVIs use the DV codec, and many AVI videos (such as video from still cameras) can cause real problems for Premiere Elements.

A good rule of thumb is that, whenever possible, use DV-AVIs as your video source video for standard definition projects. (On Macs, the ideal format is the DV Quicktime file.)

A number of free or low-cost programs will convert your files. Here are some Muvipix favorites.

Additionally, we have included in this list software for converting AVCHD files to more conventional HDV.

AVCHD are highly compressed files and can prove to be pretty challenging to work with on even the more powerful personal computers.

Converting AVCHD to HDV can make for a much less intensive high-definition video editing experience.

Windows MovieMaker

If you've got a Windows-based computer, **Windows MovieMaker** is already on your system. Despite being a rather limited video editor, **MovieMaker** can handle a wider range of video formats than Premiere Elements (including, for instance, video from still cameras). It therefore makes an excellent tool for converting many video formats into more standardized DV-AVIs.

To convert a video into a DV-AVI with **MovieMaker**:

1   Import the video into a **MovieMaker** project and place it on the timeline.

2   From the **Main Menu** select **File/Save Movie File**.

   A dialog box will open.

3   Select the option to save to **My Computer,** then click **Next**.

4   On the next option screen, name your new file and select/browse to a folder to put the file in.

   Click **Next**.

5.   On the next option screen, click the link that says **Show More Choices**.

   There will be three radio buttons to choose from.

6.   Select **Other Settings** and, from the drop-down menu, select **DV-AVI**. Click **Make Movie**.

NOTE: **Windows Live MovieMaker,** the new, online version of **MovieMaker** included with Windows 7 and Windows 8, will *not* output DV-AVIs.

Fortunately, copies of the classic **Windows MovieMaker 2.6** are still available for download on the Microsoft site. And it will still perform as discussed above.

Otherwise, to convert AVIs from still cameras to DV-AVIs for use in Premiere Elements, the best free alternative solution is **MPEG Streamclip**, as discussed on the following page.

For converting MOVs to DV-AVIs, use **Super** or **Quicktime Pro.**

MPEG Streamclip

A great tool for easily converting MPEGs and VOB files (DVD video files) to more Premiere Elements-friendly DV-AVIs.

1   Select the option to open your VOB or MPEG file(s) with **MPEG Streamclip** from its **File** menu.

2   Open the **AVI/DivX Exporter** window from **File/Export to AVI**.

3   Set **Compression** to the **Apple DV/DVPRO_NTSC** (or **DV PAL**, if appropriate) codec.

4   Set **Field Order** to **Lower Field First**.

5   Change the default sound settings from **MPEG Layer 3** to **Uncompressed**.

6   If you have widescreen footage click on **Options** at the top right.

Leave the **Scan Mode** as is but change the **Aspect Ratio** from 4:3 to 16:9.

If you would like to save these settings, click on the **Presets** button at the bottom left of then panel, then click on the **New** button to name and save your preset. The next time you run **MPEG Streamclip**, you can go directly to the **Presets** button and load your saved settings.

7   Click on **Make AVI** and choose a folder and filename for your DV-AVI file.

MPEG Streamclip is free from http://www.squared5.com

Super Video Converter

Super can convert almost any video format to almost any other video format. The latest version of the program is capable of outputting both PAL and NTSC DV files.

To use **Super** to convert virtually any video to a Premiere Elements-compatible DV file:

1   Set the **Output Container** drop-down menu to DV.

Leave everything else at its default setting.

2   To output a PAL video, ensure that *Video Scale Size* is set to 720:576
To output an NTSC video, ensure that **Video Scale Size** is set to 720:480

3   Drag the video you want to convert from your Windows Explorer panel to the area indicated, just below the **Output** specs.

Click **Encode**.

Your video will be created with a .dv suffix and should not require rendering in a standard Premiere Elements DV project.

Super is free – although finding the link to the download on its messy Web site can be very challenging.

It's available from www.erightsoft.com/SUPER.html

Quicktime Pro

Quicktime Pro is a great tool to own if your input sources tend to be MOVs (Quicktime) files. These files include video from still cameras and many MP4s.

Not only will it convert these files to DV-AVIs but the program also includes some basic video editing functions.

Quicktime Pro is available for $29 from www.apple.com.

Premiere Elements

Premiere Elements, especially current versions, can often do an excellent job of converting video. You can use the program to convert video from DVDs, hard drive camcorders and even HDV and AVCHD sources into more manageable DV-AVIs – a process that's particularly effective if you're mixing video from several sources.

Converting everything to DV-AVIs before mixing them into a final project will allow the program to work much more efficiently and with much less likelihood of problems.

To use Premiere Elements to convert your video, open a project (ensuring that the project presets match your source video), import your video into the project and place it on the timeline.

Click the **Share** tab, select click the **Personal Computer** destination and select the **AVI** output option as described on page 386 of **Chapter 31, Publish & Share Your Video**.

Virtual Dub

Virtual Dub is a terrific tool that should be on everyone's computer.

Less a conversion tool than a video processor, it will make many AVIs (including Type 1 DV-AVIs) compatible with Premiere Elements as well as converting many other file types to more standard, more editable video.

Converting your video into editable DV-AVIs with **VirtualDub** is as easy as opening your file in the program and then selecting the option to **Save As**.

Your newly saved AVI will be perfectly compatible with Premiere Elements!

VirtualDub is available from www.virtualdub.org.

Free Video Converter from KoyoteSoft

Free Video Converter will convert AVCHD video into more manageable HDV MPEG2 with virtually no loss of quality.

1   Open your AVCHD file in the **Free Video Convertor.**

2   Set the output bit rate to 25000kbs.

3   Output your file.

The output file will be 1920x1080 MPEG2.

One downside is that, when you install it, the program will automatically install a search tool to your browser toolbar – but this toolbar can easily be removed using Windows Add/Remove Programs.

The program is available from koyotesoft.com/indexEn.html

Other AVCHD converters

AVCHD UpShift, from NewBlue, will convert AVCHD video to more standard HDV (a hi-def MPEG .m2t).

AVCHD UpShift sells for $49.95 and is available from www.newbluefx.com/avchd-upshift.html

Another excellent AVCHD convertor is **VoltaicHD**. The program costs $34.99 and is available from www.shedworx.com/voltaichd

A great program for converting AVCHD to standard-definition DV-AVI, is **Corel VideoStudio Pro**, one of the best PC-based programs for working with AVCHD video.

The program sells for $59.99 and is available from www.corel.com.

Capture utilities

In the event that Premiere Elements won't capture your video no matter what you do, these free or low-cost tools will capture miniDV and HDV as perfectly compatible video files.

WinDV (free from windv.mourek.cz/) – A great DV capture utility with a simple interface.

HDVSplit (free from strony.aster.pl/paviko/hdvsplit.htm) – A great capture utility for HDV video.

Scenalyzer ($30 from www.scenalyzer.com) – A low-cost capture utility with some great extra features.

Windows MovieMaker – Video captured from a miniDV camcorder into MovieMaker is perfectly compatible with Premiere Elements.

Nero – Sometimes Nero's presence on your computer is the *reason* you can't capture from Premiere Elements. However, if you've got it on your computer, you can use it to do your capture also.

If all else fails, you can use the software that came with your camcorder to capture your video. However, if this software will not capture your video as a DV-AVI (or MPEG2 for high-definition video) or convert to one of those formats, we recommend you convert your captured video using the software above, before you bring it into a Premiere Elements project, for best program performance.

Our favorite free audio utility

Audacity (audacity.sourceforge.net) is, hands down, the best *free* audio editing software you'll find anywhere. Easy to use, loaded with preset audio filters and yet extremely versatile.

Audacity can convert audio formats as well as adjust audio levels and "sweeten" your audio's sound. You can also record into it from a microphone or external audio device and edit audio with it. A real must-have freebie that you'll find yourself going to regularly!

FTP software

FTP software uploads files from your computer to a web site and downloads files from a site to your computer. There are many great applications out there.

Here are a couple of personal favorites.

FileZilla Client is the current favorite FTP utility of a number of Muvipixers. Efficient, dependable and easy-to-use, sending files to a Web site with **FileZilla** is as simple as dragging and dropping.

FileZilla Client is available free from filezilla-project.org.

Easy FTP (free from www.download.com and other sources) – Completely free and nearly as intuitive as **FileZilla**.

Manually output a high-quality video for a video sharing site

If you prefer to manually output your video and then upload it with one of these FTP tools rather than use Premiere Elements' direct-to-site tools for YouTube, Facebook and Photoshop.com, the Muvipix.com team has come up with these very effective output settings:

From the **Share** tab, choose **Computer** and then **QuickTime/MOV**. Choose the DV preset and as a starting point and then click the **Advanced** button.

In the **Advanced** options window, set your output to the following. (You may need to turn off the chain/Constrain Aspect Ratio toggle or order to set the Frame Height/Width :

> **Video Tab**
> Video Codec: H.264
> Quality: 100
> Frame Width/Height: 1280x720
> (For standard def video set it to
> 640x480 or, for widescreen, 640x360)
> Frame Rate: 29.97
> Field Type: Progressive
> Pixel Aspect Ratio: square
> Render at Maximum Depth: checked
>
> **Audio Tab**
> Audio Code: AAC
> Output Channels: Stereo
> Sample Rate: 44100

Disc burning software

Our favorite disc-burning software is, nicely enough, absolutely free!

ImgBurn is available at imgburn.com, and it's a great tool to use to burn your DVD or BluRay files to a disc as described in Step 2 of the "Burn Disc" workaround.

The "Burn Disc" workaround

In a perfect world, you could put together a project out of any media, click the **Share** tab and burn it to a DVD or BluRay disc.

Unfortunately, for a variety of reasons – some related to Premiere Elements, most related to operating system drivers or program conflicts, this sometimes doesn't go as smoothly as it should.

There are three main reasons for a problem burning a DVD or BluRay disc:

- Challenging source video (including photos that are larger than the recommended 1000x750 pixels in size);
- Interfacing issues with your disc burner (often the result of a program like Nero not sharing the burner with other programs);
- Lack of computer resources (namely lack of available scratch disk space on your hard drive). This workaround eliminates most Burn Disc problems. And when it doesn't eliminate them, it at least helps you isolate where the problems are occurring.

The simplest solution is to break the process down into its elements and then troubleshoot each element individually.

1   **Create a "pure" AVI project.** Click on the timeline panel and then go to **Share/Personal Computer/AVI** (or **MOV** on a Mac) to create a DV-AVI or DV-MOV of your entire project.

   If this works, do a **Save As** to save a copy of your project, delete all of the video except this newly created AVI, then place the AVI on the timeline in place of the deleted video (the DVD markers should still line up).

   If you find that you are unable to create an AVI or MOV from your project, it could be that your photos are too large or you lack the resources to render the files (as discussed in step 3, below).

   Ensure that, whenever possible, your photos are no larger than 1000x750 pixels in size, as discussed in **Work with photos** in **Chapter 18, Add Media to Your Project.**

2   **Burn to a folder** rather than directly to a disc.

   Select the **Burn to Folder** option, as we discuss in **Output to a DVD or BluRay Disc** in **Chapter 31.**

This eliminates the possibility that other disc burning software is interfering with communication with your computer's burner.

Once the disc files are created, you can use your computer's burner software (or, better yet, the free utility **ImgBurn**) to burn the VIDEO_TS folder and its contents to a DVD or BluRay disc.

If this doesn't work, it could be that your computer lacks the necessary resources, as discussed below.

3   **Clear space on and defragment your hard drive**. A one-hour video can require up to 50 gigabytes of free, defragmented space on your hard drive to render and process (depending on your source files).

Even a "pure" AVI project can require 20-30 gigabytes of space.

Clear off your computer and regularly defragment it, per **Maintain Your Computer**, earlier in this chapter, and you'll reduce the likelihood of this being an issue. Assuming you've got an adequately powered computer and an adequately large hard drive in the first place.

Need some Basic Training?

Want some help with the basics of Premiere Elements?

Want some free hands-on training?

Check out my free tutorial series **Basic Training with Premiere Elements** at Muvipix.com.

This simple, eight-part series will show you how to set up a project, how to import media into it, basic editing moves, adding transitions and effects, how to create titles, how to add and customize your DVD and BluRay disc menu navigation markers and how to export your finished video.

And did I mention that it's free?

To see the series, just go to http://Muvipix.com and type "Basic Training" in the product search box.

And while you're there, why not drop by the Community forum and say hi! We'd love to have you become a part of our growing city.

Happy moviemaking!

Steve, Chuck, Ron and the whole Muvipix team

Keyboard shortcuts for Premiere Elements

These key strokes and key combinations are great, quick ways to launch features or use the program's tools without having to poke around the interface.

In virtually every workspace the arrow keys (Down, Up, Left, Right) will move the selected object in that direction. Shift+Arrow will move it several steps in one nudge.

Many of these shortcuts are slightly different on a Macintosh computer. Usually the **Command**(⌘) key is used in place of the **Ctrl** key – although a number of keyboard shortcuts may not work at all.

Program Controls

Ctrl O	Open project	Ctrl X	Cut
Ctrl W	Close project	Ctrl C	Copy
Ctrl S	Save project	Ctrl V	Paste
Ctrl Shift S	Save project as...	Tab	Close floating windows
Ctrl Alt S	Save a copy	Ctrl Q	Quit program
Ctrl Z	Undo	F1	Help
Ctrl Shift Z	Redo		

Import/Export

F5	Capture	Ctrl Shift M	Export Frame
Ctrl I	Add Media	Ctrl Alt Shift M	Export Audio
Ctrl M	Export Movie	Ctrl Shift H	Get properties for selection

Media and Trimming

I	Set in point	Page Up	Go to previous edit point
O	Set out point	G	Clear all in/out points
Q	Go to in point	D	Clear selected in point
Page Down	Go to next edit point	F	Clear selected out point
W	Go to out point	Ctrl E	Edit original
		Ctrl H	Rename

Play/Scrub Controls

Space bar	Play/stop	Shift Right	Step forward five frames
J	Shuttle left	Home	Go to beginning of timeline
L	Shuttle right	End	Go to end of timeline
Shift J	Slow shuttle left	Q	Go to in point
Shift L	Slow shuttle right	W	Go to out point
K	Shuttle stop	Page Down	Go to next edit point
Arrow Left	One frame back	Page Up	Go to previous edit point
Arrow Right	One frame forward	Ctrl Alt Space	Play in point to out point with preroll/postroll
Shift Left	Step back five frames		

Timeline Controls

Enter	Render work area	V	Selection tool
Ctrl K	Razor cut at CTI	Alt [	Set Work Area Bar In Point
+	Zoom in		
-	Zoom out	Alt]	Set Work Area Bar Out Point
\	Zoom to work area	Ctrl Alt C	Copy attributes
Ctrl A	Select all	Ctrl Alt V	Paste Effects and Adjustments
Ctrl Shift A	Deselect all	Ctrl Shift /	Duplicate
, (comma)	Insert	Shift * (Num pad)	Set next unnumbered marker
. (period)	Overlay	* (Num pad)	Set unnumbered marker
Ctrl Shift V	Insert Clip	Ctrl Shift Right	Go to next clip marker
Alt [video clip]	Unlink audio/video	Ctrl Shift Left	Go to previous clip marker
Ctrl G	Group	Ctrl Shift 0	Clear current marker
Ctrl Shift G	Ungroup	Alt Shift 0	Clear all clip markers
X	Time stretch	Ctrl Right	Go to next timeline marker
Del	Clear clip (non-ripple)	Ctrl Left	Go to previous timeline marker
Backspace	Ripple delete (fill gap)	Ctrl 0	Clear current timeline marker
S	Toggle snap	Alt 0	Clear all timeline markers
C	Razor tool		

Title Window Controls

Ctrl Shift L	Title type align left	Alt Shift Left	Decrease kerning five units
Ctrl Shift R	Title type align right	Alt Shift Right	Increase kerning five units
Ctrl Shift C	Title type align center	Alt Left	Decrease kerning one unit
Ctrl Shift T	Set title type tab	Alt Right	Increase kerning one unit
Ctrl Shift D	Position object bottom safe margin	Alt Shift Up	Decrease leading five units
		Alt Shift Down	Increase leading five units
Ctrl Shift F	Position object left safe margin	Alt Up	Decrease leading one unit
Ctrl Shift O	Position object top safe margin	Alt Down	Increase leading one unit
Ctrl Alt Shift C	Insert copyright symbol	Ctrl Up	Decrease text size five points
Ctrl Alt Shift R	Insert registered symbol	Ctrl Down	Increase text size five points
Ctrl J	Open title templates	Shift Up	Decrease text size one point
Ctrl Alt]	Select object above	Shift Down	Increase text size one point
Ctrl Alt [	Select object below		
Ctrl Shift]	Bring object to front		
Ctrl [	Bring object forward		
Ctrl Shift [	Send object to back		
Ctrl [	Send object backward		

Media Window

Ctrl Delete	Delete selection with options	End	Move selection to last clip
Shift Down	Extend selection down	Page Down	Move selection page down
Shift Left	Extend selection left	Page Up	Move selection page up
Shift Up	Extend selection up	Right	Move selection right
Down	Move selection to next clip	Shift]	Thumbnail size next
Up	Move selection to previous clip	Shift [	Thumbnail size previous
Home	Move selection to first clip	Shift \	Toggle view

Capture Monitor Panel

F	Fast forward	Left	Step back
G	Get frame	Right	Step forward
R	Rewind	S	Stop

Properties Panel

Backspace	Delete selected effect

Narration Panel

Delete	Delete present narration clip	Space	Play present narration clip
		G	Start/Stop recording
Right Arrow	Go to next narration clip		
Left Arrow	Go to previous narration clip		

Note that Premiere Elements also allows you to modify any of these keyboard shortcuts and to create your own shortcuts for dozens of other tasks. You'll find the option to do so under the Edit drop-down menu.

Section 3

The Elements Organizer

File Management with the Organizer

The Media Browser

Keyword Tags and Metadata

Smart Tags and the Media Analyzer

Storing Your Media in Albums

Identifying People, Places and Events

Chapter 33
Manage Your Files with the Organizer
Getting to Know the Media Browser

The Elements Organizer, which comes bundled with both Photoshop Elements and Premiere Elements, is Adobe's media file management tool.

It's a way to organize, to search and to create search criteria for your audio, video and photo files.

It also includes a number of great tools for creating everything from slideshows to postage stamps from your media files!

A companion program to both Premiere Elements and Photoshop Elements, the Elements Organizer is a media file management system. It includes several interesting ways for you to organize and search your still photo, video, music and audio files

Additionally, the Organizer includes a number of tools for working with your media files to create photo projects, like calendars, scrap books and online or video slideshows, as we discuss in **Chapter 34, Create Fun Pieces** and **Chapter 35, Share Your Photos and Videos**.

The Elements Organizer links directly to both Premiere Elements and Photoshop Elements and it can be launched from the **Welcome Screen** of either program – or by clicking the **Organizer** button on the **Action Bar** along the bottom left of either program's interface.

Think of your Elements Organizer as a giant search engine that can be programmed to store and retrieve the audio, video and still photo files on your computer, based on a wide variety of criteria – some of which you assign, some of which are assigned automatically and some of which are inherently a part of your photo, sound and video files when they're created.

These search criteria aren't limited to obvious details – such as the type of media or the date it was saved to your computer.

Search criteria can include **Keyword Tags** – or it can be minute technical details, such as the type of camera that was used to shoot a photo or whether the photo was shot with a flash or natural light.

Additionally, the Organizer includes features that support other tools and functions in both Premiere Elements and Photoshop Elements. The **Media Analyzer**, discussed on page 418, for instance, prepares your video files for use with the **Smart Fix** and **Smart Mix** tools in Premiere Elements.

Your Elements Organizer's media files can also be stored in **Albums**, or they can be assigned **Tags**, categorized according to the **People** in them or the **Places** they were shot, or identified by the **Events** they represent.

The Media Browser area

The main area of the Organizer's interface, in which your media files are displayed as thumbnails and which dominates the Organizer workspace, is called the **Media Browser**.

Video file

There are several types of media files, and they are each represented by slightly different thumbnail images in the **Media Browser**, as illustrated to the right:

Photo file

> **Video files** are represented as image thumbnails with a filmstrip icon on the upper right corner.
>
> **Photo files** are represented by a plain thumbnail of the image file.
>
> **Audio files** are represented by gray thumbnails with a speaker icon on them.

The size of these thumbnail images in the **Media Browser** is controlled by the slider at the bottom right of the interface.

Under the **View** drop-down on the Organizer menu bar, in the **Media Types** sub-menu, you can filter which file types are displayed in the **Media Browser**.

Audio file

Using the tabs along the top of the interface, you can set whether the **Media Browser** displays your files as categories of **People, Places** or **Events** – categories we'll show you how to build later in this chapter.

The Search Bar

A quickest way to search for a media file is to type the name of the file, any **Keyword Tag** that applies to it or the name of the **Album** that contains it in the **Search Box** along the top right of the interface. The **Media Browser** will then display all media files that match that criteria.

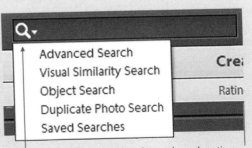

Click the magnifying glass for advanced search options.

The Organizer Catalog

The media files that the Organizer manages and displays, as well as the metadata that defines them, are said to be in the Organizer's **Catalog**. Some files and information are added to this **Catalog** automatically, while others may be added to the **Catalog** manually.

All of the video clips or photo files that you edit with Premiere Elements or Photoshop Elements are automatically added to your Elements Organizer **Catalog**. If you download or capture video or photos to your computer using any of the tools in Premiere Elements or Photoshop Elements, they too are automatically added to your Organizer's **Catalog**.

Manually add to and update your Organizer Catalog

The first time you launch the Elements Organizer, it will offer to search your computer for media files to add to the **Catalog**. (If you've had a previous version of the Organizer installed, the program will offer to simply update your existing **Catalog**.) If you're running the program on a Mac, it will even offer to use the data in your iPhoto catalog as its **Catalog**.

Import media files into your Catalog

You can manually add additional files to your **Catalog** by clicking the **Import** button in the upper left of the interface.

- To manually add files, and folders full of files, to your Organizer's **Catalog**, select **From Files and Folders**. Browse to the folder or files you would like to add and then click **Get Media**.

- To download media **From a Camera or Card Reader** or to add images **From a a Scanner**, select the respective option.

- To *automatically* add media files to your **Catalog**, select **By Searching**. The program will automatically search your entire computer (or specified folders) and add any media files it locates automatically.

- Finally, if you're storing media files in the Revel "cloud", you can add them to your computer and your **Catalog** by selecting the **From Adobe Revel** option.

The Back button

Whatever tags or filters you've applied, you can always work your way back to a display of all the media in your **Catalog** by clicking the **Back** button in the upper left of the **Media Browser**.

Resync an out-of-sync Catalog

If you move, delete or change files using Windows Explorer, Finder or a program other than one of the Elements programs, you may find your Organizer's **Media Browser** will indicate some thumbnails as broken or outdated links.

To update these connections manually or to remove the thumbnail of a deleted file from the Organizer **Catalog**, go to the **File** menu and select the option to **Reconnect/All Missing Files**.

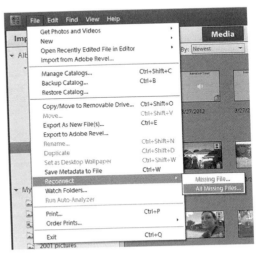

The Organizer will update your links and indicate for you all of the thumbnails in the **Media Browser** that do not have files linked to them, offering you the options of re-connecting the links or of deleting these dead thumbnails.

To avoid the program's losing track of the links to your media, it's best to use the Elements Organizer to move or remove files from your computer:

- To delete a file using the Organizer, **right-click** (**Ctrl-click** on a Mac) on the file(s) and select **Delete from Catalog**. You will then be given the option of merely removing the file from the **Catalog** or removing it completely from your hard drive.

- To move a file to a new location on your computer using the Organizer, click to select the file(s) and, from the **File** drop-down, select the option to **Move** and then browse to the new location.

Switch Folder Views

By default, the **Media Browser** displays your files according to the dates they were saved, from most recent to oldest. In default **Folder List** view, your computer's file folders are displaying running down the left side of the interface listed in alpha-numeric order.

However, if you'd prefer to navigate your folders according to their structure and location on your hard drive(s), you can switch it to **Folder Hierarchy** view by clicking the button to the right of the words **My Folders**.

To switch back to **Folder List** view, click the button on the right side of the **Folders** header.

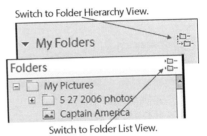

Switch to Folder Hierarchy View.

Switch to Folder List View.

Managed, Unmanaged and Watched Folders

As far as your Organizer's **Catalog** is concerned, there are three types of folders on your hard drive. These folders are indicated in your **My Folders** list or hierarchy.

Unmanaged Folders are folders whose contents do not have any links to the Organizer. The folder either does not contain any media files or the media files have not yet been added to the **Catalog**.

Unmanaged Folder

Managed Folders are folders whose contents have been added to the **Catalog** and whose media files can be viewed and searched by the Organizer.

Managed Folder

Watched Folders have a dynamic link to the Organizer's **Catalog**. As media files are added to a **Watched Folder**, they are automatically added to the **Catalog**.

Watched Folder

(Note that any media files which are used in a Premiere Elements project or are edited and saved in Photoshop Elements are automatically added to the **Catalog**, regardless of where they are stored.)

When your Organizer first deployed and it converted your old media catalogs and/or searched your computer for media files, it automatically made a number of your folders into **Managed Folders**.

You can also manually designate a folder as a **Managed Folder** or a **Watched Folder** by **right-clicking** on it and selecting either **Import Media** (to turn the folder into a **Managed Folder**) or **Add to Watched Folders**.

What is metadata?

Metadata is the hidden information embedded in virtually every computer file, including when the file was saved, who modified it last, what program created the file, etc.

The Elements Organizer uses metadata to manage, order and search your media files.

By default, all of your media files carry certain metadata. When you first open the Organizer, for instance, in the default **Thumbnail View**, you'll immediately notice that your files are categorized according to the date they were saved to your computer's drive.

If you've poked around in the Organizer at all, you've probably noted that you can display these files in the **Media Browser** from most recent to oldest or oldest to most recent.

"**Date saved**" is the simplest display of metadata and the most basic way to search through your media files – but it's far from the only way to search your file.

You might be surprised to learn how much metadata a typical photo file actually contains!

If the **Keyword Tags/Information** panel isn't displayed to the right of the **Media Browser,** click the **Tags/Info** button in the lower right corner of the interface. Then select the **Information** tab at the top of the panel and select a photo in the **Media Browser** that you've downloaded from any digital camera.

If you open the **Metadata** section of this panel, as illustrated on the right, and then click on the toggle in the upper right of this panel section to display the **Complete** metadata, you'll see an amazing amount of information – from the date and time the photo was shot to the photo dimensions, the make, model and serial number of camera that was used to take the photo, the shutter speed, if a flash was used, what settings and F-stop setting was used, if it was shot with manual or automatic focus and so on.

All of this is metadata. And it can be used – along with any additional metadata you assign manually – as search criteria in the Elements Organizer.

To search by metadata, go to the **Find** drop-down on the Organizer Menu Bar and select the option to search **By Details (Metadata)** as illustrated below.

In the option screen that opens, you can set up a search to find, for instance, all photos shot on a specific date or at a specific time, at certain camera settings – in fact, you can search by pretty much any of the metadata attached to your photo or other media file!

Also under this **Find** drop-down menu, you'll find many more search methods for your files. One of the most amazing search functions, in my opinion, is the Organizer's ability to locate files that contain **Visual Similarity with Selected Photo(s) and Video(s)** (under **Visual Searches**).

That's right: If you have a picture of the beach or the mountains or even of an individual, the Organizer will find for you all of the other photos in your collection that have similar color schemes and visual details!

It's not magic, of course. I set it to search for photos similar to a bride in her gown and my hits included a photo of a hamburger, wrapped in waxed paper. But it's still pretty amazing that it does work surprisingly well!

Some of the Metadata embedded in a typical digital photo.

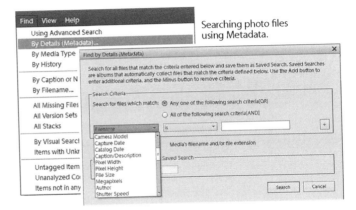

Searching photo files using Metadata.

Add your own Metadata

There are a number of ways to add searchable metadata to your media files. You can, for instance:

Place your media in an **Album** (as discussed on page 420).

Add **Keyword Tags** (as discussed on page 421). Or you can have the **Media Analyzer** automatically add **Smart Tags** to your media (as discussed below).

Apply one to five **star ratings** to your clips (by dragging across the stars that appear under the thumbnail in the **Media Browser**).

Identify your photos by the **People** in them (a process the program does semi-automatically, as discussed on page 422).

Your Place metadata can even display on a map!

Tag your photos and videos with the **Place** they were shot (as discussed on page 424).

Associate your media with a **Date** or an **Event** (as discussed on page 425).

Using both metadata you supply and metadata supplied automatically by the camera or other device you've recorded your media with, the Organizer provides you with several ways to organize and search your media files.

Smart Tag your media with the Media Analyzer

Smart Tags are **Keyword Tag** metadata (see page 421) that the Elements Organizer adds automatically to your photo and video files after **Auto Analyzing** them.

The **Auto Analyzer** (also called the **Media Analyzer**) can be used to manually analyze your video and photo files, or it can be set up to automatically analyze the media in your **Catalog** in the background, whenever your computer is idle. On most computers made in the past couple of years (dual-core or better) you shouldn't even notice the **Auto Analyzer** working. Its initial analysis of your media can take several hours, depending on how large of a collection of photos and video you have. But once it's **Smart Tagged** your **Catalog**, it only takes a few minutes (like while you're out getting lunch) to update **Smart Tags** on any new media.

To ensure that the **Auto Analyzer** is activated, go to the Organizer's **Preferences** (under the **Edit** menu on a PC or under **Preferences** on a Mac) and go to the **Media Analysis** page.

To set the **Auto Analyzer/Media Analyzer** to run automatically, check all of the boxes on the preferences panel, as illustrated on the facing page. (Likewise, if you've got a slower computer and you find the **Auto Analyzer** too intrusive, uncheck the **Analyze Photos** and **Analyze Media** checkboxes.)

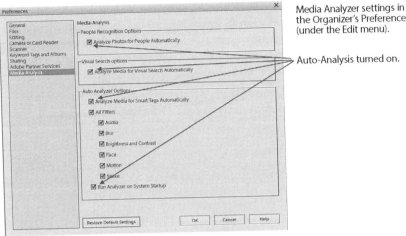

Media Analyzer settings in the Organizer's Preferences (under the Edit menu).

Auto-Analysis turned on.

The results of the program's **Media Analysis** are automatically added as **Smart Tags** to your clips and listed in the **Keyword Tags** panel (as illustrated to the right).

In addition to their use as metadata, **Smart Tags** play a role in the functionality of a couple of tools in Premiere Elements.

- **Smart Trim** (page 285) uses information gathered by the **Media Analyzer** as part of its functionality. If you have not pre-analyzed a clip before you apply a **Smart Trim**, the program will offer to run the **Media Analyzer** on the clips before launching the tool.

- The **Smart Fix** tool in Premiere Elements (page 260) will *only* function for clips that have been **Media Analyzed** and **Smart Tagged** by the Organizer prior to your adding them to your timeline. In other words, if you have disabled the **Media Analyzer** and you have not generated **Smart Tags** for the clips that you are adding to your project, Premiere Elements will not offer to **Smart Fix** them.

Even if you've disabled the automatic **Media-Analyzer,** you can *manually* run it on clips in either the Elements Organizer's **Media Browser** or in the Premiere Elements **Project Assets** panel.

To do this, **right-click** on a clip or clips (**Ctrl-click** on the Mac) in the Organizer's **Media Browser** or the Premiere Elements **Project Assets** panel and select **Run Media Analyzer** from the context menu.

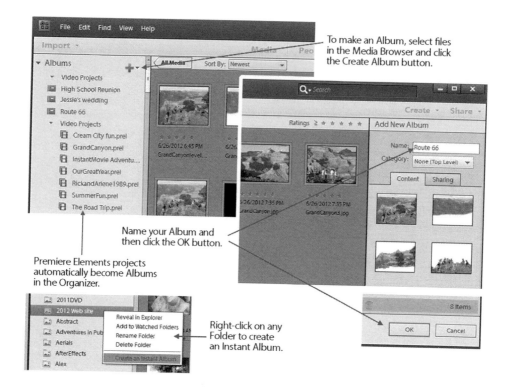

To make an Album, select files in the Media Browser and click the Create Album button.

Name your Album and then click the OK button.

Premiere Elements projects automatically become Albums in the Organizer.

Right-click on any Folder to create an Instant Album.

Assign your media files to Albums

Albums are collections of media files. When you have your media files assigned to an **Album**, only files assigned to an **Album** appear in the **Media Browser** when that **Album** is selected.

Albums are a simple way to gather photos, for instance, for creating slideshows or to gather media for a photo or video project.

An **Album** is created automatically whenever you start a new Premiere Elements project. All of the video, photo, music and audio files that have been imported into that project are included in **Albums** listed as **Video Projects**.

To create your own Album:

Select the media files you'd like to add to your **Album** in the **Media Browser** (by holding down the **Shift, Ctrl** or, on a Mac, the ⌘ key as you click on the files). Click the green **Create Album** button at the top right of the **Albums** panel. An **Edit Album** panel will open to the right of the **Media Browser,** where you can name you **Album** and add to or remove from files from it. When you're done, click **OK**.

You can also turn any **Folder** into an **Instant Album** just by **right-clicking** on it and selecting the option from the context menu.

Additional media files can be added to an **Album** just by dragging them from the **Media Browser** onto that **Album's** icon in the **Albums** panel. To re-open an **Album** in **Edit Album**, **right-click** on it and select **Edit**. (And, yes, a file can be in more than one **Album**.)

You can delete an **Album** – even a **Video Project Album** – by **right-clicking** on it and selecting **Delete**.

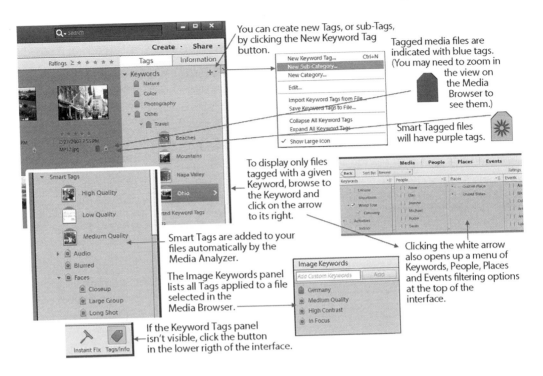

You can create new Tags, or sub-Tags, by clicking the New Keyword Tag button.

Tagged media files are indicated with blue tags. (You may need to zoom in the view on the Media Browser to see them.)

Smart Tagged files will have purple tags.

To display only files tagged with a given Keyword, browse to the Keyword and click on the arrow to its right.

Smart Tags are added to your files automatically by the Media Analyzer.

The Image Keywords panel lists all Tags applied to a file selected in the Media Browser.

Clicking the white arrow also opens up a menu of Keywords, People, Places and Events filtering options at the top of the interface.

If the Keyword Tags panel isn't visible, click the button in the lower rigth of the interface.

Manage your files with Keyword Tags

Tagging is a way to manually add custom metadata to your media files.

At first adding **Keyword Tags** to hundreds of accumulated digital photos and videos may seem like a lot of housekeeping – but the payoff is great!

The **Keyword Tags** panel lists several categories and sub-categories of **Tags**.

Creating a new **Tag** is as simple as clicking on the **+** symbol at the top right of this panel. You can create as many **Tags** and as many **Categories** – and **Sub-Categories** under them – as you'd like. You can, for instance, create a **Sub-Category** under Places and name it France. Then, within that **Sub-Category**, create **Tags** for Cousin Pierre, Landmarks, The Louvre, etc. (You can even drag your **Keyword** sub-categories in an out of categories on the **Keyword Tags** panel!)

Assigning a **Tag** to a media file is as simple as dragging the **Tag** from the **Keyword Tags** palette onto the selected file or files in the **Media Browser**. You can assign as many **Tags** as you'd like to a file. And you can assign the same **Tag** to as many files as you'd like.

When you next want to locate the files associated with a particular **Tag**, browse to the **Tag's** listing in the **Keyword Tags** panel and then click the white arrow to its right. A metadata filter menu will open at the top of the **Media Browser** (as illustrated), and only media files that associated with your selected **Tags** will appear.

If you select a major category, all of the files assigned to all of that category's sub-categories of **Tags** will appear. As you narrow your **Tag** search, only the files assigned to the **Tag** will be displayed.

Find People in your files

One of the most powerful tools for managing and searching your photo files in the Elements Organizer – and one which Adobe has clearly invested a lot of effort into developing – is the **People Tagger**.

The **People Tagger** will work with you to identify the people in your photos (identifying as many as it can on its own) so that you can easily locate all of the photos that include any one given individual.

It can take a while to work through all of your photos – but it's actually kind of fun!

To begin the process:

1   Click the **People** tab at the top of the **Media Browser**. Then click the **Add People** button at the bottom of the interface.

 The program will automatically find people in your photo files and ask you to identify them.

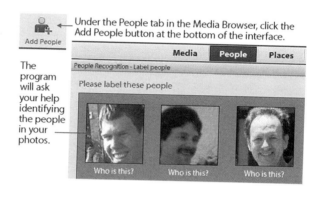

Under the People tab in the Media Browser, click the Add People button at the bottom of the interface.

The program will ask your help identifying the people in your photos.

2   Click on the "**Who is this?**" caption under each photo and type in the person's name.

 If there are people in the group you don't want to tag – or, as sometimes happens, the program includes a non-person – **right-click** on the thumbnail image and select either "**Not a Person**" or "**Ignore**".

 When you finish identifying the group, click **Save**. A new group will appear.

3   As you continue to identify people, the program will begin offering already identified names as options. If one of the names is listed correct, click on it to ID the face.

 If you begin typing in a name, the program will also list previously-added names that begin with the same letters.

Please label these people

4   The program will go on doing this – pausing occasionally to **Auto Analyze** your photos and find more faces to identify or asking your to confirm the identities of people it has found and automatically added – building its database of **People** as it does.

When you've had enough for one session, click **Cancel** rather than **Save**. (You can start a new session of identifying people just by clicking the **Add People** button again.)

When you select **Cancel**, you'll be returned to the **Media Browser** where, still under the **People** tab, you'll see all of your identified friends' faces on top of what appear to be stacks of photos.

To see all of the identified photos that include any given person, double-click on that person's stack.

Add People to Groups

Your **People** stacks are listed in alphabetic order. But, to make them a bit easier to manage (especially if you've got dozens of them!) you can also arrange them into **Groups** – and even **Sub-Groups**.

To create or browse your **Groups**, slide the switch in the upper left of the **Media Browser** from **People** to **Groups**, as illustrated below.

A **Groups** panel will open on the right side of the **Media Browser**. The groups **Colleagues, Family** and **Friends** are listed by default

To add someone to an existing **Group**, either drag their stack onto the **Group** name on this panel or drag the name of the **Group** onto their stack. You can select and add several **People** to a **Group** in one move if you'd like.

To create a new **Group**, click the **Add Group** button at the top right of the **Groups** panel.

An option panel will open in which you can name your new **Group** and select whether it will be a main **Group** (select **None**) or it will be a sub-category of an existing **Group**.

To see the **People** in a specific **Group**, either scroll down the **Media Browser** or, to jump to it, just click the **Group's** name in the **Groups** panel.

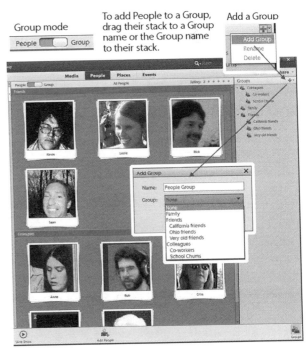

Group mode

To add People to a Group, drag their stack to a Group name or the Group name to their stack.

Add a Group

Manage your photos by Place

Just as you can manage your photo files using **Albums, Keyword Tags** and the **People** in them, you can also manage your photos or video by the location at which they were shot. Locating media shot at a given location is as clicking on a pin on a map.

Even cooler, if your camera has a built-in GPS, the Elements Organizer reads this metadata and adds the media to your map automatically!

To tag photos with a **Place**:

1   Click the **Places** tab at the top of the interface.

A map will be displayed on the right side of the **Media Browser**. Photos already tagged with **Place** metadata will appear on the map as little red squares called **Pins**. The number on each **Pin** indicates the number of photos tagged to that place.

2   Select a **Folder, Album, Keyword** or other **Tag**.

You don't need to do this. But applying a filter will limit the media files you'll have to sort through. (If you don't apply a filter, you'll need to browse through every media file in your **Catalog**.)

3   Click the **Add Places** button at the bottom of the interface.

A **Place Tagger** workspace will open. A map will dominate the workspace, and thumbnails of your media will appear along the top.

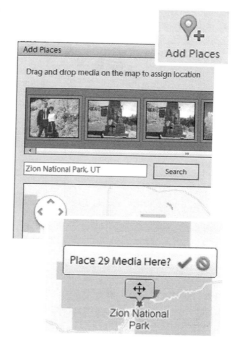

4   Search the **Map**

Type a location in the search box above left of the map. This place can be as exact as a street address. A **Place Media Here** box will appear on the map.

5   Select and place your media.

Select the media you want to add to this **Place** from the thumbnails along the top of the workspace – or choose **Select All** from the pop-up menu in the upper right.

Drag the media files to the **Place** or click the green checkmark next to the words **Place Media Here**.

And that's it! Your photo files are now tagged to this **Place**.

Retrieving all photos tagged to a given **Place** is as simple as double-clicking on a red **Pin** on the map. (Or, if you click the tab above the map, you can also search your **Places** in **List** view.)

Manage your photos by Dates or Events

Finally, you can manage your media files according to specific dates or events.

To categorize your media files by **Event**:

1   Click the **Events** tab at the top of the interface.

Any **Events** you've already created will appear in the **Media Browser** as stacks of photos.

To the right of the **Media Browser** is a **Calendar** browser. Media files will be added to this **Calendar** automatically as you create **Events**. You can then filter to a certain date using its drop-down menus.

2   Click the **Add Event** button at the bottom of the interface.

The **Events Tagger** workspace will open and, by default, the **Media Browser** will display all the media in your **Catalog**. You can filter which media files are displayed by selecting a **Folder** or **Album** from the panel along the left side of the interface.

3   Select the media files you'd like to tag as an **Event**.

You can select several files by holding down the **Shift** or **Ctrl** key or, on the Mac, the ⌘ key – or **Ctrl+a** (⌘ +a on a Mac) to select all of them.

Manage your files using Smart Events

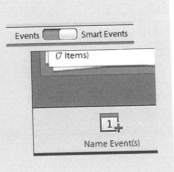

If you flip the switch at the top left of the **Media Browser** under the **Events** tab to **Smart Events** and you'll see stacks of events the Organizer has created on its own, based on the dates they were shot or created. (Part of its process of **Auto/Media Analyzing**, see page 418.)

To name a **Smart Event** stack, select the stack and click the **Name Event(s)** button at the bottom of the interface.

You can also just drag the media files you want to add to your **Event** over to the **Add New Event** panel on the right.

4   Name the **Event**.

Type the name you'd like to give your **Event** in the box at the top of the **Add New Event** panel, which appears to the right of the workspace.

You can also add dates and a description if you'd like.

Click the **Done** button at the bottom of the panel to create the **Event** and return to **Events Media Browser**.

Your **Events** will appear as stacks of photos. To see all of the files associated with an **Event**, double-click on its stack.

Printing Your Photos

Creating a Photo Book

Creating a Photo Greeting Card

Creating a Photo Calendar

Creating a Photo Collage

Creating Other Photo Pieces

Chapter 34

Create Fun Pieces
The Organizer's project templates

The Elements Organizer includes a number
of tools for creating everything from a
photo scrapbook to a greeting card, a
calendar, a US postage stamp or a DVD
cover.

Using the templates and wizards in the
Organizer (and sometimes Photoshop
Elements), creating these photo pieces is
as simple as selecting your artwork and
following the prompts.

The **Create** tab on the upper right of the Elements Organizer's interface gives you access to an array of tools for creating projects from your media files.

A number of these options are actually links to tools in Premiere Elements or Photoshop Elements, and selecting them will launch the workspace in that program. In fact, **if you do not have Photoshop Elements installed on your computer, some of these options may not even be available to you.**

Create Photo Prints

The **Photo Prints** option under the **Create** tab gives you access to several ways to output your photos.

Print Individual Prints on your local printer

As you'd expect, this option sends your selected photo(s) to your printer. But you may be surprised at the number of possible print layouts this option screen includes!

1 Select the photo or photos you'd like to print in the **Media Browser** and click to select the **Photo Prints** option under the **Create** tab.

 Then, on the **Photo Prints** option panel that appears, select **Local Printer,** as illustrated to the left.

 The **Prints** preview panel will open. The program will automatically arrange the photos you've selected so that it can print as many as possible on each page printed out.

 How many photos it fits on a page depends on the **Print Size** you've selected for photos (as in **Step 2**, below).

 The complete set of photos you've selected to print are displayed as thumbnails along the left side of the panel, and you may add or remove photos from this list.

2 Select your photo print-out options.

 As illustrated on the facing page, the **Select Print Size** drop-down allows you to set how large each photo prints. You can also select from this menu the option to print each photo at its **Actual Size.**

Whenever you print any photo, it's important to consider the resolution of the image. Printing photos smaller than their actual size will usually not be a problem. However, if you set your photo to print at a size in which its final output resolution is less than 150-200 ppi, you will likely see reduced quality and fuzziness in your output. This could definitely be a problem if you selected the **Individual Print** option and you then selected a print size much larger than the actual photo.

The Print preview panel includes settings for printing your photos in a variety of sizes and layouts as well as options for adding cool custom frames.

Select Type of Print

The **Type of Print** menu on the **Prints** option panel (illustrated above) arranges the photos in your print-out page in one of three patterns.

Individual Prints prints photos to your printer at the size you designate.

Contact Sheet prints proof-style thumbnails of your photos, according to the layout settings you provide.

Picture Package sends an arrangement of photos to your printer based on the number of photos you designate per page. This **Type of Print** also gives you the option of printing these photos with a **Frame** around each.

Print a Picture Package or Contact Sheet on your local printer

The main difference between the **Picture Package** and the **Individual Prints** print-out options is in how you set the size and number of photos that will appear on your print-out page.

When **Type of Print** is set to **Individual Prints**, you will have the option of selecting the *size* your photos will print out at. When you set the **Type of Print** option to **Picture Package** (or **Contact Sheet**), you will have the option of selecting the *number* of photos you want to print on each page.

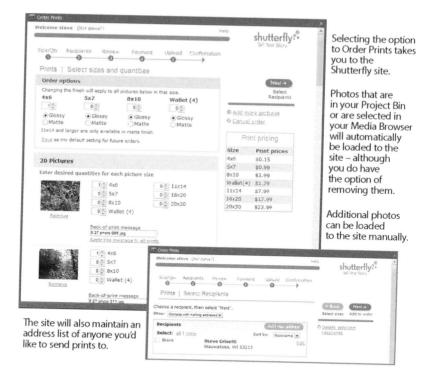

Selecting the option to Order Prints takes you to the Shutterfly site.

Photos that are in your Project Bin or are selected in your Media Browser will automatically be loaded to the site – although you do have the option of removing them.

Additional photos can be loaded to the site manually.

The site will also maintain an address list of anyone you'd like to send prints to.

Order prints through Shutterfly

When you select the **Shutterfly** option from under the **Create** tab's **Photo Prints** button, you can order high-quality prints of your photos from **Shutterfly**, an online photo service.

1   Sign on with or log on to **Shutterfly**.

2   Logging on opens an option screen at which you can add or remove photos and select the sizes of prints you would like.

   If you have photos selected in your **Media Browser** when you launch this tool, they will be included in the order unless you **Remove** them.

   If you'd like to add additional photos, click on the **Add More Pictures** button on the upper right of the screen. Click **Next**.

3   In the screens that follow, you can list the names of anyone you would like prints shipped directly to (You'll need to include your own name and address, of course).

   Select your method of payment and upload your photos.

Once you've uploaded your photos and confirmed your information, the files will be sent to Shutterfly via the Internet. You should receive your prints by mail within a week.

The Photo Book option panel.

Create a Photo Book

A **Photo Book** is a collection of photos laid out in from 20 to 80 custom-designed pages. The wizard takes you through the basic steps of setting up the book. Once the book is initially set up, you can add more photos to it and tweak the design and layout. (This tool is only available if you have Photoshop Elements.)

A **Photo Book** can be sent to **Shutterfly** for professional printing and binding, or it can be printed out on your home printer.

1   Select the photos in the **Media Browser** you'd like to include in your **Photo Book.** Then select the **Photo Book** button under the **Create** tab.

   The **Photo Book** option panel will open in Photoshop Elements.

2   Select a size and output options for your book from the **Photo Book** option panel (illustrated above). If you plan to have your book professionally printed and bound, select one of the **Shutterfly** options.

3   On this same panel, select a **Theme** for your book.

   You can designate any number of pages for your book. However, if you plan to have **Shutterfly** produce your book, there must be a minimum of 20 pages.

   Click **OK**

The photos you have selected when you launch this tool will automatically be loaded into your **Photo Book** in the order that they appear in the **Media Browser.**

The first of your selected photos will become your **Title Page Photo**.

The program will fill as many pages as possible with the photos you've selected.

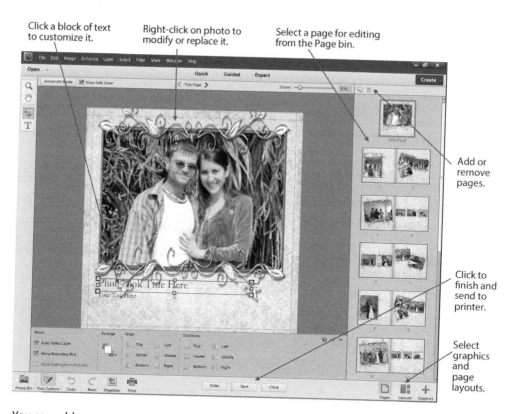

Click a block of text to customize it.

Right-click on photo to modify or replace it.

Select a page for editing from the Page bin.

Add or remove pages.

Click to finish and send to printer.

Select graphics and page layouts.

You can add pages to or remove pages from your book by clicking the icons in the top left of the **Page Bin**.

You may also change the theme and/or frames for the individual pages or add graphics by selecting options at the bottom right.

To add, edit or replace photos, **right-click** on the photo frame:

- If the frame is blank, you'll be prompted to browse for a photo on your hard drive.

- If a photo is already in the frame, options will be displayed to resize the photo or **Position Photo Within Frame**, rotate it or replace it.

By dragging on their corner handles, photos and their frames can be resized and repositioned on the page.

Along the bottom of the **Photo Book** workspace panel, you will find the options to **Order** your book professionally produced, to save the project file or to **Print** it on your home printer.

Zoom photo in/out

Rotate photo

Replace photo

Accept/Cancel

The Greeting Card option panel.

Create a Greeting Card

A **Greeting Card** can be sent to **Shutterfly** for professional printing or it can be printed out on your home printer. (This tool is available only if you have Photoshop Elements.)

1   Select the **Greeting Card** button under the **Create** tab.

The photos you have in your **Project Bin** – whether because they are open in the **Editor** or selected in the **Organizer** – will automatically be loaded into your **Greeting Card.** Photos may also be added or removed after the book is created.

2   Select a size and output option for your book from the **Greeting Card** option screen (illustrated above). You can send your card to Shutterfly for professional production or print it out on your home printer.

3   On this same panel, select a **Theme** for your card. (These features can be modified later.)

Click **OK**.

The program will generate your card.

As with the **Photo Book**, you may swap out photos and modify your **Greeting Card's** layout, graphics or text, as described on page 432.

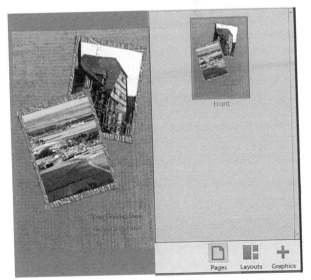

After the program generates your card, you can modify its theme, text, photos and effects.

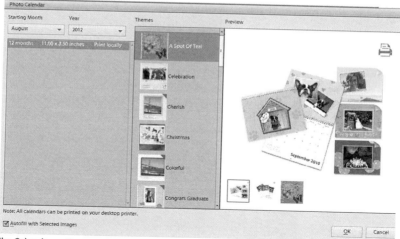

The Calendar option panel.

Create a Photo Calendar

A **Photo Calendar** can be sent to **Kodak** for professional printing or it can be printed out on your home printer. (This tool is only available if you have Photoshop Elements.)

1   Select the photos you'd like to use in your calendar in the **Media Browser**

2   Select the **Photo Calendar** button under the **Create** tab.

3   Select a starting date, size and output options for your book from the **Photo Calendar** option screen (illustrated above). You can send your card to Kodak for professional production or print it out on your home printer.

After the program generates your calendar, you can modify its layout, graphics, text and photos.

4   On this same panel, select a **Theme** for your card. (These features can be modified later.)

The photos you have in your **Media Browser** will automatically be loaded into your **Photo Calendar.** Photos may also be added or removed after the book is created.

Click **OK**.

The program will generate your card.

As with the **Photo Book**, you may swap out photos and modify your **Photo Calendar's** layout, graphics or text, as described on page 432.

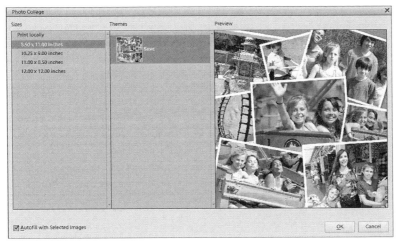

The Photo Collage option screen.

Create a Photo Collage

A **Photo Collage** is an arrangement of photos gathered together in an artful or playful way. Once you create your **Photo Collage**, you'll be able to print it out on your home printer. (This tool is only available if you have Photoshop Elements.)

1. Select the photos you'd like to use in your collage in the **Media Browser**

2. Select the **Photo Collage** button under the **Create** tab.

2. Select a size for your **Photo Collage** from the option screen (illustrated above).

3. On this same panel, select a **Theme** for your collage. (These features can be modified later.)

   Click **OK**.

   The photos you have in your **Media Browser** will automatically be loaded into your **Photo Collage.** Photos may also be added or removed after the book is created.

The program will generate your card.

As with the **Photo Book**, you may swap out photos and modify your **Photo Calendar's** layout, graphics or text, as described on page 432.

Create an Organizer Slideshow

There are actually several ways to create a slideshow in Premiere Elements and Photoshop Elements (including using the tool in the **Project Assets** panel, as we discuss on page 255.) But the Organizer's **Slide Show** creator is perhaps the most intuitive, powerful and versatile.

(Note that this feature is not available on the Mac version of the program.)

1   For best performance and results – particularly if you plan to eventually port this slideshow to Premiere Elements for use in a video project or to create a DVD – ensure that you've resized any photos you plan to use in a video project to no larger than 1000x750 pixels, as we discuss in **Use Photos in Premiere Elements** on page 240. (Photoshop Elements includes a **Process Multiple Files** feature that will do batch resizing. See page 163 for more information.)

2   Select the photos you'd like to include in your slideshow in the **Media Browser**.

3   Select the **Slide Show** option from under the Elements Organizer's **Create** tab.

This will launch the **Slide Show Preferences** window, as illustrated to below. In this window you can set preferences for many things, including the duration of each slide, the types of transitions (including **Random**) between them, elect whether or not to apply a **Pan & Zoom** over each slide and indicate whether or not you'd like to include an accompanying soundtrack.

The Slide Show creator grabs the selected photos in the Organizer's Media Browser.

Slide Show Preferences includes options for adding random transitions and Pan & Zoom motion paths to your photos.

Output slide show   Add photos to slide show

Record narration for slides

Add titles to slides

Add cartoon elements to slides

Pan & Zoom workspace

Slides

Transitions

Add music to your show

Open Quick Reorder workspace

Don't worry too much about committing to any decisions here. You can add to or revise any of your choices later.

When you've selected your options, click **OK**.

4   The program will launch the **Slide Show Editor**, the real heart of the slideshow creator (illustrated below).

If you had photos selected in the Organizer when you launched the **Slide Show Creator**, these slides will already be added to your show.

You can add more slides by clicking on the **+ Add Media** button at the top of the **Editor**, and you can remove slides by **right-clicking** on them and selecting the **Remove** option.

5   If you'd like to **Add Audio** or music to your slideshow, you can do so by clicking on the link under the slides, along the bottom of the panel.

6   If you'd like to add **Titles** to your slides, click the **Text** tab in the **Extras** panel.

If you'd like to record narration, click the **Audio** tab.

7   In the **Properties** panel, you will find the option to create or adjust your **Pan & Zoom** motion path for each slide.

Using this feature is very easy. Simply click to select the green-outlined **Start** thumbnail. This is your **Pan & Zoom** starting point – which you can define by dragging the outline's corner handles.

Then click the red-outlined **End** thumbnail and likewise define the **Pan & Zoom** ending point.

The program will automatically create a smooth motion path between those two settings – which you can preview by clicking the play button.

Setting starting and ending points for a Pan & Zoom effect.

8   If you'd like to reorder your slides, click on the **Quick Reorder** button near the bottom left of the **Slide Show Editor** workspace.

This opens a **Slide Sorter** window, in which you can drag each slide into a new position or **right-click** and delete it.

You can also return to the original **Slide Show Preferences** option panel by selecting the option from the **Edit** drop-down on the Menu Bar.

Changing the order of your slides in the Quick Reorder work space is as simple as dragging them to new positions.

Click the **Back** button to return to the **Slide Show Editor.**

9   When you're satisfied with your slideshow, click the **Output** button at the top of the window.

The **Output** window (illustrated on the facing page) will offer you a variety of file format outputs, including the option to save your slideshow as a **WMV** (Windows Media) file, a **PDF,** a **video CD** and even to output to your TV via Windows Media Center.

To output your sideshow as a video or DVD, select the option to **Edit With Premiere Elements Editor.**

If you want to create a quality video slideshow for burning to DVD, this is the option you want!

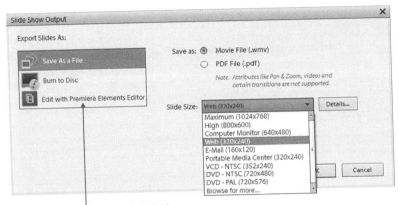

Slide Show Output options include the
option to Edit with Premiere Elements,
which sends the slides to the video editor
in an interchange format that can be
re-opened in Premiere Elements and edited further.

10 If you've selected **Edit with Premiere Elements**, you'll be prompted
to name and save the slideshow. Once you've done that, Premiere
Elements will launch and your slideshow will be added to your video
project's timeline, as a single file – in a slideshow interchange format–
complete with the transitions and motion paths you added in the **Slide
Show Editor**. The beauty of this slideshow interchange format is that it
maintains all of the integrity and quality of your original photo files.

In fact, if you **right-click** on this slideshow on your Premiere Elements
timeline and select the option to **Break Apart Elements Organizer
Slideshow**, the interchange format will break into your original photos
(with the effects you've added intact). You can then continue to edit
and refine this slideshow in Premiere Elements.

In order to see your slideshow at full quality in Premiere Elements, you
will need to render it. Press **Enter** to do so.

Your slideshow needn't be sent to Premiere Elements for output. Particularly, if
you are planning to show your slideshow on a computer, other output options
can provide you with a much higher resolution output.

Save as File – WMV or PDF. The **File Settings** for a WMV's resolution can be
set as high as 1024x768 pixels, which should fill a video monitor at full-
screen with excellent results – though it can take a while for Photoshop
Elements to create your output. PDF slideshows can be played by Acrobat
Reader, but they do not include pan & zoom animations.

Burn to Disc – VCD or DVD. A VCD is a low-resolution video file that can
pretty easily fit on a CD. In fact, it's so low in quality you probably won't
want to ever use it!

If you select the option to save to a DVD from this screen, your file will
be saved as a WMV file and then ported over to Premiere Elements
for finishing. (Though, if this is your intention, the **Edit with Premiere
Elements Editor** output option is a much better choice.)

More Create projects

There are even more "**Create**" projects available under the **More Options** button.

These photo projects are created similarly to those described in this chapter: You gather your assets (photos) by selecting them in the **Media Browser**; you select your template and generate your piece; you save your piece and then select the option of either printing it yourself or sending it to professional printers for final production.

Other **Create** projects include:

Create an InstantMovie

Selecting the option to create an **InstantMovie** gathers the photos and video clips you've selected in the Organizer's **Photo Browser** and ports them to Premiere Elements, where an **InstantMovie Theme** is applied. For more information on **InstantMovies** and **Themes**, see **Chapter 21, Make InstantMovies and Apply Movie Themes**.

Create a DVD with Menu

Selecting the option to create a **DVD With Menu** gathers the photos and video clips you've selected in the Organizer's **Media Browser** and ports them to a Premiere Elements project for further editing.

For information on adding a menu to a DVD or BluRay disc project, see **Chapter 30, Create Movie Menus**.

PhotoStamps

This tool turns your photos into customized, perfectly legal US Postal stamps! (This features is not available on the Mac version of the program.)

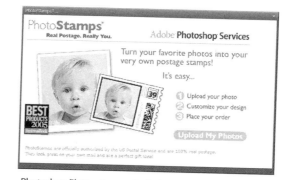

Photoshop Elements even includes a tool for creating your own, custom (and perfectly legal) US postage stamps!

CD Jacket

This tool creates a 9¾" x 4¾" image that you can print out and fit into a CD or DVD "jewel case." (Note that disc jewel cases are 4¾" x 4¾", so this artwork is designed to wrap around the case and include a ¼" spine.)

DVD Jacket

This tool creates an 11" x 7½" label for a DVD case. This template is made to fit a 5¼" x 7½" case with a ½" wide spine.

CD/DVD Label

This tool creates 4¾", circular-shaped artwork for printing onto discs. It includes the necessary spindle hole through the center. (At Muvipix, we recommend never using glue-on labels for your DVDs and CDs. They can cause any number of problems. Use this template only for printable discs and inkjet printers designed to print them.)

Sharing Your Photos as E-mail Attachments

Sharing Your Photos as Photo Mail

Sharing to Facebook, Flickr, Vimeo and Photoshop Showcase

Sharing Your Photos or Videos to a CD or DVD

Sharing Your Photos to a PDF Slideshow

Sharing to Adobe Revel

Chapter 35

Share Your Photos and Videos
The Organizer's output tools

Photoshop Elements includes a number of tools for outputting your photo and video files – from posting them online and e-mailing them to creating a DVD or PDF slideshow.

You've even got a direct link to Photoshop Showcase and Revel – Adobe sites for sharing your photo and video projects.

In addition to tools for creating photo and video projects, the Elements Organizer includes a number of tools for sharing your photos and videos.

Share your photos and videos on Facebook

If you have a Facebook account, you can upload your photos and videos directly from the Organizer's **Media Browser** to your page.

To upload to Facebook:

1   Select the photos in the **Media Browser** you'd like to include in your **Photo Book.** Then select the **Facebook** option under the **Share** tab.

    The Organizer will prepare your file(s) for upload.

    If this is the first time uploading to Facebook from the Organizer, an option screen will ask you to **Authorize** the upload. (It will also ask you if you want to download your Facebook friends to your Organizer **Contacts.** This is, of course, optional.)

2   Click **Authorize.**

    After you click the **Authorize** button, your web browser will open to your Facebook page. If you are already logged into Facebook, you're done with the authorization. You can close your web browser now. If not, you will need to log in first.

3   Back in the Organizer, click the **Complete Authorization** button.

    The program will finish preparing your files. An option panel will then open, asking you to name your file(s) and set who can see them.

4   Once you've set your options, as illustrated below, click **Upload.** Your file(s) will load to Facebook.

The Facebook option screen.

Share your photos as e-mail Attachments

The **E-mail Attachment** option optimizes your selected photo files and then sends them off, with a brief note, to the person or group of people you designate as **Recipients**.

Your photos are optimized and then e-mailed from Adobe E-mail Services.

1 Select the photo(s) you want to attach to your e-mail in your **Media Browser**.

2 Select the **E-mail Attachment** option under the **Share** tab in the Organizer.

   The **E-mail Attachment** option panel will open.

3 Drag any additional photo(s) you'd like converted into e-mail attachments from the Organizer's **Media Browser** into the **E-mail Attachments Items** bin. Remove any photos you'd like removed from the bin by selecting them and clicking the **red minus** button on the panel.

   You can add photos in any file format. The program will convert whatever you add to this bin into a JPEG for e-mailing.

   Set the **Photo Size** and **Quality**. The **Estimated Size** indicator displays the approximate loading time for your e-mail over a 56 kbps modem.

   In this age of high-speed Internet, that may not seem like a state-of-the-art measurement for load times.

   However, the point is that you *do* want to keep any files you plan to e-mail small enough that they don't bog down your recipient's account.

   When you are happy with your settings for this panel, click **Next**.

4 Create a message to accompany your photos and then **Select Recipients** from your list of contacts.

   (See the sidebar on page 449 – **Create an Elements Organizer Contact Book** – for information on creating your **Contacts** list.)

   When you are happy with your settings for this panel, click **Next**.

5 A preview of the outgoing e-mail – including your selected photo(s) – will display on your screen. This is one last chance to make any adjustments you'd like to the e-mail.

   When you are happy with your out-going e-mail, click the **Send** button.

Set up e-mail sharing for the Elements Organizer

In order to use the Elements Organizer's e-mail **Share** options, you must have an active e-mail address listed on the **Sharing** page of the Organizer's **Preferences** (under the **Edit** drop-down on the Organizer Menu Bar on a PC).

The first time you use the **Share** options for either **E-mail Attachments** or **Photo Mail**, you will be prompted to enter a **Sender Verification Number**. This number will be sent, automatically, to you at the e-mail address you've listed in your **Preferences**.

Copy and paste that number into the Organizer's **E-mail Sender Verification** screen to activate your account.

Share your photos as Photo Mail

Photo Mail creates an attractive HTML-based e-mail of your selected photo(s), on your choice of stationery backgrounds and in your preferred layout, as in the illustration on the facing page. (This feature is not available on the Macintosh version of the program.)

1 Click to select the **Photo Mail** option under the **Share** tab in the Organizer. (You can also launch this tool from the Photoshop Elements **Editor** workspace – however, the wizard itself launches in the Organizer.) The **Photo Mail** option panel will open, displaying the thumbnails of the photos that will be included in your **Photo Mail** composition.

If there are photos open in your Organizer **Media Browser**, they will automatically be added to your **Photo Mail Items** bin.

2 Drag any additional photo(s) you'd like converted into e-mail attachments into

Photos are added to the Items bin from the Organizer Photo Browser. E-mail attachments will be converted to JPEGs and should be set to an optimized size and quality.

the **Photo Mail Items** bin from the **Media Browser**. Remove any photos you'd like removed from the bin by selecting them and clicking the **red minus** button on the panel.

When you are happy with your settings for this panel, click **Next**.

3   Create a message for your recipients and then **Select Recipients** from your list of contacts.

(See the sidebar on page 449 – **Create an Elements Organizer Contact Book** – for information on creating your **Contacts** list.)

When you are happy with your settings for this panel, click **Next**.

4   On the **Stationery & Layouts Wizard**, choose the background stationery you would like to display your photos on and add captions to your pictures.

Click **Next Step**.

5   In the **Choose a Layout** screen, customize your text and add graphics and picture frames, if you'd like.

6   When you are happy with your settings for this panel, click **Next**.

Your **Photo Mail** will be sent to the recipients you indicated.

Select a theme or look for your e-mail.

Add captions to your photos.

Using the Stationery & Layout Wizard, you can select a custom layout and background for your Photo Mail.

Share your video on YouTube

When you select a video in your **Media Browser** and select the **YouTube** option under the **Share** tab, your video will be prepared, then uploaded to your account at YouTube – very much like the process described in **Share Your Videos and Photos to Facebook** on page 444.

The first time you use the tool, you will be prompted to log in to YouTube and **Authorize** the upload, as described in **Share Your Videos and Photos to Facebook**.

Videos created in Premiere Elements can also be uploaded to YouTube using the **Publish & Share Online** option described on page 383.

Share your video on Photoshop Showcase

Photoshop Showcase is Adobe's free online service into which you can upload your videos and then share them with friends or the public.

To add upload a video to **Photoshop Showcase:**

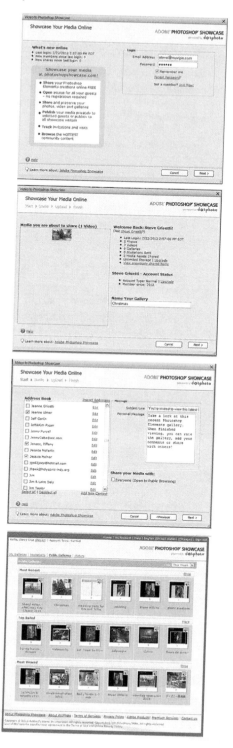

1   Select a video in the Organizer's **Media Browser** and then click **Video to Photoshop Showcase** under the **Share** tab.

    The program will prepare your file and the **Showcase** option screen will open.

2   Create a logon or log in to your **Photoshop Showcase** account.

3   Name the **Gallery** for your video, then click **Next**.

4   On the **Invite** screen, click **Import Addresses** to open your Organizer **Contact Book** (see the sidebar on the facing page) and select the people you'd like invite to see your video – or select the option to **Share Your Media** with **Everyone**.

    You can also type in a custom subject and message for your invitation.

    Click **Next**. Your video will load to the **Photoshop Showcase** web site.

Notification e-mails will be sent to the contacts you selected on the invite screen. Your videos can be viewed by following the links in these e-mails or by logging in at www.photoshopshowcase.com. You can also view others' public videos on the site.

Online Albums can also be shared on Photoshop Showcase (see page 450).

Share your video on Vimeo

When you select a video in your **Media Browser** and select the **Vimeo** option under the **Share** tab, your video will be prepared, then uploaded to your account at www.vimeo.com – very much like the process described in **Share Your Videos and Photos to Facebook** on page 444.

The first time you use this tool, you will be prompted to log in to Vimeo and **Authorize** the upload, as described in **Share Your Videos and Photos to Facebook**.

Share your photos in a SmugMug Gallery

A higher-end gallery for displaying your photos, SmugMug offers a wide variety of attractive and stylish templates for displaying your pictures. SmugMug offers their services at prices ranging from $39.95 to $149.95 per year, with a 20% discount for Photoshop Elements users.

When you select your photos in the **Media Browser** and then select the **SmugMug** option under the **Share** tab and follow the prompts, your photos will be displayed as an online slideshow – at a quality worthy of a professional portfolio.

Create an Elements Organizer Contact Book

In order to have the options to **Select Recipients** for your **E-mail Attachments** or **Photo Mail**, you will need to have these potential recipients listed in your Elements Organizer's **Contact Book**.

To create and add your contacts to this book, go to the **Edit** drop-down on the Organizer Menu Bar and select **Contact Book**:

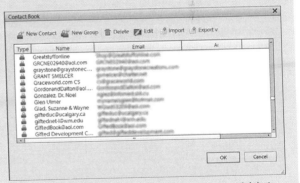

Before you can send out Photo Mail or an e-mail using Adobe's services, you'll need to build a Contact Book, an option available under the Organizer's Edit menu.

> Click **New Contacts** to manually add your contacts' names and e-mail addresses.

Or click the **Import** button to automatically add contacts from your e-mail program.

Once they have been added to your **Contact Book, these names** will be listed under **Select Recipients** whenever you select the **E-mail Attachment** or **Photo Mail** option.

Share your photos on Flickr

When you select photos in your **Media Browser** and select the **Flickr** option under the **Share** tab, your photos will be prepared, then uploaded to your account at www.flickr.com – very much like the process described in **Share Your Videos and Photos to Facebook** on page 444.

The first time you use the tool, you will need to log in to Flickr and **Authorize** the upload, as described in **Share Your Videos and Photos to Facebook**.

Create an Online Album with the Elements Organizer

An **Online Album** can be a very cool way to display your photos as a professional-looking slideshow. Your slideshow can then be burned to a CD or DVD, saved to your hard drive or uploaded to Photoshop Showcase.

1   Select your photos in the Organizer's **Media Browser** and then click **Online Album** under the **Share** tab. (You can add to this collection or remove from it later.)

Alternatively, you can just click the **Online Album** option and, on the next screen, select an existing **Album**.

The **Online Album** panel will open.

2   If you are working with an **Existing Album**, you can select it from the list.

If you are working from photos you've gathered in the **Media Browser**, select the **Create New Album** option.

Select the option to **Share To** either **Photoshop Showcase**, **Export to CD/DVD** or **Export to Hard Drive**.

Click **Next**.

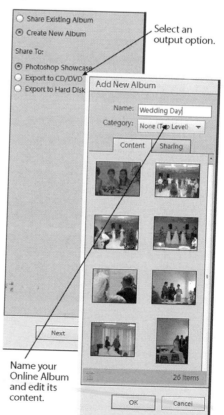

Select an output option.

Name your Online Album and edit its content.

3 On the next screen, name your **Online Album** and, if you'd like, edit your **Album's** content:

> To add photos, drag them from the **Media Browser** to the **Content** window.

> To remove photos, select them in the **Content** window and click the trashcan icon at the lower left of the panel.

Select a slideshow template.   Customize settings.

Click **OK**.

4 Select a slideshow theme, as illustrated above. Many themes allow you to customize how they play and if they include music.

Click **OK**.

5 The program will create and output your **Online Album** slideshow.

If you are uploading your slideshow, log on to **Photoshop Showcase**, name your **Gallery** and invite your viewers, as described in **Share your video to Photoshop Showcase** on page 444.

Burn a Video DVD or BluRay disc

When you click on the **Share** option to **Burn Video DVD/BluRay disc**, the program will launch Premiere Elements and the files you have selected in the Organizer's **Media Browser** will be ported to a Premier Elements project.

For information on creating menus for a DVD or BluRay disc in Premiere Elements, see **Chapter 30, Create Movie Menus**.

Share your video online

When you click on the **Share** option **Online Video Sharing**, the program will launch Premiere Elements and the files you have selected in the Organizer's **Media Browser** will be ported to a Premier Elements project.

For information on sharing your videos online with Premiere Elements, see **Chapter 31, Publish & Share Your Video Projects**.

Share your photos and videos to Mobile Phones and players

When you click on the **Mobile Phones and Players Share** option, the program will launch Premiere Elements and the files you have selected in the Organizer's **Media Browser** will be ported to a Premier Elements project.

For information on sharing your photos and videos to a portable device from Premiere Elements, see **Chapter 31, Share & Publish Your Video Projects**.

Share as a PDF Slide Show

Selecting the **PDF Slide Show** option under the **Share** tab creates a dynamic slideshow of the selected photo files you have selected in the **Media Browser** and outputs them in the PDF (Portable Document File) format, which it then e-mails your selected recipients. The slideshow can be viewed using the free utility Acrobat Reader.

Share to Adobe Revel

Revel is Adobe's "cloud" storage area for your photos. This means that any photos uploaded to Adobe Revel from any location or device can be viewed or accessed by you from any computer connected to the internet as well as from any portable devices – like smartphones, tablets, iPods and iPads – that have the **Adobe Revel** app installed. (At the writing of this book, there is an app available for desktop and laptop Macs running OSX. A Windows version of this app is in the works.)

Revel also includes tools for editing any photos you've posted to the site.

Your photos are categorized on **Adobe Revel** in galleries called **Carousels**.

When you select the **Adobe Revel** option from the **Share** tab, the program will port any selected photos – or all photos displayed – in the **Media Browser** to www.adoberevel.com.

Revel is a subscription service from Adobe (starting at $5.99 a month). There is a free 30-day trial.

Index